BRAVES ON THE WARPATH

BRAVES ON THE WARPATH

The Fifty Greatest Games in the History of The Washington Redskins

by Alan Beall

With a Foreword by Sammy Baugh

KINLOCH BOOKS
WASHINGTON, D.C.

For my mother
Bonita Wilson Beall
Whose lifetime of love and kindness
Made this book possible

This book is not endorsed by, or authorized by, the
National Football League or the Washington Redskins.

Library of Congress Cataloging-in-Publication Data

Beall, Alan, 1949-
    Braves on the warpath.

    Includes index.
    1. Washington Redskins (Football team)—History.
I. Title.
GV956.W3B38   1988   796.332'64'09753   88-81470
ISBN 0-929639-00-6

ISBN 0-929639-00-6 (cloth)
ISBN 0-929639-01-4 (paper)

CONTENTS

FOREWORD

When I first started playing for the Washington Redskins in 1937, I had only 22 teammates, about half of what they have today. Because everybody played both ways, teams were forced to cut some real good offensive boys because they couldn't play defense. But pro football really opened up when the free substitution rule went into effect. All of a sudden, a real good end could make the team and it didn't matter if he could play defense. And because he didn't have to play all 60 minutes, he would still be fresh in the fourth quarter.

Teams started keeping more players, and, in 1943, Coach Dud DeGroot divided the Redskins into two platoons. One platoon would play one quarter, then a fresh squad would take its place. Later on, we started using particular players in particular situations, and everything eventually became specialized. Now you have the best players on the field at all times, and I think that's good for the fans. But I enjoyed playing both ways.

Over the years, other changes in the rules have opened up the game and made for a lot more scoring, which I like. In 1938, George Preston Marshall was responsible for putting in the rule that prohibited defenders from roughing a passer after he had gotten rid of the ball. Sometimes I think the "in the grasp" rule has gotten a little out of hand, but I guess the refs have to be stricter today because defensive players are so much bigger, faster, and stronger than when I played. I know that if I was an owner, I sure wouldn't want a boy I was paying a million dollars to getting hurt and missing half the season. People want to see those good quarterbacks play, and so do I.

I'd say the T-Formation added about eight years to my career. Before Clark Shaughnessy installed it in 1944, I was planning to play only one more season of Single Wing ball. Although it took everyone about a year to get it down, the T-Formation made my life a lot easier because I no longer had to carry the ball or block on running plays. By mixing up our plays and doing the unexpected, we moved the ball pretty well. In fact, we often used the passing game to set up our running attack. That was our whole philosophy in Washington for years and years. If we weren't as strong as the other team, I wasn't going to spend a lot of time trying to establish our running game when I knew we weren't going to get anywhere with it. We wanted the other team to know we were going to throw the ball because, after they spread out their defense, it was a lot easier to run on them.

Like everything else in football, the passing game has evolved greatly over the years, but the basics remain the same. When you go into a ballgame, you first have to figure out if your linemen can protect the passer. If the other team is putting on a good rush, you'd better have a short passing game or you're going to be in trouble. You have to take what the defense is willing to give you. For some reason, young quarterbacks have a hard time learning that. Just like when I was playing, all the quarterbacks coming out of college want to throw long. I guess it's the same mentality as a baseball player wanting to hit a home run.

But you can't throw long unless you've got time. The worst thing that can happen is to have your passer get thrown for a loss. It really kills your momentum. So show me a quarterback with good, quick feet who can move left or right and throw from any position, and I'll take him every time. But those skills don't come easy. They only come with practice and experience.

The thing I liked best about playing quarterback was calling the plays. It was a real test to figure out how to beat the defense, especially when you were still seeing stars from the last play. At the end of the game, it was real satisfying to look back and see which plays had worked. I think quarterbacks who don't call their own plays are missing the most interesting part of the game.

This may sound strange, but the best bunch I ever played for was the 1940 Redskins team that the Chicago Bears whipped in the Championship game, 73-0. Just two weeks earlier, we had beaten those same Bears, 7-3. But in the title game we just couldn't do anything right. After we fell behind, 28-0, in the first half, we started gambling on every series. It backfired every time. I think the Bears scored more when we had the ball than when they had the ball.

But I thought players like Dick Todd, Wilbur Moore, Bob Seymour, and Ki Aldrich were just as good as the boys on our '37 Championship team: Cliff Battles, Riley Smith, Turk Edwards, and Wayne Millner. And they proved it two years later when we beat that same Bears team for the 1942 Championship.

My biggest thrill in football came in 1947 when the Touchdown Club honored me with a "Day" at Griffith Stadium and gave me a new Packard stationwagon. Our opponents that Sunday were the Chicago Cardinals, who were on their way to winning the Championship that season. I guess they came into Washington figuring they would have an easy game, but they were in for a big surprise. The boys on our line had gotten together before the game and promised themselves that I wouldn't get a speck of mud on my uniform. Well, they kept their word. I ended up throwing six touchdown passes, and we just beat the living hell out of those Cardinals.

That was the same kind of game that Doug Williams had in Super Bowl XXII. Believe me, you can play football all your life and never have a game like that. Everything went just right for him. He was throwing balls so perfectly that the receivers never even had to shorten their stride to catch them. And what made it even better was the fact that he had never received much credit when he was with Tampa Bay and that nobody besides the Redskins offered him a contract when the USFL closed down. You couldn't have written a script any better than that. I was just tickled to death for him. I know exactly how he feels.

Sam Baugh
Rotan, Texas
April, 1988

INTRODUCTION

I am a Redskins fan. Like millions of other fans, I celebrate when the 'Skins win and I sulk when they lose. The night before the 1972 NFC Championship game against Dallas, I fell off an 8-foot wall and landed awkwardly on a log. I went into shock, and my lower back locked itself into a tight fist of pain. Nevertheless, the next morning I drove 150 miles from Charlottesville to Washington and stiffly took my place in the upper deck of RFK Stadium alongside my old friend Charley. By the fourth quarter of the Redskins' brilliant 26-3 triumph, I was jumping up and down as if nothing was wrong with me.

I grew up in the Fifties listening to Eddie Gallaher, Dan Daniels, and Jim Gibbons broadcast the games on radio and television. Although I was born too late to cheer for Redskins legends like Sammy Baugh, Cliff Battles, Wayne Millner, Bill Dudley, and Bones Taylor, I learned of their exploits from my older brothers. Eddie LeBaron was my first hero; Dick James remains the only person to whom I've ever sent a fan letter.

Throughout the victory-barren Fifties and Sixties, I remained faithful, always waiting patiently for "next year" while taking whatever solace I could find in individual achievements. As an adult I cried as the shattered promise of the Lombardi era reached its nadir a few months after the great coach's death when the Giants, trailing by 19 points, scored three touchdowns in the fourth quarter to beat the 'Skins, 35-33. A year later, I was in the delirious crowd at Dulles Airport when George Allen's victorious "Over-the-Hill Gang" returned from Dallas. I was also there when the Redskins returned from Kansas City smarting from their first defeat of the season. In 1979, I threw a chair across the room when the 'Skins were edged out of the playoffs because they could not hang onto a 34-21 lead in the last 3 minutes of the season.

All of the suffering seemed worthwhile, though, when John Riggins broke loose for those 43 glorious yards in Super Bowl XVII. In the final moments of Washington's 27-17 triumph, I called my old friend Charley long-distance and together we watched the Washington Redskins reclaim the NFL Championship for the first time in our lives. No victory was ever sweeter.

Over the next five seasons, the Redskins added to their success, compiling the best record in the league, but never quite winning it all. Until January, 1988. Doug Williams' amazing achievement in the second quarter of Super Bowl XXII provided a perfect exclamation point for a tale that began half a century ago with an equally brilliant performance by Sammy Baugh in the 1937 NFL Championship game. Great moments like those deserve to be remembered.

Washington, D.C.
February, 1988

BRAVES
ON THE
WARPATH

WELCOME TO WASHINGTON

East-West Championship Game

Washington Redskins vs. Chicago Bears

December 12, 1937

"We do things a lot differently in the pro league," warned Washington Redskins Coach Ray Flaherty as he greeted the rookie from Texas Christian University. "For instance, on forward passes the receivers don't want to bend for the ball, and they don't like it too high. They like 'em right around the eye." The rookie, Sammy Baugh, had only one question: "Which eye, Coach?"

Baugh's brashness was quickly excused by his performance as he led the National Football League in passing in 1937. Slingin' Sam played tailback in Washington's Single Wing, a formation that thrived on spins, fakes, criss-crossing backs, and tricky ball-handling. Besides Baugh, who received the hike from center and either passed, ran, or handed off, the Redskins offense featured three backs: quarterback Riley Smith, who called the plays in the huddle and yelled out the signals from his position 2 yards behind the tackle, fullback Ernie Pinckert, who blocked or plunged into the line, and all-pro wingback Cliff Battles, who was split out to the side and was used as a trap blocker, a receiver, or a sweeping outside runner.

In 1937, the 'Skins won seven of their first ten games, then met the New York Giants on the last day of the regular season in a showdown for the Eastern Division championship. Redskins Owner George Preston Marshall, who had moved the team from Boston to Washington after the 1936 season because of a lack of support, arranged a chartered excursion to New York and 12,000 enthusiastic fans responded. When the armada of 15 trains arrived at Penn Station, Marshall seized the moment by organizing an impromptu parade down Seventh Avenue to Columbus Circle. The mob happily followed, and bemused New Yorkers on their way to church were treated to the sight and sound of thousands of drunken Redskins fans extolling the virtues of their favorite team in language somewhat less decorous than a minister's. Bill Corum of the *New York Journal-American* described it this way: "At the head of a 150-piece band and 12,000 fans, George Marshall slipped unobtrusively into town."

During the week prior to the game, Giants Coach Steve Owen had been asked to name his personal all-pro list. When Owen neglected to include Baugh or Battles or any other Redskin on his list, the Washington players vowed to make him pay for his snub. On Sunday, with those 12,000 unruly fans cheering them on at the Polo Grounds, the 'Skins, led by league-leading rusher Cliff Battles, who accounted for over 200 yards, routed the Giants, 49-14, to earn a shot at the Chicago Bears for the East-West Championship.

The following week when George Halas was asked

to name his all-pro team, the Bears' head coach unhesitatingly replied:

> "Left End: Wayne Millner, Redskins
> Left Tackle: Turk Edwards, Redskins
> Left Guard: Swede Olsson, Redskins
> Center: Ed Kawal, Redskins
> Right Guard: Jim Karcher, Redskins
> Right Tackle: Jim Barber, Redskins
> Right End: Charles Malone, Redskins
> Quarterback: Riley Smith, Redskins
> Tailback: Sammy Baugh, Redskins
> Wingback: Cliff Battles, Redskins
> Fullback: Ernie Pinckert, Redskins."

Obviously, Halas knew the inflammatory power of words and wanted to make sure his would have a soothing effect on the hot-tempered Redskins. "That's the greatest football team ever put together," said Halas, winking. "Please see that these selections get in the paper before Sunday."

Halas' Bears were a dangerous, hard-hitting team epitomized by legendary fullback Bronko Nagurski, who had once been described by *Washington Post* writer Shirley Povich as a 6-foot 2-inch, 238-pound "riot in cleats." A 3-time all-pro who reigned as Heavyweight Wrestling Champion during the off-season, Nagurski was feared as much for his devastating blocking and linebacking as for his punishing line charges that had averaged 4.4 yards per carry over the course of his 8-year career.

With all-pros Joe Stydahar, Dan Fortmann, Frank Bausch, and George Musso manning the offensive line, the Bears averaged 212 pounds from tackle to tackle, making them the biggest bunch of brutes in the league. Nevertheless, Chicago was equally capable of using finesse to bury an opponent, as they had demonstrated the week before against their cross-town rivals, the Chicago Cardinals, when Ray Buivid had thrown six touchdown passes to Les McDonald. Considering the fact that the Bears also sported the stingiest defense in the league, the leading scorer (Jack Manders), and the best record (9-1-1), it was no surprise that bettors had made Chicago an 8-5 favorite.

Still, the Redskins were confident. The day before the big game, Redskins quarterback Riley Smith told reporters, "We are going out tomorrow to pass the Bears into the ground . . . Tomorrow you will see the best passing exhibition of all time. Washington will beat the Bears, and Baugh will be the man who will be responsible."

On a bleak and frosty 20-degree afternoon, only 15,878 of an expected 42,000 fans braved Chicago's biting winds to witness the 1937 East-West Championship of the National Football League. And that total included 3,000 Washingtonians who had paid $23.20 roundtrip to ride the B & O Special train to Chicago to cheer for their new team. For Washington sports fans who had waited 24 years for the Senators' first baseball pennant, having an opportunity to root for a football champion in the Redskins' first year in the Nation's Capital was too delicious an opportunity to miss.

The day before, in an attempt to thaw the frozen soil at Wrigley Field, the groundskeeper had drenched the field with gasoline and set it on fire. Not only did the ground remain frozen, but the scorched field made it appear as if a battle had been fought there overnight. Both teams had no choice but to abandon their football cleats in favor of rubber-soled basketball shoes.

The Championship game started auspiciously for the Redskins. After yielding one first down, the Washington defense stopped Bronko Nagurski on a third-and-2 smash up the middle, forcing the Bears to punt. From his 7, Baugh took the hike from center Ed Kawal, faded back into his end zone, and looped a screen pass to Cliff Battles, who dashed to the Bears 49 before Ray Nolting stopped him. The drive stalled, though, and Baugh punted to the Bears 6.

After keeping Chicago bottled up inside its 10, the Redskins regained possession on their 47 and began the first sustained drive of the game. A 14-yard completion from Baugh to Riley Smith and an 18-yard strike to fullback Ernie Pinckert advanced the ball to the Bears 21. Unfortunately, Pinckert was injured when the Bears' Bernie Masterson used his knees like piledrivers on the already-fallen fullback. When play resumed, the 'Skins used a smart mixture of runs and passes to move the ball to the Bears 7, where they faced third and goal. Baugh handed off to Battles on a reverse, and Cliff skirted end and soared over the front corner of the end zone for a touchdown to give the Redskins the early lead. [Fig. 2] Placekicker Riley Smith added the extra point, and Washington went on top, 7-0.

Fig. 2   *AP/Wide World Photos*

Apparently, that only made the Bears mad. Chicago's Bernie Masterson passed to Ed "Eggs" Manske, who picked the ball cleanly off his shoetops, galloped to the Redskins 40, slipped, got up, and skittered over the frozen field for another 20 yards before Baugh knocked him down at the 19. (In those days, players performed on both offense and defense; many played the entire 60 minutes.) Bronko Nagurski swept left end for 9 yards, then Jack Manders scored on a 10-yard burst through a big hole over right guard. Touchdown, Bears! With 4 minutes remaining in the

first quarter, Manders' conversion tied the game, 7-7.

After the kickoff, Sammy Baugh took charge again, passing and bootlegging the ball to the Redskins 48, but George Wilson intercepted at midfield and Chicago had a chance to take the lead. Three plunges into the line earned a first down at the Washington 39. The Redskins bunched six men at the line in anticipation of another infantry charge, but Masterson fooled them by passing to Manders at the 25. The only Redskin with any chance of tackling Manders was Cliff Battles, but he was wiped out on a devastating block by Wilson and Manders galloped into the end zone with his second touchdown of the game. His extra point gave the hometown Bears a 14-7 lead as the first quarter ended.

The Single Wing was custom-made for Sammy Baugh. A classic triple threat, Baugh was a deadly passer, the league's best punter, and a hard-nosed runner. Unfortunately, that last talent got him into trouble on the 'Skins' second possession of the second quarter. After a punt by the Bears gave Washington the ball at its 20, Baugh faked a pass and ran 17 yards up the middle before being slammed to the rock-hard field by four Bears defenders. [Fig.3] When Baugh rose slowly to his feet, blood was dripping steadily from a deep gash in his right palm. He took a step and staggered from the sharp pain stabbing his left leg. Baugh hobbled to the bench for treatment on his leg, but, fearing he would not be allowed to continue, hid his bloody hand from the trainer. Cliff Battles took over Baugh's ball-handling duties, but, without Slingin' Sam, Washington's offense became icebound.

The demoralized Redskins desperately needed a break, especially after a short punt gave Chicago excellent field position at its 44. When Battles picked off a pass by Ray Buivid at his 36, it appeared that the 'Skins had sidestepped disaster. But the Bears got the ball right back when Battles threw an interception to Gene Ronzani, who returned it all the way to the Washington 20. The Redskins defense, which had limited six opponents to 8 points or less during the regular season, rallied again, pushing Chicago back to the 26. Not wanting to risk losing any more ground, Coach Halas ordered a 37-yard field goal attempt on

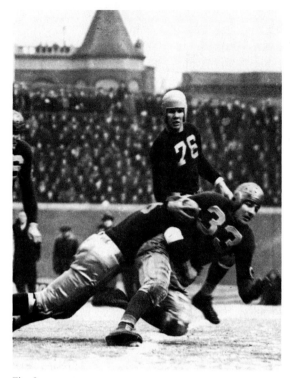

Fig. 3   *AP/Wide World Photos*

returned the ball to his 47. Riley Smith completed a 17-yard pass to Battles at the Chicago 36, then tempted fate once more. The result: Jack Manders' third interception, and the first half ended with the Bears on top, 14-7.

After surrendering that early touchdown, the Bears had taken complete control of the game. Their runners were chewing up large chunks of ground with each carry; their receivers were averaging 25 yards per catch; and their defense had stymied Washington with three interceptions and a fumble recovery. To have any hope of winning, the Redskins needed Sammy Baugh, whose injured left leg was so sore that he could not put any weight on it. Nevertheless, when the second half started, Baugh limped back into the game.

The 'Skins returned the second half kickoff to their 30, and Baugh tested himself immediately. Instead of transferring his weight to his injured left leg, Baugh improvised a 9-yard pass to Wayne Millner by throwing entirely off his right leg. Two plays later, Slingin' Sam surprised everyone by firing a long spiral to Wayne Millner over the middle. [Fig. 4] The big end grabbed the perfect pass on the dead run at the Chicago 35 and sprinted into the end zone for a 55-yard touchdown! Riley Smith kicked the extra point, and the game was deadlocked, 14-14.

The Bears' offensive linemen maintained control of the line of scrimmage, opening gaping holes for their running backs. Starting from the Chicago 27, it was Nagurski for 6 yards, then Manders for 17, Nolting for 8, then 8 more, and Nagurski for a yard and a half to give the Bears a first down at the Washington 4. Somehow, the overmatched Redskins defenders withstood Chicago's assault for the next three downs, but, on fourth and goal, Masterson faked a run up the middle and threw a jump-pass to Eggs Manske for a touchdown. Manders converted, and the scoreboard read: Bears 21, Redskins 14.

After the kickoff, the Washington Redskins tried the same play that had given them their last touchdown. It clicked again. Wayne Millner caught Baugh's long, arching bomb at midfield and outraced Bronko Nagurski to the goal line for an 80-yard touchdown!

third down, but Manders missed and the Redskins still trailed by only a touchdown, 14-7.

Without Baugh, the 'Skins couldn't manage a single first down, and Battles punted from his goal line. When Ray Buivid bungled the catch, Washington fans leapt to their feet, but Manders recovered for the Bears on the Redskins 39. Again the Redskins resisted and Manders tried a field goal on third down; again the kick was too low and the 3,000 Washington fans at Wrigley Field cheered and jeered. Inheriting the Bears' squandered momentum, the revitalized Redskins drove to midfield, but Battles slipped on the icy field and fumbled the ball away to Jack Manders at the Washington 44. At this point, Manders had accounted for two touchdowns, two extra points, and two fumble recoveries, but, luckily for the Redskins, had also missed two field goal attempts.

On the Bears' next play, Masterson threw an interception to Washington linebacker Ed Kawal, who

Fig. 4   *UPI/The Bettmann Archive*

Riley Smith's extra point tied the score at 21 apiece.

The game had developed into a match between Washington's quick-scoring passing attack and Chicago's rushing juggernaut. But the Bears broke that pattern when Bernie Masterson launched a deep pass to Manske over the middle. With a clear path to glory, Manske dropped it!

The Redskins got the ball back at their 20 and, thanks in part to a successful fake punt by Don Irwin, marched to the Bears 36. On second and 3, Baugh pump-faked a pass to Malone and threw 25 yards downfield to Ed Justice, who caught the ball at the 11 and bulled into the end zone for the score! That put the Redskins ahead, 28-21. Sammy Baugh's accomplishment bordered on the miraculous. On a leg so painful that he could hardly stand, and with every Chicago defender doing his best to put him out of the game for good, Sam had passed for three touchdowns in a single quarter against the best defense in the league.

The final quarter began. The Bears gained excellent field position at their 45 when a punt by Baugh was partially blocked. Ray Buivid completed a 32-yard pass to Pug Rentner, but his next four throws fell incomplete in the end zone and Washington took over at its 23. Baugh continued to carve up the Chicago secondary with a pair of 20-yard tosses to Ed Justice and Cliff Battles. But Millner ruined the 'Skins' chance of icing the game when he fumbled at the Bears 14.

Keith Molesworth replaced Masterson and completed a 35-yard pass to Dick Plasman, who was ridden out of bounds by Sammy Baugh. Upset by his rough treatment, Plasman took a poke at Sam and a fight broke out. Both teams met for the obligatory shoving and growling, but the officials restored order and everyone returned to their places with their honor intact. Masterson returned and hit Les McDonald with a 30-yard strike at the 12. A few minutes later, though, the Bears failed to score for the fourth time in the game when Jack Manders couldn't reach a fourth-down pass in the end zone.

With 4 minutes remaining, things started getting crazy. On first down, Baugh fumbled the snap but fell on it. On third down, he tried to quick-kick out of trouble, but his punt was blocked. Luckily, Washington's Bill Young retrieved the live ball at the 22, giving Sam an opportunity to kick again on fourth down. This time, Baugh got the punt away cleanly, yet it traveled only 20 yards. Ray Buivid raced upfield to catch the ball before it could bounce but miscalculated slightly, and the ball glanced off his arm and into the hands of a Redskin!

With 2 minutes left in the game, Washington merely had to hang on to the ball to earn the championship. (In 1937, neither team was allowed to call a time-out after the 2-minute warning.) But on third down, a Chicago defender tackled the ball, ripping it from Cliff Battles' tight grip. The ball bounced crazily on the slippery field as Redskins and Bears dove for it. Finally, Chicago's Ray Nolting recovered on his 42, and the Bears, trailing 28-21, had one last chance to salvage a tie.

Less than a minute remained. Masterson faded back and pegged the ball to Jack Manders, but the great wingback couldn't reach it. On second down, Masterson aimed a pass toward Ed Manske, who was streaking down the field all alone. At the last instant, Riley Smith swooped in from his safety position and intercepted! The Redskins were NFL champions, 28-21!

Despite injuries to his throwing hand and left leg, Sammy Baugh had pinpointed his receivers like an archer, completing 17 of 34 passes for 335 yards and three touchdowns to fulfill Riley Smith's prediction that he would single-handedly defeat the Bears. Washington's defense had played brilliantly, too, turning back four Chicago scoring threats and keeping the game close during the second quarter while Baugh recuperated from his injuries. Even though they received a winner's share of only $234 for their efforts, every member of the 1937 Washington Redskins earned something far more valuable on that cold, windy day in Chicago: the right to be called a champion.

DOWN TO THE WIRE

Philadelphia Eagles vs. Washington Redskins

November 1, 1942

While the Washington Redskins were playing the final game of the 1941 season, news of another drama—so devastating that officials at Griffith Stadium decided it was necessary to withhold the full story to prevent a stampede to the gates—was being indirectly revealed to the crowd through an alarming stream of announcements. Rumors grew increasingly close to the truth as every few minutes an admiral, or general, or ambassador, or high-ranking Pentagon official was paged over the public address system and asked to "Call your office— Urgent!"

It was Sunday, December 7, 1941—Pearl Harbor Day. The United States was at war with Japan.

Hundreds of NFL players, including Redskins Jim Barber, Frank Filchock, and Wayne Millner, immediately joined the Armed Forces. Team owners, whose rosters were decimated by the call to arms, debated whether or not to suspend play until the war was over. A few overzealous patriots even demanded that all nonessential activities like movies, plays, and professional sports be cancelled for the Duration. However, the Office of Civilian Defense, citing that such diversions were an important escape for people under the constant distress of war, ruled that pro football was one of America's essential pastimes and thus could continue to be played.

That was good news for Redskins Owner George Preston Marshall, who, by the early Forties, had parlayed a nationwide radio network and his natural flair for entertainment into a promotional triumph. As the first NFL team to broadcast its games nationwide, the first to employ a marching band, and the first to have a fight song, the Washington Redskins quickly became the most popular professional football team in the country. Marshall's love of pageantry revealed itself in his highly acclaimed halftime shows. In those days, marching bands were a popular novelty, and Marshall's choreographed shows were as keenly anticipated as the games. On occasion, Marshall even hired the National Symphony Orchestra to knock out a few numbers between halves.

In 1938, Barnee Breeskin, whose fashionable local swing band dressed up as Indians on game day and played in front of a teepee perched atop Griffith Stadium, and Corinne Griffith Marshall, the owner's wife, wrote *Hail to the Redskins* (with a little help from the old spiritual, *Yes, Jesus Loves Me*). Although it has since been sanitized of any words objectionable to American Indians, the exuberance of the song remains. The original version went like this:

> HAIL TO THE REDSKINS, Hail Vic-to-ry,
> Braves on the war-path, Fight for old D.C.
> Scalp 'em, Swamp 'em

Another halftime extravaganza at Griffith Stadium   *Abbie Rowe Photo, Courtesy Washington Redskins*

We will take 'em big score.
Read 'em, weep 'em,
Touch-down we want heap more.
Fight On. Fight on till you have won.
Sons of Wash-ing-ton (Rah! Rah! Rah!)
HAIL TO THE REDSKINS, Hail Vic-to-ry
Braves on the war-path, Fight for old D.C.

Published by Leo Feist, Inc., New York

After their glorious inaugural season in 1937, the 'Skins remained powerful but had been unable to repeat as champions. They had come awfully close, though. With the Eastern Division title on the line in the final game of the 1939 season, the Redskins, trailing 9-7, moved the ball inside the New York Giants 10 yard line with less than a minute to play. On fourth down, Washington's Bo Russell tried a 15-yard field goal that appeared to be good as it soared high over the stubby upright. Some of the Giants players threw their helmets on the ground in disappointment; others offered their congratulations to the 'Skins. But the referee hesitated—then called it wide!

Despite the Redskins' anguished protests, the ref stuck with his call and Washington went home a loser.

The following year, the Redskins made it to the Championship game but soon wished they hadn't when their arch-enemy, the Chicago Bears, lined up in the T-Formation with a man in motion. Although the T-Formation was invented by Amos Alonzo Stagg before the turn of the century, it had rarely been used in the pros, and the new wrinkle of putting a man in motion made it even more alien. Without a clue of how to defend against the new formation, the bewildered Washington team was embarrassed, 73-0. "The unluckiest guy in the crowd," wrote Bob Considine, "was the five-buck bettor who took the Redskins and 70 points." Before it turned into a rout, though, Washington was threatening to take the early lead as Sammy Baugh led the 'Skins smartly down the field. But Charley Malone dropped a perfect pass at the Chicago 5, and the Redskins never threatened again. After the game, Baugh was asked if he thought it would have made any difference had Washington scored that early touchdown. "It sure would have," replied Baugh. "It would have been 73-6."

In the early Forties, pro football was slowly emerging from its roots as a push-and-shove contest into the highly strategic and specialized game we know today. The switch from the Single Wing to the T-Formation was a milestone in the evolution of the game. By going into motion, a speedy halfback could become either a receiver or a devastating crackback blocker. With a larger area to cover, defenders were forced to spread out, especially when coaches retooled their basic rushing plays to take advantage of the extra running room. But more importantly, the T-Formation opened up the passing game, which, until then, had been considered a dangerous frill — exciting but unnecessary. As the shape of the football became more streamlined, the forward pass became easier to throw and the T-Formation became its showcase.

But even though the Redskins had the greatest passer in the game in 1942, they were one of the few clubs to continue using the Single Wing. When asked why he hadn't switched to the T-Formation, Coach Ray Flaherty replied that Sammy Baugh would be effective in any formation, and he liked the way the Single Wing allowed quick kicks and utilized the talents of hard-charging fullback Andy Farkas. Washington's 5-1 record, the best in the division, proved his point.

By 1942, Baugh, who was the highest paid player in the league, had already won three passing crowns and led the league in punting twice. Known as "Mr. Redskin," Sam had even led the team in interceptions from his defensive safety position. No wonder that when Baugh trotted onto the field by himself one day, a reporter in the pressbox cracked, "There goes the Redskins' first team on the field."

Actually, Baugh had some excellent co-stars. Andy Farkas, Washington's first-ever draft choice who had led the league in scoring in 1939, suffered a serious knee injury the following year, causing him to miss the entire 1941 season. However, by 1942 Farkas was once again crashing into the line with the same furious abandon that had characterized his early years. Wilbur Moore and Dick Todd, both of whom had joined the 'Skins in 1939, completed the Redskins' powerful backfield.

Dick Todd   *Courtesy Washington Redskins*

The Philadelphia Eagles, led by their one-eyed quarterback, "Machine Gun" Tommy Thompson, arrived in Washington midway through the 1942 season intent on upsetting the division-leading Redskins. Their coach, Earl "Greasy" Neale, who earned his unusual nickname in college for his uncanny knack of slipping tackles, was one of the most innovative tacticians of his era. The author of the shifting defensive line and the naked reverse, Neale had also played major league baseball, starring for the Cincinnati Reds in the infamous 1919 "Black Sox" World Series. Shortly thereafter, Neale left baseball to become football coach of tiny Washington & Jefferson College, where he gained nationwide fame for leading his laughably undersized team to an incredible 0-0 tie against mighty Southern Cal in the 1922 Rose Bowl.

In 1941, the Eagles hired Neale to overhaul a team that had never experienced a single winning season in its 9-year history. Eventually, Neale would lead the Eagles to two NFL championships before the decade was out, but, for now, Philadelphia was still struggling. Nevertheless, the Washington Redskins, although heavily favored to win their eleventh consecutive game against the lowly Eagles, were far from complacent. They knew that anything could happen against a team coached by Greasy Neale.

3 2,658 Washington fans jammed into Griffith Stadium to watch the Redskins administer a few lessons in the manly art of football to the Philadelphia Eagles. But the Eagles turned the tables on Washington. On their first possession, Fred Meyer raced 60 yards on an end-around, and only a desperate tackle by Ed Justice prevented a Philadelphia touchdown. Although the Eagles failed to score, they had served notice that the 'Skins were in for a fight.

The Redskins marched steadily down the field as fullback Andy Farkas hammered the Philadelphia defense with his pounding runs. However, like Philadelphia, Washington came away empty-handed when placekicker Bob Masterson missed a 39-yard field goal attempt. The Eagles took over at their 20, and "Machine Gun" Thompson used quick, short passes to drive his team to the Washington 8. But safety Sam Baugh ruined Philadelphia's scoring opportunity when he picked off a pass in the end zone.

Andy Farkas continued to rip through the Eagles defense, picking up 5, then 6, then 9, then 12 yards with slashing runs. On third and 10 at the Philadelphia 31, Baugh launched a deep pass to Farkas, who made an acrobatic over-the-shoulder catch at the 5 and ran into the end zone for the first touchdown of the game. Masterson converted, and the 'Skins broke on top, 7-0.

The Eagles stormed back in the second quarter with a 65-yard drive that was capped by an 8-yard touchdown pass from Thompson to Larry Cabrelli. The score remained 7-6, however, when Len Barnum's extra point attempt bounced off the crossbar. A few minutes later the first half ended, and the Redskins trotted off the field accompanied by the nervous applause of their fans at sold-out Griffith Stadium who realized that a 1-point lead was an invitation to disappointment.

The third quarter opened like a Mack Sennett comedy. Philadelphia's Bob Davis fielded Bob Masterson's second-half kickoff and headed upfield. At the 30, Davis lateraled to teammate Ted Williams, who had looped behind him. However, Williams was under the impression that Davis was going to fake the lateral, and the ball bounced off his hands. Washington's Ed Cifers alertly scooped up the free ball and charged into the end zone, giving the 'Skins a 14-6 lead only 12 seconds into the third quarter.

After shutting down the Eagles offense and forcing a punt, the Redskins engineered a steady 71-yard drive, alternating short passes by Baugh and strong runs by Andy Farkas. On first down from the Philadelphia 20, Farkas blasted through center, twisted out of the grasp of two tacklers, and dragged an Eagles defender the final 5 yards before diving into the end zone for his second touchdown of the afternoon. Masterson missed the PAT, though, and Washington had to be satisfied with its 20-6 lead midway through the second quarter.

Philadelphia's Bosh Pritchard fielded Masterson's kickoff at his 3 and veered to his right. Once again,

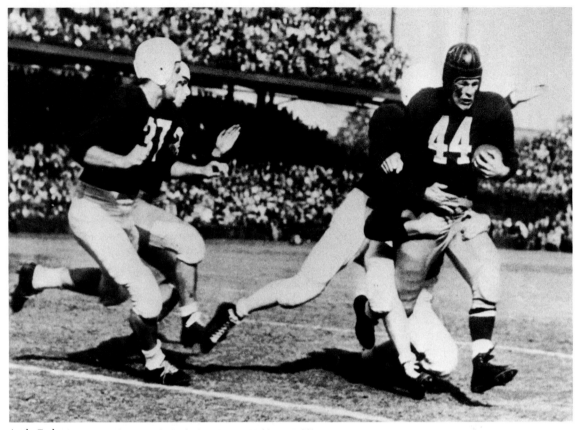

Andy Farkas   *Nate Fine Photo/Nate Fine Productions, Courtesy Washington Redskins*

the Eagles set up a crisscross, but this time there was no breakdown in communication. As planned, Pritchard faked the handoff and continued up the right sideline. The Redskins bit hard on the fake; Pritchard broke into the clear and sprinted to the goal line for a 97-yard touchdown! Dick Erdlitz, replacing the benched Len Barnum, succeeded on the extra point, and the Eagles trailed by only a touchdown, 20-13.

Fearing a long runback, Philadelphia Coach Greasy Neale ordered a squib kick, but that tactic backfired when tackle Wee Willie Wilkin returned it from his 15 to the Redskins 45. On first down, Sammy Baugh completed a pass to Ed Justice in the flat, but linebacker Rupert Pate slammed into him and knocked the ball loose. Scrambling to his feet,

Pate grabbed the fumble and raced 53 yards into Washington's end zone to tie the game, 20-20.

On the ensuing kickoff, Coach Neale called for another squib, but Ed Kasky, the Eagles' third-string placekicker, inexplicably drove the ball deep to Ray Hare at the 5. Racing straight up the middle, Hare shook off a tackler at the 20 and burst into the open. By midfield, there wasn't an Eagle within 20 yards of him, and Hare galloped into the end zone accompanied only by the happy shouts of the crowd at Griffith Stadium. Masterson converted, and the 'Skins were back in front, 27-20. In all, five touchdowns had been scored in the wild third period, four of which had been packed into a space of just 3½ minutes.

At the beginning of the fourth quarter, quarterback Tommy Thompson orchestrated a long Philadelphia drive, but the Washington defense held at the goal line and the Redskins took over at their 2. Undaunted, the Eagles quickly regained possession and headed for the Washington end zone again. After completing long passes to Bob Davis and Fred Meyer, Thompson lateraled to Davis, who swept into the end zone from 3 yards out to bring the Eagles to within 1 point of the fast-fading Redskins. A moment later Erdlitz booted the conversion, and the score was tied, 27-27, with 5:35 left on the clock.

Washington's Ki Aldrich returned Philadelphia's short kickoff just past midfield. On first down, Sammy Baugh fired a 22-yard strike to Ray Hare. Andy Farkas swept right end for 22 more, giving him a total of 184 yards rushing in the game. Thinking he was out of bounds, Farkas released the ball when he hit the ground and made no attempt to retrieve it. But the referee ruled he was still in bounds, and the Eagles took over at their 3. Although Washington's exasperated defenders kept Philadelphia bottled up inside the 10, a long punt by Barnum left the Redskins 65 yards away from victory with only 2 minutes remaining in the game.

Baugh dropped back and passed to Hare for a 23-yard gain at the Philly 42, then uncorked another beauty to Andy Farkas at the 12. After an incompletion in the end zone, the Redskins lined up for a field goal attempt on second down. Sammy Baugh spotted the ball for Masterson—but it was a fake! Baugh rolled to his right and threw to Masterson, who was tackled at the 4. On third down, with 1 second showing on the unofficial stadium clock, Baugh laid a perfect pass into Masterson's hands in the end zone—and Masterson dropped it! Coach Neale and the rest of the Eagles assumed the game was over, but, according to the official timekeeper, there still were 2 seconds left in the game.

In the Redskins huddle, Sammy Baugh looked at Masterson and said, "You get back, and we'll kick on 2." Faced with a severe 45-degree angle that allowed no room for error, Masterson stepped into the ball and connected. As the gun sounded, the ball sailed over the outstretched hands of the Eagles and slipped through the slender gap between the goal posts while the crowd roared in hoarse delight. Washington had escaped, 30-27!

"**M**asterson had no time to gloat, his life was in danger," wrote Merrell Whittlesey in Monday's *Washington Post*. "His overjoyed teammates lifted him to their shoulders and those without an arm or a leg pounded him with clenched fists and they were joined by an excited mob of well wishers who pushed and shoved like madmen. They had just seen the football game by which all others must be measured from this time on. There will not, there cannot be another like it."

BEAR TRAP

National Football League Championship Game

Chicago Bears vs. Washington Redskins

December 13, 1942

On the eve of their 1942 Championship game against the Washington Redskins, the undefeated Chicago Bears, champions of the National Football League for two straight years, were getting angrier by the minute. The Bears had just been informed that whoever won the championship would have to face a team of all-stars the following week in an exhibition to benefit the Armed Forces. Now, the Bears didn't mind playing the game, but they did object to the fact that they had donated their usual fees to the cause without the courtesy of being consulted. It never even occurred to the mighty Bears that the Redskins might be the ones contributing their services the following week in Philadelphia.

It's easy to see why Chicago was looking past the Redskins. Unbeaten for 24 straight games over two seasons, the 1942 Bears had outscored their collective opponents 521-126, and, in their last six games, had surrendered a total of 14 points. Chicago's complete domination of the league was reflected in the fact that it ranked first in 8 major statistical categories. Even if the Bears had spotted each of their opponents two touchdowns, they still would have been undefeated. No wonder the disgruntled Chicago

players assumed they would be playing the all-stars the following week in Philadelphia.

The war had taken its toll on the Bears, most notably in the person of their founder and head coach, George "Papa Bear" Halas, who had enlisted in the Navy. But the powerful Bears never missed a beat as they collected their third straight Western Division crown with two assistants, Luke Johnsos and Hunk Anderson, sharing the head coaching duties.

Quarterback Sid Luckman was to the Bears what Sam Baugh was to the Redskins: the heart of his team. Known as "Brain Trust," Luckman quickly mastered Chicago's complicated T-Formation offense and terrorized defenses with his sharp passing and clever ball-handling. Like Baugh, Luckman also excelled on defense and was a fine punter. If the 15-point underdog Redskins were to have any chance of winning, they would have to control Luckman and his favorite receiver, Scooter McLean, who was averaging 30 yards per catch. "Shut them down," said Redskins Coach Ray Flaherty, "and we can win."

Clearly, Washington and Chicago were the class of the league, their rivalry the equal of any in sports.

Although not quite in the same superhuman category as the Bears, the Redskins had cruised to a 10-1 record and their third Eastern Division championship in 6 years. During that period, the 'Skins had compiled an impressive 47-16-3 record (second only to the Bears' 52-13-1), and had won nine straight games since a freakish loss to the Giants in the second week of the 1942 season. In that game, the Redskins defense had allowed only one pass completion, 1 yard rushing, and no first downs. Unfortunately, the pass completion went for a touchdown on the first play of the game, and an interception was returned for another TD, giving the Giants all the points they needed for a 14-7 victory.

Washington's foundation was its rock-solid offensive line, a tough and mobile unit that protected Sammy Baugh and opened gaping holes for running backs Andy Farkas, Ray Hare, and Dick Todd to crash through. "I never did play behind lines like we've got this year," said Baugh, who, besides Ed Justice, was the only current Redskin to have played on the 1937 championship team that had beaten Chicago, 28-21. "I figure they'll make it awfully tough on the Bears . . . The teams we've been playin' say the Redskins are rougher than the Bears, but the Bears make it look rougher because four or five of 'em hit a ball-carrier at the same time. But you can't condemn 'em for that."

Coach Flaherty believed that the team that controlled the line of scrimmage would win the game. "Farkas and the line are the keys," said Flaherty. "We are going to run at them because they're sure we're going to pass. The line must control the Bears defense, and Farkas will do the brunt of the work. And any time they look like they're expecting the run, then Sam will give them a taste of the pass. We don't want them to expect a thing."

On a bitingly cold afternoon at Griffith Stadium, the Washington Redskins received the opening kickoff of the 1942 NFL Championship game. 36,006 well-wrapped fans rose to their feet in unison as the Chicago Bears' Lee Artoe booted deep to Ray Hare, who returned the ball to the 29 before Bulldog Turner slammed him to the frozen ground. On the Redskins' first play, Andy Farkas tested the Chicago front line. He got a yard. On second down, Sammy Baugh surprised everyone by quick-kicking. The punt sailed past the startled safety, and, after a journey of 59 yards, finally rolled out of bounds at the Bears 10.

The Redskins regained possession at their 30, and, in an attempt to pin Chicago to its goal line, Baugh quick-kicked again. This time, though, the Bears nearly blocked it, and Sammy's hurried punt traveled only 30 yards to the Chicago 40. The Bears began to move. Halfback Ray Nolting followed crisp blocking on a quick-opener to gain 18 yards up the middle, then quarterback Sid Luckman connected with Nolting on a pass for 11 more, giving Chicago a first down at the Washington 28. The Redskins defense stiffened, though, and forced a field goal attempt from the 45. Lee Artoe's kick was straight enough but short, and Washington took over at its 20.

Baugh finally decided to try a pass, but the ball was tipped at the line and Ray Nolting intercepted at the Redskins 30. Fortunately, on first down, Washington defensive tackle Wee Willie Wilkin charged into Nolting and caused a fumble, and the Redskins recovered both the ball and their composure at the Washington 26.

Astonishingly, Sammy Baugh quick-kicked again on first down! After taking a hop, skip, and a jump, the ball wobbled to rest at the Chicago 17. The Stone Age strategy paid off, though, as the Redskins defense forced the Bears to punt again, and Washington took over near midfield as the first quarter ended in a scoreless tie. Although Baugh's surprise punts had kept the Bears at bay, field position would eventually become meaningless if the Redskins kept giving the ball back without ever trying to score.

Realizing this, Coach Flaherty decided to open things up. Cecil Hare (Ray's brother) rushed for 4 yards. Then Baugh flipped a 10-yard pass to Dick Todd, who caught it but fumbled when he was hit. Chicago's Lee Artoe scooped up the ball and, with a convoy of six Bears, lumbered 52 yards into the end zone! Artoe must have been leg-weary, though, because he botched the extra point and the score remained 6-0, Chicago.

Washington's Wilbur Moore received the kickoff and escaped every Bear but Ray Nolting, who saved a touchdown with his sure tackle at the 28. Once more, Sammy Baugh trusted his toe, his defense, and the surprise factor as he quick-kicked 61 yards to the Chicago 11 yard line. The Washington defense came through again, stopping the Bears inches short of a first down at their 20. Chicago dropped back in punt formation but surprised Washington when signal-caller Bill Osmanski took a short hike, dove into the line, and made the first down by an inch. However, even the success of that desperate maneu-

ver failed to ignite the Bears. After one more first down, the Redskins' Wilbur Moore intercepted a Luckman pass at the 28 and brought it back to the Chicago 42.

This was the moment the Redskins had been waiting for. On second down, Slingin' Sammy Baugh unleashed his famous arm and hit Wilbur Moore with a perfect pass at the goal line 38 yards away. Touchdown, Redskins! Bob Masterson kicked the extra point, and, midway through the second period, the underdog Washington Redskins forged ahead, 7-6.

Three plays after the touchdown, the Redskins

Wilbur Moore   *Nate Fine Photo/Nate Fine Productions, Courtesy Washington Redskins*

had another opportunity to score when Cecil Hare intercepted a Luckman pass at the Bears 38. Dick Todd swept end for a first down at the 28, but, three plays later, Washington faced a fourth-and-2 at the Chicago 20. With the nerve of a safecracker, Baugh drilled the ball to Masterson at the 14 for a first down. But with their backs to the wall, the Bears turned from Teddies into Grizzlies and stopped the Redskins cold on the next three plays. On fourth down, Flaherty disdained the field goal and ordered a pass to big Bob Masterson. The ball, Masterson, and the Bears' Scooter McLean arrived in the south corner of the end zone at the same time. Both players leaped, but it was McLean who got a hand on the football and knocked it away, quashing the Redskins' hopes for a comfortable lead.

With only 2 minutes to go in the half, the once-cocky Chicago Bears were reduced to using up the clock to prevent further damage. They succeeded, and the first half ended with Washington on top, 7-6. The Redskins' ultra-conservative strategy of quick-kicking whenever they had been saddled with unfavorable field position had worked, but most reporters in the pressbox were predicting a savage counter-attack by the Bears in the second half. However, they didn't fully consider the effect of 36,000 fans at Griffith Stadium pleading for the biggest upset in the 22-year history of the National Football League.

A huge ovation greeted the Redskins as the players returned to the frozen field for the second half. Chicago received the kickoff, but Washington's defense continued to dominate as it pushed the Bears back to their 1 yard line. Luckman punted to the Chicago 43, and the Redskins' momentum increased as fullback Andy Farkas became a human battering ram, rushing for 8 yards and then 3 more. Two scrambles by Baugh and another Farkas plunge produced a fourth-and-2 at the Bears 24. Coach Flaherty responded to the pleas of the crowd and ordered the 'Skins to go for it. Baugh handed off to Farkas, who climbed up right tackle Bill Young's back, sprang over the line, and landed at the Chicago 20 for a first down. [Fig. 9]

The Bears bunched themselves into an 8-man line, but Farkas still picked up 5 yards on a slant through left tackle and 7 more on a reverse to the 8 yard line. Two more carries moved the ball to the 1. On third down, Andy charged into the line once more. Just as he reached the goal line, he was hit hard and the ball squirted loose. The Bears pounced on it and began rejoicing, but the referee ruled that

Fig. 9   *AP/Wide World Photos*

Farkas had already crossed the goal line before the fumble occurred and awarded a touchdown to Washington! Redskins 14, Chicago 6.

Down by 8 points as the fourth quarter began, the Bears replaced the ineffective Luckman with Charley O'Rourke. On his first play, O'Rourke tossed a screen pass to Frank Maznicki, who ran down the right sideline for 40 yards. Then O'Rourke threw a 9-yard strike over the middle to John Siegel at the Washington 14. The overworked Redskins defense looked as if it was about to crack, but Sammy Baugh provided a tonic by intercepting an option pass from Maznicki, who had thrown to a spot in the end zone 15 yards from any of his receivers. For Maznicki, it was one of those unexplainable lapses of talent that strike an athlete from time to time. For the Redskins, it was a case of perfect timing.

With 12 minutes left in the game, the Bears knew that they had to stop the Redskins in a hurry and did so. However, on fourth down, a Chicago player was too anxious to block Baugh's punt and jumped offside, giving Washington a first down and more time with the football. Trying to catch the Bears napping, Slingin' Sam fired a long pass intended for Wilbur Moore, but Charley O'Rourke was wide awake and intercepted it at the Chicago 34. Despite O'Rourke's success on the previous drive, Luckman was sent back in with 8 minutes remaining in the championship. However, the breather had done nothing to rejuvenate the Chicago quarterback, and, after losing 19 yards, the Bears had to relinquish the ball again.

When the 'Skins took over at their 43, Baugh called a few conservative, time-consuming running plays, then punted into the Chicago end zone. To have any chance of winning, the Bears needed to score in a hurry then pray for an onside kick recovery. O'Rourke replaced the frustrated Luckman again and hit McLean with a bullet, giving the Bears a first down at the Washington 33. Then O'Rourke passed to Osmanski, who escaped Baugh's tackle and ran to the 2 yard line. From there, fullback Hugh Gallarneau bulled his way into the end zone, but the touchdown was nullified when Chicago was penalized 5 yards for having a man in motion. Osmanski crashed for 3 but lost a yard on third down due to a bone-rattling tackle by Dick Farman. Fourth down. Only 4 yards

separated the Bears from a 1-point game. O'Rourke took the snap from center Bulldog Turner and looked for Osmanski in the end zone. Seeing the 200-pounder from Holy Cross get open for an instant, O'Rourke threw. The football and Osmanski converged; Osmanski stretched out his hand—and the ball bounced off it!

The jubilant Redskins took over at their 20. With only a minute and a half remaining and the Bears unable to call a time-out, Washington guaranteed its victory by gaining one final first down. The mighty Bears could only watch helplessly as the hands on the big scoreboard clock met at zero, ending their 24-game unbeaten streak and two-year stranglehold on the rest of the league. By the final score of 14-6, the Washington Redskins were crowned champions of the National Football League!

Victory-crazed fans stormed onto the field to congratulate their heroes as the ecstatic Redskins ran to their locker room accompanied by Ki Aldrich's recurring shouts of: "We beat their pants off! We beat their pants off!" Head Coach Ray Flaherty, who was about to enter the Navy, went around the room and congratulated every Redskins player for his valiant effort. Finally, the shouting tapered off enough for the greatly admired coach to address his team. "Half of us are going into the service in a couple of weeks," said Flaherty in a hoarse, emotion-choked voice. "Hit the enemy just half as hard as you hit the Bears today, and this war won't take long to finish, and we can get back here pretty quick."

Three factors had combined to upset a Bears team that was essentially unchanged from the championship club that had beaten the 'Skins by 73 points only two years before: Baugh's 52-yard average on six punts, Andy Farkas' strong running, and a defense that allowed Sid Luckman to gain only 2 yards through the air. "They might have beaten us 73-0," exclaimed Redskins Owner George Preston Marshall, "but we beat 'em twice out of three times when the chips were down."

Nobody knew it at the time, but it was a moment that the Washington Redskins and their fans would have to savor for the next 30 years.

CRUEL AND UNUSUAL

National Football League Championship Game

Washington Redskins vs. Cleveland Rams

December 16, 1945

Pro football players were not always as well-known as they are today. When Red Grange, the most famous player in the early days of the NFL, was brought to the White House in 1925 to meet President Calvin Coolidge, the great halfback was introduced as "Red Grange, who plays with the Bears." The president shook Grange's hand earnestly and said, "Nice to meet you, young man. I've always liked animal acts."

Obviously, President Coolidge was not a football fan, but if he had been in office 20 years later, even he would have known about the Washington Redskins' greatest star: Slingin' Sammy Baugh. In 1945, Baugh set an NFL record for passing accuracy when he completed an incredible 70.3% of his passes (128-182 for 1,669 yards and 11 touchdowns) while winning his fourth passing crown. In addition, the 3-time all-pro had already established league records for best punting average in a season (51.4 yards in 1940) and intercepting the most passes in a single game (4 against the Lions in 1943), and had further distinguished himself by leading the league in passing, punting, and interceptions in 1943. Over 40 years later, those records still stand.

The reason Slingin' Sam threw only 182 times in

'45 was because second-year Coach Dudley DeGroot used a two-platoon offensive system, alternating one complete offensive squad led by Baugh with an entirely different squad headed by Frank Filchock, an excellent passer in his own right. DeGroot believed that alternating his platoons on each series would maximize the team's effectiveness while everyone learned the finer points of the T-Formation, which special assistant Clark Shaughnessy had installed in 1944.

At first, Baugh objected to the T-Formation even though he realized it would probably extend his career. Once, in a midseason game in 1944, the Redskins were having trouble moving the ball, and Sam could stand it no longer. "Listen fellers," said the frustrated Baugh in the huddle, "let's git back to the old Single Wing. We'll use the old plays, the old formations, and the old assignments." His teammates readily agreed. Freed from having to concentrate on unfamiliar footwork and ball-handling, Baugh recaptured his passing touch, and the Redskins cruised to victory. Nevertheless, once learned, the T-Formation offered greater flexibility, and Baugh eventually mastered it, although not as quickly as Filchock, who won the passing crown in 1944. Baugh came in second, the only time in NFL history that two passers from the same team finished 1-2.

In their 9 years in Washington, the Redskins had compiled the best record in the league (70-26-5), earned five Eastern Division titles, and won two NFL championships. At one point, from 1942-43, Washington played 17 games in a row without a loss. Their tremendous success worked against them, though, when a local newspaper report insinuated that they had thrown a late-season game in 1943 against the lowly Phil-Pitt Steagles. Enraged by the thinly veiled allegations, Redskins President George Preston Marshall, Coach Dutch Bergman, and the entire team marched into the editor's office and confronted the reporters who had written the story. It turned out that a gambler had supplied the information to the newspaper but had been unwilling to sign an affidavit to that effect. "You mean you printed it on the front page on hearsay?" shouted Marshall. An embarrassed silence followed, and Marshall stormed out, thinking a retraction would surely be printed the next day.

He was wrong, and the rumors continued to grow. As a result, the demoralized Redskins lost their last two games of the regular season to the New York Giants, which forced a playoff for the Eastern Division championship the following week. The stench of suspicion finally dissipated a few days before the game when the newspaper apologized to Marshall and the team for its unsubstantiated allegations, and the exonerated Redskins smashed the Giants, 28-0, to win their fourth Eastern Division crown in 7 years. Unfortunately, in the NFL Championship game against the Chicago Bears, Baugh suffered a concussion in the first quarter, and Chicago romped by the 'Skins, 41-21.

In 1944, Coach Bergman resigned to pursue a career in radio, and Marshall hired Dudley DeGroot. The switch in coaches and the problems of adjusting to the new T-Formation caused Washington to slip to third place with a 6-3-1 record. But, once Slingin' Sam got the hang of things in 1945, the 'Skins returned to the top of the Eastern Division with an 8-2 record, clinching the title with a 17-0 whitewashing of the Giants at Griffith Stadium in front of a sellout crowd that included General Dwight D. Eisenhower.

Baugh's passing artistry remained the key to Washington's success because it forced defenses to spread their men over such a wide area that they were unable to contain Washington's running attack. Fullback Frank Akins, who had barely lost the rushing title to Philadelphia's Steve Van Buren, provided the forward thrust of the Redskins' strong running game while swivel-hipped halfback Steve Bagarus provided the thrills.

In addition, Washington's roster had been bolstered by the return from the war of all-pro end Wayne Millner, centers Al Demao and Ki Aldrich, guard Clem Stralka, tackle Fred Davis, and halfbacks Cecil Hare and Dick Todd. Left end Joe Aguirre, right guard Marvin Whited, and right end Doug Turley completed the big and mobile line that was coached by the 'Skins' former all-pro tackle, Turk Edwards.

For the first time in five appearances in the Championship game, the Redskins would not face their arch-rivals, the Chicago Bears. In their place stood a young Cleveland Rams team headed by the league's Most Valuable Player, quarterback Bob Waterfield. Even though he was only a rookie, "Beautiful Bob" (who was married to actress Jane Russell) had almost single-handedly lifted the Rams from 4-6 mediocrity to 9-1 superiority. Like Sammy Baugh, the 6-foot 1-inch, 190-pound Waterfield was the complete player, leading his team in passing, scoring, kicking, and interceptions. After serving in World War II, Waterfield returned to UCLA, spurning a job with the Rams, who had drafted him in 1944. After starring for the Bruins and earning his degree, Waterfield joined the Rams in 1945 and made his presence felt immediately. "On the second day he joined us," said Cleveland Coach Adam Walsh, "he started to take charge of the club. He plays like a 60-minute head coach."

Cool under pressure, Waterfield excelled at throwing deep to either Steve Pritko or Jim Benton, a tricky all-pro receiver whose 45 receptions was second only to the great Don Hutson's 47. Halfbacks Fred Gehrke and Jim Gillette shared rushing duties, combining equally for 857 yards in 137 carries for a remarkable 6.25 average. The quick Rams line could not match the Redskins' in size even though it was spearheaded by the biggest man on the field, 6-foot 4-inch, 265-pound tackle Eberle Schultz, and "Rattlesnake"

Riley Matheson, a 4-time all-pro guard who had earned his nickname by surviving the bite of a rattlesnake. Twice.

One reason the Rams were favored by 3 points in their first appearance in a Championship game was because they would be playing at home at Cleveland Municipal Stadium, a mammoth lakeside coliseum known for its tricky winds and arctic conditions. Sure enough, a massive cold front hovered over Lake Erie all week prior to the game. Maintenance crews tried to prevent the field from freezing by mulching it with $7,200 worth of straw and scrap paper, but, when it was removed on game day, the unprotected field quickly turned into a hockey rink. With the temperature at minus-8 degrees and a stiff intermittent wind blowing off the lake, it was not surprising that the reeds on the Redskins Marching Band's wind instruments froze and only 32,178 fans out of a possible 80,000 showed up to root their team to victory.

The Redskins, who had had the foresight to bring along sneakers to maintain a modicum of traction on the icy surface, were not overly concerned about the weather. "Hell, those Rams have to play on the same field as we do," said Washington halfback Bob Seymour, "and nasty weather figures to bother Waterfield more than it does Baugh." Amazingly, though, the Rams had neglected to provide their players with sneakers. More amazingly, when Cleveland Coach Adam Walsh explained his predicament to Dud DeGroot, the Washington coach agreed that it would be an unfair advantage for his players to wear their sneakers and ordered them to take them off. Apparently, in those days there was some crazy notion that it mattered "how you played the game."

Blasts of frozen wind whipped the unshoveled remnants of 5 inches of fresh snow into the corners of Municipal Stadium as Cleveland's Pat West kicked off to open the 1945 NFL Championship game. Washington's Merle Condit fielded the ball at his 10 and skated 34 yards over the frozen gridiron to the 44. On first down, fullback Frank Akins charged through a big hole over left tackle for 8 yards before a punch to the nose knocked him down. Even though blood was pouring out of his broken nose, Akins refused to leave the game. Three more plunges into

the line moved the ball to the Cleveland 40, but a 2-yard loss on third down forced the 'Skins to punt.

The Rams started at their 21. Halfback Fred Gehrke broke through tackle for 16 yards, then notched 17 more as Cleveland surged into Washington territory. On first down, quarterback Bob Waterfield surprised the Redskins by launching a deep pass to Jim Benton, who caught it at the Washington 14 before being tackled. The Redskins defense stiffened, though, and, three plays later, the Rams faced fourth and 4 at the 8. Rather than attempt a field goal, Coach Walsh decided to go for the first down. Waterfield handed off to halfback Jim Gillette. For a moment it appeared he had an opening, but the 'Skins shut the gate and brought him down just short of the first-down marker at the 5.

As was the custom then, Sammy Baugh lined up deep in his end zone on first down to punt the 'Skins out of trouble. But he dropped the snap from center and had to throw the ball away intentionally to avoid a safety. With the ball moved back to the 2 due to the penalty, Baugh again set up in punt formation. This time, Slingin' Sam had a surprise waiting for the unwary Rams. Instead of punting, Baugh unleashed a pass to Wayne Millner, who was racing upfield completely uncovered. But the ball never reached him; it hit the goal post and bounced back into the end zone for a safety! At that time, the rule specified: "When a forward pass from behind the goal line strikes the goal posts or the cross bar . . . it is a safety if the pass strikes the ground in the end zone." Instead of getting the points for a 98-yard touchdown, the forlorn Redskins trailed, 2-0.

Late in the first quarter, Sammy Baugh lurched to the sideline holding his ribs. For the past month, Baugh had been denying rumors of problems with his ribs and continued to play despite the pain. Now he could play no more—two of his ribs were broken.

Frank Filchock replaced Baugh at quarterback, and, a few minutes later, Washington's sagging spirits were rejuvenated when Washington linebacker Ki Aldrich intercepted a Waterfield pass and returned it to the Redskins 43. An unnecessary roughness penalty gave Washington a first down at the Cleveland 38, then, two plays later, Filchock threw deep. Halfback Steve Bagarus, who had streaked down the right sideline after going in motion, caught up to the perfectly thrown pass at the 12, braked to allow a Rams defender to skid by, turned 360 degrees, straight-armed safety Bob Waterfield at the 5, and scored! Joe Aguirre kicked the extra point, and Washington led, 7-2.

After an exchange of punts, the Rams regrouped at their 3. Halfback Jim Gillette raced 24 yards through a gaping hole over left tackle before being shoved out of bounds at the Washington 46. A pass to Benton gained 9 yards. On fourth and 1 at the 37, Coach Walsh decided to gamble again. The Redskins bunched their strongest players at the line, but Waterfield surprised them by faking a handoff and firing a perfect pass down the middle to Jim Benton, who caught it at the 10 and raced into the end zone for a touchdown! On the extra point attempt, a bad snap from center upset the timing, and Waterfield topped the ball. Washington lineman John Konizewski got a hand on it, but the ball continued to float like a knuckleball toward the goal post, where it landed on the crossbar, teetered for a moment, then finally crawled over. That gave the Rams a 9-7 lead.

After the kickoff, Cleveland's pass rushers swarmed in on Frank Filchock, sacking him twice. On third and long at his 14, Filchock finally managed to get off a pass, but it was intercepted by Pat West at the Washington 30 and brought back to the 13. The 'Skins averted disaster, however, when Ki Aldrich picked off another Waterfield pass with a minute left in the half, and both teams gratefully repaired to their locker rooms to thaw out. The numbers on the scoreboard reflected the difficulty of the conditions as much as the closeness of the two teams' abilities: Cleveland 9, Washington 7.

George Preston Marshall stormed into the Redskins' locker room and shouted, "Who the hell decided not to wear the sneakers?"

"I did," admitted Dud DeGroot.

"Why?"

"Because I made a gentleman's agreement with Coach Walsh," replied DeGroot calmly.

Glowering, Marshall shot back: "This is no gentleman's game! That's the last decision you'll ever make as coach of the Redskins!"

In the embarrassed silence that followed Marshall's loud departure, the Washington players suddenly longed for the comparative warmth of the wind-swept field. Although they realized that DeGroot would remain fired no matter what happened in the second half, the Redskins vowed to exonerate their coach by winning without the sneakers. Handicapped further by the loss of their two greatest stars, Sammy Baugh and fullback Frank Akins, the 'Skins hoped that their righteousness would be rewarded, not in heaven, but on the hard, frozen field of Municipal Stadium.

The Cleveland Rams proved that right does not always make might by driving mercilessly down the field on their first possession of the second half. Halfback Jim Gillette broke loose for two big gains, then grabbed a long pass from Waterfield at the Washington 15, skipped out of the grasp of a diving tackler, and ran into the end zone for a 44-yard touchdown! Waterfield missed the conversion, but the Rams were still in control, leading 15-7.

Late in the third quarter, the Redskins cranked up their stalled offense. From the 30, reserve halfback Bob DeFruiter swept end for 15 yards. One play later, Filchock faded back and fired a pass to Steve Bagarus at the Rams 40. Bagarus tucked the ball away and raced toward the end zone but was finally hauled down at the 6 by Fred Gehrke. Three plays lost 3 yards. On fourth and goal at the 9, the Rams double-covered Bagarus, leaving Bob Seymour wide open in the end zone. Filchock hit him on the numbers for a touchdown, and Aguirre's conversion closed the gap to a single point, 15-14.

After another exchange of punts, the Rams threatened to widen their lead as they drove to the Washington 29. On first down, Waterfield passed to fullback Pat West, who then tried to lateral to Gillette. Instead, the ball bounced into the hands of linebacker Ki Aldrich, and the resurgent Redskins took over at their 24 with less than 8 minutes left in the game. Filchock passed to Pat Dye, who caught the ball at his 40, escaped a tackle, and dashed to the Rams 31. However, Cleveland surrendered only 7 yards on the next three plays, so on fourth down Joe Aguirre, the league-leading kicker, set up for a 32-yard field goal attempt. Stepping forward gingerly on the hard, slippery field, Aguirre sunk his toe into the frozen ball, sending it spinning end over end toward the wooden goal posts. [Fig. 10] At first, the kick appeared to be on target, but a sudden gust of wind blew it off course and the ball sailed wide of the left upright by a foot. The luckless Redskins still trailed, 15-14.

After forcing the Rams to punt, Washington took over at its 43 with 2 minutes left in the game. Halfback Cecil Hare took a pitchout and skirted end for 12 yards. The next three plays netted only 7 yards, and Aguirre went in to try another field goal from the 45. This time, his kick was far short, and a Cleveland safety returned it to the 26.

Trusting his defense's ability to stop the Redskins more than his offense's ability to hang on to the football so close to its goal line, Walsh ordered another punt, and Waterfield booted it out of bounds at the Washington 16. The strategy paid off as Frank Filchock's last desperate heave was intercepted by Albie Reisz at the 45, allowing the frost-bitten Cleveland Rams to defeat the snake-bitten Redskins, 15-14.

Although they had been outplayed in every area, the Washington Redskins could have won the game if Dame Fortune had been even slightly impartial with her gifts. If both Sammy Baugh and Fred Akins had not been injured; if Bob Waterfield's blocked extra-point kick had been one inch shorter; if Joe Aguirre's 32-yard field goal attempt had not been blown off course; or if Baugh's first-quarter pass had not bounced off the upright, giving the Rams 2 points for a safety, the Redskins, even though they had been limited to eight first downs, would have been the ones laughing and shouting in their locker room instead of the victorious Rams.

Luck, however, has always played an important role in football, and, in this game, Washington had been completely star-crossed. "It was the first time we've ever been licked by a goal post," lamented George Marshall. It was the last time, too. "I'm sure as hell going to change that rule at our next league meeting," vowed Marshall. The Redskins' owner kept his promise, but, unfortunately, even George Preston Marshall could not legislate against broken ribs and untimely gusts of wind.

Fig. 10   *AP/Wide World Photos*

NEVER SAY DIE

Pittsburgh Steelers vs. Washington Redskins

October 5, 1947

There is a culling process in the development of an NFL player that corresponds quite nicely to the process of natural selection that Charles Darwin described in *Origin of the Species*. Like the long-legged deer that is better adapted than his short-legged cousin to outrun wolves on the open plains, so too do only the fastest, strongest, and most coordinated athletes survive the ever sterner tests of skill that accompany his advancement from high school to the pros. Currently, there are more than 1 million high school football players, but only 5.5% of those will have the size and ability to play in college. Four years later, only 2% of those 55,000 collegiate players will make it to the pros. In other words, only one in every 850 football players has everything it takes to play in the NFL.

With those kind of odds, you would think that any player drafted in the first five rounds would be a superstar. He would be if there were some infallible method of identifying which athletes were truly the best football players. But there isn't. Scouting combines like QUADRA, United, and BLESTO-V (an acronym for its members—Bears, Lions, Eagles, Steelers, Tampa Bay, Oilers, and Vikings) that share information on collegiate players, tend to rely on technology to solve the problem. Numbers are assigned to every aspect of a prospect's physique and performance —sprint times, height, weight, strength, reflexes, intelligence, even vertical jump—and fed into a computer. The final tally often determines a player's draft position, which determines his salary, which, in turn, determines how many chances he will get to prove himself. This system places so much emphasis on a player's physical attributes that an inch in height can mean the difference between having a lucrative 10-year career in the NFL and getting a plane ticket to anonymity.

However, for all their wizardry, the computer programmers have yet to discover a way to assign numbers to the amount of desire in a player's heart or his ability to perform under pressure. "If I were a scout," said Jack Lambert, the Pittsburgh Steelers' great middle linebacker, "the first thing I would look for is heart. I'll take 22 guys with heart over 22 guys with great athletic ability any day." In judging those intangible traits, scouts are no better off today than they were half a century ago.

In the Thirties and Forties, the college draft was a disorganized grabfest populated by men like Redskins President George Preston Marshall, whose only preparation was to scan the latest copy of *Street & Smith Football Yearbook*. Rather than let his scouts and newly hired general manager, Dick McCann, choose players whose ability had been verified by first-hand observations, Marshall believed he could discern a player's talent by the pose he had struck for his publicity photo in *Street & Smith*. Marshall's ineptness cost him. Of the thirty players he chose in the 1946 draft, only one made the team.

It became common knowledge around the league that Marshall was not above spying on his competitors. On draft day, he would wander around the room, paying his respects to the other owners while trying to get a peek at the names on their lists. Little did he know that they were laying in wait for him, letting him look at lists of bad players in whom they had no interest. Sure enough, Marshall would squander his choices on washouts while everyone else in the room shared a good laugh.

To make matters worse, Marshall often neglected to determine whether a prospect met even the most basic requirements before drafting him. In 1946, Marshall wasted his #1 choice on UCLA running back Cal Rossi, who was ineligible to be drafted because he was still a junior. Undeterred, Marshall picked Rossi in the first round again the following year, then learned, too late, that the UCLA star had no interest in pursuing a career in pro football.

Marshall's conceit also extended into the coach's realm, where his meddling became a constant nuisance. In 1946, Marshall hired Turk Edwards, a former Redskins tackle and team captain who had earned all-pro honors four times in his 9-year career, to replace Coach Dud DeGroot. But Marshall never really gave Edwards a chance. Having recently sold his Palace Laundry, Marshall had nothing better to do than undermine Edwards' authority with his incessant kibitzing—especially after the 'Skins blew a 24-0 halftime lead and lost to the Eagles, 28-24, midway through the 1946 season.

The Redskins' Big Chief was equally renowned for his thriftiness. In the Forties, pro football was considered a part-time job with afternoons free for pursuing more conventional careers. The low salaries, ranging from $3,000 for linemen to $25,000 for a few stars like Sammy Baugh, Bob Waterfield, Sid Luckman, and Steve Van Buren, reflected that attitude. Even worse, during training camp the Redskins were essentially slaves, playing six or seven exhibi-

tion games every season for free. Once, in the early Fifties, when it was learned that the Bears and the Lions had been paid $50 per man to play an extra exhibition game, the Washington players, who also were being asked to play an extra game, got together and decided to petition Marshall for equal treatment.

A trio of veteran players—Sammy Baugh, Bill Dudley, and Al Demao—approached Marshall in his office at Occidental College, where the 'Skins trained during the summer. No sooner had Baugh said, "We've formed a committee . . .," than Marshall sprang from his seat shouting, "Committee? That means a union! I won't have it! I don't recognize any of you!" and escaped out a back door.

General Manager Dick McCann was as startled by Marshall's outburst as the "committee" and intervened on the players' behalf. When Marshall found out that the players would settle for $10 per man, he returned and told Baugh he would talk to the entire squad before the start of afternoon practice. At 3:00, Marshall placed himself in the center of a large circle of expectant players and announced, "There will be no extra money for exhibition games. If any of you don't like it, the exit is over there." End of negotiation.

Injuries and defections to the new All-America Football Conference took a heavy toll in '46, and Washington wound up with its worst record to date: 5-5-1. Somewhat to his credit, Marshall resisted the temptation to fire Edwards, and, in 1947, the 'Skins inaugurated a youth movement. When the season began, only 4 of the 35 players on the roster—Sammy Baugh, Dick Todd, Doug Turley, and Ki Aldrich—had more than two years' experience. Gone were stars like Joe Aguirre, Frank Akins, Ed Cifers, Frank Filchock, Cecil Hare, Wayne Millner, Bob Seymour, and Clem Stralka, many of whom had left because Marshall refused to pay them a decent wage.

In the first game of the 1947 season, 33-year-old quarterback Sammy Baugh completed 21 of 34 passes for 364 yards and five touchdowns, yet the Redskins lost to the Philadelphia Eagles, 45-42. Three of those touchdown passes landed in the hands of a rookie end, Hugh Taylor, whose blade-like physique had earned him the nickname "Bones." How had the Redskins known to draft Taylor? *Street & Smith*, of

Bones Taylor   *Abbie Rowe Photo, Courtesy Washington Redskins*

course. Coach Edwards had read an article in the magazine about the Oklahoma City College star and convinced Marshall to spend a draft choice on him. Over the next eight seasons, Taylor would justify his selection by catching 272 passes for 5,233 yards and 58 touchdowns.

The Redskins' opponent for their 1947 home opener at Griffith Stadium was the Pittsburgh Steelers, a 1-1 team on the rebound from a disastrous merger with other undermanned franchises during World War II. In 1943, the Steelers and Eagles had spliced themselves together to form the Phil-Pitt Steagles. After going 5-4-1, the Steagles committed polygamy the following year by uniting with the 0-10 Chicago Cardinals. The mutant Card-Pitts were so awful they became known as the "Carpets" while 10 straight opponents walked over them.

After the war ended, all three teams had resumed their original identities, and new Coach Jock Sutherland led the Steelers back to respectability with a 5-5-1 record in '46. Sutherland's hard-hearted approach to the game rejuvenated the soft-nosed Steelers, but it also cost them the services of their greatest star, halfback Bill Dudley, the league's Most Valuable Player, who demanded to be traded after Sutherland forced him to play the final four games of the season with broken ribs.

Sutherland also drew criticism for being the only coach in the NFL to continue using the Single Wing. When asked why he stuck with the outdated formation, Sutherland would quote Columbia Coach Lou Little, who had once said, "The best system is the human system. Give me the big, strong, fast, smart boys and I'll win with any system."

Maybe Charles Darwin should have been a football coach.

36,565 Redskins fans, the largest crowd ever to attend a football game in Washington, D.C., wedged into newly enlarged Griffith Stadium to see if the 'Skins could avenge the 14-7 defeat that the Pittsburgh Steelers had handed them the year before. That didn't appear very likely when the Steelers took the opening kickoff and drove 60 yards through the Redskins defense without having to resort to a single pass. Runs by fullback Steve Lach, wingback Bob Sullivan, and tailback Johnny Clement, who racked up 43 yards on a keeper, moved the Steelers to the Washington 8. The 'Skins defense finally held, but Joe Glamp's 15-yard field goal gave Pittsburgh a 3-0 lead.

Neither team mounted a serious threat during the rest of the first period; in fact, the Redskins could not even make it out of their own territory. However, on the first play of the second quarter, Sammy Baugh took the snap at his 46, dropped back into the pocket, and pegged the ball to Bob Nussbaumer, who gathered in the wobbly pass at the Pittsburgh 27 without breaking stride and outraced safety Paul White to the goal line for a 54-yard touchdown! Dick Poillon converted, and the 'Skins led, 7-3.

Late in the second quarter, the Steelers got the first break of the game when Walt Slater recovered a Redskins fumble at the Pittsburgh 40. A 19-yard pass from Clement to Val Jansante sparked the Steelers, and they drove 45 yards in seven plays. On first down at the 15, Clement threaded the needle to Steve Lach, who caught the perfect pass between three Redskins defenders at the 8 and dragged all three plus the referee into the end zone for a touchdown! That put the Steelers back on top, 10-7.

Unable to stop the clock with 59 seconds remaining in the half, Sammy Baugh passed the Redskins quickly down the field. Unfortunately, time ran out on him with the ball at the Pittsburgh 14, and Washington trudged to its locker room, trailing 10-7.

The second half got off to a rousing start as Redskins halfback Dick Todd returned the kickoff 50 yards to the Steelers 43. Sammy Baugh picked up right where he had left off by passing to Nussbaumer for 6 yards and to Eddie Saenz for 28 more. On third and goal at the 3, Baugh faded back and fired a bullet to Dick Poillon in the end zone. Touchdown, Washington! Poillon missed the extra point, though, ending his streak of 30 straight conversions, and the Redskins had to be satisfied with their 13-10 lead.

Linebacker Ki Aldrich thwarted the Steelers on their next drive by intercepting a Clement pass, but Washington's offense couldn't capitalize on the turnover. After an exchange of punts gave the 'Skins good field position at their 41, Slingin' Sam decided it was time to go deep. Spotting Bones Taylor pulling away from his defender, Baugh cocked his arm and fired. Just as Taylor reached for the long pass, Pittsburgh safety Bob Compagno arrived on the scene and plucked the ball out of his grasp. A convoy of blockers formed and escorted Compagno down the right sideline, knocking over Redskins like dominoes as Compagno dashed 64 yards for a touchdown! Glamp converted, and the Steelers forged ahead, 17-13.

Eddie Saenz fielded Pittsburgh's kickoff at his 6, darted past the first wave of tacklers, and nearly broke away for a touchdown but was tripped up at the 38. Fullback Sal Rosato blasted through the line four times, picking up two first downs and taking the heat off Baugh, who had been under a heavy rush all day. On first down at the Pittsburgh 35, Baugh spotted Bones Taylor getting free again. This time Sam's pass arrived without mishap, and Taylor hauled it in at the goal line for a 35-yard touchdown! [Fig. 12] Washington 20, Pittsburgh 17.

The Steelers roared back. On first down at midfield, Clement rifled the ball to halfback Bob Sullivan, who caught it at the Washington 25 and outran safety Jim Youel to the goal line for a stunning 50-yard touchdown! Glamp kicked the extra point, and, for the sixth time in the game, the lead changed hands: Steelers 24, Redskins 20.

Pittsburgh gained more momentum when linebacker Frank Sinkovitz intercepted a Baugh pass at the Washington 21. The Steelers carefully worked the ball to the Washington 2 but came away empty-handed when a fourth-down gamble failed. The Redskins took over at their 1, and Baugh dropped back into the end zone to punt out of danger. Instead of punting, though, Sam looked downfield for an open receiver. Unfortunately, the Steelers were not fooled, and he had to scramble to avoid being sacked. Just before he got rid of the ball, Sammy stepped on the backline of the end zone and the referee called a safety, giving Pittsburgh 2 points to increase its advantage to 26-20.

Following Baugh's free kick, the Steelers marched rapidly down the field, but, when Glamp missed a

Fig. 12   *Nate Fine/NFL Photos*

40-yard field goal attempt, lost their chance to go ahead by two scores. With 9 minutes left in the game, Washington took over at its 20 and surged into Steelers territory. A 35-yard pass from Baugh to Saenz gave the Redskins a first down at the 11. However, the next three plays gained only 2 yards. On fourth and 8 at the 9, Baugh gunned a pass to Sal Rosato at the goal line. Rosato grabbed the ball, and, although he was tackled before he could get into the end zone, succeeded in making the first down. On the next play, fullback Tom Farmer plowed into the end zone, and

Poillon boomed the crucial extra-point kick between the uprights, putting Washington back on top, 27-26.

Pittsburgh had one more chance. With 3 minutes remaining in the game, the Steelers regrouped at their 30 and quickly drove to the Washington 23, where they faced fourth and a foot. With 25 seconds remaining, Coach Sutherland decided to send in Bob Glamp for the game-winning field goal attempt from the 29. 36,000 Redskins fans roared discouragement as Glamp tried to steady his nerves. The snap and hold were perfect. Glamp stepped forward and swung his leg. The ball soared over the outstretched hands of the Washington defenders and headed for the goal post, spinning end over end over end. With plenty of distance to spare, the ball smacked into the left upright and bounced back onto the field. No good! As the jubilant fans celebrated in the stands, the Washington Redskins ran off the field with their first victory of the 1947 season. Washington 27, Pittsburgh 26.

With seven lead changes, five touchdown passes, three missed field goals, and one safety, this topsy-turvy game foreshadowed the wide-open brand of football that would soon captivate the nation. Sammy Baugh's performance (13 completions in 28 attempts for 275 yards and three touchdowns) was typical for the man who, more than anyone else, was bridging the gap between pro football's formative stage and the pass-happy modern era on the horizon.

Slingin' Sam would eventually retire in 1952 after 16 glorious seasons in a Redskins uniform, and, in 1963, would enter the Hall of Fame as a charter member. The only player in history to lead the league in passing, punting, and interceptions in a single year, Baugh was arguably the greatest all-around player in the history of professional football. When he retired, his many NFL records included:

> Highest percentage of completed passes in a season: 70.33% *
> Most seasons leading the league in passing: 6*
> Most passes attempted in a career: 3,097
> Most passes completed in a career: 1,751

Sammy Baugh addresses the crowd at his induction into the Pro Football Hall of Fame   *UPI/The Bettmann Archive*

> Most seasons leading the league in completions: 5*
> Most yards gained passing in a career: 22,717
> Most years leading the league in passing yardage: 4
> Most touchdown passes in a career: 193
> Most passes completed in a season: 210
> Most yards gained passing in a season: 2,938
> Most seasons leading the league in punting: 4*
> Highest punting average in a season: 51.4*
> Highest punting average in a career: 45.1*
> Most interceptions caught in a game: 4*
> *still NFL records

For those who were lucky enough to see him play, Sammy Baugh will always be "Mr. Redskin."

SPONTANEOUS COMBUSTION

Washington Redskins vs. Philadelphia Eagles

October 1, 1955

From 1948-1954, Washington Redskins head coaches had about as much job security as a food taster for a South American dictator. In that 7-year span, six different coaches discovered the impossibility of being forceful enough to lead 35 grizzled football players while remaining docile enough to kowtow to Redskins President George Preston Marshall. "Marshall didn't keep his coaches around long enough to have any continuity," said halfback Bill Dudley. "I was in Washington three years (1950, '51, and '53) and we had, what, three different coaches. He'd always try to hire someone he could boss around. His coaches didn't have the guts to tell him where to go."

In 1949, Marshall fired Coach Turk Edwards (16-18-1) and, in a step out of character, tried to sign Paul "Bear" Bryant. Unfortunately, the University of Kentucky refused to release Bryant from his new contract, and Marshall ended up hiring Admiral Billick Whelchel, a war hero with limited coaching experience. Seven games later, Marshall replaced Whelchel with assistant coach Herman Ball, who guided the hapless 'Skins to only 4 victories in their next 20 games. After the Redskins opened the 1951 season with three straight defeats, Ball "resigned" in favor of Dick Todd, a former star halfback with the Redskins, who posted a respectable 5-4 record down the stretch.

During the 1952 preseason, Coach Todd made the mistake of standing up to Marshall, who was upset that 16-year veteran Sammy Baugh had not played in an exhibition loss to the San Francisco 49ers. When Marshall confronted him on the train to Los Angeles the next day, Todd defended his decision, saying, "I know what Baugh can do. I wanted to try out my other quarterbacks. Now, do you want me to coach the team, or do you want the job?" Startled by Todd's audacity, Marshall backed off. Nevertheless, a few days later, Todd decided that the job was not worth the aggravation and resigned during halftime of the Rams game. "You can't do this to me," screamed Marshall, but Todd refused to change his mind. In a rage, Marshall returned to his seat in the stands and impulsively offered the job to one of his guests, former Green Bay Packers Coach Curly Lambeau.

At first glance, the choice seemed inspired. After all, Lambeau had founded the Packers and led them to six NFL championships in his 31 years as head coach. However, Lambeau, who had been out of coaching for several years, soon discovered that recent refinements in the game had evolved beyond his grasp. In addition, his frequent outbursts of temper cost him the respect of his players. "Nobody on the team was certain of his job or his position," said linebacker Chuck Drazenovich. "Nobody knew whether he was going to play, or whether he was going to get cut. As a result, everybody was looking for a hole to crawl into."

Under Lambeau, the '52 'Skins skidded to a 4-8 record, their fourth straight losing season. To be fair, though, Lambeau's coaching was only one of several factors undermining the Redskins' fortunes. George Marshall's refusal to integrate his team not only left Washington with a much smaller pool of talent from which to choose, but also made the 'Skins the favorite target of black players throughout the league. Moreover, the recent rule change allowing free substitution favored those clubs with productive scouting systems. Now that a great punter or receiver did not have to play a full 60 minutes, teams with the greatest depth of talent on and off the field began to pull away from old-fashioned clubs like the Redskins.

Instead of choosing the best players available, Marshall continued to draft Southern collegians because he thought it would please his large constituency of fans in the Deep South. Marshall's antiquated policy cost the Redskins dearly in the 1952 draft when he bypassed Frank Gifford of USC and Hugh McElhenny of the University of Washington in order to choose Larry Isbell of Baylor in the first round. Gifford and McElhenny ended up in the Hall of Fame. Isbell never played a down for Washington, choosing to play baseball instead. "I guess there was some merit in picking Southern players," said Bill Dudley. "I don't doubt for a minute that it helped put people in the stands. But in the long run, people come if you win. And we weren't winning. The people eventually started staying away."

Falling attendance meant lower revenues, which, in turn, meant low salaries for the players. Unwilling to pay for the kind of talent that could lead the 'Skins back to the top of the standings, Marshall let the Redskins slip into a vicious circle where failure fed on itself, acting as both cause and effect. "Marshall was a showman most of all," explained quarterback Eddie LeBaron. "He wanted entertainment. That's how he looked at his draft picks. We never had very good defensive teams but we kept drafting offensive players. He wanted big names, people who would draw fans and bring excitement."

To that end, Marshall acquired "Bullet" Bill Dudley from the Detroit Lions in 1950. Dudley, who had been the league's Most Valuable Player in 1946, came to Washington near the end of his career after starring in Pittsburgh and Detroit, where he had been the highest paid player in the NFL. That same year, the Redskins drafted all-America halfback Charlie "Choo-Choo" Justice out of the University of North Carolina, another in a long line of highly touted Southern running backs like Rob Goode of Texas A & M and Leon Heath of Oklahoma. Goode set a Redskins record in 1951 by rushing for 951 yards, then spent the next two years in Korea. Heath led the team in rushing in '52, followed by Justice in '53. However, Michigan State's Billy Wells finally broke up the Southern hegemony in '54 when he rushed for 516 yards, seventh best in the league.

With the legendary Sammy Baugh nearing retirement, the Redskins began to search for a quarterback who could fill his hightop cleats. In 1948, Marshall brought two excellent prospects to camp: Harry Gilmer and Charlie Conerly. Unwilling to keep both, Marshall sold his rights to Conerly to the New York Giants, where he would star for the next 14 years. Typical of Redskins luck, Gilmer injured his leg a week later and never attained the stardom that was predicted for him.

In 1950, the Redskins drafted another quarterback, this time in the tenth round. However, before he could take his place as Baugh's successor, this 5-foot 7-inch product of the College of Pacific would have to overcome two Korean War shrapnel wounds and Coach Lambeau's preconceived conviction that he was too short for the job. His name was Eddie LeBaron, the "Li'l General." In college, LeBaron's slick ball-handling and ability to throw on the run had compensated for his lack of height and earned him Little All-America honors. As a sophomore, Eddie pioneered the Belly Series, a ploy that required quick hands and quicker thinking. "I kept seeing how the defensive end would come in and stop our off-tackle slant play," said LeBaron. "So I started to put the ball in the belly of the fullback, then kept it there until the end reacted. When he did, I'd flip it out to the trailing halfback."

After being cited for heroism in the Korean War, LeBaron rejoined the Redskins in 1952 only to have his ruggedness called into question by Coach Curly Lambeau. Not that there weren't problems. "Making the switch from Sam to Eddie was an adjustment for all the receivers," remembered Bones Taylor. "Sam was the greatest, the best. Eddie was a fine man, too, a great competitor. But his size was a problem. When he threw the ball, it would look like it was coming out of a tent. You couldn't see his motion or see him, for that matter. So you had to adjust differently." Despite a good showing in his rookie season, LeBaron began to feel unwanted after the Redskins chose quarterbacks Larry Isbell, Jack Scarbath, and Al Dorow in successive drafts. Forced to share playing time with Scarbath in 1953, LeBaron became more and more disgruntled and finally, in 1954, defected to the Canadian Football League along with all-pro defensive end Gene Brito.

That same year, two great Redskins veterans retired: center/linebacker Al Demao and halfback "Bullet" Bill Dudley. Demao, the only remaining member of Washington's 1945 championship team and one of the last Redskins to play both ways, received a special honor in 1952 when he became the first Redskins lineman to be given a "day" at Griffith Stadium. Like Demao, Dudley played both offense (halfback) and defense (safety) and also place-kicked and returned punts. In 1946, when he played for the Pittsburgh Steelers, "Bullet" Bill became the only man in history to lead the NFL in rushing, interceptions, and punt returns in a single year, and, for that, was named the league's Most Valuable Player. In 1966, he was inducted into the Hall of Fame.

With so many major changes in personnel, Coach Lambeau knew he was on shaky ground, especially after the 'Skins limped to a 6-5-1 season in '53. It turned into quicksand during the summer of 1954 when Lambeau got into a shouting match with Marshall in the lobby of the Senator Hotel in Sacramento. After watching the 'Skins lose to the 49ers in an exhibition game, Marshall, who had a strict rule prohibiting players from drinking in public, noticed a couple of Redskins walking through the lobby with six-packs of beer under their arms. Marshall accosted

Eddie LeBaron   *Courtesy Washington Redskins*

them, but the players explained that Coach Lambeau allowed them to drink beer after games as long as it was done in private, which was their intention. Marshall stormed after Lambeau, who happened to be in the lobby at the time, and the two men nearly came to blows. Goodbye, Curly; Hello, Joe Kuharich.

Kuharich, who had been the Chicago Cardinals' head coach in 1952, took charge immediately, and

Coach Joe Kuharich (on right) with Assistant Coach Mike Nixon   *Abbie Rowe Photo, Courtesy Washington Redskins*

the Redskins responded to his professional, organized approach. "The first problem is to gain the squad's confidence that the things you teach are sound and workable," said Kuharich. "Many of your players have been in the league a long time. They have played under many coaches and have their own ingrained ideas of the right way to do things. Their skepticism of a new coach's principles is understandable. The big job is to convince them you're solid. Sometimes it's a task not completed even in an entire season." That last statement proved prophetic as the 1954 'Skins slipped to a 3-9 record while giving up 432 points, the seventh highest total ever surrendered by an NFL team—before or since.

To restock the Redskins roster after the retirements of Bones Taylor, end Joe Tereshinski, tackle Paul Lipscomb, and Charlie Justice, Coach Kuharich traded for running backs Bert Zagers and Leo Elter, linebacker Laverne "Torgy" Torgeson, tackle J.D. Kimmel, and end Ralph Thomas. In addition, fullback Vic Janowicz, a Heisman Trophy-winner from Ohio State, decided to trade in his Pittsburgh Pirates baseball cap for a Redskins helmet. Then safety Norb Hecker, an ex-Ram who had spent a year in Canada, joined Scooter Scudero, Dick Alban, and Nick Adduci in the Washington secondary. "I like the spirit of this team," said Leo Elter. "I liked the way we came from behind to beat the Packers [in preseason]. This team doesn't quit. The boys didn't stop trying even when we were losing to the Bears, and with that kind of spirit we can have a winner."

The Redskins roster was further bolstered by the return of Eddie LeBaron and Gene Brito, both of whom asked to rejoin the team when they learned Lambeau had been fired. Sporting a new defense called the 4-3, the Washington Redskins opened the 1955 season by ambushing the World Champion Cleveland Browns, 27-17. Although Tom Landry is generally given credit for designing the 4-3 when he was an assistant with the Giants, Kuharich was actually the first coach to shift the nose guard (Chuck Drazenovich) of the 5-2 to a spot just behind the line and try to funnel every play toward him, which was the essence of the formation. Within a few years, every team in the NFL would adopt the 4-3, and

middle linebackers like Sam Huff, Bill George, Ray Nitschke, Chuck Bednarik, Dick Butkus, and Joe Schmidt would become household names.

Unlike Curly Lambeau, Kuharich had no qualms about starting LeBaron, and his faith was rewarded when Eddie passed for two touchdowns and ran for another in the opener against the Browns. "People looked at his size," said Kuharich, "but I never had to be convinced. I had never seen a man handle a ball any better—and I mean handle it like you couldn't even tell where it was, even when you knew where it was supposed to wind up."

Washington's next opponent, the Philadelphia Eagles, had also experienced some coaching difficulties. First, Greasy Neale had been canned in 1950 for slugging team owner James P. Clark in the locker room. Then the Eagles went through two other coaches before settling on Jack Trimble in 1952. After finishing second in the Eastern Conference three years in a row with records of 7-5, 7-4-1, and 7-4-1, the Eagles were determined to regain the championship that had eluded them since 1949, when they won their second NFL title in a row. "They're tough and they're deep," said Redskins assistant coach Joe Tereshinski. "They are as good as their record, and they haven't been beaten yet [in either the exhibition or regular season]."

Although Washington and Philadelphia had split their 34 games over the past 17 years, the Eagles had won 14 of the last 20, including a 49-21 massacre the year before in which quarterback Adrian Burk had thrown seven touchdown passes. However, in Philadelphia's opening game against the New York Giants, Burk had been ineffective and was replaced by Bobby Thomason, who completed 10 of 17 passes for 209 yards and a touchdown as the Eagles rallied to win, 27-17. When Philadelphia Coach Jack Trimble announced that Thomason would start at quarterback against Washington, there was no unrest in the locker room. "I think we have the two best passing quarterbacks in the league," bragged Eagles tackle Bucko Kilroy. "If one has an off-day, the other usually comes through."

No matter who was playing quarterback, the key to Philadelphia's passing attack remained 6-time all-

Chuck Drazenovich   *UPI/The Bettmann Archive*

pro wide receiver Pete Pihos, who was on his way to leading the NFL in receptions for the third year in a row. The league's leading scorer, halfback Bobby Walston, who had started his career as an end, gave the Eagles another excellent target coming out of the backfield. And on running plays, rookie fullback Dick Bielski provided the kind of line-busting power unseen in Philadelphia since the retirement of Hall of Famer Steve Van Buren.

If nothing else, Coach Joe Kuharich would quickly discover whether the success that his 4-3 defense had enjoyed against the Browns was a fluke or a glimpse of the future.

On a pleasant Saturday evening in Philadelphia, 31,891 fans, including a large contingent of excited Redskins supporters who had paid a total of $10 for a game ticket and round-trip accommodations on the B & O, gathered at Connie Mack Stadium to see which undefeated team would get the jump on the rest of the Eastern Conference. For the entire first half, the answer appeared to be painfully clear.

With Bobby Thomason throwing and Dick Bielski running, the Philadelphia Eagles marched 79 yards on their first possession of the game. The overmatched Washington defense finally dug in and stopped the Eagles at the 18, but Philadelphia took a 3-0 lead on Bobby Walston's 25-yard field goal. Late in the first quarter, Redskins quarterback Eddie LeBaron fumbled while being sacked by Norman "Wild Man" Willey, and Jesse Richardson recovered for the Eagles at the Washington 15. On first down, right halfback Jerry Norton swept end for 6 yards, then left halfback Skip Giancanelli darted to the 2. However, three plunges into the line left Philly an inch shy of the goal line. On fourth down, Thomason handed off to veteran fullback Jim Parmer, who crashed into a solid wall of Redskins. For a moment, it was unclear whether Parmer had broken through, but, after the officials peeled enough bodies off the pile, there was no doubt that he had been stopped short of the goal line. Washington's 4-3 had held.

After forcing LeBaron to punt from his end zone, the Eagles steamed downfield again. On first down

at his 41, Thomason fired to Skip Giancanelli for 21 yards. A sweep gained 7 more, but, on second down, Giancanelli fumbled and Washington cornerback Nick Adduci pounced on it at the 10. The Redskins could not stay out of trouble, though. Late in the second quarter, halfback Leo Elter fumbled, and Philadelphia recovered at the Washington 43.

Racing against the clock, Thomason completed four straight passes to four different receivers as the Eagles rolled to the Washington 14. With 13 seconds left in the half, the Redskins blitzed, but Thomason got rid of the ball an instant before he was snowed under. The soft pass floated into the arms of Giancanelli, who slipped at the 3 but still managed to crawl into the end zone with three Redskins defenders on his back! Touchdown! (In 1955, runners had to be pinned to the ground before the whistle would blow.) Philadelphia had to be satisfied with its 9-0 halftime lead, though, when Walston's extra-point attempt hit the right goalpost. Although the Redskins had worked hard throughout the first half, they had not come close to scoring, and the way the Eagles defense was playing, that 9-point lead looked insurmountable.

Picking up right where they had left off, the Philadelphia Eagles took the second-half kickoff and roared down the field in five plays. Two long completions to Bobby Walston accounted for 51 yards, then Thomason hit Pete Pihos with a 15-yard touchdown pass to stretch the Eagles' lead to 16-0.

Still unable to generate anything on offense, the disheartened 'Skins had to punt back to Philadelphia again. Washington finally got a break, though, when middle linebacker Chuck Drazenovich smashed into Eagles halfback Jerry Norton, causing a fumble. Gene Brito recovered at the Philly 32, and the Redskins offense came to life. Eddie LeBaron fired to split end John Carson for 10 yards; Vic Janowicz bulled for 3; then, from the 19, LeBaron tossed a short flair to Janowicz, who raced into the end zone for a touchdown! Janowicz added the extra point, and the Redskins were back in the game, 16-7.

Norb Hecker kicked off. The ball landed in the coffin corner, and Philadelphia's Jerry Norton, assuming it would roll out of bounds, did not try to field it. Suddenly, though, the ball took an unexpected hop away from the sideline, and Norton failed to react. Washington's Ralph Thomas dove on the free ball at the 3 and rolled into the end zone for a touchdown! Janowicz's conversion cut the Eagles' lead to 16-14.

Jerry Norton's troubles were not over. On the first play after the kickoff, he fumbled again, and Torgy Torgeson pounced on it at the 13, giving Washington a chance to take the lead. LeBaron whipped a pass to Vic Janowicz for 9 yards, then, after a penalty and a quarterback sneak advanced the ball to the 1, Janowicz squeezed into the end zone for the score! In the most astounding 2 minutes and 17 seconds of their history, the Redskins had gone from 16-0 misery to 21-16 delirium. In the stands amid thousands of shocked Eagles fans, the Washington rooters hollered and clapped and whistled, then made complete pests of themselves by giving an *a cappella* performance of *Hail to the Redskins*.

-Despite their sudden collapse, the Eagles regained their footing when Thomason fired to Pihos for 17 yards. Then Giancanelli ran for 20 more. On first down at the Washington 36, Thomason gave the benighted Norton another chance, and Norton made the most of it, grabbing a perfect pass in the end zone to put Philadelphia back in the lead, 23-21. That score didn't last very long either. After the kickoff, Eddie LeBaron launched a 57-yard bomb that Bert Zagers hauled in at the 1 foot line. On the last play of the third quarter, LeBaron scored on a quarterback sneak, and Washington went back on top, 28-23.

The Redskins' 4-3 defense finally shut down the Eagles' attack in three plays, and Washington took over at its 40. A trio of Redskins running backs—Leo Elter, Dale Atkeson, and Bert Zagers—ground out four consecutive first downs. When the 'Skins were stopped at the Philadelphia 10, Vic Janowicz kicked a 20-yard field goal to increase Washington's lead to 8 points. With the Philadelphia fans urging them on, the Eagles quickly drove the length of the field and scored on a 5-yard pass from Thomason to Bill Stribling. Walston booted the extra point, and Philly trailed, 31-30.

With 3:20 remaining in the game, Washington set out to protect its 1-point lead. Atkeson, Elter, and Zagers took turns crashing through the line, forcing Philadelphia to use all of its time-outs in a futile effort to stop the clock. Finally, the Eagles ran out of time-outs, and the undefeated Washington Redskins ran off the field, celebrating their remarkable 31-30 victory.

Although the Eagles had outgained Washington in virtually every statistical category, the Redskins deserved to win for two reasons: they had refused to cave in after trailing by 16 points, and they capitalized on almost every scoring opportunity. Eddie LeBaron's numbers (10 completions in 14 attempts for 168 yards and one touchdown) were not nearly as gaudy as Bob Thomason's (25 of 37 for 349 yards and four touchdowns), but his passing had been a model of efficiency. In that same vein, fullback Vic Janowicz had accounted for only 37 yards of total offense, yet had scored 19 points on two touchdowns, a field goal, and four conversions.

Although he could easily have blamed the loss on the three consecutive turnovers in the third quarter, Philadelphia Coach Jack Trimble refused to downgrade Washington's accomplishment. Congratulating Coach Kuharich at midfield, Trimble simply said, "Joe, you've got the hardest working team in the NFL—that's why you beat us."

The 1955 Redskins went on to finish second in the Eastern Conference with an 8-4 record, their best showing in a decade. In light of the fact that Coach Kuharich's 4-3 defense gave up only 222 points all season, down from the 432 it had surrendered in 1954, General Manager Dick McCann proclaimed that "Joe Kuharich has done the greatest reconstruction job since the Civil War." He was not alone in that opinion. At the end of the 1955 season, Kuharich was chosen the NFL Coach of the Year. George Preston Marshall had finally found a coach he could live with.

OUT OF TIME

Detroit Lions vs. Washington Redskins

November 11, 1956

Tragedy struck on August 17, 1956. After celebrating an exhibition victory over the Los Angeles Rams, halfback Vic Janowicz was returning to the Redskins' training camp at Occidental College when the car in which he was riding crashed into a telephone pole. Janowicz was thrown from the car and, for two days, remained in a coma. At last he awoke, and he eventually recovered, but his promising football career was over.

Ironically, quarterback Al Dorow was injured in another car accident that same week, but he would be sidelined for only a month. Because Eddie LeBaron had wrenched his left knee in an earlier preseason game, the quarterbacking job fell to rookie Fred Wyant, whose inexperience contributed to a 30-13 loss to the Pittsburgh Steelers on Opening Day. Dorow returned the following week, but the Redskins offense continued to founder, scoring only 9 points and 3 points in consecutive losses to the Philadelphia Eagles and Chicago Cardinals. However, the 'Skins rebounded with convincing victories over both the World Champion Cleveland Browns and the unbeaten Cardinals, and were now eager to test themselves against the undefeated Detroit Lions.

NFL champions in 1952 and '53, Western Conference champs in '54, and undefeated in six games thus far in '56, the Lions boasted four players who would eventually be inducted into the Pro Football Hall of Fame: safety Jack Christiansen, linebacker Joe Schmidt, safety and punter Yale Lary, and quarterback Bobby Layne. After a disappointing 1955 season in which Layne was injured, Coach Buddy Parker refurbished the Lions by installing a ball-control offense to complement his tight-fisted defense. No matter how the coach devised his game plan, though, the fortunes of the Lions would continue to rest on the shoulders of Layne, whose competitive fires and appetite for fun could never be quenched.

"Whether it was playing cards or playing football," said one of his teammates, "all Bobby Layne ever wanted to do was bash your brains in." A prototype of Billy Kilmer, Layne wobbled his passes and generally racked up more interceptions than touchdowns. Yet Coach Paul Brown of Cleveland called him "the best third-down quarterback in football." And when a game was on the line, he was nearly unstoppable. "Bobby Layne could get in more plays in the last two minutes of a game than any other quarterback in history," marveled linebacker Bill Pellington of the Baltimore Colts. "He was smart. He knew what to do against every defense."

As renowned for his drinking and practical jokes as he was for his gridiron heroics, Layne once visited 320-pound middle guard Les Bingaman in the hos-

Bobby Layne   *Courtesy Detroit Lions*

pital after the big man had broken his leg. While commiserating with Bingaman over how uncomfortable it must be to have his leg elevated and harnessed in traction, Layne pulled out a bottle of cold beer, walked to the foot of the bed, and poured every drop of it down the helpless giant's cast.

Layne's reputation for staying up all night before a game, playing cards and drinking bourbon, may have been exaggerated, but not by much. Every season during training camp, Layne threw a party for the Lions rookies. Those who could keep up with Bobby as he downed beer after beer were welcomed to the team. Those who couldn't soon would be looking for other work. "Football is a team game," explained the irrepressible Layne, "and the guys have to belong."

One rookie who had passed every test on and off the field was a Heisman Trophy-winning halfback from Ohio State, Howard "Hopalong" Cassady. After gaining 78 yards in a relief role against the 49ers the week before, the heir-apparent to the great Doak Walker was about to get his first starting assignment against the Redskins. Only 5-foot-10 and 183 pounds,

Cassady relied on guile and speed to avoid being pounded, something his gigantic running mate did not have to worry about. At 6-foot-5 and 257 pounds, fullback Leon Hart could absorb hits like a blocking sled.

For all their offensive skill, though, the Lions were at their ferocious best when on defense. Coach Parker had followed Washington's lead by replacing his 5-2 defense with the more versatile 4-3. That meant moving Lions captain Joe Schmidt to middle linebacker, where he would thrive for the next decade. Because of his uncanny ability to diagnose a play, Schmidt would become a perennial all-pro despite his unimposing size. The Detroit secondary, nicknamed "Chris's Crew," featured Jack Christiansen, who was leading the NFL with 6 interceptions, and Yale Lary, whose last-minute interception in the end zone the week before had preserved a 17-13 victory over the 49ers.

With so much talent on both sides of the ball, the undefeated Lions were sure to unmask any hidden weaknesses of the 2-3 Washington Redskins. Despite scoring only 62 points in five games (compared to Detroit's 128), the Redskins offense was beginning to show promise. Rookie halfback Dick James had introduced himself to Washington fans by returning the first kickoff of the season 83 yards. "I think we've found ourselves a back!" exclaimed backfield coach Mike Nixon as he watched the indomitable James break tackle after tackle and fight for every inch. Another halfback, Billy Wells, the 'Skins' Most Valuable Player in 1954, who had just returned from two years of military service, was hoping to recapture his former elusiveness. Leo Elter, Washington's leading ground-gainer, could play either halfback or fullback, but, like James and Wells, was not very big. Without a powerful fullback like Vic Janowicz in the lineup, Washington had to rely on fancy ball-handling and clever diversions to get its runners past the line of scrimmage.

As a replacement for the injured LeBaron, quarterback Al Dorow had worked hard to improve his passing and, against the Cardinals, had thrown touchdown passes of 40 and 34 yards. Even though LeBaron was now healthy enough to play, Coach Joe

Dick James *Courtesy Washington Redskins*

Kuharich decided to stick with Dorow, who had led the team to two straight victories over top-notch competition. "Our club was disappointing at first," said Redskins Owner George Preston Marshall, "but in the last two games their execution has been excellent. We are in better shape than we've been all sea-son and we have a top player [Wells] back. I believe we have a good enough team to beat the Lions."

Coach Kuharich was more cautious in his appraisal of Washington's chances: "There's only one way to know what will happen in Sunday's game. That's to go out and see it."

After years of dwindling support, Washington fans were catching Redskins Fever again as a result of the consecutive victories over the Browns and Cardinals. Over 28,000 excited fans, the largest crowd in years, nearly filled Griffith Stadium to see if the 'Skins could continue their string of upsets against the 6-point favorite Detroit Lions.

When the game began, Washington's staunch 4-3 defense, which had surrendered the fewest points in the NFL, smothered the Lions on their first two possessions. The Redskins took over at their 36, and, after a 45-yard pass interference penalty against Yale Lary, jumped out to a 3-0 lead on a 17-yard field goal by placekicker Sam Baker. Lions quarterback Bobby Layne countered with a 27-yard completion to left end Dorne Dibble, but, four plays later, Washington safety Norb Hecker thwarted Detroit's plans for a touchdown by making a leaping interception in the end zone.

Late in the first quarter, Scooter Scudero picked off another Layne pass, and the Redskins took over at Detroit's 41. Quarterback Al Dorow lateraled to Dick James, who swept around end, slipped three tackles, picked up a block by guard Red Stephens, and sprinted down the sideline. At the 10, 230-pound linebacker Bob Long collared the 175-pound James with a headlock and tried to yank him down, but James twisted out of his helmet and ran into the end zone bare-headed. Touchdown, Washington! Baker converted, and the 'Skins led, 10-0.

Bobby Layne wrestled some of the momentum away from the high-flying Redskins by completing four out of five passes as Detroit drove relentlessly down the field. Washington's defense finally held at its 15, though, and Layne salvaged 3 points with a 22-yard field goal, putting the Lions on the board, 10-3.

After completing only one pass in five attempts for minus-5 yards, Al Dorow was replaced by Eddie LeBaron—who promptly fumbled on his first hand-off to fullback Sam Baker. Fortunately, Detroit failed to capitalize on the turnover, and several punts were exchanged.

With 1 minute to go before halftime, Dick James returned Yale Lary's punt to midfield. Working quickly,

LeBaron fired to Johnny Carson for 15 yards. James scampered for 11. The excited fans groaned, though, as LeBaron hobbled off the field favoring his reinjured left knee. Dorow returned and threw a perfect strike to Steve Meilinger, but the big rookie dropped it at the goal line and Washington had to settle for Sam Baker's 29-yard field goal and a 13-3 halftime lead.

The happy cheers of the partisan crowd at Griffith Stadium were directed mainly toward Dick James, Sam Baker, and the entire Redskins defense, which had limited the powerful Lions to a total of 123 yards and 3 points. The excited fans wanted George Preston Marshall to know that this was the kind of football Washingtonians would gladly support.

On the first play of the second half, the fans realized their celebration may have been premature when middle linebacker Joe Schmidt recovered a Redskins fumble at the Washington 13. Hopalong Cassady, Bobby Layne, and fullback Gene Gedman, who was substituting for the injured Leon Hart, gained 3 yards apiece. On fourth and 1, Gedman plowed into the line again. A great cheer arose as the line judge indicated Washington had held its ground, but another official overruled him and awarded a first down to the Lions. As the crowd booed, Gedman wedged into the end zone, and Detroit, though still trailing, 13-10, was back in the game.

Although the Lions knew Washington wanted to keep the ball on the ground, they were unable to stop the Redskins' undersized backs. Seven straight running plays, a 25-yard pass from Dorow to Carson, then eight more rushes gobbled up 75 yards, leaving Washington with a fourth-and-3 at the Detroit 5. Unfortunately, Billy Wells, who had entered the game moments before to a tremendous ovation, was thrown for a 1-yard loss, and the Lions took over on downs.

Although disappointed, the Redskins defense kept Detroit bottled up, and, after a punt, Washington moved into scoring position again. However, Sam Baker missed a 29-yard field goal attempt at the beginning of the fourth quarter, and the 'Skins continued to lead by only 3 points. Detroit gathered itself and began to drive. Bobby Layne completed three

Leo Elter picks up 6 yards   *Vic Casamento/Washington Post Photo*

straight passes, but two major penalties and a sack by defensive end Gene Brito moved the Lions back into their own territory. Then, on second and 30, Norb Hecker intercepted Layne again, and the fans began to smell an upset.

Detroit's defense forced the 'Skins to punt from midfield. Rather than let Baker's punt sail into the end zone, Yale Lary caught it at the 2 and tried to run it out. He was plastered at the 6. Three straight passes by Layne fell incomplete, and Washington got the

ball back at its 40. Again the Lions held, and Lary repeated his mistake, fielding Baker's punt at his 7 and running backwards to escape the onrushing Redskins. He was nailed at the 1! After watching Bobby Layne throw three more incompletions, Coach Parker ordered Lary, the punter, to take an intentional safety on fourth down. Leading, 15-10, the Redskins inherited excellent field position when Billy Wells returned Lary's free kick to midfield. Five straight runs moved the ball to the Lions 29, but Washington missed an opportunity to salt away the game when Baker missed another field goal attempt, this one from 36 yards out.

Trailing by 5 points with 3 minutes left in the game, Detroit geared up for one of its patented rallies. Layne gunned the ball to Dibble for 15 yards. Then, noticing Redskins cornerback Art DeCarlo playing deep, Layne threw short to Jug Girard. But DeCarlo had been playing possum. Timing his move perfectly, he cut in front of Girard, intercepted at the 40, and dashed to the Lions 29! Three careful running plays worked the ball to the 22, and, with just under 2 minutes remaining in the game, Sam Baker connected on a 31-yard field goal, boosting Washington's lead to 18-10.

Fans began heading toward the exits, but were quickly reminded of what Tobin Rote had said: "Bobby Layne never loses a game. Time just runs out on him sometimes." On first and 10 from his 20, Layne connected on a long pass to right end Jim Doran, who raced to the Washington 10 before finally being hauled down from behind. Art DeCarlo's touchdown-saving tackle gave Washington a reprieve, but for only one play. On second down, Layne threw a flare to Dave Middleton, who ran into the end zone for the score. Layne converted, and the Lions trailed by only a point, 18-17.

One minute remained as the two teams lined up for the crucial kickoff. Detroit made no attempt to disguise its onside intentions, and Washington assembled its best ball-handlers at midfield. Jim Martin bunted the ball on a squirming path, and both sides dove for it. At the bottom of the pile lay the man with the ball—Washington's Ralph Thomas! Seconds later, the game was over. The Redskins had prevailed, 18-17.

"I was playing to win. I didn't want a tie," explained Lions Coach Buddy Parker when asked about his decision to take an intentional safety while his team was trailing, 13-10. "I didn't think Yale Lary had been punting well. I thought we might wind up punting to the 30 or 35 and they would be in position to score. Two points didn't make any difference unless they scored again. If we hold them, we'd have a shot at a touchdown. I'd call it again." Parker's error was not so much that he had given up the points, but that he had underestimated the Redskins defense, which intercepted four passes, gave up only 52 yards rushing, and limited Bobby Layne to 15 completions in 40 attempts. Parker had also underestimated the Washington rushing attack, which continued to grind out big yardage (205 yards in 54 carries) and kept Layne off the field for long stretches of time.

In the next two weeks, the surprising Redskins extended their winning streak to five games with victories over the Giants and Browns, but then faltered down the stretch, losing three of their last four to finish at 6-6. Nevertheless, by knocking off two undefeated teams (the Lions and Cardinals), the current champions (the Browns) twice, and the champions-in-waiting (the Giants) on five consecutive Sundays, the 1956 Washington Redskins regained the goodwill of their fans and the respect of every team in the NFL.

CLIFFHANGER

Baltimore Colts vs. Washington Redskins

November 8, 1959

The widely divergent fates of two teams going in opposite directions pivoted on one desperate pass in the last 15 seconds of the final game of the 1956 season. With his team trailing the Washington Redskins, 17-12, rookie quarterback Johnny Unitas of the Baltimore Colts took the snap at his 47, shuffled quickly back into the pocket, pumped once, and sailed a deep pass toward the goal line, where Redskins defenders outnumbered Colts receivers two to one. When the high, arching spiral finally came down, Washington safety Norb Hecker was in perfect position to intercept it. Incredibly, though, the ball bounced off Hecker's shoulder pad and into the hands of Baltimore's Jim Mutscheller, who grabbed it and dragged two defenders into the end zone to win the game, 19-17!

In a sport full of funny bounces, no other play had as much impact on the future of the two neighboring teams. If Hecker had intercepted, the Redskins would have finished at 7-5, their second consecutive winning season, and the Colts management would have fulfilled its threat to fire Head Coach Weeb Ewbank. As it turned out, Washington would not have another winning season until Vince Lombardi became head coach in 1969 while Baltimore, which finished at 5-7, would not suffer another losing season until 1972. In fact, with Ewbank as their coach, the Colts would soon emerge as a league power, winning the 1958 NFL Championship in overtime against the New York Giants, 23-17, in what is generally considered the greatest game in the history of the league.

In 1959, Baltimore was driving toward its second championship. Chocked with star players at almost every position, the Colts were as devastating in their heyday as the Packers of the Sixties and the Dolphins and Steelers of the Seventies. Six of their 22 starters —Johnny Unitas, wide receiver Raymond Berry, halfback Lenny Moore, offensive tackle Jim Parker, defensive end Gino Marchetti, and defensive tackle Art Donovan—would eventually be enshrined in the Hall of Fame. And Coach Ewbank would join them in 1978.

Unitas was the Colts' leader, the greatest passer in the game, the man who almost single-handedly initiated pro football's pass-happy modern era. "Unitas is the best quarterback I've ever seen," said first-year Coach Vince Lombardi after "Johnny U" had dismantled his Green Bay Packers, 38-21. "He picks you apart. With Unitas throwing, his receivers don't have to beat the defense by much because he lays it right in there. He's just a helluva player." Marveling at the fact that Unitas had thrown 17 touchdown passes in the first six games, New York Giants safety Jimmy

Patton said, "With every other quarterback, you look at his eyes and you know where he's going to throw. Not Unitas. He looks one way and throws another."

In the late Fifties and early Sixties, Unitas-to-Berry was the hottest passing combination in the game. Through long practice and detailed analysis, they honed their skills to a deadly edge. "It takes me 1.2 seconds to retreat 7 yards behind the line of scrimmage," explained Unitas. "Now I've got 1.3 seconds to get rid of the ball. Then, if it's not too long a pass, the ball's in flight for 1 second. It should be in Raymond's hands at 3.5." That kind of precision had resulted in Unitas throwing at least one touchdown pass in 31 straight games, an NFL record that would eventually stretch to 47 games.

Raymond Berry, the league's leading receiver with 40 receptions, specialized in the unstoppable sideline catch: his rigid body cantilevered at a 45-degree angle like an airborne ski jumper, both toes tapping the ground just inside the painted stripe, both hands glued to the ball six feet out of bounds. So complete was Berry's concentration that, in 13 seasons in the NFL, he fumbled only once. In 1957, he caught 12 passes in a single game against the Redskins, then matched that effort with 12 more in the '58 Championship game.

When the Colts ran the ball, Unitas had the luxury of choosing between two of the best backs in the game. Halfback Lenny Moore—fast, elusive, explosive, and tough—ran with liquid grace, swerving and twisting at full speed as he paralyzed defenders with his eye-popping feints and cuts. Equally dangerous as a pass receiver, Moore had averaged 9.5 yards every time he touched the ball in three previous games against the Redskins. Fullback Alan "The Horse" Ameche, who had kicked off his NFL career with a 79-yard touchdown run, is perhaps best remembered for his game-winning plunge into the end zone that capped Baltimore's sudden-death victory over the Giants. Colts fans remember much more, though. A Heisman Trophy-winner from Wisconsin, the durable Ameche led the NFL in rushing in his rookie season with 961 yards and had averaged 4.6 yards per carry in five years of pounding up the middle.

Baltimore's defensive line would have boasted three Hall of Famers had defensive tackle Gene "Big Daddy" Lipscomb not been addicted to drugs and alcohol. Despite a heroin habit that sapped his vitality and finally killed him in 1963, Big Daddy terrorized the league with his tremendous strength, surprising agility, and fearsome intensity. Although there is no question that both Gino Marchetti and Art Donovan earned their spots in Canton, it was always the 6-foot 6-inch, 290-pound Lipscomb who starred in opposing quarterbacks' nightmares. One can only imagine how good Big Daddy might have been had he not played in a drug-induced stupor.

There were no future Hall of Famers on the 1959 Washington Redskins. In fact, when new Head Coach Mike Nixon commented at a Touchdown Club luncheon that "the fans don't ask for much in this city," there was general agreement among his audience that "they don't get much, either." After watching his team lose four of its first six games while giving up an average of 28 points, Redskins President George Preston Marshall was understandably upset. "Offensively, I don't find too much fault with the team," said Marshall. "What I want to know is why we're so lousy on defense. I'm getting fed up. I just can't take it."

During the off-season, the Redskins had lost the services of their only coach in recent history who had combined enough backbone to stand up to Marshall with enough charm to get away with it: Joe Kuharich. Even though Kuharich had recently signed a 5-year contract with the 'Skins, Marshall allowed Joe to accept the head coaching job at his alma mater, Notre Dame. In five seasons with the Redskins, Coach Kuharich compiled a 26-32-2 record, but the team had been in a tailspin since 1955, winning fewer games every year. In 1958, the Redskins finished with a lackluster 4-7-1 record. With no funds allotted for scouting, the foundation of the team was eroding quickly, and Kuharich was smart enough to get out before the inevitable collapse.

After spending 20 years as an assistant, the last 5 with the Redskins as backfield coach, Mike Nixon leaped at the chance to be the head man. After the 'Skins lost the 1959 season opener, 49-21, to the Chicago Cardinals, Nixon shed his nice-guy image by instituting long practices, daily meetings, and even full scrimmages every Wednesday. At first, the extra work paid off with victories over the Steelers and Cardinals, but the 'Skins rediscovered their losing touch on the following three Sundays.

In an attempt to revitalize his slumbering defense, Nixon gave nine new players a chance to start. Only Ralph Felton and 5-time all-pro Chuck Dravenovich kept their linebacking jobs. A midseason trade for cornerback Gary Glick bolstered the secondary, but the defense remained porous, surrendering points faster than any other team in the league.

On offense, Nixon tried alternating quarterbacks Ralph Guglielmi and Eddie LeBaron, but it soon became obvious that Goog needed more seasoning. Finally recovered from a series of leg injuries, LeBaron was recapturing the form that had made him the NFL's leading passer in '58. But while the passing

Eddie LeBaron and Joe Walton team up for a touchdown against the Packers on October 19, 1958
Copyright Washington Post; Reprinted by permission of the D.C. Public Library

game was beginning to come together, Washington's running game was producing bittersweet results. In the 'Skins' last game, fullback Don Bosseler had gained 168 yards against the Philadelphia Eagles, yet, in the final seconds, he was stopped three times inside the 1 as Washington lost, 30-23.

It seemed that no matter what it took, the Redskins of the late Fifties could always find a way to lose.

To the great delight of George Preston Marshall, every wooden seat at sold-out Griffith Stadium was filled except the one reserved for Vice President Richard M. Nixon, who was still en route from California. Once common in the Redskins' halcyon days, sellouts at the old stadium now occurred about as often as Marshall lost a salary negotiation with one of his players. But the Colts always drew a good crowd. Even though an imbalance of power currently existed between the two teams, the proximity of Baltimore and Washington fostered a natural rivalry that Marshall had envisioned when he wisely refused to block the Colts' entry into the league in 1950.

Redskins co-captain Sam Baker won the toss and elected to receive. On Washington's first play, halfback Dickie James was smothered at the line, and, after two sweeps proved equally unproductive, Baker boomed a 61-yard punt that pinned the Colts at their 15. Johnny Unitas trotted onto the field in his trademark high-top cleats. After an incompletion, Unitas handed off to Lenny Moore, who zig-zagged past three Washington defenders for an 18-yard gain. Under a heavy rush by the Redskins front four, Unitas overthrew open receivers on four out of his next five passes, yet the Colts still managed to drive to the Washington 14. When the 'Skins finally dug in, Baltimore's Steve Myrha drew first blood with a 21-yard field goal.

Late in the opening quarter, Eddie LeBaron engineered the Redskins' first sustained drive. Starting from his 23, LeBaron completed six straight passes, dividing them among fullback Don Bosseler, ends Jim Podoley and Bill Anderson, and halfback Eddie Sutton. On first down at the Baltimore 19, LeBaron drilled a pass to Joe Walton at the 5, and Walton

muscled his way into the end zone to give Washington a 7-3 lead.

Coach Mike Nixon had a surprise planned for his guests from Baltimore: an onside kick. But Baker flubbed it. Instead of bunting the ball, Baker sent a spinner past the first row of Colts. Nevertheless, the squirming ball finally came to rest in the arms of Washington's Ken MacAfee at the Baltimore 31! Trying for a quick knockdown before the Colts could steady themselves, LeBaron uncorked a deep pass toward the goal line, but Baltimore's Ray Brown intercepted at the 2.

The Redskins returned the favor late in the second period when middle linebacker Chuck Drazenovich thwarted the Colts by picking off a Unitas pass at the Washington 31. Constantly hounded by the Redskins' pass rushers, "Johnny U" had struggled throughout the first half, connecting on only 4 of 14 throws for 60 yards. When halftime arrived, the Washington Redskins reveled in the rarely heard cheers of 32,773 supporters as they trotted proudly off the field with their 7-3 lead.

The charged-up Redskins kept the pressure on the Colts with three third-quarter drives, but picked up only 3 more points for their efforts. Sam Baker, who succeeded on a 42-yard field goal, missed two other attempts: one from 52 yards away and the other from midfield, which had enough distance but was wide to the left by a foot.

After overthrowing his first four passes of the second half, Johnny Unitas finally zeroed in. Starting from his 20, Unitas took turns connecting with Jim Mutscheller and Lenny Moore on four consecutive slant patterns over the middle. Then, on the twelfth play of the drive, Unitas hit Mutscheller in the corner of the end zone for a 19-yard touchdown, and the game was tied, 10-10.

As the fourth quarter got underway, the Redskins were marching again. After taking over near midfield, LeBaron completed passes to Jim Podoley for 12 yards and to Bill Anderson for 19 yards, giving Washington a first down at the Baltimore 22. LeBaron handed off to halfback Eddie Sutton, who ran to his right, stopped, and threw a perfect option pass to Joe Wal-

Fig. 20   *Vic Casamento/Washington Post Photo*

ton for a touchdown! [Fig. 20] While the crowd cheered in delighted disbelief, Baker converted, and the 'Skins were back on top, 17-10.

The Colts retaliated immediately. Lenny Moore galloped 65 yards down the right sideline with a swing pass, and Unitas finished the job with a 3-yard touchdown toss to Mutscheller. Myrha added the point-after to pull Baltimore even at 17-all. Not to be outdone, though, LeBaron led the 'Skins on a 10-play, 80-yard excursion that ended with Bill Anderson catching a 17-yard scoring pass, and Washington reclaimed the lead, 24-17.

With 3:20 left, Unitas nearly gave the game away when he fumbled on first down. Redskins defensive end Art Gob got his hands on the ball for a moment, but Baltimore center Buzz Nutter recovered at the Washington 11. On third and 19, Unitas fired to Berry, who was dragged down at the 29, a yard short of the first-down marker. Demonstrating a confidence that bordered on arrogance, Coach Ewbank let his team go for the first down. The Redskins defenders bunched together at the line in anticipation of a charge by Ameche, but Unitas faked a handoff to the big fullback and flipped the ball to Moore for an easy 22-yard gain. Unitas followed with a 37-yard completion to Mutscheller, then hoodwinked the 'Skins again, calling for a halfback option pass from Moore to Jerry Richardson that clicked for a 12-yard touchdown. The game was tied, 24-24.

Less than 2 minutes remained. Eddie LeBaron tried two short passes and a quarterback keeper, but the Colts defense clamped down and forced Washington to punt with 30 seconds left in the game. On first down at his 38, Unitas just missed Berry on a sideline pattern. On second down, he overthrew Richardson. On third down, Unitas fired over the middle. Dickie James, who had been inserted as an extra defensive back, leaped and deflected the ball to linebacker Tom Braatz, who intercepted at the Redskins 40 and barreled his way to the Colts 39.

Only 8 seconds remained on the scoreboard clock. Unwilling to risk a sack or a turnover, Coach Nixon ordered his field goal unit onto the field. The shouting fans in the stands quieted themselves as Sam Baker concentrated on his task. Center Jim Schrader snapped the ball to LeBaron, who placed it on its point at the 46. Baker stepped forward and swung

his right leg. [Fig. 21] The ball cleared the line and headed for the goalposts as the collective voice of the hopeful crowd quickly swelled, urging it onward. Finally, the spinning ball completed its journey, falling over the crossbar like an exhausted marathoner as the stadium erupted in joyful disbelief. The Redskins had knocked off the World Champions, 27-24!

"I never saw a more exciting professional football game," exclaimed Vice President Richard Nixon, who had arrived in time to see the second half. "How could any football game be more exciting?" After accepting the congratulations of the vice president,

Fig. 21   *Vic Casamento/Washington Post Photo*

Coach Mike Nixon savored his biggest victory with his happy assistant coaches. "When you beat the world champions, you don't have a hero. You have heroes. We finally got everything working. Everybody played a beautiful game. This is what makes coaching worthwhile."

Coach Nixon admitted that "until the last two minutes, I would have settled for a tie. When you're losing a lot of games and you're playing the champions, what the hell is wrong with a tie? I was afraid of what happened to them—an interception and then getting within field goal range. The Colts went for it when they got the ball and lost the game. That could have happened to us."

As in 1956, the Redskins' upset of the Colts marked a turning point for both teams, but not in the way one would expect. Baltimore went on to capture the Western Conference crown by winning its last five regular season games, then, in the NFL Championship game, outclassed the New York Giants, 31-16. The Redskins, on the other hand, lost their last five, closing out the decade with the same record with which they began it: 3-9. Once again, the Colts had used the annual game with Washington as a springboard to their success while the Redskins ended up walking the plank.

FIGHT FOR OLD D.C.

Washington Redskins vs. New York Giants

October 16, 1960

If experience is what tells us we've just made the same mistake all over again, then the Washington Redskins were by far the most experienced recruiters in the National Football League. On Draft Day, 1960, the Redskins chose a quarterback with their #1 pick for the fifth time in a decade. The latest prospect, Richie Lucas, followed four other first-round picks —Larry Isbell (1952), Jack Scarbath (1953), Ralph Guglielmi (1955), and Don Allard (1959)—in the Redskins' continuing quest to fill Sammy Baugh's high-top cleats. But, like Allard and Isbell, Lucas never played a down for the Redskins.

Since Slingin' Sam's arrival in 1937, the passer has always been the centerpiece of Washington's highly entertaining offense. Redskins Owner George Preston Marshall believed it was far more important (and lucrative) to put on a snazzy passing show for a packed house than to assure a low-scoring victory with lots of defense and monotonous line plunges. Unfortunately, by 1960, that stategy had produced only three winning seasons for the Redskins in the past 14 years, enough to make an occasional boring victory sound pretty enticing to Washington's long-suffering supporters.

Eddie LeBaron, the man who had quarterbacked the Redskins through most of the Fifties, was now wearing the star-spangled uniform of the NFL's new-est expansion team, the Dallas Cowboys. When Lucas (obtained with Dallas' first pick in exchange for LeBaron) failed to pan out, the mantle of leadership was subleased to Ralph Guglielmi.

Even though his college coach, Frank Leahy, called him "the greatest quarterback I coached at Notre Dame," Guglielmi (pronounced Gool-YAH-mee) had yet to make a solid impression in the NFL. Just as he began getting comfortable in his new starting role, Ralph injured his knee in an exhibition game, and, with Eagle Day at quarterback for the opening game of the season, the punchless Redskins were shut out by the World Champion Baltimore Colts, 20-0. Fortunately, Guglielmi healed quickly and returned to the lineup two weeks later to lead the 'Skins to a 26-14 victory over the newborn Cowboys. That long-awaited triumph ended an 11-month victory drought and was cause for considerable celebration in the Capital. The fans soon returned to their senses, though, when they remembered that the New York Giants were on deck as the 'Skins' next opponent.

Bullies of the Eastern Conference, the Giants loved nothing better than to run up the score against weaker teams like the Redskins. It seemed as if everyone on New York's talent-rich squad was a household name. Not that it was surprising that offensive stars like quarterback Charlie Conerly, halfback Frank Gifford, split end Kyle Rote, halfback Joe Morrison, and full-backs Mel Triplett and Alex Webster were famous; after all, their names filled headlines in the media capital of the world. But Giants fans could also reverently tick off the melting-pot names of their defensive heroes: Andy Robustelli, Jim Katcavage, Dick Modzelewski, Roosevelt Grier, Cliff Livingston, Sam Huff, Harland Svare, Jimmy Patton, Dick Nolan, Lindon Crow, and Dick Lynch.

Nine of New York's eleven defensive starters had been playing together since their NFL Championship victory in 1956 and were in great part responsible for the team's 34-13-1 record over the past four years. (Over that same period, the anonymous Redskins were 18-28-2.) Eastern Conference champs the last two years, the Giants had beaten the Redskins ten out of the last twelve times they had played and were 13-point favorites to do it again.

"No," laughed Redskins Coach Mike Nixon in response to a reporter's question after the win over the Cowboys, "I don't think overconfidence will be one of our problems this Sunday." To ensure their continuing humility, 17 Redskins, including quarterback Ralph Guglielmi, came down with colds the week of the Giants game. Said Nixon: "We'll be okay if our guys run on Sunday the way their noses are running now."

On a warm and breezy October afternoon at Yankee Stadium, Pat Summerall got the game underway by kicking off to Washington's most versatile player, Dick James, who returned the ball to the 22. On the Redskins' first play, the tone of the first half was set when Ralph Guglielmi was sacked for a loss of 5 yards by middle linebacker Sam Huff. Two plays later, the Redskins punted to just beyond midfield. Surprisingly, the Giants didn't score immediately; instead, they traded punts with the 'Skins — then scored on Summerall's 48-yard field goal to take an early 3-0 lead.

The Giants were trying to rattle Guglielmi with blitzes, but, even though they got to him twice more, Ralph remained unruffled and guided the 'Skins into New York territory. However, the drive stalled at the 44, and placekicker Bob Khayat was short on a 51-yard field goal attempt. The Giants took over at their 20 and moved to midfield on a 26-yard pass from Charlie Conerly to Joe Morrison. Then, after baiting Washington's pass rushers into chasing him, Conerly lobbed a screen pass over their heads to all-pro halfback Frank Gifford, who dashed 24 yards to the Washington 19. A 17-yard pass to Kyle Rote advanced the ball to the 2, and Gifford plunged into the end zone on the following play to stretch New York's lead to 10-0.

Early in the second quarter, the Giants sacked Guglielmi twice more and regained possession at midfield. Conerly tried a long pass to Kyle Rote, but Washington's Pat Heenan intercepted at the 15. Not that it did the sluggish Redskins much good; three plays later they were punting again. But Conerly threw another interception to linebacker Dick Lasse, and, after the 'Skins lost 10 yards on three plays, Bob Khayat kicked a 50-yard field goal to put Washington on the board, 10-3.

Disgusted by Conerly's two interceptions, New York Head Coach Jim Lee Howell replaced the 39-year-old veteran with George Shaw. Under Shaw's steadier hand, the Giants pounded out five consecutive first downs before they were stopped at Washington's 28. Pat Summerall tried a 35-yard field goal —but it was blocked! Washington's Dick Haley picked up the spinning ball at his 15 and raced to midfield, handing the Redskins a gift-wrapped opportunity to tie the game with 1:10 left in the second quarter. However, for the sixth and seventh times of the first half, Guglielmi went down under the Giants' furious pass rush. On fourth down, Day's punt traveled only 28 yards to the New York 47, and, with 20 seconds left in the half, the Giants had one more chance to score.

Shaw threw a long pass to Gifford, who was blanketed by Pat Heenan. As both men fought for position, the ball hit Heenan in the back. To the delight of the 60,000 Giants fans, the official on the scene called pass interference against the Redskins rookie, giving New York a first down at the Washington 6. With only seconds left in the first half, Kyle Rote found an open spot in the end zone and caught Shaw's perfect pass for a touchdown. Trailing 17-3,

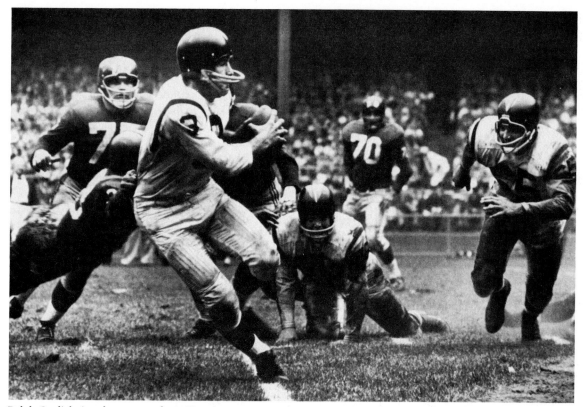

Ralph Guglielmi under pressure from Giants' strong pass rush   *Dan Rubin/NFL Photos*

the downcast Redskins trudged to the visitor's locker room to lick their wounds and blow their cold-infected noses.

As usual, the 'Skins were being outclassed in every department. After subtracting the 40 yards they had lost on seven quarterback sacks, the Redskins had netted only 15 yards on offense while giving up 92 yards in penalties. But their flickering hopes were brightened a bit at the start of the second half when Pat Summerall missed a 44-yard field goal attempt.

Suddenly, the Redskins offense started to jell. Running backs Dick James, Jim Podoley, Don Bosseler, and Johnny Olszewski took turns gaining 6 and 7 yards on each carry. With the Giants having to pay attention to the Redskins' rushing attack for a change, Guglielmi had time to complete a 9-yard swing pass to Podoley and a 16-yard bullet to James at the Giants

2. On first and goal, fullback Don Bosseler slanted through right tackle for Washington's first touchdown, and the Redskins, although still trailing, 17-10, were back in the game.

After trading punts, the two teams traded fumbles deep in Washington territory. On first down at the Redskins 23, New York halfback Frank Gifford darted through the line for 13 yards. Then, after a pass to Morrison moved the ball to the 3, Gifford scored his second touchdown of the game on a quick burst up the middle. With a minute left in the third quarter, the Giants were sitting on a comfortable 24-10 lead.

But Washington fought back. Using the same formula of three rushing plays for every pass that had been successful on the previous drive, the 'Skins moved deep into New York territory. On fourth and 7 at the 23, Coach Nixon, figuring 3 points wouldn't

Don Bosseler leaps over line for short gain against Giants   *UPI/The Bettmann Archive*

do his team any good this late in the game, decided to forgo the field goal in favor of a pass to Don Bosseler. Bosseler made the catch—but was tackled a yard short of the first down marker.

Despite their disappointment, the Redskins refused to fold. Instead, their defense forced New York to punt from its 17, putting Guglielmi & Co. back in business at midfield. Cleverly alternating passes and runs, Washington marched to the Giants 22, where it faced another desperate fourth-and-7 situation. This time Guglielmi made sure his pass was long enough, hitting Joe Walton on the sideline for a first down at the 10. Guglielmi nearly scored on the next play on a bootleg to his right, but was brought down at the 1.

On second down, fullback Johnny Olszewski hurdled the line and landed in the end zone for a touchdown [Fig. 24], and Khayat's extra point closed the gap to 24-17. 2:07 remained in the game.

With the shouted warnings of 60,000 Giants fans making his intentions clear, Washington placekicker Bob Khayat dribbled an onside kick the necessary 10 yards to midfield, where New York's Jimmy Patton fielded it cleanly. But the ball squirted loose when Patton was clobbered by Ben Scotti, and Vince Promuto fell on it to give the Redskins the break they desperately needed. Knowing Guglielmi would pass, New York's crack linebacking corps stormed after the young quarterback. Ralph misfired on his first two passes, and his third gained only 2 yards. But on fourth and 8 at the Giants 47, Guglielmi found Joe Walton open again and hit him at the 37 for a critical first down.

Two consecutive pass interference penalties against New York gave the Redskins a first down at the Giants 24. With less than a minute to play, Guglielmi threw a strike to Tom Osborne at the 13, but was sacked on the next play for a 7-yard loss. Thirty seconds remained as Guglielmi analyzed the defense before taking the snap from center Jim Schrader. As expected, the Giants blitzed their linebackers. But instead of keeping halfback Jim Podoley in the backfield to block, Guglielmi sent him into the just-vacated area in the middle of the field. Ralph quickly released his pass. The ball, Podoley, and Giants safety Lindon Crow arrived at the goal line at the same instant. Both players fought for possession, but Podoley pulled it in and landed in the end zone! Touchdown, Washington!

With the precision of a surveyor, Bob Khayat lined up his crucial extra-point attempt, then kicked the ball squarely between the uprights to give the ecstatic Redskins a 24-24 tie with the disbelieving Giants. On the final play of the game, Shaw completed a short pass to Kyle Rote, but he was brought down shy of midfield just as the line judge fired his pistol to end the game. On the sideline, Ralph Guglielmi, sick and exhausted, collapsed.

The Redskins didn't win another game all season, finishing 1-9-2. Nevertheless, on that one enchanted October afternoon in 1960 against one of the greatest teams in the history of the NFL, the Washington Redskins knew how it felt to play like champions.

Fig. 24   *UPI/The Bettmann Archive*

THE MARSHALL PLAN

Philadelphia Eagles vs. Washington Redskins

October 29, 1961

There were two Marshall Plans. The first, named after Secretary of State George C. Marshall, involved airlifting food and supplies to starving Europeans after World War II. The other Marshall Plan, named after Redskins Owner George Preston Marshall, involved giving away professional football games on Sunday afternoons.

Although the 1961 edition of the Washington Redskins had acquired a new head coach, a new stadium, and a new quarterback to help celebrate their Silver Anniversary season, they still played the same old brand of football—a lukewarm mishmash of busted plays, stunted drives, and untimely penalties —that had produced 12 losing seasons in the previous 15 years and 14 consecutive visits to the loss column. After compiling a composite 4-18-2 record in 1959 and '60, Head Coach Mike Nixon was fired, replaced by offensive backfield coach Bill McPeak. Continuing the longstanding Washington traditions of losing early and losing often, the Redskins under Coach McPeak dropped their first six games—the last two being shutouts at the hands of the Steelers and Cardinals. The 'Skins' closest brush with victory so far in 1961 had been in their debut at Washington's new stadium when they blew a three-touchdown lead against the New York Giants and lost, 24-21.

Officially named District of Columbia Stadium, the new 50,000-seat playground gave Redskins fans something besides the team's ludicrous play to complain about. The first customers at the $24 million palace of undulating concrete griped about the steep prices ($6.00 for the cheapest seat), the lack of intimacy, and the scarcity of hot dog vendors and restrooms. (Beer-drinking fans, it seemed, prized accessibility over sanitation and quickly became nostalgic for the convenient but acrid facilities of Griffith Stadium.)

In truth, the only advantage that the old stadium held over the new one was its element of intimacy. Sadly, though, good old Griffith Stadium was a crumbling wooden relic that had been forsaken by the Calvin Griffith family when they uprooted the Washington Senators baseball team and slithered off to Minnesota. To their credit, the city fathers decided to sever any relationship with the Griffiths, and, with the help of some Federal dollars, built the imposing new stadium next to the National Guard Armory. Griffith Stadium was left to rot.

Able to hold only 36,000 customers, the ancient park was one of the old line of asymmetric stadiums such as Ebbets Field, Fenway Park, and Wrigley Field that gave spectators a close-up view of their heroes. But that's not all.

Exhilaration greeted you the moment you escaped the city street and entered the ancient grounds of Griffith Stadium. Up the wide, gently sloping entrance ramp past the ticket booths on the right you'd go, past the Hall of Fame plaque of Walter Johnson, through the tight, chrome turnstiles and into the cool, dark, crowded area beneath the stands. Carried along with the tide of jostling fans, you hurried to find your aisle and, like Alice, gasped as you stepped from the bustle of mundane life into the carefree wonderland of that vast, bright green grassy field framed by dark green grandstands.

The startling sounds of exploding beer cups, whistles, shouts, and bugle blasts accompanied the vendors' hypnotic songs— ''Get your red-hot peanuts'' ''They're nutritious and delicious'' ''COLD beer'' ''Coke, coke, coke'' —and punctuated the undertone of shuffling shoeleather and 15,000 words spoken at once.

Aromas of popcorn and peanuts, hot dogs and Cracker Jacks saturated the city air as you joined the thousands of happy, animated people milling about in a vivid exchange of colors and noise. Matching your ticket stub to the number on a hard wooden seat, you'd take your place and eavesdrop on your noisy neighbors as they told their favorite tall tales of legendary ballplayers or made boastful predictions about the game at hand. As a fan, you were a bit player in the day's drama, a member of the chorus sharing the stage with your heroes. You could claim Griffith Stadium as your own.

Nevertheless, one aspect of the retired stadium's intimacy would surely not be missed: the lingering stench of cheap cigars, stale beer, and sweating bodies that had soaked the wooden seats of Griffith Stadium for half a century. Charges that the new stadium was too antiseptic could only have been made by fans with terminal cases of nasal congestion. When combined with the customary overdose of junk food, those smells could test the strength of any stomach.

A similar queasiness crept up on the winless Washington Redskins as they prepared for their midseason game against the World Champion Philadelphia Eagles. With their 5-1 record and league-leading quarterback, Sonny Jurgensen, the Eagles unsettled opponents' stomachs wherever they traveled. One statistic demonstrates the reasonableness of the Redskins' fears: Philadelphia had scored more points the previous week (43) than Washington had totaled in all six games (38).

Opposing the offensive artistry of the Eagles was a Redskins defense that could contain running backs fairly well, but could never be trusted to cover a pass. Although they didn't receive a lot of publicity, Washington's defensive line was one of the best in the business. Left defensive end "Mean" John Paluck had been voted Redskin of the Year in 1960, but had lost two years of playing time while serving in the Army and, from time to time, still had to trade his high-top cleats for combat boots on weekend maneuvers with the Army Reserve. All-pro defensive tackle Bob Toneff lined up next to rookie Joe Rutgens, a first-round draft choice who was showing promise at right tackle. Completing the front four was 250-pound defensive end Andy Stynchula, a second-year player from Penn State who specialized in rushing the passer.

As usual, Washington's offense was "in transition." Rookie quarterback Norman Snead had somehow survived his first six games in the NFL despite little or no assistance from his blockers, but his main task—leading the team to victory—had proven more difficult. Besides the strong-armed Snead, the Redskins offense featured Fred Dugan, a rookie receiver who had caught an 80-yard touchdown pass in the first Philadelphia game, Don Bosseler, a fullback best suited for blocking, and center Jim Schrader, one of the few Redskins linemen to actually make contact while throwing a block.

Then there was the hero of the team: Dick James, a 5-foot 9-inch, 175-pound halfback from Oregon who played both offense and defense and nearly gave his life on every down. When tackled, James never succumbed without a fight as he struggled and stretched and squirmed for every possible inch. Now in his sixth season with the Redskins, James continued to be an inspiration with his courage and dauntlessness.

So it was not an entirely incompetent Redskins team that ran out to face the Eagles on the dyed-green grass field of D.C. Stadium—just mostly.

George Preston Marshall with William Shea (*left*) and minority stockholder Jack Kent Cooke (*right*)
Nate Fine Photo/Nate Fine Productions, Courtesy Washington Redskins

On an Indian Summer afternoon in late October 1961, 31,066 hopeful sunbathers cheered the Redskins about as vigorously as supporters of an 0-6 team can be expected to cheer. Earlier, when the two teams met in the second week of the season, the Eagles had triumphed thanks to a couple of customary Washington gifts—a fumble that terminated a long Redskins drive at the 7, and another bobble that set up an easy Philadelphia score. As the game began, redemption and revenge were uppermost on Washington's mind.

Both teams appeared jittery in the early going, but, after an exchange of punts, the Redskins offense ignited. Starting from his 20, Snead passed to Dugan for 30 yards, then handed off to Dick James, who shook off seven Eagles tacklers while gaining 28 yards to the Philadelphia 17. One play later, Snead fired a strike to halfback Sam Horner, who caught the perfect pass between two defenders at the 2 and squeezed into the end zone for a touchdown! John Aveni added the extra point, and the aroused Redskins led the startled Eagles, 7-0.

Dick James   *UPI/The Bettmann Archive*

Philadelphia's Sonny Jurgensen replied in kind. After marching his team to the Washington 46, Jurgensen drilled a 20-yard pass to tight end Pete Retzlaff, who out-maneuvered Steve Junker and Fred Hageman at the 25 and raced into the end zone with Philadelphia's first touchdown. Bobby Walston hit the point-after, and the game was even at 7 apiece.

Soon after the second quarter got underway, the Redskins were forced to punt. Sam Horner booted to Teddy Brown, but Brown muffed the catch and John Aveni recovered for Washington in Eagles territory. After a penalty advanced the ball to the Philadelphia 24, split end Fred Dugan hauled in a pass from Snead at the 3 [Fig. 27], and, on the next play, fullback Don Bosseler plunged into the end zone, scoring Washington's first rushing touchdown of the season to put the 'Skins back on top, 14-7.

A few optimists in the grandstands were starting to believe the Redskins might actually win this game —especially when Jurgensen stumbled and lost control of the ball as he handed off to Billy Barnes. The crowd roared happily as Washington's John Paluck pounced on the fumble at the Eagles 40. On three successive plays, though, Philadelphia repelled Washington's ball carriers—in fact, the 'Skins lost 5 yards. But that merely positioned the ball perfectly for John Aveni's club-record 52-yard field goal that gave the giddy Redskins a 17-7 lead.

Washington's defensive line was controlling Philadelphia's running attack so well that Jurgensen abandoned it and began to rely exclusively on his gifted right arm. Two long completions—one to Barnes and the other to Tommy McDonald—proved the wisdom of that strategy and moved the ball to the Washington 11. Then, on first down, Pete Retzlaff faked out defensive back Dale Hackbart and caught his second touchdown pass from Jurgensen to shorten the Redskins' lead to 17-14.

When the period ended with no further scoring, Washington rooters gleefully celebrated the 'Skins' surprising first-half achievements. Merrily joining in with the Redskins Marching Band, the happy patrons were robust once again in their off-key singing of *Hail to the Redskins*.

Fig. 27   *UPI/The Bettmann Archive*

The Philadelphia Eagles must not have had a pleasant halftime experience with their new head coach, Nick Skorich. Embarrassed by the first-half handiwork of the winless Washington team, the Eagles came out flying in the second half. Using his aerial attack almost exclusively, Jurgensen swept his team swiftly down the field. Just before they reached the end zone, though, the Eagles were shot down by a Dale Hackbart interception. Unfortunately, Philadelphia safety Don Burroughs returned the favor a few minutes later by stealing an errant Snead pass, and the Eagles went back to work deep in Redskins territory.

Jurgensen threw a strike to Retzlaff in the end

zone, but the big receiver dropped it, botching the opportunity to catch his third touchdown pass. So Sonny gave Bobby Walston a shot, but he bungled his chance also. On third down, Jurgensen, perhaps a little miffed, put too much zing on a bullet to Retzlaff and overthrew him in the end zone. Having to settle for 3 points, Walston made partial amends by placekicking a 14-yard field goal which knotted the game at 17-all. Although reeling badly, the Redskins were still on their feet.

Five minutes into the fourth quarter, Walston nudged the Eagles ahead with another field goal, and Philadelphia's backers began to relax, especially when the Redskins stalled again on their next possession. But the Eagles players knew they still had a tough job on their hands—a point driven home like a spike

when Jurgensen was sacked for a big loss and Philadelphia was forced to punt on fourth and 35.

Starting from his 19 with 5 minutes left in the game, Norman Snead pieced together a magical Redskins drive. First, Stormin' Norman passed to Don Bosseler for a 10-yard pickup, then hit Fred Dugan on a crucial third-down pass to advance the chains again. Halfback Dick James got the next call and twisted through the entire Philadelphia secondary for 22 yards and another first down at the Eagles 26. Moments later, Snead found Dugan again for 14 more, but, on first and goal at the Philadelphia 6, Sam Horner was trapped and lost a yard. On second and goal, Snead avoided a furious rush but overthrew Jim Cunningham in the end zone. On third down, Norm went back to Cunningham again, throwing the

Joe Rutgens (72) makes Sonny Jurgensen pay for his 4-yard gain   *UPI/The Bettmann Archive*

ball low and to the outside. Chuck Weber and Jimmy Carr of the Eagles lunged, but the ball slipped through their crisscrossing arms. Cunningham dove —and grabbed the ball in a full stretch just inches off the ground. Touchdown, Washington! Aveni's kick was good, and, with only 40 seconds to go, the Redskins were back on top, 24-20.

Washington's players and coaches pounded each other's backs and let out war whoops of joy and relief. After six hard losses, the lowly Redskins were about to win their first game of the 1961 campaign —and against the World Champs, no less! All they had to do was hold on for 40 seconds. With that in mind, Coach McPeak inserted seven defensive backs to thwart Jurgensen's inevitable passing barrage.

When Sonny hit Walston with a 19-yarder, the partiers in the stands hardly noticed. But when Jurgensen connected with Walston for another 20 yards, the fans quickly became interested again. With the frantic shouts of 31,000 Redskins partisans nearly drowning his signals, Jurgensen barely managed to get the next play started. Spotting his favorite receiver, Tommy McDonald, slanting to the left sideline, Jurgensen released a long, arching spiral just before he was snowed under by several Redskins rushers. To the dismay of the crowd, the ball sailed straight into the arms of McDonald, who tucked away his prize at the 20 and sprinted into the end zone ahead of a half-dozen flabbergasted Redskins! Walston's extra point was good, and the Eagles reclaimed the lead, 27-24.

Philadelphia's incredible 81-yard touchdown drive had used only 35 of those 40 remaining seconds. For 31,000 shocked and heartbroken Redskins fans, that touchdown pass had the same effect as a kick in the stomach. Their only hope now was for a miracle, but, sadly, it was not to be. Dick James galloped 44 yards with a Snead pass, but was finally dragged down at the Eagles 36 as the gun fired to end the game. Surrounded by silence, the snake-bitten Washington team trudged dejectedly off the field, averting their eyes from the scoreboard that read: Philadelphia Eagles 27, Washington Redskins 24.

Just when the Redskins thought they were finally going to feast at the victor's table, Sonny Jurgensen and Tommy McDonald had pulled their chairs out from under them. In view of the fact that Jurgensen had completed 27 of his 41 passes for 413 yards and three touchdowns, it was small consolation that Washington's defenders had intercepted him twice and bottled up Eagles runners for an overall loss of 12 yards. Jurgensen's artistry had been all that Philadelphia needed.

Norman Snead had been quite successful too, hitting on 21 of 31 passes for 296 yards and two touchdowns. Normally, statistics like those belong to a winning quarterback, but Snead would have to wait until the fourteenth and final week of the 1961 season for his first taste of victory in the NFL. Until then, the Marshall Plan would still be in effect.

PAYBACK

Washington Redskins vs. Cleveland Browns

September 23, 1962

In the early days of the National Football League, there was no rigid color line like the one in major league baseball. Black stars like Fritz Pollard, Paul Robeson, Duke Slater, and Ink Williams played in the NFL 20 years before Jackie Robinson ever put on a Brooklyn Dodgers uniform. In the Forties and Fifties, every team in the NFL but one recruited players on the basis of ability, not color. Finally, after 25 years of representing the capital of the United States of America, the Washington Redskins ended the ignominy of being the last team in the NFL to allow a black man to play for them.

On December 14, 1961, Redskins President George Preston Marshall traded the rights to Ernie Davis, Syracuse's Heisman Trophy-winning halfback (who had declined the honor of breaking Washington's color line), to the Cleveland Browns for Bobby Mitchell, making Mitchell the first black player to wear the Burgundy and Gold. Until that time, George Marshall, the only NFL owner to broadcast his team's games into the Deep South, had kept the Redskins white-only because he was afraid of offending his large radio and television audience. In fact, Marshall was so solicitous of Southern Redskins fans that he altered the lyrics of *Hail to the Redskins* from "Fight for old D.C." to "Fight for old Dix-ie"—a change that was not lost on Washington's large black population.

It finally took an ultimatum from Secretary of the Interior Stewart L. Udall to force Marshall to open his locker room doors to black athletes. When Udall ordered Marshall to integrate his team or clear out of the federally-funded D.C. Stadium, the Redskins owner reluctantly capitulated. However, Marshall made the best of his predicament by obtaining Mitchell, a star halfback who had once rushed for a record-setting 232 yards in 14 carries against Washington, and Cleveland's #1 draft choice (Leroy Jackson) in exchange for the rights to Davis. Tragically, Davis died of leukemia soon thereafter without ever playing a single down in the NFL.

Washington Head Coach Bill McPeak figured the best way to utilize Mitchell's speed and eye-popping moves was to position him outside as a flanker. In his first game as a Redskin, Mitchell justified McPeak's reasoning and clearly exposed what Washington's attack had been missing when he returned a kickoff 92 yards for a touchdown, scored twice more on pass receptions of 81 and 6 yards, and set up two other touchdowns with long catches as the Redskins tied the Dallas Cowboys, 35-35. Suddenly, with Mitchell in the lineup, Washington had a potent offense.

But Bobby Mitchell wouldn't have a soft defense like the Cowboys' to compete against the following week. Instead, he would be facing his former teammates, the rock-hard Cleveland Browns. Returning to Cleveland for the first time since the big trade,

Mitchell denied he had an ax to grind with his former coach, the imperious Paul Brown. "I'm not interested so much in impressing Paul Brown this Sunday," said Mitchell, who had scored 38 touchdowns in four seasons as a Brown. "He knows what I can do. But I have many fans in Cleveland and throughout Ohio. I want them to know that I'm still a good ballplayer."

Before Mitchell's arrival, good ballplayers on the Washington Redskins were in noticeably short supply. In 1961, first-year Head Coach Bill McPeak had experienced mostly McValleys as the 'Skins bottomed out with a 1-12-1 record. Only the performances of quarterback Norman Snead and halfback Dick James, who was named Outstanding Redskin of 1961, had consoled Washington's long-suffering fans. The Redskins' 5-30-3 record over the previous three years (not including their 1-20 mark in preseason games) made them, along with the woeful Dallas Cowboys, the co-patsies of the league. In fact, had it not been for two victories over the newly-formed Cowboys, the 'Skins would have been riding a 28-game losing streak.

The Cleveland Browns, on the other hand, had won three NFL Championships in their 12 years in the league while compiling a 94-38-4 record. To maintain his team's winning tradition after the retirement of one of the greatest passers in history, quarterback Otto Graham, Coach Brown had built a new offense around the greatest running back in NFL history, Jimmy Brown. A 6-foot-2, 228-pound fullback who would lead the league in rushing nine times in his 10-year career, Brown combined the shiftiness of a rabbit with the power of a charging rhino. And the poor-tackling Redskins were Brown's favorite doormats.

So when the oddsmakers made the Cleveland Browns 16-point favorites to defeat the Redskins for a ninth consecutive time, there was no outpouring of indignation, no flood of Washington bettors backing the 'Skins. Redskins fans knew better. And Coach McPeak was not exaggerating when he said, "If we don't do better against the Browns [than we did against the Cowboys], we'll get run right out of Cleveland Stadium."

5 7,491 spectators partially filled Cleveland's vast Municipal Stadium to witness what they assumed would be another easy victory for the Browns. Such a crowd would have been a sellout at D.C. Stadium, but, in Cleveland, 30,000 seats remained unoccupied.

After receiving Bob Khayat's opening kickoff, the Browns moved from their 20 to their 43 in four plays. Then something strange happened. After taking a handoff from quarterback Jim Ninowski, Jim Brown was trapped in his backfield. Rather than swallow the 4-yard loss, Brown lateraled—to nobody! Redskins defensive back Jim Steffen, who had just arrived on the scene to help wrestle Brown to the turf, intercepted the ball at full speed and carried it into the end zone 39 yards away! Khayat converted, and the giddy Redskins pocketed their 7-point handout.

After an exchange of punts, Cleveland's offense began to click. Ninowski passed to tight end Johnny Brewer for 17 yards, then Jim Brown swept around left end for 18 more to the Washington 20. However, three straight incompletions brought out 16-year veteran Lou (The Toe) Groza, and the 6-time all-pro booted a 32-yard field goal to shorten Washington's lead to 7-3.

The Browns continued to dominate. Just before the end of the first quarter, a Norman Snead pass was picked off by Cleveland cornerback Jim Shofner at the Washington 36. Seizing the opportunity, Jim Brown blasted for 9 yards, and Ninowski passed for 17. The Redskins defense stiffened inside its 5, but, on fourth down, halfback Tom Wilson plunged into the end zone from a yard out to give Cleveland a 10-7 lead.

Snead's next pass was also intercepted when Cleveland's other cornerback, Bernie Parrish, cut in front of Bobby Mitchell, snatched the ball at the 45, and ran to the Washington 8. The Redskins defense managed to keep the Browns out of the end zone, but Groza kicked a short field goal to extend Cleveland's lead to 13-7. In the remaining 6 minutes of the first half, both teams missed medium-range field goals, and, when intermission came, the Redskins trotted to their dressing room, relieved to still have a chance in a game that could easily have turned into a Cleveland rout.

After gaining only 1 yard rushing in the first half, Washington's somnambulant running backs suddenly awoke. On the Redskins' first series of the third quarter, fullback Don Bosseler carried five times for 32 yards, and Jim Cunningham added 14 more on an off-tackle burst. When the Redskins were finally stopped at the Cleveland 26, Bob Khayat salvaged 3 points with a 33-yard field goal to shrink the Browns' lead to 13-10.

Cleveland retaliated with a long drive highlighted by a 21-yard pass from Ninowski to Jim Brown. Surprisingly, with a first down at Washington's 3, the Browns could gain only 1 yard on three consecutive running plays. On fourth down, Cleveland shunned another field goal to go for the touchdown. Figuring that the Redskins would be keying on Jim Brown, Coach Paul Brown ordered a handoff to Tom Wilson. Wilson dove into the right side of his line—and was knocked back for a loss! The jubilant Redskins took over at their 3. Washington couldn't muster a first down, though, and Cleveland got the ball again near midfield as the fourth quarter began. A short drive produced a 37-yard field goal by Groza, and, with 10 minutes left in the game, the Browns led, 16-10.

Groza kicked off deep to Bobby Mitchell, who nearly broke free but was tripped at his 38. Continuing their unprecedented success, Bosseler and Cunningham took turns sweeping the ends as the Redskins marched steadily into Cleveland territory. But the drive ended when Snead threw his third interception of the game, and Cleveland took over at its 43. After Ninowski passed to Rich Kreitling for a first down at the Washington 45, the Redskins figured the Browns would resort to time-consuming running plays. But Ninowski fooled them by throwing a swing pass to Jim Brown. Cradling the ball in his right hand, Brown swept gracefully out of the backfield at full throttle and galloped to the Washington 33, where linebackers Dale Hackbart and Bob Pellegrini crashed into him. The violent impact knocked the ball out of Brown's grasp, and Eddie Khayat fell on it for the Redskins!

3:33 remained. Having gained only 64 yards through the air while throwing three interceptions, Snead wisely chose to stay with his newfound run-

ning attack. Bosseler and Cunningham continued their fine work, advancing the ball to midfield on five carries. Faced with a crucial third and 4, Snead dropped back and flipped a short pass to Bobby Mitchell over the middle. With the first down already in hand, Mitchell headed toward the left sideline, ostensibly to get out of bounds to stop the clock. Spotting two Cleveland defenders closing in on him from his right, Mitchell suddenly braked. Both defenders reversed their direction but quickly realized they had been tricked. Instead of cutting back, Mitchell continued toward the sideline [Fig. 29] and in a few steps was heading down the field at top speed. At the 20, Mitchell dodged to his right to avoid an incoming defender while leaping out of a diving tackle from behind—all in the same motion! Leaving the tangled bodies of all 11 Cleveland players in his wake, Bobby Mitchell completed the dazzling 50-yard touchdown play by racing into the end zone! To his former boss, Paul Brown, Mitchell's touchdown must have felt like a dagger in the ribs; to Washington fans, it felt like salvation. Placekicker Bob Khayat booted the crucial extra point, and the ecstatic Redskins went back on top, 17-16!

Only one more miracle was required: prevent the powerful Browns from scoring in the final 1:25. Starting from his 27, Jim Ninowski fired to Ray Renfro for 13 yards, then followed with a 14-yard completion to Johnny Brewer at the Redskins 46. After a quick huddle, Rich Kreitling caught Ninowski's next pass at the Washington 38. Finally, Ninowski hit Brewer for another 10 yards, and the Browns were comfortably within Groza's field goal range at the Redskins 28. A first-down incompletion stopped the clock with 7 seconds remaining in the game, and ''The Toe'' came in for the kill. Taking the snap from center, Bobby Franklin set the ball on its nose, and Groza swung his talented leg. A heartbeat after Groza connected, Redskins linebacker Dale Hackbart broke through the line and blocked the kick! The ball skittered back to the Cleveland 43, where Franklin recovered for the crestfallen Browns.

Thinking the game was over, the Redskins started to celebrate, but the official timekeeper ruled that 2 seconds still remained even though no time-out had

Fig. 29   *AP/Wide World Photos*

been called. And since Cleveland had recovered the blocked kick on second down, the Browns had one final shot at snatching victory from the clutches of the incredulous Redskins. Once again, Groza aimed his famous toe at the crossbar—this time from 50 yards away—and once again, it was blocked! Bobby Freeman, a former Brown, did the honors, and the Redskins fell all over themselves in a joyous back-slapping free-for-all. Justice, and the Washington Redskins, had triumphed, 17-16.

In Washington and Bethesda; Alexandria and Gaithersburg; Richmond and Charleston; Memphis, Louisville, and Winston-Salem—wherever the game was shown on television—excited young boys swarmed out of their homes after the game to toss a football with their pals. As they played, they kept re-enacting the amazing touchdown run they had just witnessed, impatiently taking turns impersonating the star. And each time they scored their make-believe touchdowns, they visualized their American dream—that someday, even if they were not the same color, they would grow up to be the next Bobby Mitchell.

FIGHT ON, FIGHT ON

Dallas Cowboys vs. Washington Redskins

November 28, 1965

In September of 1963, Head Coach and General Manager Bill McPeak quickly squelched a growing rumor that his third-year quarterback, Norman Snead, was on the trading block. "If Snead goes, I go," said McPeak emphatically. So it came as no surprise that seven months later, on April Fools Day, 1964, McPeak traded Stormin' Norman to the Philadelphia Eagles for quarterback Sonny Jurgensen.

Although Snead had performed commendably in his three seasons as a Redskin, the opportunity to acquire Jurgensen, one of the premier quarterbacks in the league, proved irresistible to McPeak. Jurgensen had become available when the Eagles, who won the 1960 NFL Championship in Norm Van Brocklin's last year as quarterback, plummeted to last place in 1963 with a 2-10-2 record. Looking for somebody besides themselves to blame for the team's sudden decline, the Eagles management decided to get rid of Sonny, who had been the target of unrelenting abuse by the legendary boo-birds of Franklin Field. No matter how well Jurgensen played, Philadelphia "fans" had only one reaction—booing. They even booed when he threw five touchdown passes in a single game.

"People in Philadelphia don't look on me with too much favor," said Sonny. "The feeling is mutual." But not everyone in the City of Brotherly Love was anti-Jurgensen. The day after the trade was announced, a Philadelphia newspaper headline questioned whether the exchange had been a "SWAP OR SWIPE?", and the accompanying story implied that the Eagles' braintrust had flown north in a snowstorm.

The trade was an instant hit in Washington. With Jurgensen at quarterback, long-suffering Redskins fans anticipated an immediate return to the glories of the Sammy Baugh era. In his first season, Sonny certainly made a positive impact, but the 1964 'Skins could do no better than 6-8. Still, that was enough improvement for Washingtonians to believe that in 1965 the Redskins were ready to contend for the Eastern Conference championship. They were quickly brought back to earth, though, when the Redskins dropped their first five games. However, after new team President Edward Bennett Williams hosted a players-only meeting "to clear the air," the offense finally jelled and Washington won four of its next five games.

With the season nearing completion, even the 'Skins' defense, traditionally the weak link of the team, was gaining respect. For that, credit new players like safety Paul Krause, who as a rookie in 1964 led the NFL with 12 interceptions, former Colts cornerback Johnny Sample, and Chris Hanburger, an undersized but over-achieving linebacker who had been

Sonny Jurgensen in action against his former team for the first time, Oct. 11, 1964. Sonny made the Eagles regret their decision to trade him by throwing 5 TD passes in Redskins' 35-20 victory

Paul Fine Photo/Nate Fine Productions, Courtesy Washington Redskins

Sam Huff (70) and Johnny Sample (24) overpower Joe Morrison of Giants in 23-7 victory, Nov. 7, 1965
Paul Fine Photo/Nate Fine Productions, Courtesy Washington Redskins

drafted in the 18th round. Plus one more. A week after the Jurgensen-for-Snead swap, the Redskins astounded their fans once more by trading two of their most popular players, halfback Dick James and defensive lineman Andy Stynchula, to New York for the centerpiece of the Giants defense, middle linebacker Sam Huff. Although shocked and angered by the trade, Huff reluctantly reported to Washington and soon became captain of the defense.

The new-look Redskins were definitely improving, but not as quickly as their next opponent, the 4-6 Dallas Cowboys, who were systematically assembling the core of a team that, over the next 20 years, would win more games than any other club in the NFL. Soon, men like Don Meredith, Bob Hayes, Dan Reeves, Don Perkins, Ralph Neely, Jethro Pugh, Bob Lilly, Lee Roy Jordan, Mel Renfro, Cornell Green, and Chuck Howley would become very familiar to football fans throughout the country. But, in 1965, those future stars were playing on a somewhat disjointed Cowboys team that was a 3-point underdog to the spruced-up Washington Redskins.

As Edward Bennett Williams and his 50,204 co-rooters at D.C. Stadium could attest, Sonny Jurgensen's afternoon began with a thud. In the first 8 minutes of the game against the Cowboys, Jurgy misfired on all four of his passes, threw two interceptions, lost a fumble, and was sacked. Halfback Charley Taylor, NFL Rookie of the Year in 1964, was just as star-crossed, fumbling twice in his first three carries. Here's the damage report: Bob Lilly, the Cowboys' giant defensive tackle, picked up Jurgensen's fumble and returned it 41 yards to the Washington 6. From there, Don Meredith passed to Perry Lee Dunn for a touchdown, and the Cowboys grabbed an easy 7-0 lead. Taylor recovered his first fumble, but not his second. When Charley coughed up the ball on third and 33 at his own 2, Cornell Green scooped it up and ran 5 yards into the end zone to give Dallas an ill-deserved 14-0 advantage.

By the end of the first quarter, the harassed Jurgensen had completed just one of five passes—and that was for minus yardage. Finally, though, the Redskins got a break when middle linebacker Sam Huff recovered a Pete Gent fumble at the Washington 46.

Jurgy came alive, completing passes to Bobby Mitchell, Angelo Coia, and Pat Richter. But Sonny was sacked at the Cowboys 28, so placekicker Bob Jencks came in for a 35-yard field goal attempt. The Redskins' guardian angel must have been ogling a Redskinette at that particular moment because Dallas safety Mike Gaechter blocked Jencks' kick, recovered the ball himself, and raced 60 yards into the end zone for a touchdown! After Danny Villanueva booted the extra point, the Cowboys, with more touchdowns than first downs, were coasting, 21-0.

The Redskins' chances depreciated even further when Dallas forced a punt and surged to the Washington 18. But Villanueva blew a 25-yard field goal, and, for the first time in the game, the Redskins stopped feeling like case studies at a voodoo workshop. Throwing on every down, Jurgensen led his troops on an 80-yard march that was capped by a 26-yard touchdown pass to Charley Taylor. But the 'Skins had to be satisfied with only 6 points when Jencks' conversion attempt was blocked.

Mercifully, halftime arrived before the Redskins could embarrass themselves further. Trailing 21-6, they escaped to their locker room accompanied by the mutters and snorts of 50,000 disgruntled fans.

What else could go wrong for Washington? Well, how about Rickie Harris fumbling the Cowboys' first punt of the second half? Or Charley Taylor fumbling after catching a pass at the Redskins 42? Or Don Meredith escaping a horde of Redskins rushers and scrambling 19 yards? Or Danny Villanueva kicking a 29-yard field goal to increase the Cowboys' lead to 24-6 lead midway through the third quarter?

On top of all that, a clipping penalty on the ensuing kickoff forced the snake-bitten Washington Redskins to start at their 10. Suddenly, though, the Redskins bit back. Sonny fired a strike to Angelo Coia for 21 yards, and Charley Taylor broke through the line for 16 more. Then Jurgensen passed to Mitchell for 22 and to Coia for another 14. After using only five plays to travel 82 yards, the 'Skins needed seven plays to cover the last 8 yards, but Jurgensen finally sneaked in from the 1. After Jencks' conversion, Washington trailed by 11 points, 24-13.

As the fourth quarter began, the Redskins were

boring down the field again. An 11-yard completion to Taylor and a 9-yard bullet to Jerry Smith moved the ball close to midfield. Then Jurgensen connected with Smith twice more before hitting Charley Taylor at the 2 with a 21-yard strike. When journeyman halfback Danny Lewis plunged into the end zone for Washington's third touchdown, the one-sided affair suddenly became two-sided. Although still leading, 24-20, the Cowboys were in serious trouble.

Dallas' next drive looked like the boom-or-bust performance of a volatile penny stock: big gains followed by big losses. The Cowboys raced from their 24 to the Washington 19 in four plays, then backtracked to midfield on their next five plays before Villanueva had to punt. Dallas reclaimed some of its lost momentum, though, when linebacker Dave Edwards intercepted a Jurgensen pass, putting the Cowboys only 53 yards away from the Washington goal line. It didn't take them long to get there. Don Meredith tossed a short pass to split end Frank Clarke, who raced untouched into the end zone for a touchdown. 50,000 voices were silent as the Cowboys celebrated their 31-20 lead.

Less than 6 minutes remained as Jurgensen & Co. regrouped at their 36. Sonny passed to Bobby Mitchell for 15 yards. Then Angelo Coia made a nifty catch of a 39-yard bomb before falling out of bounds at the Dallas 10. One play later, Jurgensen fired to Mitchell in the end zone for a touchdown, and Washington, though trailing, 31-27, still had a chance with 3:32 remaining in the game. The buoyant mood of the born-again partisan crowd quickly sank, though, when Dallas' Mel Renfro returned Jencks' kickoff 56 yards to the Washington 41. However, with the game squarely on the line, the Redskins defense came through, stopping the Cowboys on three plays. On fourth down, Dallas Coach Tom Landry ordered a long field goal attempt, but Villanueva missed from the 45 and Washington took over, still trailing by 4 points with 1:41 left in the game.

Needing to cover 80 yards in a hurry, Jurgensen dropped back in his pocket—and fumbled. This time the Redskins' guardian angel was on active duty, and Sonny recaptured the ball on a convenient bounce and scrambled for a 9-yard gain. Then a pass interfer-

ence penalty gave Washington a first down at its 38. Suspecting that the defender who had fouled Jerry Smith would give him some extra room, Jurgy went right back to his sure-handed tight end for a 22-yard gain at the Cowboys 40. [Fig. 32] On first down, Jurgensen spotted Bobby Mitchell getting open deep and hit him at the 5 an instant before Cornell Green knocked him to the ground with a devastating tackle. With 1:14 left in the game, Washington took its final timeout.

The frenzied sellout crowd hushed on command to allow Jurgensen to call his signals. At the snap, split end Angelo Coia slanted toward the middle as if to make a crackback block, then cut back sharply to the outside. While still backpedaling away from center, Jurgensen lofted a soft pass over the heads of the frozen Cowboys defenders and into Coia's arms as the tense crowd exploded in joyous relief. The Redskins, after falling into a 21-0 hole, had finally climbed into the lead, 34-31!

Ironically, Washington's offense had been too efficient. By scoring in only 37 seconds, the 'Skins had left the Cowboys more than a minute in which to retaliate. Once again, it would be up to the much-maligned Washington defense to save or squander a victory. On the second play after the kickoff, Redskins defensive tackle Joe Rutgens set off a thunderous volley of cheers by sacking Meredith for a 6-yard loss. Undaunted, Dandy Don overcame the temporary setback by passing to Pete Gent for 20 yards at the Cowboys 34. Then, after an incompletion, Sam Huff sacked Meredith again, marking the sixth time the Redskins had dumped the Dallas quarterback. With 40 seconds remaining, Meredith fired deep to speedster Bob Hayes, who, despite double coverage, grabbed the ball at Washington's 37 for a 35-yard gain!

With 7 seconds on the clock, Redskins fans steeled themselves for another in a long line of bitter disappointments as Dallas Coach Tom Landry sent in Danny Villanueva to tie the game with a 45-yard field goal. At the snap of the ball, Washington's Fred Williams and Sam Huff power-blocked like offensive linemen, clearing a path through the Dallas line. Lonnie Sanders charged through the hole and dove.

Fig. 32   *Richard Darcey/Washington Post Photo*

Villanueva swung his leg, and the ball took off toward the goal post. An instant later, it smacked into Sanders' outstretched arm, and 50,000 ecstatic Redskins fans roared in grateful disbelief. When Jim Steffen recovered the ball for Washington, the Redskins' 34-31 miracle was complete.

Sonny Jurgensen's sparkling statistics—26 completions in 42 attempts (17 of 22 in the second half) for 411 yards and three touchdowns—were all the more remarkable because they had been earned against a defense whose only chore was to guard against his passes. With that performance, Sonny forever endeared himself to Redskins fans, who now could at least hope for occasional victories by way of miraculous comebacks and unlikely finishes.

General Manager McPeak had certainly chosen wisely when he traded Norman Snead for Sonny Jurgensen. And shortly after the 1965 season ended, he even made good on his promise that "If Snead goes, I go." After 21 wins, 46 losses, and 3 ties in his five years as head coach, Bill McPeak was fired.

COWBOYS AND INJUNS

Dallas Cowboys vs. Washington Redskins

November 13, 1966

The headline on the front page of *The Washington Post* on January 25, 1966, brandished the news: "Otto Graham to Coach Redskins." Emphasizing that "we were looking for a crack-down coach with a winning background," Redskins President Edward Bennett Williams described how he had finally lured Graham away from his comfortable post at the U.S. Coast Guard Academy with a fat 5-year contract and the autonomy that went with being both coach and general manager of the Washington Redskins. Without hesitation, Washington fans accepted Graham as the One True Savior of a ragamuffin Redskins team that had staggered to five straight losing seasons under the previous One True Savior, congenial Bill McPeak. "Maybe that was the problem," said one of McPeak's players. "He was such a nice guy—probably too nice a guy."

Otto Graham certainly had a winning background. No other quarterback in history came close to his record of appearing in 10 consecutive Championship games. A crack-shot passer, Graham had been instrumental in the Cleveland Browns winning the All-America Football Conference Championship all four years the league was in existence. When the Browns (along with the Baltimore Colts and the San Francisco 49ers) merged into the NFL in 1950, the older league's chauvinists predicted that Cleveland's

success would evaporate. Typical of that group, Redskins Owner and laundry magnate George Preston Marshall scoffed: "The only job Otto Graham could get in Washington is driving one of my laundry trucks." With Graham in the driver's seat, the Browns responded to the taunts by cruising to six straight National Football League Championship games—and driving off with three titles. In six seasons in the NFL, Otto Graham was named all-pro five times, and he later was inducted into the Hall of Fame.

Prowess on the field, however, does not automatically convert into success on the sideline. Before going off to New London, Connecticut, each fall to instruct the Coast Guard team, Graham would reappear briefly at the edge of the national limelight as the coach of the College All-Stars. Over the years, he had earned a measure of respect by leading the All-Stars to occasional victories against the previous year's NFL champions in the *Chicago Tribune* charity game, which, at that time, kicked off each season. Much of that esteem was thrown away, however, when Graham started spouting his arrogant and dumbfounding opinions. A strong believer in hard practices at his All-Star training camp, Otto criticized Charley Taylor in 1964 for being "lazy." Then he refused to let Gale Sayers play a single down after accusing the future Hall of Famer of not giving his best in practice.

Coach Otto Graham   *Paul Fine Photo/Nate Fine Productions, Courtesy Washington Redskins*

Later that year, Graham even lambasted Jim Brown, the Cleveland Browns' peerless fullback, saying "Jimmy Brown doesn't block and he won't help with fakes, and I'd trade him for the good of the team."

Of course, the rest of the football world merely considered Brown to be the greatest running back in history. His high-octane mixture of speed, power, balance, size, and agility made him almost unstoppable. Redskins quarterback Sonny Jurgensen said, "[If I had him in my backfield,] I'd just take the snap from center, hand off to Jim Brown and watch him do his own blocking for himself. He's good at that." A bit of a nut on the importance of backfield blocking, Graham, an active member of the Fellowship of Christian Athletes, was remembered vividly by a teammate who said, "Otto loves his fellow man. It's just that if they don't block for him, he wants to cut their hearts out."

Graham had starred in an era when men played both offense and defense, and every player blocked no matter what his position. For Graham to make such an outlandish statement about Jim Brown shows the degree to which he had been spoiled by his old Cleveland teammate, Marion Motley, whose offensive and defensive play was arguably the greatest one-man combination of running, blocking, and tackling ever seen on a gridiron.

But there were no Marion Motleys (nor Jim Browns) on the 1966 Washington Redskins. Instead, Graham inherited a soft-nosed squad that scored easily but made their own end zone far too accessible. Over the previous 20 years, an apathetic attitude had corroded team spirit, and the Redskins' lackadaisical play gave birth to their most common nickname: the "Deadskins." Otto Graham, disciplinarian, set out to change that. In his first act as head coach and general manager of the Washington Redskins, Graham left for a six-week vacation.

That summer, when he gathered his troops at Dickinson College for his first training camp, Coach Graham quickly discovered that the 1966 Washington Redskins would never win a defensive battle. His only hope for a winning season was to create a high-powered offense that could outscore the enemy. To that end, Coach Graham designed a wide-open aerial attack to take advantage of the pin-point passing of Christian Adolph (Sonny) Jurgensen. It was once said that "if you wanted one quarterback to throw one pass with whatever money and prestige you care to imagine on the line, if that pass had to get through the tightest coverage and the wildest rush, if the margin for error over 30 yards was three inches . . . you'd take Jurgy."

If that wasn't enough to scare opponents, Jurgensen was also blessed with three gifted receivers: flanker Bobby Mitchell, tight end Jerry Smith, and Charley Taylor, whom Graham had just switched from halfback to split end to take advantage of his impressive open-field running ability. The combination of Mitchell's speed and shiftiness, Smith's impeccable hands, and Taylor's strength and speed left enemy defenders with an unsolvable puzzle of whom to double-cover.

Unfortunately, Washington's porous defense surrendered points as quickly as Jurgensen & Co. put them on the board. So it was not surprising that by midseason, the 5-4 Redskins, with their high-performance offense and low-performance defense, had become a model of inconsistency, winning and losing games by equally lopsided margins. At the start of the season, Graham had tried to prepare Washington fans for that by saying, "Instead of winning games 3-0, I'd rather risk losing some games by, say, 35-28 and have the fans up off their seats with excitement."

Graham's next opponent, the Dallas Cowboys, were anxious to give him his wish. It had taken 7 years, but Tom Landry had finally molded his team into an NFL contender. The 5-2-1 Cowboys were not only leading the league in rushing defense and total defense, but also in passing, scoring, and total offense. Coach Landry, a former defensive back with the New York Giants, was especially pleased with his defense. "When it plays its best, our defense can do almost anything it wants to," said Landry. "It forces the opposition to do things it does not want to do." Although the Redskins were leading the series, 5-4 with 2 ties, a comparison of the two teams' average scores in 1966 explains why the Cowboys were listed as 7½ point favorites. Dallas' average game thus far had been a 36-13 victory; Washington's average game had been a 22-20 loss.

An overnight rain had softened the natural sod at D.C. Stadium, giving hope to the 50,927 Redskins fans, the largest crowd ever to watch the 'Skins in Washington, that the soggy field would bog down the speedy Dallas Cowboys. Among that sixteenth consecutive sellout crowd was Jack Kent Cooke, proud new owner of 25% of the Washington Redskins, who was attending his first game in that capacity. Cooke must have believed his presence had a curative effect on his new employees when Mel Renfro fumbled the opening kickoff into the hands of Washington's Don Croftcheck at the Dallas 26. Hoping to quickly knock the Cowboys on the seats of their silver pants, the Redskins instead were forced to settle for a 35-yard field goal by their #1 draft pick from Princeton, Charley Gogolak. The fans, however, weren't choosy; they were delighted that the 'Skins had scored first, even if it was only a field goal.

After Renfro returned Washington's kickoff to his 25, the Cowboys embarked on a graceful and untroubled voyage down the field, reeling off six first downs in 16 well-rehearsed plays. Perkins and Reeves cruised through the line for a total of 38 yards on nine carries, and Meredith completed five of six passes on the 75-yard excursion that finally concluded when Meredith dove into the end zone from the 1. Danny Villanueva kicked the PAT, and Dallas led, 7-3.

Sonny Jurgensen's reply came in three parts: a 24-yard strike to Jerry Smith, an 11-yarder to Taylor, and a 12-yard completion back to Smith. When the Dallas defense stiffened at its 26, Gogolak used his new-fangled soccer-style kicking motion to cash a 33-yard field goal, tightening the score to 7-6, Dallas, at the end of the first quarter.

The second period evolved into a punting contest with each team kicking four times. But Dallas managed to wedge in one devastating play: a 52-yard touchdown bomb to Bullet Bob Hayes that extended its advantage to 14-6 at halftime. The Redskins had been outclassed in every area—passing, rushing, and defense—and things would only get worse at the start of the second half.

Before Bob Hayes joined the Dallas Cowboys, he was known as the World's Fastest Human, owner of the lowest times in history for both the 100-meter and 100-yard dashes. When he won the 100-meter dash at the 1964 Olympics, he buried the finest sprinters on the planet with his record-setting time of 10.0 seconds. However, in the anchor leg of the 4×100-meter relay, Hayes forced himself to run even faster in order to mow down a Russian who had started with a 5-meter lead. In the most exciting race of the Tokyo Olympics, Hayes blazed past the Russian at the wire, winning his second gold medal and unquestionably establishing himself as the fastest man on earth.

When he wasn't running track, the 190-pound Hayes played fullback at Florida A & M, but when he joined the Cowboys Coach Landry moved him to wide receiver to utilize his speed and lengthen his career. The opening play of the second half demonstrated Landry's wisdom. From a standing start at his own 5 yard line, Hayes flashed by defensive back Lonnie Sanders, grabbed Don Meredith's long spiral near midfield, and accelerated. Then accelerated some more. Five seconds later, Bullet Bob scored, and the awe-struck Redskins trailed, 21-6.

Although intimidated by the 95-yard touchdown, Washington didn't quit. Ricky Harris received Villanueva's kickoff 4 yards deep in his end zone and weaved his way to midfield. Jurgensen took advantage of this unaccustomed field position with a 16-yard pass to Joe Don Looney and a 31-yard strike to Charley Taylor inside the Cowboys 5. On first down, tight end Jerry Smith found a vacant spot in the Dallas end zone and caught Sonny's 4-yard touchdown pass, narrowing the score to 21-13.

Unable to sustain their next drive, the Cowboys punted back to the 'Skins. From his 22, Jurgensen spotted Taylor getting open over the middle and fired. Taylor snagged the ball in stride, ricocheted off two Cowboys defensive backs, and sprinted into the end zone for a 78-yard touchdown! After Gogolak's conversion, Dallas' lead was down to a single point, 21-20.

Meredith mobilized his forces, and the Cowboys zipped downfield until defensive end Ron Snidow

As a halfback in 1964, Charley Taylor ran for 755 yards, caught 53 passes, and was named Rookie of the Year

AP/Wide World Photos

jolted the ball out of Dan Reeves' hands and into the arms of Sam Huff, who recovered for Washington at the Redskins 23. 50,000 fans stomped and yelled as Jurgensen continued to carve up the Dallas secondary. First, Bobby Mitchell caught two identical 14-yard bullets. Then Jurgy connected with Smith on a 21-yard beauty. Fifteen yards were tacked on for roughing the passer, and Washington was suddenly knocking on the door at the Dallas 13. Two plays later, on third and 10, Jurgensen hit Smith again, but the tight end was tackled inches short of the first down. Playing it safe, Coach Graham ordered Gogolak to kick an 11-yard field goal, and the resurgent Redskins climbed back on top, 23-21.

As the third quarter ended, defensive back Jim Shorter staved off another Cowboys threat by intercepting a Meredith pass at the Redskins 5. [Fig. 35] But the Cowboys defense kept the 'Skins pinned to their goal line, and Dallas got the ball again at its 41. Meredith threw to Reeves for 29 yards, then hit Hayes with a 27-yarder at the Washington 3. Dan Reeves charged into the end zone from there, and the Cowboys vaulted back into the lead, 28-23.

With 10 minutes left in the game, the determined Redskins fought back again. Three straight pass completions earned a first down at the Dallas 36. Then Jurgy connected with Mitchell for 8 yards and again for 5 more. From the Cowboys 18, Sonny threw into the corner of the end zone for Charley Taylor, who had attracted double coverage. In a tangle of twisting bodies, Taylor leapt and—caught the ball for a touchdown! Leading 30-28, the Redskins now only had to sweat out the final 5½ minutes.

After the Washington touchdown, rookie Walt Garrison fielded Gogolak's short kickoff at the 15 and ran it back to the Dallas 41. On first down, with every Redskins fan praying for Divine intervention, defensive tackle Joe Rutgens heard the call and sacked Meredith for a 4-yard loss. A quick pass to Hayes recouped 12 yards, but, on third and 2, Don Perkins was stacked at the line for no gain. On fourth and 2 at midfield, Coach Landry decided to go for the first down. Surrounded by 50,000 screaming maniacs, Don Meredith handed off to Perkins again. The Cowboys halfback stabbed into the heart of the Washing-ton line, where defensive end Ron Snidow smashed into him and threw him to the ground. No gain! The Redskins defenders ran to the bench in triumph as their excited teammates added their congratulations to the cheers of the grateful fans in the packed stadium.

With 2 minutes left in the game, the 'Skins needed to make only one more first down to seal their victory. On second and 9, Joe Don Looney was caught behind the line for a loss of 3. On third and 12, Jurgensen completed a pass to fullback Steve Thurlow in the flat, but Cowboys linebacker Lee Roy Jordan wrestled him down after a gain of only 4 yards. After Dallas took its final time-out, Washington was forced to give up the ball.

Pat Richter's perfect punt was downed by Jerry Smith at the Dallas 3, and the Cowboys, trailing by 2 points and with no time-outs, went into their hurry-up offense. Otto Graham ordered a prevent defense, exchanging one of his pass rushers for an extra defensive back, and told his men to protect against the bomb even if it meant conceding the short pass. That was fine with Don Meredith. Throwing from his end zone, Meredith hit Pete Gent with a short toss that turned into a 26-yard gain because the 'Skins were playing so deep. On the next play, Meredith was spooked from his pocket yet managed to pick up 12 yards before the Redskins secondary could double back and force him out of bounds. Two plays later, the Cowboys faced a third-and-9 at their 42 with 48 seconds remaining in the game.

Given plenty of time to look for an open receiver, Meredith waited for Gent to get open again and hit him with a perfect strike 25 yards downfield. That put the Cowboys at the Washington 33 with half a minute remaining. On first down, Meredith scampered out of bounds after a 6-yard gain, and the referee tacked on 15 yards for unnecessary roughness. That was all the Cowboys needed. With 19 seconds left on the clock, Danny Villanueva lined up a 20-yard field goal. The Redskins charged in furiously to block the kick, but Villanueva was too quick. The spinning ball sailed over the outstretched hands of the leaping Washington linemen and between the metal uprights for the 3 points that sank the Redskins.

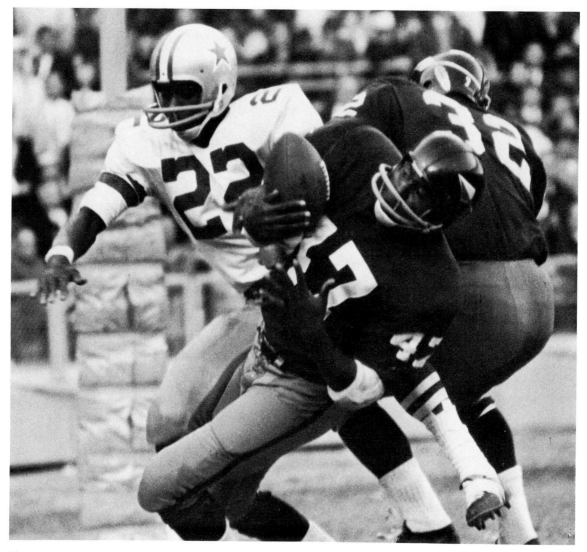

Fig. 35   *Jim McNamara/Washington Post Photo*

50,000 mourners watched helplessly as the scoreboard changed to Dallas 31, Washington 30. There was only enough time for the kickoff, and no miracle runback saved the day for the Washington Redskins. When the inevitable shot from the timekeeper's gun killed their final hope, Washington's disappointed fans filed out of D.C. Stadium, shaking their heads in bitter silence.

When he first took over the job as Redskins head coach, Otto Graham had promised high-scoring excitement, not victories. That may have been acceptable to fans in places like Cleveland, where championships were as routine as Midwestern accents. But in Washington, where Redskins fans had been dispirited by years and years of losing, one of those 3-0 victories that Graham had so casually denounced would have been met with rave reviews.

THRUST & PARRY

Washington Redskins vs. Dallas Cowboys

December 11, 1966

Without a doubt, Joe Don Looney was the MIP (Most Interesting Player) on the 1966 Washington Redskins. "Never was a man more aptly named," quipped George Sauer, who had teamed with the muscular 6-foot 1-inch, 224-pound halfback at the University of Texas. Before arriving in Washington, Looney had consternated seven consecutive coaches —four in college and three in the NFL—with his outrageous behavior. Blessed with an outstanding physique but cursed with a bewildering attitude, Looney never mastered the art of staying on one football team long enough to realize his tremendous potential.

In his college days, Looney bounced from Texas to TCU to Cameron Junior College to Oklahoma. Despite his wacky reputation, Looney was drafted in the first round by the New York Giants, who soon learned that the stories about Joe Don's daffiness had not been overstated. During preseason practices, Looney ran through guard when he was supposed to run through tackle because "anyone can run where the holes are; a good football player makes his own holes." Then Joe Don refused to toss his used socks and jock into the laundry hamper because "no damn sign is going to tell me what to do." He lasted 28 days with New York before he was traded to the Colts. Baltimore shipped him to Detroit. And the Lions

traded him to the Redskins. The final outrage in Detroit had occurred when Lions Coach Harry Gilmer told Looney to take in a play to quarterback Milt Plum and Looney replied, "If you want a messenger, call Western Union."

As a Redskin, Joe Don immediately became the darling of Washingtonians, who were used to rooting for underdogs and outcasts. Momentarily forgetting that a good rushing attack begins with a strong offensive line, the fans hoped Looney would be the long-awaited cure for the 'Skins' chronically anemic running game. There was no doubt that Looney had a burning desire to excel, but his wild antics, bad luck, and inability to deal with authority would continue to overshadow his considerable talents.

Two weeks after their heartbreaking loss to the Cowboys, the Redskins demolished the New York Giants in the highest scoring game in NFL history. After Brig Owens collected three interceptions and a fumble, which he parlayed into two long touchdowns, after halfback A.D. Whitfield scored three touchdowns in his first four carries, after Rickie Harris returned a punt 52 yards for a TD, and after Sonny Jurgensen threw three touchdown passes, including two to Charley Taylor, Coach Otto Graham did the only gentlemanly thing. Leading by four touchdowns with 3 seconds left in the game, Graham ordered a 29-yard field goal. In the least pressurized last-second field goal attempt in history, Charley Gogolak pumped it through the uprights, and the sore-fingered score-keeper gave his final accounting: Washington Redskins 72, New York Giants 41.

"We were like a starving man who is suddenly treated to a smorgasbord," said a sheepish Edward Bennett Williams in a lame attempt to justify Washington's final field goal. Thanks in small part to those last 3 points, six NFL records, four Redskins records, and eight series records (Redskins vs. Giants) had been tied or broken. "Don't worry," laughed quarterback Sonny Jurgensen after the massacre, "I promise not to run up the score against the Cowboys."

Given the fact that the Dallas Cowboys occupied first place in the Eastern Conference with a 9-2-1 record while the Redskins were struggling at 6 and 6, Dallas had little to fear on that count. But if anyone could pick apart the Cowboys' complex defense, it was Sonny Jurgensen, Washington's co-captain and just-elected Player of the Year in 1966.

Coach Don Shula of the Baltimore Colts simply called Jurgensen "a great pocket passer." To compensate for his lack of speed, Sonny had learned to get rid of the ball quickly, which allowed him to wait until the last possible moment before committing to a receiver. When combined with his talent for reading defenses and his knack for improvisation—on several occasions he had completed passes behind his back or with his left hand—Sonny's quick release made him one of the most dangerous quarterbacks ever to play the game. So there was really no need for Sonny to be particularly mobile. All he needed to do was drop back in the pocket, plant his right foot, and fire perfect strikes to his receivers, which he did with more precision and frequency than anyone else in the game. "When Jurgensen's right," said Cowboys Owner Clint Murchison, Jr., "there's no better quarterback in the league."

Before Sonny joined the Redskins, Washington's offense had relied on one man: flanker Bobby Mitchell. If a team stopped Mitchell, they stopped the Redskins. With the addition of Jurgensen and halfback Charley Taylor in 1964 and tight end Jerry Smith in

1965, the Redskins offense became more diversified and unpredictable, but the team ended up 6-8 in both years. In mid-1966, new Head Coach Otto Graham switched Taylor from halfback to split end to take greater advantage of his open-field running ability. Although Charley had shown talent as a halfback —he won Rookie of the Year honors in 1964— Graham believed that his full potential would never be reached until he was no longer dependent on an offensive line to spring him into the secondary.

With Taylor split out wide as a receiver, opposing pass defenses could no longer afford to double-team Mitchell and Smith, and Washington started putting on the best aerial show in the NFL. All three Redskins receivers were among the top 10 in the race for most receptions, led by Taylor, who had made 60 catches so far. Along the way, Charley had also set a club record by grabbing 11 passes for 199 yards in a single game. "In all my years in pro football," said Graham, "I never had more good ends on one squad."

Washington's defense had a few stars, too: 5-time all-pro middle linebacker Sam Huff, defensive tackle Joe Rutgens, outside linebacker Chris Hanburger, and safety Paul Krause. At first bitter over being traded to the Redskins from the highly successful New York Giants, Huff found himself on a losing team for the first time in his career. "It's hard when you're successful with one organization, and that's all you've ever known, to come with a losing organization," said Sam. "That was the hard part about it, giving up all those things you'd worked so hard for." But Huff was too much of a professional to let his resentment toward Giants Coach Allie Sherman affect his play, and, along with the two other newcomers and one old veteran, he was helping to transform Washington's leaky defense into a fairly respectable unit.

Free safety Paul Krause had the speed to keep up with the swiftest receivers in the NFL, and, at 6-3 and 195 pounds, the size to bring them down. In 1964, he finished second in the Rookie of the Year balloting (behind Charley Taylor) and was selected to start the Pro Bowl after leading the league with 12 interceptions (7 of which occurred in consecutive games). Linebacker Chris Hanburger, 6-foot-2 and 218 pounds, had been considered so small for his

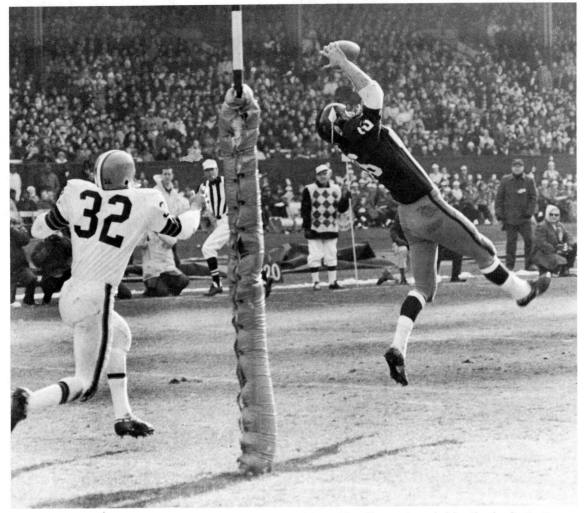

Paul Krause, who made 28 interceptions in his 4 years as a Redskin, picks off a pass intended for Cleveland's Jim Brown
Paul Fine Photo/Nate Fine Productions, Courtesy Washington Redskins

position that he wasn't chosen until the 18th round of the 1965 draft. But he compensated for his lack of bulk with savvy, anticipating the flow of a play and positioning himself where he could do the most damage.

Then there was 6-year veteran defensive tackle Joe Rutgens, who was Washington's working class hero. A #1 draft choice in 1961, Joe endeared himself to every middle-aged man in the Capital area with his prodigious beer belly, sloppy shirttail, and outstanding defensive play. Perhaps more than any-

one else, Joe Rutgens symbolized the Washington Redskins in the Sixties—disheveled, out of shape, but surprisingly indomitable.

Unfortunately, the Redskins were not indomitable very often. In his role as general manager, Otto Graham had done his best to make the team more competitive by completing 11 trades, but his players resented his Scrooge-like response to their salary requests. Having played in the days when professional football was a part-time job, Graham could not get used to the idea of paying a minimum wage of

$12,000 to his second-string players, or paying stars like Sam Huff and Sonny Jurgensen $30,000 and $45,000 per year. After squeezing his players dry at the negotiating table, Graham could not understand when those same players refused to give blood in his drawn-out practices.

As his first season in Washington was coming to a close, Coach Graham recanted his statement that he preferred high-scoring defeats to low-scoring victories. "I'd like to get ahead and stay ahead just once," said the frustrated Graham, who had watched helplessly as the 'Skins surrendered over 300 points for the seventh consecutive year. Nevertheless, the Redskins still had a chance to pull out a winning season, something they hadn't accomplished in over a decade. They just needed to win their final two games, the first of which was against the Dallas Cowboys.

After 5 years of building from scratch, Dallas had blossomed into one of the top clubs in the league and needed just one more victory to clinch the Eastern Conference title. The Cowboys were especially tough at home, where they had never lost a game to Washington even when they were the door-mats of the league. "Most everyone here has been through some long years," said Dallas' veteran fullback Don Perkins. "So it's pleasing to have something to battle for, for a change."

As usual, the 13-point underdog Washington Redskins were battling only for a bit of self-respect.

64,198 eager fans filled the Cotton Bowl expecting to witness another high-scoring shootout between the Washington Redskins and the Dallas Cowboys. CBS shared their expectations. For the first time ever, a Redskins game was being telecast to a nationwide audience, and Washington hoped to ratify the network's belief that they could keep up with the fast-scoring Cowboys. Surprisingly, though, both teams got off to a slow start. In the early going, the Redskins squandered two scoring opportunities when they could not improve on excellent field position and gained only one first down in four possessions. Yet that was one more than the Cowboys could manage.

The scoreless spell was finally broken early in the second quarter when fullback Don Perkins burst

through right tackle and sprinted 20 yards into the end zone to give the Cowboys a 7-0 advantage. A few minutes later, Washington got a break when Dallas quarterback Don Meredith fumbled as he was being sacked by defensive end Ron Snidow. Linebacker Carl Kammerer fell on the loose ball at the Cowboys 40, and, three plays later, Gogolak came through with a 42-yard field goal, cutting Dallas' lead to 7-3.

After Washington's defense thwarted the Cowboys for the sixth time in seven possessions, Jurgensen and his receivers started connecting. A beautiful pass to tight end Jerry Smith was good for 34 yards and a

Chris Hanburger

Copyright Washington Post; Reprinted by permission of the D.C. Public Library

first down at the Dallas 27; then two short tosses worked the ball to the 14. Unfortunately, halfback Joe Don Looney fumbled at the Cowboys 5, and Dallas linebacker Lee Roy Jordan scooped it up and returned it 28 yards to the 33. After two holding penalties against the Cowboys nullified two long pass completions, and a sack by Ron Snidow nearly caused a safety, Dallas was faced with fourth and 43. Standing at the back edge of his end zone, Danny Villanueva hurried to get his punt away, but Carl Kammerer broke through the line and blocked it! The ball skittered tantalizingly around the end zone until John Reger finally fell on it for a Washington touchdown! Gogolak's PAT was good, and the Redskins celebrated their 10-7 lead while 64,000 Dallas fans muttered amongst themselves.

With 2 minutes left in the half, the Cowboys marched from their 37 to the Washington 37 in three plays. On first down, Meredith hit halfback Dan Reeves with an apparent touchdown pass, but it was called back due to an ineligible receiver downfield. Two plays later, middle linebacker Sam Huff blitzed, smashing into Meredith a split second after he had released his pass. The Cowboys quarterback fell flat on his back. His head snapped back and cracked into the rock-hard Cotton Bowl field, knocking him unconscious for a few moments. After regaining a few of his senses, Meredith was helped to the sideline, and the star-crossed Cowboys had to settle for a 42-yard field goal attempt. To Washington's surprise, Villanueva's kick sliced to the right, and the first half ended with Washington still on top, 10-7.

Without a doubt, the Redskins defense had just played its best half of the season, giving up only 23 yards through the air to the high-scoring Cowboys while sacking Meredith three times. Dallas' defense had been almost as effective, though, limiting the 'Skins to three first downs.

Shortly after intermission, the Cowboys got the first break of the second half when safety Mike Gaechter intercepted a Jurgensen pass and returned it 18 yards to the Washington 19. With the disoriented Meredith unable to continue, Coach Tom Landry alternated his two rookie quarterbacks, Craig

Morton and Jerry Rhome, on a play-by-play basis. The charged-up Redskins defense didn't surrender a yard, and Dallas had to settle for a 26-yard field goal and a 10-10 tie.

Mistakes continued to cost the 'Skins. Late in the third period, a roughing-the-punter penalty extended a Dallas drive that eventually produced a touchdown on a 23-yard pass from Morton to Bob Hayes. Although somewhat deflated to be trailing, 17-10, the Redskins refused to go under. Passes to Mitchell and Taylor gave Washington a first down at its 48, then former Cowboys halfback A.D. Whitfield burst through a hole at left tackle and ran 41 yards before Cornell Green finally brought him down. A moment later, Jurgensen struck again with a perfect toss to Mitchell in the end zone, and the game was tied, 17-17.

The Redskins defense continued to play well, but, early in the fourth quarter, rookie halfback Dan Reeves took a pitchout and broke loose for 67 yards down the right sideline, and Dallas surged back in front, 24-17. Jurgensen responded with six straight passes, including a 53-yard bomb to Charley Taylor and a 17-yard bullet to tight end Jerry Smith. After two incompletions, Sonny fired an 11-yard touchdown pass to Smith, and the game was deadlocked, 24-24.

With the excited Cotton Bowl crowd shouting encouragement, the Cowboys roared back down the field. Quarterback Jerry Rhome drilled a pass to Hayes for 12 yards; Dan Reeves ran for 21 more; then Rhome hit Pete Gent with a 47-yard bomb. On first and goal at the Washington 6, fullback Don Perkins slanted through left guard and dove into the end zone for a touchdown, tipping the see-saw battle back in Dallas' favor, 31-24. Twenty-one seconds later, the game was tied again. That was all the time Sonny Jurgensen needed to complete a beautiful 65-yard scoring pass to Charley Taylor. "It was a broken play," said Otto Graham after the game. "It was supposed to be a down-and-out to Taylor, but, when the safety came up, Taylor took off deep and Jurgensen was sharp enough to pick it up." It was the fourth touchdown that had been scored in the last 7 minutes. And there was still 3:19 left for one of the teams to break the 31-31 tie.

Coach Landry led off with Craig Morton, who

skipped a pass to Hayes, incomplete. Rhome's turn produced 6 yards on a determined run by Perkins. On third and 4, Morton was flushed out of the pocket and threw on the run—from beyond the scrimmage line! The Cowboys had to give up the ball.

Just before the 2-minute warning, Danny Villanueva got off a short punt that Rickie Harris faircaught at the Washington 46. Coach Landry sent in extra defensive backs to clog the passing lanes, but Sonny Jurgensen countered by handing off to halfback A.D. Whitfield, who turned the corner and raced 30 yards to the Dallas 24. Needing only a field goal, Jurgensen wisely called for three straight line plunges. They gained only 2 yards but accomplished the far more important task of using up time. With 25 seconds left in the game and the clock moving, Jurgensen

sauntered over to referee George Ronnix and started shooting the breeze. Sonny's nervous teammates begged him to call a time-out, but Jurgensen kept talking. Finally, with 8 seconds left on the scoreboard clock, Sonny asked for a time-out.

Rookie placekicker Charlie Gogolak had succeeded on 21 of 26 field goals over the season, but had missed twice earlier in the game and had never faced pressure like this. With 64,000 rabid Cowboys fans screaming at him and a nationwide television audience on the edge of their seats, Gogolak waited for his holder, Dick Shiner, to spot the ball, then swung his leg and sent it spinning toward the uprights 29 yards away. [Fig. 38] It was as perfect as the final score: Washington 34, Dallas 31.

Fig. 38   *Copyright Washington Post; Reprinted by permission of the D.C. Public Library*

"The Cowboys may go on to the championship," said Sam Huff in the happy Redskins locker room, "but we should have beaten them twice. That was the most exciting game for me since I've been playing in Washington." When asked about the quarterback sack that had knocked Don Meredith out of the game, Huff said, "Sure, I hit him. I had a clear shot at him, so I hit him. It's my job to hit people. There was nothing wrong about it. We were blitzing, baby. You've got to keep the pressure on. We blitzed two out of three plays in the first half."

Bobby Mitchell's seven catches for 79 yards and one touchdown, Charley Taylor's four receptions for 145 yards and a TD, and Jerry Smith's five catches for 79 yards and a touchdown point directly to the man who made the remarkable victory possible—quarterback Sonny Jurgensen. All three touchdown passes had come on broken plays that Jurgensen stitched together on the run. And his last pass, the 65-yard touchdown to Taylor, was his 235th completion of the season, tying his own NFL record.

By the end of 1966, Charley Taylor would lead the league in receiving, and Sonny Jurgensen would set club records for passing attempts, completions, yardage, and touchdowns. Clint Murchison had told the truth: "When Jurgensen's right, there's no better quarterback in the league."

LUCKY WITH LOVE

New York Giants vs. Washington Redskins

October 1, 1967

America's two favorite team sports, football and baseball, offer a perfect contrast. Whereas baseball is essentially a game of control with wonderful moments of abandon, football is a game of abandon with wonderful moments of control. In 1958, pro football began a swift rise in popularity when the Baltimore Colts captured the attention of the nation with their sudden-death victory over the New York Giants in the NFL Championship game. In comparison, baseball suddenly seemed too tame, too predictable, and too slow. Football's pace was better suited to television, and, with the advent of slow-motion instant replays, fans could fully appreciate the grace and fury that formerly had been hidden in the swirl of 22 colliding bodies.

In 1960, the American Football League expanded the horizons of the pro game westward, placing franchises in non-NFL cities such as Oakland, Houston, Kansas City, and Denver. Led by innovative thinkers like Al Davis and Lamar Hunt, the young league succeeded, in part, by signing top college players like Billy Cannon, Abner Haynes, John Hadl, Paul Lowe, Lance Alworth, Don Maynard, Mike Garrett, Otis Taylor, and Joe Namath. Although originally scoffed at as a pass-happy league with permissive defenses, the AFL captivated fans with its high-scoring, exciting games. A salary war ensued, draining the coffers of both leagues. Finally, in June, 1966, NFL Commissioner Pete Rozelle announced a plan for a merger with the AFL that would take place in several stages and be completed by 1970.

As an intermediate step, the NFL divided its Eastern and Western Conferences into four divisions — Capitol, Century, Coastal, and Central. The Washington Redskins, naturally, belonged to the Capitol Division along with Dallas, Philadelphia, and New Orleans. The rest of the Eastern Conference — Cleveland, Pittsburgh, St. Louis, and New York — fell into the Century Division. At the end of the season, two playoff games between the winners of the four divisions would determine who would represent the two conferences in the NFL Championship game. Luckily, the Washington Redskins and their next opponent, the New York Giants, didn't have to worry about such confusing matters. They would be watching it all on television.

By 1967, the New York Giants had fallen far from their once-habitual perch atop the Eastern Conference of the NFL. But, like the Washington Redskins, the Giants could occasionally remind their fans of their glorious past with one or two masterful games each season. In an attempt to make that happen more often, New York traded two first-round draft choices and a #2 pick to the Minnesota Vikings for

Fran Tarkenton, a scrambling quarterback whose improvisational escapades could disrupt the most disciplined defense. With receivers like Homer Jones (a 9.3 sprinter averaging 33 yards a catch), Del Shofner, Aaron Thomas, and Joe Morrison to throw to, Tarkenton's job was to put more points on the scoreboard than the woeful Giants defense would surrender.

That was precisely the dilemma that Washington quarterback Sonny Jurgensen faced each Sunday. Sometimes the magic worked, and Jurgensen and his teammates would ambush an overconfident opponent; more often, though, the Redskins would shoot themselves in the foot. Overall, in the 3 years since Jurgensen joined the team, the Redskins had limped to a 19-23 record. Obviously, Sonny couldn't win by himself. To balance his attack, Otto Graham drafted Ray McDonald, a 6-foot-4, 238-pound all-America fullback from Utah. That investment began paying dividends when McDonald rushed for 98 yards and three touchdowns against the New Orleans Saints. Still not satisfied, though, Coach Graham further increased his options by shifting 32-year-old flanker Bobby Mitchell back to his old halfback position.

Despite their inconsistent performances, the Redskins were the hottest ticket in town—so hot that every home game had been sold out for the second season in a row. And so hot that 252 season tickets that had been mailed to their owners were "missing." If you were not a season ticket holder, the only way to get into D.C. Stadium to see the 1-1 Redskins' 1967 home opener against the 1-1 Giants was to beg, borrow, or steal.

The New York Giants belied their status as 10-point underdogs by taking the opening kickoff and skillfully driving 72 yards. A 14-yard pass to Joe Morrison and a 15-yard scramble by Fran Tarkenton set the stage for fullback Ernie Koy's 14-yard burst and, finally, his 22-yard touchdown run. The Giants offensive unit trotted off the field with a 7-0 lead. Then, after stopping the Redskins short of midfield, New York regained possession at its 20. Not known for his breakaway speed, Ernie Koy surprised even his own teammates by racing 61 yards to the Washington 19. The drive fizzled after a holding penalty, but placekicker Les Murdock boosted New York's lead to 10-0 with a 30-yard field goal.

Rickie Harris returned Murdock's kickoff 37 yards to midfield, but the Redskins offense could not get on track. Washington's ineptitude turned to its advantage, though, when the Giants' Spider Lockhart fumbled Pat Richter's punt and Dave Crossan recovered for the 'Skins at the New York 20. However, Washington still couldn't get into the end zone. The best they could do was have John Love, a rookie flanker filling in for injured placekicker Charlie Gogolak, kick a 27-yard field goal that shortened New York's lead to 10-3.

The Giants continued to falter as the second quarter got underway. First, they missed a 42-yard field goal, then they coughed up another fumble, which Washington safety Tom Walters returned 15 yards to New York's 43. Finally, the Redskins offense began hitting on more than one cylinder at a time. Halfback Bobby Mitchell dashed for 11 yards. A personal foul by the Giants added 15 yards, and a pass to tight end Jerry Smith was good for 7 more. Then, from the Giants 14, Jurgensen delivered a touchdown pass to John Love, and the game was even, 10-10.

The Redskins continued to roll. On their next possession, Sonny Jurgensen completed four straight passes, including a 43-yarder to Smith. After an interference penalty gave the 'Skins a first down at the 1, Sonny dove into the end zone on a quarterback sneak, and Washington went ahead for the first time, 17-10.

Fran Tarkenton struck back with a 57-yard bomb to Homer Jones. Several good defensive plays by the Redskins secondary defused the Giants threat, but Murdock salvaged 3 points with a 29-yard field goal, cutting Washington's lead to 17-13. Just 45 seconds remained in the first half, but Jurgensen wasn't satisfied. Two completions—a 37-yarder to Charley Taylor and a 12-yarder to Smith—gave Washington a last-second field goal opportunity at New York's 21. Love missed, though, and the first half ended with the score: Redskins 17, Giants 13.

Sonny Jurgensen   *Paul Fine Photo/Nate Fine Productions, Courtesy Washington Redskins*

Washington received the second-half kickoff and immediately got in gear. Jurgensen opened with a 10-yard pass to Charley Taylor; halfback Bobby Mitchell jitterbugged for 16 yards [Fig. 40]; and Sonny threw to Love for 35 more. On first and goal at the 6, Mitchell dashed into the end zone, and the Redskins were in command, leading 24-13. The Giants retaliated with a solid drive that was capped by a spectacular 35-yard touchdown pass from Tarkenton to Homer Jones. A few minutes later, John Love missed another short field goal attempt, and the third quarter ended with Washington ahead, 24-20.

Realizing he couldn't afford to sit on such a slender lead, Coach Graham told Jurgensen to keep passing. Happy to oblige, Sonny threw to Charley Taylor for gains of 21 and 23 yards, giving Washington a first down at the New York 11. One play later, Jurgensen whipped the ball to Jerry Smith in the end zone for another TD, and the Redskins, now leading 31-20, started to think they had the game in hand.

Fig. 40   *Paul Fine Photo/Nate Fine Productions, Courtesy Washington Redskins*

Fran Tarkenton making life miserable for Ron Snidow   *Paul Fine Photo/Nate Fine Productions, Courtesy Washington Redskins*

But the New Yorkers had a nasty surprise waiting for their Washington hosts. On the first play after the kickoff, Ernie Koy took a pitchout and headed for the sideline. Suddenly, he stopped and threw a pass to Homer Jones, who grabbed it at midfield, shook off a tackler, and raced into the end zone to complete a 68-yard scoring play. With almost 9 minutes left in the game, the Giants, trailing only 31-27, were once

again breathing down the Redskins' neck. And, as Washington fans knew only too well, that neck was liable to start choking at any moment.

Rickie Harris returned Murdock's kickoff 47 yards to midfield, but his fine effort was wasted when Spider Lockhart recovered a Bobby Mitchell fumble at the 50. Koy bulled for 9 yards, but the Giants failed to make a first down on their next two plays. Not surprisingly, Coach Allie Sherman decided to go for it on fourth and 1. With the crowd doing its noisy best to rattle him, Tarkenton faked a handoff and threw a soft pass to Homer Jones. Fortunately, the dangerous Giants receiver couldn't reach it, and Washington took over at its 41 with just under 7 minutes remaining in the game.

Even though the Giants knew the Redskins would keep the ball on the ground to use up time, running backs Ray McDonald and Bobby Mitchell managed to pound out a first down at the New York 45. Then, figuring he could surprise the Giants, Jurgensen threw deep to John Love. Not realizing the ball was already in the air, the rookie flanker broke his pattern to try a freelance move. New York safety Spider Lockhart taught Love a lesson by backpedaling to the goal line and easily intercepting Jurgensen's pass at the spot where Love should have been. But the play wasn't over. Lockhart's momentum caused him to fall awkwardly on his back. He hit the ground so hard that the ball popped loose and bounced into the end zone. Turning his bonehead play into a triumph, Love redeemed himself by falling on the ball, and the Redskins had their touchdown—the lucky way. After accepting a ribbing from his teammates, Love added the conversion, and the score changed to: Redskins 38, Giants 27.

5:08 remained in the game. Leading by 11 points, the 'Skins went into their "prevent" defense, an alignment of six defensive backs playing so deep that Tarkenton could complete any pass he wanted except the bomb. Taking full advantage of Washington's generosity, Tarkenton threw five straight completions, and New York drove 86 yards in 3 minutes. With just under 2 minutes remaining in the game, Aaron Thomas' 11-yard touchdown catch put the Giants back within reach of the Redskins, 38-34.

The 'Skins needed to make only one first down to ice the game, but, with New York calling a timeout after each play, they came up a yard short and had to punt. When the Giants took over at their 18 yard line, there were 47 seconds left in the game. 50,266 nervous Redskins fans held their breath as Tarkenton missed on his first pass, then hit fullback Tucker Frederickson for a 6-yard gain. On third down, Washington defensive linemen Bill Briggs and Joe Rutgens stormed past New York's blockers and dumped Tarkenton for a 7-yard loss. So with 15 seconds left in the game, the Giants were down to one last play. Tarkenton dropped back and threw as far as he could for the sprinting Aaron Thomas. As the long pass started to descend, haunting memories of games lost on similar last-second passes flooded to mind. This time, however, the ball sailed over Thomas' head, and the fans released their bated breath with shouts of joy. For once, the 'Skins had held on to win, 38-34.

True to their favorite method of winning, the Washington Redskins had simply scored more points than their defense frittered away. Bobby Mitchell's 110 yards rushing, Rickie Harris' 150 yards returning kicks, and Sonny Jurgensen's 285 yards passing had barely been enough to outlast the Giants. In fact, those feats wouldn't have been enough if it had not been for the luck-enhanced performance of John Love, whose 20 points (two touchdowns, five PAT's, and a field goal) was the second highest single-game total in Redskins history, behind Dick James' record of 24 points.

Admittedly, neither the Washington Redskins nor the New York Giants were outstanding teams in the mid-Sixties. But on the last day of the 1967 baseball season, on the same afternoon the Boston Red Sox won the tightest pennant race in American League history, the 'Skins and Giants put on the kind of crowd-pleasing show that had enabled professional football to surpass major league baseball as the most popular team sport in America.

IRRESISTIBLE FORCE

Washington Redskins vs. Los Angeles Rams

October 22, 1967

"To say that I'm disappointed is putting it mildly," snapped a furious Otto Graham moments after the lowly Atlanta Falcons had tied his Washington Redskins, 20-20, in the fifth week of the 1967 season. "We have the passer and the receivers to complete throws against anybody. We should have won." When asked if he had tried to change anything at halftime, Graham sarcastically replied, "Yes, their spirit." This, after all, was the year the Redskins were supposed to challenge for the Eastern Conference crown, but, due to wildly uneven performances, they had frittered away the opportunity to assert themselves, producing only a mediocre 2-2-1 record. Looking great one week and terrible the next, the inconsistent 'Skins could blame most of their problems on one chronic affliction: carelessness.

To be fair, part of the Redskins' problems stemmed from injuries. When injured placekicker Charlie Gogolak's replacement, John Love, also got hurt, Coach Graham was reduced to having Charley Taylor kick off and having safety Brig Owens kick field goals. (Not surprisingly, Owens had missed an extra point and two field goals in the Atlanta debacle.) The following week, after several days of hastily arranged tryouts, the Redskins signed former Maryland linebacker Dick Absher to take over the placekicking duties in time for the upcoming Rams game on Sunday.

Washington's running backs had also suffered a string of injuries, leaving 32-year-old Bobby Mitchell, A.D. Whitfield, and rookie Gerry Allen as the only healthy runners on the team. Although the Redskins were more dangerous with Mitchell at flanker, the former Cleveland halfback was needed in the backfield to prevent Washington's next opponent, the fierce Los Angeles Rams, from directing all their defensive energies toward quarterback Sonny Jurgensen.

"The number one objective of the defensive line is always to get to the passer," asserted Lamar Lundy, a member of the Rams' Fearsome Foursome defensive line. "If you flatten him often enough, he'll start throwing wildly and the interceptions will come. Not many quarterbacks can keep their poise under a heavy battering." The Fearsome Foursome—Roger Brown (6-foot-5, 300 pounds), Merlin Olsen (6-foot-5, 276), David "Deacon" Jones (6-foot-5, 260), and Lamar Lundy (6-foot-7, 260)—were not just bigger, stronger, faster, and meaner than any defensive line in the NFL, they also had the best nickname. And with all-pro linebackers Jack Pardee, Maxie Baughan, and Myron Pottios behind them guarding against the run, the Rams' front four were free to concentrate on making life miserable for enemy quarterbacks.

The creator of that defensive powerhouse, Coach George Allen, had taken over the Rams in 1966 following their seventh straight losing season. Saying, "I don't know what fuzzy-faced kids can do; I like bald-headed men," Allen immediately upgraded the team by trading future draft choices for proven veterans. Endlessly preaching the joys of mistake-free football, Allen installed a conservative, ball-control offense that featured the legs of running backs Les Josephson and Dick Bass far more often than the arm of quarterback Roman Gabriel. The overnight transformation proved successful as Los Angeles earned a respectable 8-6 record in Allen's first year as head coach.

By 1967, George Allen believed his 3-1-1 Rams were ready to make a run for the playoffs, a prognosis that was substantiated by their 24-24 tie with the undefeated Baltimore Colts in the fifth week of the season. Although both the 'Skins and the Rams had tied their opponents that week, the fact that the Falcons had been 0-4 while the Colts had been 4-0 pointed out the considerable difference in strength between the Washington and Los Angeles clubs. That difference was underlined when the odds-makers picked the Rams by 13½ points. Defiantly, Redskins Coach Otto Graham predicted, "It will be a tough ball game. It'll take a tremendous effort on our part, but if we play our best football it's possible to beat the Rams." Unfortunately, there was about as much chance of that happening as there was of George Allen becoming head coach of the Washington Redskins.

In 1965, while his team was staggering through its seventh consecutive losing season, Rams Owner Dan Reeves had installed 65,000 plush theater-style seats in the Los Angeles Coliseum to "be sure our fans suffer in comfort." Two years later, 55,381 fans filled most of those comfortable seats to watch their newfound heroes duel the Washington Redskins on another boringly perfect, 76-degree Southern California afternoon.

The game started slowly as neither team was able to get beyond midfield on its first two possessions. Then, with 4 minutes left in the opening period, Jurgensen sent split end Charley Taylor straight downfield from his 14 yard line. Taylor got exactly two steps on cornerback Clancy Williams but that was all he needed as Sonny laid the ball in his hands so perfectly that he was able to catch it at midfield without upsetting the flow of his stride. [Fig. 42] Williams continued the chase but never closed the gap, and Taylor ran into the end zone for an 86-yard touchdown! A moment later, in his first act as a Redskin, Dick Absher kicked the extra point, and Washington trotted off the field with a 7-0 lead.

Throughout the rest of the first quarter, the Redskins held the Rams at bay, but, early in the second period, Los Angeles' offense began to click. Roman Gabriel passed three times to wide receiver Bernie Casey for a total of 44 yards. Then a 12-yard gain by fullback Les Josephson on a shovel pass pushed the ball to the 2, and, from there, Dick Bass knifed into the end zone for the score. The game was tied, 7-7.

The Redskins offense continued to struggle. Los Angeles' aggressive defense was completely shutting down their running attack, and, whenever Jurgensen dropped back to pass, the Fearsome Foursome swarmed in and forced him to rush his delivery. On top of that, penalties were nullifying the Redskins' few instances of forward progress. Washington was getting into trouble defensively, too. After the Rams got the ball back at their 39, Roman Gabriel launched a deep pass to his favorite receiver, Jack Snow, who grabbed it at the 25 and ran into the end zone for a dazzling 61-yard touchdown. L.A. led, 14-7.

It looked as if the game was about to degenerate into a rout, but Jurgensen rejuvenated the faltering Redskins by firing a 55-yard bomb to Charley Taylor at the Rams 25. Three plays later, though, the Terrible Twosome of Deacon Jones and Roger Brown sacked Jurgy for an 11-yard loss, and Coach Graham was forced to call on his new placekicker to try a 44-yard field goal. The nervous Absher's kick was so short that it rolled dead at the Los Angeles 4.

The Rams continued to dominate as Les Josephson broke free on a 22-yard run. However, three plays later, middle linebacker Sam Huff gave the 'Skins a much-needed break when he intercepted a Gabriel pass and returned it 5 yards to the Rams 30. The Redskins scored in two plays: a 16-yard screen pass to A.D. Whitfield, and a lob to Jerry Smith at the very

Fig. 42   *Paul Fine Photo/Nate Fine Productions, Courtesy Washington Redskins*

back of the end zone that tied the game, 14-14. [Fig. 43] Three minutes later the first half ended, and the underdog Redskins went to their dressing room delighted with their performance. The Los Angeles Rams were somewhat less amused.

The fact that Sonny Jurgensen had been the Redskins' leading ground gainer in the first half (one carry for 6 yards) demonstrates how well Washington's front line was faring against the Fearsome Foursome. Realizing that Washington's only chance lay in going to the air, Coach Graham switched halfback Bobby Mitchell back to his old flanker position. On the 'Skins' first possession of the second half, the offensive line fended off L.A.'s pass rushers long enough for Jurgensen to complete four throws to four different receivers, which put the ball at the Los Angeles 21. One play later, Jurgy floated a feather-soft pass to Jerry Smith, who caught it all alone in the end zone, and Washington surged ahead, 21-14. As the points went up on the scoreboard, the Coliseum patrons began to twist nervously in their soft, upholstered seats.

Absher mistimed his kickoff and sent a spinner down to the Los Angeles 20. Thinking it would roll out of bounds, the Rams' return team stood by and

Fig. 43   *Paul Fine Photo/Nate Fine Productions, Courtesy Washington Redskins*

watched the ball teeter at the sideline. Alertly, Jerry Smith raced downfield and fell on the free ball at the 18 before it went out of bounds! Unfortunately, the Redskins couldn't capitalize on the Rams' blunder. After one sack and two incompletions, Coach Graham sent in John Love (in place of the unsteady Absher) to try a 32-yard field goal. Without a warm-up, the injured Love hooked his kick to the left, and Los Angeles remained just 7 points behind.

Freshly motivated by a few well-chosen words from Coach Allen, the Rams offense marched 80 yards in 13 plays. Les Josephson ran the final 4 yards into the end zone for a touchdown, and Bruce Gossett kicked the extra point, deadlocking the game, 21-21. Then, after stopping the Redskins, Los Angeles began another long drive as the fourth quarter got underway. In twelve careful plays, Gabriel led his teammates from their 15 to the Washington 29, where the 'Skins finally stood their ground. On fourth down, placekicker Bruce Gossett tried a 37-yard field goal, but, like his Redskins counterparts, missed.

Midway through the final period, Washington's Rickie Harris returned a punt 51 yards to the Rams 39. With the instincts of a leopard, Jurgensen pounced. Under a fierce rush, Sonny stepped up into the pocket and fired a long pass to Jerry Smith at the Rams 5. Defensive back Claude Crabb immediately slammed into him, but Smith held on and dragged Crabb into the end zone. Touchdown, Washington! It was Sonny's fourth touchdown pass, and, with it, the 'Skins reclaimed their 7-point lead, 28-21.

Just 3 minutes remained as the Rams offense

Roman Gabriel under attack   *Paul Fine Photo/Nate Fine Productions, Courtesy Washington Redskins*

came back on the field, bent on retaliation. Starting at his 25, Gabriel threw to Casey for 12 yards, then hit tight end Billy Truax with a quick toss in the flat. The play was designed for short yardage, but Truax brushed off Brig Owens' tackle, swerved past linebacker Jim Carroll, got a good block from Jack Snow, and ended up with a 41-yard gain before safety Paul Krause pulled him down at the Washington 22.

After the 2-minute warning, the Redskins flushed Gabriel from his pocket on successive plays, but both times the big quarterback escaped and gained 4 yards. Then, on a crucial third and 2, halfback Les Josephson sidestepped a tackler in his backfield and picked up 8 yards and a first down at the Washington 6. 1:10 was left in the game as Gabriel dropped back again. Wide receiver Bernie Casey ran into the end zone, and Gabriel threw—complete! Touchdown, Rams. The crowd roared, then fell silent as Gossett lined up his critical extra point, then cheered again when the ball sailed through the uprights to give the relieved Rams a 28-28 tie.

With a minute left in the game, the Redskins had one final chance to win. Halfback Joe Don Looney surprised the Rams with a 20-yard burst on a draw play, but Deacon Jones snuffed out Washington's last hope when he sacked Sonny Jurgensen at the Redskins 25. Final score: 28-28, in favor of the Washington Redskins.

Los Angeles Coach George Allen called Sonny Jurgensen's four-touchdown performance "the greatest exhibition of long passing I've ever seen." As luck would have it, three of his touchdown passes went to Jerry Smith, whose family was watching him in person for the first time in his professional career. "Smith is the most underrated tight end in football," said Allen. "We expected they would throw long to him, as well as to Taylor, because he's fast, has good moves and great hands. We didn't bother about their running [in preparing for the game]. But that passing—whew. They've got more speed than any team in the league, and if you dog Jurgensen he'll hurt you with the short one."

Because of the caliber of the opponent, Redskins Coach Otto Graham, in striking contrast to his feelings of the week before, was overjoyed to come away with a tie. George Allen was simply relieved. "We weren't playing for a tie," admitted the Rams coach. "We were playing to avoid a loss."

DEFLECTED GLORY

Washington Redskins vs. Cleveland Browns

November 26, 1967

"The Redskins' momentum is pretty good," admitted Dallas Cowboys Coach Tom Landry moments after his division-leading team had lost to the upstart Washington Redskins, 27-20. "But their big test is in Cleveland this week. After that they have a chance to win them all." Was this really the Redskins Landry was talking about? The same Redskins who had put together only two winning seasons in the last 20 years? The same Redskins whose idea of a good defensive effort was to prevent opponents from scoring touchdowns longer than 90 yards? The same Redskins who had lost 28 of 33 games to the Cleveland Browns, including the last 8 in a row?

Apparently so. By virtue of beating the Cowboys in the tenth week of the 1967 season, the 4-4-2 Washington Redskins had rekindled their flickering hopes for a spot in the playoffs. And at least one Washington player believed the 'Skins were close to being a major force in the NFL—if they could break out of their Catch-22-like dilemma. "All the Redskins need is to get in the habit of winning," said Washington middle linebacker Sam Huff, who had starred on the New York Giants' championship teams from 1956-63. "Like the Redskins, the Giants did not have a great team but we were a tight unit. Everybody was always convinced we would win because everybody was sure somebody would make the big play. The Packers have

the same confidence. That is why they keep playing their game, no matter what." In other words, in order to win consistently a club must have a winning attitude, but the only way to attain that attitude is by consistently winning.

Not known for their skills in manipulating abstract paradoxes, Washington's offensive and defensive lines decided it would be far easier to come up with some snazzy nicknames. The offensive line, justly proud of their ability to protect quarterback Sonny Jurgensen from incoming blitzers, tabbed themselves "The Guardian Angels." The defensive line—Joe Rutgens, Ron Snidow, Walter Barnes, and Carl Kammerer—wanted to draw attention to the fact that they were leading the league in sacks, but the best nickname they could come up with was "The Four Furies." How well those nicknames are remembered today proves how well they actually described the Redskins' play.

Despite its real or imaginary shortcomings, Washington had generated enough firepower with its passing game to win half its games. League-leading quarterback Sonny Jurgensen, named AP's Offensive Player of the Week for his four-touchdown performance against the Cowboys, and his three excellent receivers—Jerry Smith, Charley Taylor, and Bobby Mitchell—were the scourges of the NFL. "I haven't seen a passing game that good in years," marveled Landry. "Not since Norm Van Brocklin has anyone passed with that much accuracy." Jerry Smith, with seven touchdown catches in his last five games, was threatening to become the first tight end to lead the league in receiving. Bobby Mitchell, back at his flanker position after a brief stint at halfback, had just moved ahead of Don Hutson into third place on the all-time receiving list with his 490th catch. And Charley Taylor, the defending league-leader in receptions, was back in top form after sitting out a few games with a pulled hamstring.

Unfortunately, the rest of the team was in disarray. Injuries to fullbacks Steve Thurlow and Ray McDonald had reduced Washington's running game to a walk. Dick Absher, the surrogate placekicker who had relieved Brig Owens, who had supplanted Charley Taylor, who had filled in for John Love, who had pinch-hit for Charlie Gogolak, was himself replaced by Gene Mingo. The final bit of bad news was that, due to an ankle injury, middle linebacker Sam Huff was expected to see only limited action against his old rivals, the Cleveland Browns.

Coached by Blanton Collier (who had been Otto Graham's backfield coach when Graham played quarterback for Cleveland in the Fifties), the 6-4 Browns were a well-balanced team that liked to keep the ball on the ground. Jolted by the sudden retirement in 1966 of fullback Jim Brown, who had led the league in rushing eight of the nine years he played, the Browns had turned over most of their ball-carrying duties to a rookie halfback, Leroy Kelly, who had responded by racking up 1,141 yards and 15 touchdowns. Currently leading the NFL in rushing, Kelly was averaging 5.2 yards per carry, a figure matched, amazingly, by his blocking back, Ernie Green. Quarterback Frank Ryan, with his doctorate in mathematics, could win on brains as easily as with a touchdown pass to all-pro flanker Gary Collins. And when the Browns needed 3 points, 22-year veteran placekicker Lou "The Toe" Groza could still boot 'em through the uprights from anywhere inside the 50.

As usual, it all added up to a betting line favoring the Cleveland Browns, but this time by only 4 points.

The icy wind sweeping in from frozen Lake Erie was no colder than the reception the Browns gave the Washington Redskins in the first quarter of their game at Cleveland Municipal Stadium. The Browns did not have to rely on trickery or sleight-of-hand to accomplish their objectives; they simply ran the ball down the Redskins' throat. Leroy Kelly and Ernie Green took turns beating a path through the Washington front line as Cleveland marched from its 22 to the Redskins 42 in nine well-executed plays. On second and 10, Leroy Kelly took a lateral from Frank Ryan and headed to his right. Just past the line, Kelly cut inside a block by Green, shifted into high gear, and raced into the end zone without a hand being laid on him. Lou Groza kicked the extra point, and the Browns trotted off the field with a 7-0 lead.

The Washington Redskins responded by driving 59 yards in nine plays, mostly on the arm of Sonny Jurgensen. On third and 2 at the Cleveland 23, Jurgensen dropped back again. Browns defensive end Paul Wiggin charged in and leapt as Sonny released his pass. The ball smacked into Wiggin's outstretched hand and ricocheted into the arms of linebacker Johnny Brewer, who chugged 70 yards for a touchdown as 72,798 Cleveland fans hooted and cheered. 14-0, Cleveland.

When the chastened Redskins took over at their 20, Jurgensen surprised the Browns by handing off to halfback Gerry Allen, who shook free for 30 yards. Three more rushes and a screen pass to fullback A.D. Whitfield advanced the ball to the Cleveland 31, where, on fourth and 2, Coach Graham decided to go for the first down. But before Jurgensen could get his pass off, he was swamped by a group of blitzers.

The Browns took over at their 37 but were driven back. On the last play of the first quarter, Gary Collins shanked a punt, and the ball fluttered out of bounds only 11 yards downfield. Taking advantage of the excellent field position, Jurgensen fired to tight end Jerry Smith for a first down at the Browns 24, then, one play later, hit Charley Taylor for a touchdown. Mingo converted, and the 'Skins were on the board, trailing 14-7.

On the Browns' next possession, fullback Ernie Green gave the Redskins an opportunity to tie the game when he fumbled to cornerback Rickie Harris at the Washington 43. However, despite a 24-yard completion to Whitfield, the 'Skins could only harvest a 27-yard field goal that reduced the Browns' lead to 14-10. A moment later, Carl Ward fielded Mingo's kickoff 4 yards deep in his end zone and headed upfield. Cutting to his right, Ward burst past the first wave of Redskins tacklers, broke into the clear, and outran everyone to the end zone for a 104-yard touchdown! Cleveland was back in control, 21-10.

The Redskins regrouped, but a promising drive degenerated into a comedy of errors and Pat Richter finally had to punt on fourth and 27. Four plays later, the Browns scored again when Frank Ryan lofted a perfect pass to wide receiver Paul Warfield, who caught it on the sideline and sprinted into the end zone for a 48-yard touchdown. Cleveland 28, Washington 10.

With the first half drawing to a close, Jurgensen quickly drove the Redskins 80 yards by completing five of six passes—the last one a quick-out that Charley Taylor transformed into a 15-yard touchdown with some spectacular dodging. [Fig. 45] Trailing 28-17, Washington escaped to the locker room to await the second half.

Fig. 45   *Copyright Washington Post; Reprinted by permission of the D.C. Public Library*

Fig. 46   *Paul Fine Photo/Nate Fine Productions, Courtesy Washington Redskins*

In the first half, Sonny Jurgensen had compiled the kind of numbers (16-25 for 210 yards and two TD's) that most quarterbacks would be proud to have for an entire game. Unfortunately, Cleveland halfback Leroy Kelly (eight carries for 101 yards) was enjoying the same kind of lavish success. Both teams had scored on big plays, but the Browns, with their 104-yard kickoff return and 70-yard touchdown on an interception off a tipped pass, had simply gotten more of them.

On Cleveland's first possession of the second half, that pattern continued as Kelly gathered in a swing pass from Ryan, broke several tackles, and ended up with a 48-yard gain to the Washington 21. Then, two plays later, fullback Ernie Green sliced into the end zone from the 1, and the Browns were sitting on an 18-point cushion, 35-17.

Following the kickoff, Jurgensen dropped back to pass on third and 9 at his 26. Finding no one open, Jurgy escaped a horde of Cleveland rushers and ran up the middle for a 21-yard gain. Two plays later, Sonny hit A.D. Whitfield in the flat for another 21 yards at the Cleveland 31. An 11-yard bullet to Whitfield and an interference penalty gave the 'Skins a first down at the Browns 1. Halfback Gerry Allen dove over the goal line [Fig. 46], and the Redskins, though still trailing, 35-24, were once again within sight of the powerful Browns.

After an exchange of punts, Cleveland marched 65 yards into the Washington end zone, with Kelly extracting the last 21 yards on sheer extra effort. As the fourth quarter began, the Browns held a commanding 42-24 lead. But 2 minutes later, the scoreboard changed to 42-31 when Washington flanker Bobby Mitchell transfixed rookie cornerback Ben Davis with some sleight-of-foot and grabbed a Jurgensen pass for a 48-yard touchdown. Three punts and 6 minutes later, the Redskins embarked on another drive from their 26. Jurgensen couldn't miss; he completed five straight passes as the 'Skins rolled to the Cleveland 1. Gerry Allen vaulted over the goal line for his second touchdown, but Mingo's extra-point kick bounced off the crossbar and the score remained 42-37, in favor of Cleveland.

With 3 minutes left in the game, the Browns only needed to keep possession for a couple of first downs to sew up their victory. Kelly turned the corner for an 18-yard gain, but Cleveland's next three plays produced only 9 yards. Although tempted to go for it on fourth and 1 at his 47, Browns Coach Blanton Collier decided it was too risky and ordered Gary Collins to punt.

1:33 remained as Jurgensen brought the Redskins to the line at their 23. With 72,000 Cleveland fans shouting and cursing at him, Sonny whipped a 17-yard pass to Jerry Smith. After a sack by Paul Wiggin, Jurgensen found Smith open again for 21 yards and another first down. Then, with 58 seconds left on the clock, Jurgensen delivered a 19-yard strike to Charley Taylor, who was tackled at the Cleveland 25. (It was Taylor's eleventh catch and gave Sonny over 400 yards passing for the day.)

Coach Otto Graham sent in rookie flanker John Love in order to get some fresh, young legs into the lineup. Jurgensen sent Love into the end zone and fired. The pass was on target, but, as it was about to settle into Love's hands, cornerback Erich Barnes arrived on the scene and deflected it away. [Fig. 47] On second down, a bullet to Gerry Allen was broken up at the 6. On third down, Allen caught a screen but was forced out of bounds at the 26. Fourth down. Eleven yards to go. Twenty-eight seconds left in the game. Jurgensen took the snap and dropped back into the pocket one last time. The Browns swarmed in after him. Sonny looked for an open receiver, but, before he could get his pass away, defensive end Bill Glass tackled him and the Redskins' heroic quest was over.

The Browns had survived, 42-37.

After watching the game on television in Dallas, the wife of Cowboys quarterback Don Meredith sat down and wrote Sonny Jurgensen a letter. "You played such an outstanding game—always coming from behind and never losing your spirit—that by the end of the game we were jumping up and down, screaming and yelling, really pulling for you to make that last touchdown. When that last drive

Fig. 47   *Wally McNamee/Washington Post Photo*

died, Don turned to me and said, 'You don't know how he feels . . . it's something you'll never understand . . . I feel sick.'"

Sonny Jurgensen would finish the year as the #1 passer in the league, setting NFL records for attempts, completions, and yardage. And Charley Taylor, Jerry Smith, and Bobby Mitchell would become the first set of receivers from a single team to finish in the top five in the race for most receptions. But the Washington Redskins were never the same after the heartbreaking loss to the Browns. With a chance to earn a winning record for the first time in 12 years, the Redskins collapsed in the last game of the season, losing to the just-born New Orleans Saints, 30-14.

Old habits die hard.

LOMBARDI

Washington Redskins vs. New Orleans Saints

September 21, 1969

In the winter of 1969, three major events within a two-week period reshaped history in the Nation's Capital: Richard Nixon's first presidential inauguration, the purchase of the Washington Senators by Robert Short, and the hiring of Vince Lombardi as head coach and executive vice president of the Washington Redskins.

"Lombardi is to football what God is to religion," testified Red Mack, one of Lombardi's Green Bay Packers. Having coached the Packers to six Western Conference titles, five NFL Championships, and two Super Bowl victories in 9 seasons, Vince Lombardi was frequently linked to the Divinity, especially in Wisconsin. For instance, in the 1967 NFL Championship game that became famous as the Ice Bowl, Lombardi's Packers defeated the Dallas Cowboys, 21-17, in Green Bay's minus-13-degree weather, a climate that distinctly favored the winter-hardened Packers. "I figure Lombardi got on his knees to pray for cold weather," said Green Bay tackle Henry Jordan, "and stayed down too long."

The legend of Vince Lombardi grew out of his unmatched winning record and his reputation for toughness tempered by fairness. The volcanic coach was a man of emotional extremes, arousing both love and anger in his players but always winning their respect and unswerving loyalty. A strict disciplinarian, Lombardi ruled predominantly through fear.

In his book, *Instant Replay*, former Packers guard Jerry Kramer recalled the Lombardi Method of Motivation. "This is a game of abandon and you run with complete abandon," the uncompromising coach began. "When you get close to the goal line, your abandon is intensified . . . Nothing, not a tank, not a wall, not a dozen men can stop you from getting across that goal line. If I ever see one of my backs stopped a yard from the goal line, I'll come off that bench and kick him right in the can." Above all, Vince Lombardi's players learned to obey. "When Lombardi said 'Sit down,'" attested all-pro safety Willie Wood, "I didn't even look for a chair."

Lombardi's teams dominated the league simply because he demanded more from his players than any other coach would dare. "Lombardi treated us all alike—like dogs," said Henry Jordan. But the great coach also could be generous when his players pleased him. Twice, after NFL Championship victories, Lombardi gave each of the Packers' wives a mink coat or diamond ring.

Then, after Green Bay won Super Bowls I and II, the 54-year-old Lombardi shocked the football world by resigning as head coach to devote full time to his role as general manager. That was the moment the Packers Dynasty ended. One year later, though, a combination of desires led Lombardi to reconsider his choice. The fabled coach wanted to live on the

East Coast near his family; he wanted more action; he "missed the rapport with the players"; and he wanted to build a financial estate for his family. With that in mind, the Washington Redskins offered to make him their head coach at $110,000 per year, which would give him plenty of money and all the action and rapport he could stand. And as a 5% team owner, Lombardi could assure his family of a generous continuing income after his death.

After some understandable foot-dragging, the Packers grudgingly acceded to Lombardi's request to be excused from the remaining 5 years of his Green Bay contract, and, on February 7, 1969, Vince Lombardi became head coach of the Washington Redskins. To sweeten the deal, Redskins President Edward Bennett Williams even handed over his personal office to Lombardi, who, according to his former employees, would soon redecorate it in "Dictator Modern."

Why had Lombardi chosen Washington instead of the other NFL cities that were after him? "Because this is the capital of the world. And I have some plans to make it the football capital." Probably equally appealing was the challenge of transforming a chronic loser into an immediate winner, a task not unlike the one he had encountered in his first year at Green Bay. In order to accomplish this, Lombardi was given total authority. "I will have control of the club—everything," declared the grinning, snaggle-toothed coach at his first Washington press conference. Standing to the coach's side, Williams meekly stage-whispered, "I've just asked Vince if I could have my same season tickets." Lombardi laughed, but quickly became serious again, saying, "I will demand a commitment to excellence and to victory." Those unvarnished words held a long-overdue message for Redskins veterans: losing would no longer be tolerated. Period.

More than any football coach since Knute Rockne, Vince Lombardi understood the power of inspirational words, and he motivated his players with convictions as basic and effective as the Packers Sweep. "Winning isn't everything . . . It's the only thing." "Winning is not a sometime thing; it's an all the time thing." "Winning is a habit. Unfortunately, so is losing."

After 13 consecutive seasons without a winning record, the Washington Redskins were painfully familiar with the self-perpetuating nature of losing. Exasperated fans, who had watched the bedeviled Redskins lose by every agonizing method imaginable (and unimaginable), believed that Lombardi would need something stronger than adages to turn the team around, perhaps something more on the lines of a mass exorcism. To that end, Lombardi purged the Redskins of their bad habits and losing attitudes on the sun-baked training camp fields of Dickinson College in Carlisle, Pennsylvania. After six weeks in Vince Lombardi's version of Hell, the Washington Redskins couldn't wait to prove themselves against their first opponent, the New Orleans Saints.

In their first two years, while weeding out most of the hand-me-down players the other teams in the NFL had donated to help get them started, the Saints had upset seven opponents, including some of the top clubs in the league. With newcomers like tight end Dave Parks and fullback Andy Livingston teaming with original Saints like wide receiver Danny Abramowicz and quarterback Billy Kilmer, New Orleans had developed a respectable offense. But, like Washington teams of the past, the Saints repeatedly lost as a result of self-inflicted wounds: mental mistakes, turnovers, untimely penalties, and plain bad luck.

And what of Otto Graham? After 17 wins, 23 losses, and 3 ties in his three years as head coach, Graham went out the same way he had come in—on an extended golfing vacation in the California desert. "Everyone was so disappointed in Otto Graham," said middle linebacker Sam Huff. "I guess all of us felt that when he came here we were really going places. He had a great background and some great ideas. But we wasted too much time on things we never used, on incidentals that were not going to help us in a game. We never understood him, and I guess he never understood us. What it really took was someone who could come in and say, 'This is my way, and we do it that way. And we do it until it's right.'" In Vince Lombardi, the Washington Redskins finally had such a man.

Vince Lombardi   *AP/Wide World Photos*

Decked out in new uniforms that made them look like Burgundy and Gold cousins of the Green Bay Packers, the Washington Redskins faced off against the New Orleans Saints in the opening game of the 1969 season. Surrounding them were 73,147 rowdy fans at Tulane Stadium, which was known throughout the country as the Sugar Bowl. Both teams started cautiously, like boxers trying to protect their scar tissue. After 5 minutes of tentative runs and incomplete passes, New Orleans finally orchestrated a drive. Six handoffs to Andy Livingston and a 24-yard pass from Billy Kilmer to Ray Poage propelled the Saints from their 37 to the Washington 5. On the tenth play of the drive, Kilmer hit Poage with a pass in the end zone, and the Saints' drunken and disorderly rooters celebrated their team's 7-0 lead.

The Redskins continued to imitate their old blundering selves. First, they missed an opportunity to tie the game when Sonny Jurgensen overthrew a wide-open Charley Taylor, then, on their first possession of the second quarter, fullback Henry Dyer lost a fumble at his 12 yard line. Luckily, New Orleans was equally inept and had to settle for Tom Dempsey's 13-yard field goal and a 10-0 lead.

That was enough foolishness for Vince Lombardi. He replaced his starting backfield of Dyer and Gerry Allen with rookie halfback Larry Brown and newly-acquired fullback Charley Harraway. The switch ignited the Redskins offense. Starting at the 16, it was Harraway for 4 yards and Brown for 5. On third and 1, Jurgensen faked a handoff and threw deep to wide receiver Bob Long, who caught the long spiral at the Saints 43 and ran 20 more yards to the 23. After two Redskins Sweeps advanced the ball to the 10, Jurgensen fired into the corner of the end zone to Charley Taylor, who made a sensational leaping catch for a touchdown! [Fig. 49] On the conversion, place-kicker Curt Knight scored his very first NFL point, and Washington was back in the game, trailing 10-7.

Even though Knight boomed his kickoff 8 yards deep into the end zone, return specialist Carl Ward decided to run it out. At the 14, Ward realized his mistake when a vicious tackle dislodged the ball and Mike Bass recovered, giving the 'Skins a first down at the New Orleans 13. Taking immediate advantage of the turnover, Sonny Jurgensen passed to Jerry Smith for a touchdown, and, as Coach Lombardi congratulated his excited team, the scoreboard changed to: Washington 14, New Orleans 10.

Throughout the rest of the second quarter, the Redskins defense, led by player-coach Sam Huff, who had come out of retirement for the chance to play for Lombardi, dominated the Saints, and the first half came to an end with Washington in front, 14-10.

First-game jitters and the pressure of playing for Vince Lombardi had taken its toll on the Redskins in the beginning of the game. "We really were tight," said Jurgensen. "We tried to calm down in the huddle and ended up getting called for too much time in the first series." Neither Jurgensen nor the Saints' Kilmer had been on target in the first half. Sonny had hit on only five of fourteen passes, but two of them had worked for touchdowns. The Saints' dominating runners, 236-pound fullback Andy Livingston and halfback Tony Baker, were averaging over 5 yards per carry, but that was exactly what Washington's new tandem of Brown and Harraway were averaging. The only difference was that New Orleans' rushers had carried 19 times while the 'Skins' duo had run only seven times.

On their first possession of the third quarter, the Saints called on Livingston and Baker eight times in the first ten plays, and New Orleans rolled from its 20 to Washington's 35. But Sam Huff broke up a third-down pass to Danny Abramowicz, and New Orleans Coach Tom Fears sent in Tom Dempsey, a club-footed escapee from the semi-pro ranks, to try a 43-yard field goal. Dempsey's kick was good, and the Redskins' lead was whittled down to 1 point, 14-13.

Washington retaliated by marching from its 21 to midfield. On second and 8, Jurgensen launched a bomb to Charley Taylor, who caught the perfect pass at the 10 and dashed into the end zone for a 51-yard touchdown! When Knight made the extra point, the Redskins reclaimed their 8-point lead, 21-13, just as the third quarter came to an end.

Undiscouraged, the Saints kept coming. Livingston ripped for 15 yards on two carries, then Kilmer

Fig. 49   *Nate Fine/NFL Photos*

threw to wide receiver Al Dodd for a 30-yard pick-up. New Orleans even overcame its customary holding penalty with a 22-yard sweep by reserve halfback Don Shy. With a first down at the Washington 6, Livingston banged into the line three times, finally scoring from the 1, and the Saints were back within a point, 21-20.

The Redskins replied with a well-balanced drive of their own. Larry Brown's sweeps and Sonny Jurgensen's passes (notably a 31-yard completion to Brown and a 28-yarder to Smith) worked the ball to the New Orleans 10. On fourth and 3, Lombardi ordered Knight to kick an 18-yard field goal. Knight obeyed, and Washington took a 24-20 lead into the last 4 minutes of the game.

Instead of falling apart in the late going like so

many Redskins teams of the past, Lombardi's men kept their composure. And rather than install a leaky umbrella defense that conceded any pass short of a bomb, Lombardi ordered the 'Skins to increase their pressure on quarterback Billy Kilmer. It worked. On third and 14, defensive tackle Frank Bosch broke through and sacked Kilmer for a 10-yard loss at the 2. Coach Fears, formerly an assistant to Lombardi at Green Bay, made a smart move on fourth down by ordering his punter to take an intentional safety. (Trailing by 4 points, the loss of another 2 points was meaningless, but the Saints would have a chance to get decent field position if their defense could stop the Redskins.) The strategy paid off as Washington failed to make a first down, and New Orleans took over again at its 20. However, to win the game, the Saints would have to travel 80 yards in 1 minute and 22 seconds.

Instead of passing, Kilmer crossed up the 'Skins on first down by handing off to Livingston for an 11-yard gain (giving him 142 yards rushing on the day). Then Billy completed five short passes to advance the ball to midfield. But the Saints paid a high price for those small successes in the form of time. Only 2 seconds remained as Kilmer dropped back one last time and heaved the ball in the direction of his fastest receiver, Al Dodd. Matching Dodd step for step, Redskins cornerback Pat Fischer waited for the ball to come down, then knocked it away at the last moment to preserve Washington's 26-20 victory.

Appropriately, Vince Lombardi's first game as head coach of the Washington Redskins had ended in triumph, and, although it wasn't a thrilling upset nor an improbable comeback, it was counted as an important first step in the establishment of a winning habit. Under Lombardi's taut leadership, the 1969 Redskins went on to compile a 7-5-2 record, their first winning season since 1955.

Tragically, less than a year later, on September 3, 1970, Vince Lombardi died of cancer. Too soon, the great man was gone.

Arnie Sachs/Consolidated News Pictures

DELIVERANCE

Washington Redskins vs. Dallas Cowboys

October 3, 1971

"Dear God," began Reverend Thomas Kane, "in the last 30 years we fans have developed a great deal of patience in the discouragement of defeat. This year we fans would feel privileged if You would teach us to be more humble in the glory of victory." With those holy words, Rev. Kane consecrated the Redskins Alumni Association's annual Welcome Home luncheon at the beginning of the 1971 season. It may have been the only invocation ever given a standing ovation.

Sports fans in the Capital area were sick of rooting for athletic misfits dressed in Washington uniforms. The baseball Senators, for instance, had been the laughingstock of the American League for decades. Then, in 1960, just as they began showing some talent, the Nats had moved to Minnesota, replaced by a team of cast-offs and minor-leaguers renamed the Senators who continued their predecessors' losing ways. In the fall of 1971, the "new" Senators owner, Robert Short, short-changed Washington fans again by absconding to Arlington, Texas. Professional(?) basketball teams had come and gone in the Nation's Capital with the regularity of administrations. And the Redskins, playing at a .355 clip, had posted losing records in 14 of the last 15 years. The only man to have coaxed a winning season out of a Washington team since 1955 was Vince Lombardi —and he died.

To the rescue came George Allen. Allen began his professional coaching career with the Los Angeles Rams as an assistant to Sid Gillman, then joined the Chicago Bears as defensive coach under George Halas. In the 1963 NFL Championship game, Allen was given an unprecedented honor for an assistant coach when he was awarded the game ball in the Bears' 14-10 victory over the New York Giants. Los Angeles hired Allen as head coach the following season, and George quickly built the Rams into an NFL powerhouse spearheaded by the defensive line known as the "Fearsome Foursome." Then at the height of his success in L.A., Allen was fired by team owner Dan Reeves. However, when Rams players threatened a walkout, Reeves relented and reinstated Allen for one more year. But the shaky truce didn't last, and Allen became available in 1971.

Hired by Redskins President Edward Bennett Williams as both head coach and general manager, Allen immediately started transforming his new team into winners through professionalism, trades, and a shift in attitude. Part of the Redskins' problem was that they didn't have a permanent practice field. Allen cured that by obtaining land in an industrial area near Dulles Airport and building Redskin Park, a modern training facility with offices, two practice fields, and a state-of-the-art weight room. Williams' favorite line that year was, "I gave George Allen an unlimited budget—and in a week he had exceeded it." But on that expensive foundation in suburban Virginia, Allen started to build a winner.

General Manager Allen's next goal was to bolster the Redskins' soft-hearted defense. Declaring, "The future is now," he traded draft choices for proven veterans, including 10 of his former Rams players. Jokingly, people started calling his team the "Ramskins" and "The Over-the-Hill Gang," a reference to the advanced age of so many of Allen's new players. But there was no question that Allen, who acquired 7 new starters for his defense, had upgraded the Redskins in record time.

A great believer in positive thinking, Coach Allen infused his team with enthusiasm and confidence. He refused to equivocate. "Nothing will stop us—bad calls, bad breaks, injuries, nothing," preached Allen. "We will win!" Then, just as the Washington Redskins and their pessimistic fans were starting to believe, catastrophe struck. Two weeks before the season began, quarterback Sonny Jurgensen broke a bone in his left shoulder. The injury would sideline Jurgensen, who had led the league in passing five times, for 6 weeks. Suddenly, Billy Kilmer, a journeyman quarterback for whom Allen had traded in the offseason, was thrust into the starting position.

Hopes for a quick start in the tough Eastern Division faded, and even Allen became disconsolate. "If we win 6, 7, or 8 games," said Allen, "that would be something." The following day when he realized that he had impugned Kilmer's ability and undermined the Redskins' shaky new positive attitude, Allen denied giving the statement and, with the zeal of a new convert, became Kilmer's biggest booster.

Although Billy Kilmer may have lacked Jurgensen's artistry with the forward pass, he excelled in leadership, ball-handling, and tactics. Kilmer's ruddy complexion betrayed his emotions so much that his teammates tagged him "Furnace Face," but they responded to his gung-ho attitude and Washington opened the 1971 season with a 24-17 victory over the St. Louis Cardinals. The following week, Kilmer surprised his critics by throwing for over 300 yards as the 'Skins squashed the New York Giants, 30-3. But now the undefeated Redskins had to travel to

Dallas to play the NFC Champion Cowboys, a team that had whipped them six straight times, including a 34-0 trouncing the year before. The game would pit the NFC's leading offense (Dallas) against the NFC's leading defense (Washington), but bookies were giving 10 points on the assumption that the Cowboys would make it seven in a row over the Redskins.

61,554 confident fans watched Curt Knight kick off to the Cowboys on a warm and rainy October afternoon at the Cotton Bowl in Dallas. The Cowboys, who always tried to score immediately to demoralize their opponents, were stopped after three plays, and the Redskins got the ball at their 27. Larry Brown, the NFL's leading rusher the year before, skirted right end for 13 yards. Then fullback Charley Harraway took a handoff from Kilmer, burst through left tackle, slanted to the sideline, picked up blocks from Walter Rock and Roy Jefferson, and raced 57 yards for a touchdown! With Curt Knight's extra point, the 'Skins went up, 7-0. Surprise!

Dallas began at its 18 and used fifteen computer-driven plays to move to Washington's 41. On fourth down, placekicker Mike Clark tried a 48-yard field goal, but the ball was tipped by a Redskin and Washington kept its 7-point lead. Late in the first period the Cowboys got a break when they recovered a fumble by punt-returner Ted Vactor at the Redskins 21. Washington's defense rose to the occasion, though, and, three plays later, Clark was called on to salvage 3 points with a 22-yard field goal, which narrowed the score to Washington 7, Dallas 3.

The second quarter began with the Redskins and Cowboys trading punts, but Washington got the better of the exchange when Vactor returned Dallas' punt 30 yards to midfield. On first down, Billy Kilmer dropped back and threw to Roy Jefferson on a quick post pattern. Fifteen yards downfield, Jefferson caught Kilmer's strike at the seam in Dallas' zone defense, cut to the right to avoid Charlie Waters' desperate lunge [Fig. 51], and sprinted into the end zone for a 50-yard touchdown! Surprise, surprise. Knight hit the extra point, and the 'Skins were in control, 14-3.

Fig. 51   *Dick Darcey/Washington Post Photo*

Normally, it was the Cowboys who scored quick touchdowns while forcing opponents to salvage field goals at the end of long drives, but Allen's sky-high Redskins were turning the tables. Cowboys quarterback Craig Morton used short runs and even shorter passes to move his team from its 33 to the Redskins 2, but, when linebacker Chris Hanburger stopped Calvin Hill for no gain on third and goal, Dallas had to settle for Mike Clark's 9-yard field goal. With 5 minutes left in the half, Washington led, 14-6.

After the kickoff, Larry Brown picked up 21 yards on three carries. But he fumbled on the next play, and Jethro Pugh recovered for Dallas at its 46 with 1:45 remaining in the half. Working quickly, Morton

completed three straight passes—a 16-yarder to Gloster Richardson, a 6-yarder to Walt Garrison, and a 26-yarder to Bob Hayes—to advance the ball to the Washington 6. After a holding penalty moved the Cowboys back to the 21, Morton threw three times into the end zone. He missed all three, and Clark had to kick his third field goal. Seconds later, the first half ended with Washington still on top, 14-9.

Although Billy Kilmer completed only one pass in the first half, it had been good for a 50-yard touchdown. Craig Morton, on the other hand, had thrown 25 times, yet the Cowboys were unable to get into the end zone. And even though Dallas had recovered two Washington fumbles and run 30 more plays,

Verlon Biggs (82) and Richie Petitbon (16) force Calvin Hill out of bounds at the 4

Paul Fine Photo/Nate Fine Productions, Courtesy Washington Redskins

George Allen's pack of spry senior citizens were in the lead, and the crowd at the Cotton Bowl was silent.

After receiving the second-half kickoff, the Washington Redskins began to play with greater confidence. Larry Brown ran off left tackle for 11 yards, over right tackle for 12 yards, then back through the left side for 12 more. Billy Kilmer hit Jerry Smith with a 10-yard pass. Charley Harraway ran for 9. A 17-yard pass to Jefferson moved the ball to the Dallas 18, but it all went for naught when Billy threw an

interception to Cowboys linebacker Dave Edwards at the 5.

Sunken Washington hearts were quickly lifted, though, when Morton fumbled the next snap and Richie Petitbon recovered for the 'Skins at the Cowboys 5. Dallas' Doomsday Defense rose to the occasion, stopping Brown twice and sacking Kilmer for a loss, but Curt Knight increased Washington's lead to 17-9 with a 25-yard field goal. Again, the Cowboys offense couldn't budge (in the entire third quarter they kept the ball less than 2 minutes), and, as the fourth quarter began, the Redskins were marching into Dallas territory. When the drive stalled at the Cowboys 24, Knight collected his third field goal of the game to give the 'Skins an 11-point lead. The scoreboard seemed to blink in disbelief as the new numbers were posted: Redskins 20, Cowboys 9.

After watching Craig Morton contribute a total of one fumble and one incomplete pass in the third quarter, Coach Tom Landry replaced him with Roger Staubach. As usual, Staubach came in hot. He started with an 18-yard strike to the World's Fastest Human, Bob Hayes, and followed with a 25-yarder to Bullet Bob at the Washington 37. Alarmed that the momentum they had worked so hard to gather was slipping away, Washington's defense dug in and forced two incomplete passes. On third and 10, Coach Allen inserted pass-rushing specialist Bill Brundige. At the snap of the ball, both Brundige and fellow defensive tackle Diron Talbert broke through the Cowboys line, forcing Staubach to abandon his pocket. Famous for his devastating scrambles, Staubach ran backwards and to his left. When Talbert closed in, Staubach reversed his direction. Talbert doggedly pursued, and Staubach doubled back again—right into the arms of Brundige, who wrapped him up for a 29-yard loss. While the Redskins rejoiced, Dallas punted.

The 'Skins were unable to sustain a drive, and the Cowboys regained possession at their 31 with 7:44 remaining in the game. Needing two quick scores, Staubach, a Heisman Trophy-winner at Navy, rekindled Dallas' smoldering offense. Fullback Calvin Hill ran for 11 yards up the middle, then Staubach fired a pass to wide receiver Lance Alworth for 24 more. Three quick tosses to tight end Mike Ditka gained 12, 16, and 8 yards. Finally, Calvin Hill scored from the 1, and Dallas climbed to within 4 points of the tiring Redskins, 20-16.

Three minutes remained as Speedy Duncan returned Mike Clark's kickoff to the Redskins 26. Even though the Cowboys were prepared for a dose of time-consuming running plays, halfback Larry Brown dashed 14 yards up the middle. Unfortunately, Brown aggravated an old leg injury and had to be replaced by 11-year veteran Tommy Mason.

With 2 minutes to go, the Redskins needed one more first down to avoid having to face Staubach & Co. again. On second and 5, Mason met a wall of Cowboys at the line but refused to go down. He broke loose for a step, then was hit again. Somehow, Mason twisted free of that tackle also and made the first down that sealed the Cowboys' fate. With only one time-out remaining, Dallas could not prevent the clock from reaching zero, and, when it did, the exultant Redskins ran off the field with their 20-16 victory!

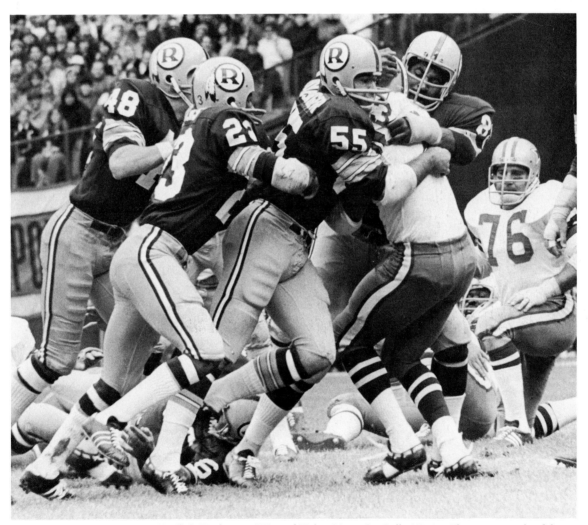

Jon Jaqua (48), Brig Owens (23), Chris Hanburger (55), and Verlon Biggs give Dallas' Duane Thomas a sample of the Redskins' new defensive strength   *Paul Fine Photo/Nate Fine Productions, Courtesy Washington Redskins*

For the first time in 28 years, the Washington Redskins had started a season with three victories. Their formula for success was simple—1 ball-control offense + 1 steadfast defense = sole possession of first place in the NFC East. Charley Harraway's 111 yards on 18 carries and Larry Brown's 81 yards on 21 rushes were made possible in large part by the outstanding efforts of the Redskins offensive linemen: Snowden, Schoenke, Hauss, Wilbur, and Rock. Washington's defensive secondary had excelled also, shutting down Dallas' long passing game and forcing the Cowboys to settle for three field goals instead of three touchdowns—a long-awaited turnaround for a Redskins team playing Dallas. Wearing a Texas-sized smile as he congratulated his players in the dressing room, George Allen called it "a great, great victory. A complete victory." And so it was.

At Dulles Airport that night, the airplane carrying the triumphant Redskins was met by 5,000 delirious supporters shouting, "DEFENSE! DEFENSE! DEFENSE!" and "WE'RE NUMBER ONE!" After 30 years of patience in the discouragement of defeat, Washington fans could be forgiven for not being humble in the glory of victory.

RECEPTION

Washington Redskins vs. Kansas City Chiefs

October 24, 1971

"*Good afternoon, ladies and gentlemen, and welcome to Municipal Stadium in Kansas City, Missouri, where 51,989 spectators, a record attendance for any sports event here, have gathered to witness the clash between the undefeated Washington Redskins and the powerful Kansas City Chiefs. It's a warm and overcast afternoon here in Kansas City as we await the kickoff. I'm Biff Poplin, and I'll be your host today for a game that pits the Redskins, who are 5 and 0 under new Head Coach George Allen, against Hank Stram's Chiefs, who are 4 and 1.*

"As I'm sure you'll remember, it's been just two years since the Chiefs' surprising 23-7 victory over the Minnesota Vikings in Super Bowl IV, and this year's team looks like they have a good chance of returning to New Orleans for Super Bowl VI. Right now, let's go down to the field to hear more about the Kansas City Chiefs from my colleague, Goose Johnson."

"Thanks, Biff. The Chiefs are big. How big? Well, just take a look at their defensive line: Buck Buchanan at 6-foot-7, 275 pounds; Aaron Brown, 6-6 and 255; Curley Culp at 6-1, 265 pounds; and Marvin Upshaw at 6-4, 265. The Chiefs are also talented. How talented? Well, on defense they lead the AFC in stopping the rush, and have the best set of linebackers in the NFL. On offense, they are led by quarterback Len Dawson, a man with over 200 touchdown passes in his career; wide receivers Otis Taylor and Elmo Wright; and running backs Ed Podolak and Wendell Hayes. And when the Chiefs need 3 points, they

can count on Jan Stenerud, probably the best placekicker in the game today. The Chiefs are strong, aggressive, balanced, and well-coached. But so are the Washington Redskins. How strong, aggressive, balanced, and well-coached? Well, to find out let's go to my colleague, Blimp Peterson."

"Thanks, Goose. The Washington Redskins are the surprise team of the NFL this year. George Allen has assembled a group of aging veterans, free agents, and so-called problem players from around the league and forged them into an enthusiastic, cohesive unit that is threatening to make a runaway of the Eastern Division race. Billy Kilmer, who replaced the injured Sonny Jurgensen at quarterback, is in charge of a new ball-control offense that is equally efficient whether he is handing off to NFL rushing champ Larry Brown or throwing to all-pro wide receiver Charley Taylor. But the big news in the Nation's Capital is about the six new players who have rejuvenated Washington's once-porous defense: Verlon Biggs, Diron Talbert, Ron McDole, Jack Pardee, Myron Pottios, and Richie Petitbon. The Redskins defense is now ranked first in the NFC and should cause plenty of problems for the Chiefs today. Coach Allen's boys are pretty excited about being undefeated, and you can bet they'll give it all they have as they try to win their sixth game in a row. Right, Biff?"

"Right, Blimp. Well, it looks like we're ready to go. Jan Stenerud has teed up the ball. There's the referee's whistle. Stenerud kicks, and we're under way!"

Larry Brown   *Paul Fine Photo/Nate Fine Productions, Courtesy Washington Redskins*

Both the Redskins and the Chiefs stumbled coming out of the chute. On the first play of the game, Larry Brown fumbled, and Kansas City linebacker Willie Lanier recovered at the Washington 28. However, the Redskins escaped an early grave when cornerback Mike Bass intercepted a Len Dawson pass at the Washington 4 yard line. A few minutes later, on the Chiefs' second possession, Dawson gave up another interception to Washington cornerback Pat Fischer, who returned it all the way to the Kansas City 4. On first down, Billy Kilmer hit Charley Taylor with a quick pass in the end zone, and the Redskins broke on top, 7-0.

Len Dawson was obviously having problems. The 'Skins front four was putting so much pressure on him that his first five attempts had produced two interceptions, two tipped passes, and a scrambling escape. So, after Robert Holmes' 41-yard return of Knight's kickoff, it was not surprising that Dawson decided to rely exclusively on his running backs to advance the ball to the Washington 30. On third and 7, though, Ron McDole and Myron Pottios trapped Kansas City halfback Ed Podolak for a 2-yard loss, and Hank Stram called on Jan Stenerud to kick a 39-yard field goal. The kick was good, and the Chiefs were on the board, 7-3.

Kansas City got a break when linebacker Willie Lanier intercepted a Kilmer pass and returned it to the Washington 17. (In all, the wild first period produced four turnovers, which was either a testimonial to both defenses or an indictment of both offenses.) With Ed Podolak and Wendell Hayes continuing to take turns running with the ball, the Chiefs surged to the Redskins 9. On third and 2, Podolak tried to squeeze through a small hole over right guard, but Ron McDole and Jack Pardee clobbered him a yard short of the first down. Ignoring the pleas of the home crowd, Coach Stram ordered Stenerud to salvage 3 points with a 15-yard field goal. When the ball sailed between the uprights, Washington's lead was cut to 1 point, 7-6.

Both teams missed field goal attempts on their next possessions—Knight from the 46 and Stenerud from the 47. Washington took over at its 20, and, on

third and 12, Billy Kilmer belied his conservative image by throwing long to Charley Taylor. The high, arcing pass soared down the field and settled into Taylor's hands at the Chiefs 33 for a 49-yard gain! But the promising drive bogged down at the 26, and the field goal unit was called into action again. This time, Knight succeeded on his 33-yard kick, and, with 3 minutes left in the half, the scoreboard changed to: Washington 10, Kansas City 6.

The 'Skins' defense survived a scare when Dawson overthrew Elmo Wright, who had gotten wide open in the Washington secondary. So with just over a minute to go in the half, the Chiefs punted to the Washington 29, and the Redskins went to their hurry-up offense. Three short passes by Kilmer and a run by Harraway worked the ball into Kansas City territory. On third and 6 at the 36, Kilmer threw a short pass to Charley Taylor, who bobbled the ball momentarily, then latched onto it and headed toward the end zone with a one-step lead on cornerback Emmitt Thomas. Just before Charley reached the goal line, Thomas dove and snared Taylor's left foot. Determined to get a touchdown, Taylor lunged for the end zone, stretched over the line—and scored!

SNAP! Charley's left ankle, trapped in Thomas' tight grasp, cracked apart. [Fig. 55] Taylor's happy teammates rushed to his side to congratulate him, but their smiles quickly turned into tight grimaces when they saw the exorbitant price he had paid for the touchdown. As Charley was carried to the dressing room, Curt Knight kicked the extra point, and, a few seconds later, the first half ended with Washington on top, 17-6.

Besides Taylor's two spectacular touchdowns, the key to the Redskins' success so far had been their ability to shut down the Chiefs' high-octane passing attack. Amazingly, Len Dawson had completed only 1 of his 10 passes in the first half. In contrast, Kilmer had hit on 10 of 17 throws for 165 yards and two touchdowns. But the satisfaction that the Redskins would normally have felt was muted by the knowledge that their co-captain, Charley Taylor, would be on crutches for the rest of the season.

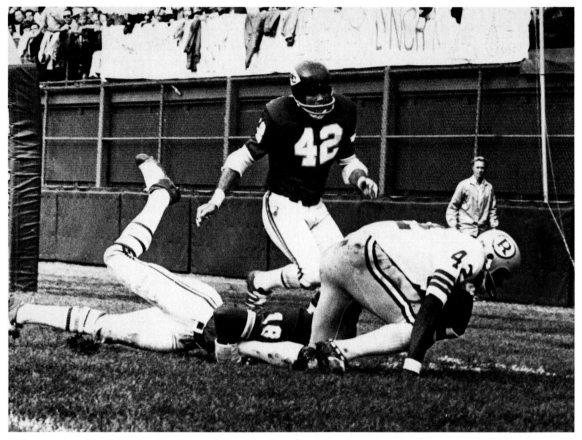

Fig. 55   *Paul Fine/NFL Photos*

On their first possession of the second half, the Kansas City Chiefs looked as if they had installed a supercharger as they zoomed down the field. Dawson opened with a pass to Otis Taylor for 22 yards and followed with a 26-yard completion to Elmo Wright. Ed Podolak swept right end for 21 more. Then Dawson spotted Taylor getting open on a post pattern and nailed his big receiver with an unstoppable 25-yard touchdown pass, and the Chiefs climbed within 4 points, 17-13.

After an exchange of punts, the Redskins began to overcome the gloomy inertia that Charley Taylor's injury had produced. From his 47, Kilmer threw to tight end Mack Alston for 12 yards, then completed a 10-yarder to Taylor's replacement, Boyd Dowler, for a first down at the Kansas City 30. One play later, Billy threw long to Alston, who had gotten open near the goal line. Kilmer's pass was a little behind the big tight end, but Alston managed to get both hands on it—and dropped it! Curt Knight tried a 33-yard field goal but missed, and the score remained 17-13, in favor of the increasingly frustrated Washington Redskins.

On the Chiefs' next series, defensive tackle Bill Brundige sacked Lenny Dawson twice, and Jerrel Wilson punted to Washington at midfield. Fullback Charley Harraway, best known for his devastating blocks, now displayed his versatility by catching a pass for 10 yards, running 19 yards on a draw play, and sweeping left end for 7 more. However, on third and 3 at the Chiefs 14, Kilmer fumbled the snap and, although he fell on it, Washington's chance for a comfortable lead was ruined. Knight's 23-yard field goal raised the score to 20-13, but the Redskins were disappointed to be sitting on only a one-touchdown cushion as the fourth quarter got underway.

Kansas City put the ball in play at its 18. After an incompletion, defensive end Ron McDole caught Dawson in his backfield for an 8-yard loss. Needing to reach the 28 on third and long, Dawson threw a flare to Otis Taylor, who caught it at the 15 and ran to the 25 before three Redskins hit him. Refusing to go down, Taylor dragged all three defenders to the 29 and made the first down! Taylor's second effort took on added significance a moment later when the Chiefs' other wide receiver, Elmo Wright, got loose over the middle and caught a 51-yard bomb at the Redskins 20. Then, before the stunned Washington secondary could regroup, Dawson whipped a touch-

down pass to Wright in the end zone, and the game was deadlocked, 20-20.

With the excited crowd at Municipal Stadium roaring on every play, the Chiefs defense paralyzed the 'Skins on their next series, and Mike Bragg punted to Ed Podolak at the K.C. 36. Seven minutes remained in the game as Kansas City began a steady drive to the Washington 28. On second and 9, Dawson launched what appeared to be an overthrown pass to Otis Taylor at the goal line. The Redskins' 5-foot 9-inch cornerback, Pat Fischer, draped himself on Taylor's back like an extra jersey, but the 6-foot 2-inch Taylor stabbed his right arm into the air—and caught the ball one-handed! [Fig. 56] Touchdown! After trailing the 'Skins for 56 minutes, the Chiefs vaulted into the lead for the first time, 27-20.

Billy Kilmer tried to rally the 'Skins in the re-

Fig. 56   *AP/Wide World Photos*

maining 1:34, but Washington couldn't get past its own 30, and, when the gun sounded, the Redskins' 5-game winning streak was over. Final score: Kansas City Chiefs 27, Washington Redskins 20.

On Saturday, just before the Redskins had flown to Kansas City, 3,000 enthusiastic well-wishers gathered at Dulles Airport to give the team a noisy send-off. Co-captain Charley Taylor had thanked the crowd for their support, then ended his short speech by proclaiming, "With fans like you, we can't do anything but come back as winners from Kansas City!" At midnight on Sunday, when the injured Taylor and the rest of the bitterly disappointed Redskins arrived back at Dulles, they were amazed to find over 8,000 cheering fans waiting for them at the gate with hastily-drawn signs reading, "YOU'RE STILL # 1" and "WE STILL LOVE YOU." The Washington Redskins had come home as winners after all.

Harry Naltchayan/Washington Post Photo

THE FUTURE IS NOW

Washington Redskins vs. Los Angeles Rams

December 13, 1971

Roman Gabriel could barely contain his fury. After repeatedly being asked what he planned to do when he crossed paths with George Allen for the first time since his former coach had left Los Angeles, the Rams quarterback snapped, "George Allen might walk off the field with a football in his mouth." Ironically, only three years earlier when Los Angeles Owner Dan Reeves had fired Allen following the 1968 season, Gabriel was among a group of Rams players so enamored of their coach that they threatened a walkout if Allen was not reinstated. When Reeves realized the players were serious, Allen was quickly rehired, and Los Angeles went on to win the 1969 Coastal Division championship with an 11-3 record. Gabriel was named the league's Most Valuable Player.

One year later, Allen, despite having coached the Rams to two division titles and compiling winning records in each of his five seasons, was fired again. But this time there were no protests from his players. What had changed during those two years? In a word, trust. "I have a lot of respect for Allen as a coach," explained Gabriel. "I used to as a man, but I felt he was insincere as a person."

Given a fresh start in Washington, George Allen quickly became the toast of the town. Allen's quick-fix trades (including deals for 10 former Rams), his ge-

nius for defense, and his infectious enthusiasm transformed the "Deadskins" into instant winners. The turnaround earned the team visits to the White House, overpowering ovations at RFK Stadium, and several emotional greetings at Dulles Airport by thousands of devoted fans.

With two games left in the season, the 8-3-1 Washington Redskins, after 26 years of non-participation, were only one victory away from making the playoffs. So whom did the football gods conjure up as the watchguard the Redskins would have to vanquish in order to gain entrance to the NFL's sanctum sanctorum? Why, none other than Coach Allen's former confederates, the Los Angeles Rams. Since both teams were in direct competition for the single wild-card spot, the nationally televised Monday night game would be both a reckoning of different philosophies and a chance for one side to destroy the other's season. It was the kind of game George Allen lived for.

Statistically, the two teams were evenly matched, but, due to their superior passing game, the 7-4-1 Rams were declared 6-point favorites. Although Billy Kilmer sometimes answered his critics with a topnotch performance, the Redskins relied almost exclusively on all-pro halfback Larry Brown to move the football. For example, in a game against the New York Giants the week before, Brown had rushed for

129 yards while Kilmer struggled to accumulate just 54 yards with his 4-for-14 passing. Luckily, Washington's ball-hawking defense had rescued the 'Skins' "Sputtering T-Formation" by intercepting four Tarkenton passes, and the Redskins waltzed to a 23-7 triumph.

But Kilmer knew he would have to perform much better if he were going to lead the Redskins to victory against Los Angeles. Coach Allen agreed, saying, "The Rams are an explosive team. We've got to move the ball and get points on the board—lots of points. The offense knows this." Ex-Rams defensive tackle Diron Talbert, now a Redskin, added, "We've got our hands full. They've got a shot at the championship, too. We've got to play a hell of a game."

In his incessant quest for victory, George Allen always was on the lookout for fresh ways to motivate his men. One of his favorite methods was to find insulting remarks about his team printed in the newspaper and post them on a bulletin board in the locker room. "George tries to find as much information as he can for his bulletin board," said Gabriel. "He's probably got all kinds of things on the Rams. He didn't get along very well with the organization. He's probably got a whole bedroom full of stuff."

Sure enough, George Allen had accumulated plenty of interesting reading material for his beloved bulletin board that week. A quote by Rams linebacker Isiah Robertson—"I play football in cold blood. I like to hurt people"—was read so often that it became engraved on the mind of every Redskin. And Deacon Jones, the Rams' perennial all-pro defensive end, couldn't resist throwing a verbal jab even though he knew his words would land on Allen's bulletin board. "The Rams," preached the Deacon, "will blow the Redskins out of the Coliseum on Monday night!"

Conversely, as the league-leader in disinformation, George Allen was being especially careful not to add fuel to the Rams' emotional fires. When asked about Roman Gabriel's derogatory statements, the wary coach replied, "Gabe's always ready for the big games." Concerning the Rams, Allen merely said, "They'll have the advantage playing at home." By being dull, Allen was being bright.

Captain Crunch, linebacker Jack Pardee
Copyright Washington Post; Reprinted by permission of the D.C. Public Library

The sky-high Washington Redskins won the coin-toss and elected to receive the opening kickoff. With 80,402 Southern Californians providing background vocals, Los Angeles' David Ray kicked off, and his teammates tore down the field, each man eager to strike a blow against George Allen's new team. A member of the Redskins blocking wedge, Harold McClinton, fielded the short kick and held on for dear life as he lumbered to the Washington 23.

Halfback Larry Brown quickly established the Redskins running game with three carries for a total of 20 yards. On second and 1, Kilmer faked a handoff to Brown and zipped a 27-yard pass to tight end Jerry Smith at the Rams 30. Three plays later, Kilmer dropped back again and threw to wide receiver Roy

Jefferson, but Rams safety Kermit Alexander intercepted and dashed 82 yards for a Los Angeles touchdown! As the fans in the Coliseum celebrated, Ray converted, and the Rams led, 7-0.

The dazed Redskins regrouped at their 20. After Brown and Harraway rushed for a first down, Kilmer called for the bomb. Running a straight fly pattern, Roy Jefferson broke into the clear as Kilmer reared back and threw as far as he could. Never breaking stride, Jefferson caught the perfectly thrown pass at the Rams 27 and ran triumphantly into the end zone. Touchdown, Redskins! The 70-yard play was the perfect antidote to L.A.'s shocking score, and, after Curt Knight booted the extra point, the game was deadlocked, 7-7.

Now the Rams offense had a turn with the ball. Running backs Larry Smith and Willie Ellison ripped through the line for 47 yards in six carries. But Gabriel missed his first five passes, and the Rams eventually had to settle for David Ray's 32-yard field goal and a 10-7 lead. After an exchange of punts, Washington moved the ball to the Los Angeles 45. On fourth down, Curt Knight tried a 52-yard field goal —and made it, tying John Aveni's club record and knotting the score at 10 apiece.

As the second quarter got underway, Roman Gabriel missed two more passes (making him 0-7) but finally connected with wide receiver Jack Snow on a 44-yard bomb at the Washington 27. Three more plays left Los Angeles a yard shy of a first down at the 18. Disdaining the field goal on fourth down, Gabriel, as big and strong as any running back, rolled to his right with the option of running or passing. He decided to run, but Redskins Ron McDole and Jack Pardee gang-tackled him at the line of scrimmage just short of the first down marker. The 'Skins took over, but the Rams got the ball again at the Washington 45 when Charley Harraway fumbled. Los Angeles moved to the Redskins 22, yet failed to score when Ted Vactor blocked Ray's 29-yard field goal attempt.

From his 38, Billy Kilmer threw a 27-yard pass to Jefferson, then followed with a 32-yard touchdown strike to Clifton McNeil, who made a diving catch in the end zone! As the Coliseum scoreboard registered

Paul Fine Photo/Nate Fine Productions, Courtesy Washington Redskins

Washington's 17-10 lead, 80,000 witnesses sat in stunned silence. With 2½ minutes remaining in the first half, Knight kicked off to deep man Roger Williams, who muffed the catch, and Ted Vactor dove on the free ball at the Rams 4 yard line! It took the Redskins seven plays (and a defensive holding penalty), but Larry Brown finally scored from the 1 on a fourth-down sweep. A few seconds later, the curtain fell on the first half, and the Washington Redskins marched off the field with a solid 24-10 lead.

Just as the bookies had predicted, the score was reflecting the comparative skills of the two quarterbacks. But, so far, it was Gabriel who had struggled (5-15 for 76 yards) while Kilmer soared, hitting on 8 of 11 for 191 yards and two touchdowns. Billy's only interception was long forgotten in the noisy Redskins locker room. The game, however, was far from over.

After enduring a few sarcastic remarks by their acerbic coach, Tommy Prothro, the Los Angeles Rams returned to the field intent on redeeming themselves. Washington kept the upper hand, though, when cornerback Mike Bass picked off a Roman Gabriel pass and returned it to the Los Angeles 45. Kilmer went right for the Rams' jugular with a 36-yard completion to Clifton McNeil. Then Roy Jefferson grabbed a 5-yard touchdown pass, and the Redskins took a seemingly insurmountable 31-10 lead over the flustered Rams.

A few minutes later, Los Angeles finally got a break when Bob Klein recovered a fumbled punt near midfield. Completions to Matt Maslowski and Lance Rentzel advanced the ball to the 3, and Gabriel hit Klein, who was lying flat on his back in the end zone, for a touchdown. Although trailing, 31-17, the Rams finally appeared to have found the throttle.

L.A. maintained its pressure and began another drive at the beginning of the fourth quarter. Gabriel connected with Jack Snow on passes for 12 and 19 yards. Then, after Rentzel caught a 9-yard bullet at the Washington 16, halfback Willie Ellison took over. The NFL's newly crowned single-game rushing champ (247 yards on 26 carries the week before against New Orleans) sliced through the Washington defense four times and scored. Now the Rams were in striking distance, 31-24.

Several minutes later, the Redskins, thanks to some defensive heroics by linebacker Chris Hanburger, inherited terrific field position at the Los Angeles 38. After three safe running plays failed to earn a first down, Curt Knight tried to ice the game with a 43-yard field goal. But he missed, and the Rams took over with 4 minutes left in regulation. Led by cornerback Pat Fischer and defensive end Ron McDole, Washington's defense forced the Rams into a fourth-and-12 at their 34. Trailing by a touchdown so late in the game, Los Angeles had to go for it. Gabriel dropped back and threw to Rentzel, who was covered tightly by safety Richie Petitbon. When the pass arrived, both men bumped into each other as they grappled for the ball. The ball fell to the ground; a moment later, a yellow flag joined it. Pass interference. On the sideline, angry Redskins started to complain—until they heard the rest of the call. "Pass interference—against the Rams!"

Washington took over at the Los Angeles 34 with 1:52 remaining. Three running plays consumed a minute. On fourth down, Knight came in for the coup de grace from 39 yards away. But he missed again! Roman Gabriel celebrated the Rams' stay of execution with a 10-yard flare to Les Josephson. Then, with the Redskins covering deep, Gabe flipped another short pass to Josephson, who carried it to his 39. With 35 seconds remaining, Gabriel dropped back and threw to fullback Larry Smith. The ball never reached him. Washington nickel back Speedy Duncan cut in front of Smith, picked off the pass, and raced 46 yards into the end zone! That was it! By the final score of 38-24, the Washington Redskins had earned a spot in the playoffs for the first time in over a quarter century.

"It was a complete team victory," proclaimed Coach George Allen in the delirious Washington locker room. "This Redskins team has tremendous character. We've overcome adversity all year. When it looked like we might fold, we pulled together and won." Amid cheers and laughter, game balls were awarded to Billy Kilmer (14-19, 246 yards, and three touchdowns), Roy Jefferson (eight receptions, 137 yards, and two TD's), Speedy Duncan (game-clinching touchdown), Chaplain Tom Skinner (for his inspirational help), and George Allen (in the name of justice).

After the game, Roman Gabriel's wish nearly came true. However, instead of walking off the field with a football in his mouth, Coach George Allen walked out of the Los Angeles Coliseum with a game ball under his arm. And a playoff berth in his pocket.

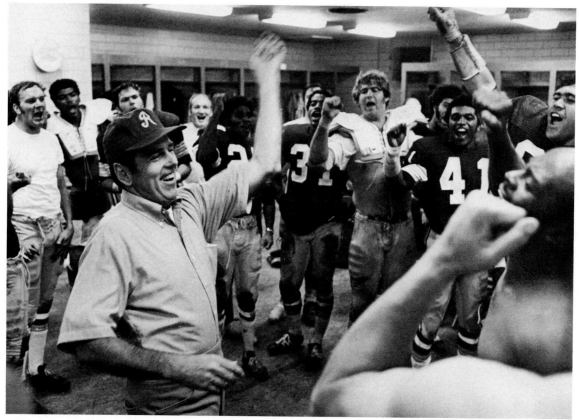

Coach George Allen leads the cheers for his playoff-bound Washington Redskins
Paul Fine Photo/Nate Fine Productions, Courtesy Washington Redskins

MONDAY NIGHT SPECIAL

Washington Redskins vs. Minnesota Vikings

September 18, 1972

Howard Cosell spotted Billy Kilmer eating breakfast in a Minneapolis hotel coffee shop and decided to have a little fun. Thrusting an imaginary microphone at his table companion, Redskins tight end Jerry Smith, Cosell mimicked himself perfectly. "Is it true, Jerry Smith," inquired Cosell in a staccato voice loud enough to pierce armor, "that you said without Sonny Jurgensen at quarterback the Redskins offense is woefully inept?" Smith, of course, had never said any such thing, and Billy laughed at Howard's little joke, but the gibe held a kernel of truth. With Kilmer at quarterback, the Washington Redskins offense seemed unable to get out of low gear.

Many Washington fans were upset that, with Sonny Jurgensen healthy and available, Kilmer had been named to start the first game of the 1972 season. After all, wasn't Jurgensen the NFL's #1 passer of all time? And wouldn't the threat of a Jurgensen aerial bombardment spread out opposing defenses that had learned to congregate around all-pro halfback Larry Brown? In other words, why drive a Chevy, functional as it may be, when you could burn up the streets with a Ferrari?

Responding to the barrage of criticism, George Allen claimed, "It doesn't make any difference who's quarterback as long as we play together and work as a team." Seemingly unconcerned with scoring a lot of points as long as he could field a first-rate defense,

Allen's idea of a perfect game was a 2-0 victory. Most fans realized that by starting Kilmer, Allen was rewarding Billy for his fine work in '71, when he had replaced the injured Jurgensen and led the 'Skins to the playoffs for the first time since 1945. It was also suggested that the Redskins seemed to play harder for Kilmer to compensate for his more modest talents.

But those who noted the relish with which George Allen drank from the trough of celebrity speculated that he preferred to keep Jurgensen in a low-visibility role to prevent Sonny's star from outshining his own. Then again, perhaps Allen was simply afraid that Jurgensen would trust his arm too often for the good of the coach's ulcerous stomach. George certainly made it plain that he preferred lackluster conservatism, believing that "when you pass, three things can happen—and two of them are bad." He neglected to mention that the same could be said of a running play.

Jack Pardee, the Redskins' all-pro linebacker who had played for Allen at Los Angeles, took the diplomatic high ground by saying, "The key to George Allen's success is getting 40 men to play as one. There are no superstars." That certainly had been the case in 1971 when a host of crusty old vets known as "The Over-the-Hill Gang" produced the Redskins' most successful season in 25 years. Even though they lost to the San Francisco 49ers, 24-20, in the first round of the playoffs, the 'Skins had emerged as a league power by transforming three chronic weaknesses—defense, rushing, and special teams—into their greatest strengths.

Despite the fact that 20% of the plays in a football game involve a kick, most NFL teams in the early Seventies paid little or no attention to their "suicide squads." Redskins special teams Coach Marv Levy changed that. He created an esprit de corps by treating his players with the kind of respect normally reserved for first-stringers. And he designed actual plays instead of just telling his troops to "run down the field and hit someone." No longer mere cannon-fodder, Levy's specialists blocked seven field goal attempts in 1971 and led the conference in punt returns and kickoff coverage. "With most other clubs, players aren't crazy about being on the special teams," said George Burman. "Levy has changed that. He made the special teams into something important. That's the difference."

The Washington Redskins' first test of the 1972 season came on Monday night against the Minnesota Vikings. In 6 years as a head coach, George Allen had never lost an opening game, and his Redskins players desperately wanted the streak to continue. "We've got a real big opportunity," said Kilmer. "Monday night could tell us how the season will go. With an all-out effort and a win over Minnesota, we can have a tremendous season."

Expertly coached by Bud Grant, the Vikings had won four straight Central Division crowns and were the bookies' leading candidate to represent the NFC in Super Bowl VII. Over the previous 3 years, Minnesota had posted a league-best 35-7 record despite mediocre performances by three successive quarterbacks: Joe Kapp, Gary Cuozzo, and Norman Snead. But without a strong passing attack the Vikings had not been able to win a Super Bowl. So when Coach Grant got the chance to reacquire Fran Tarkenton, one of the greatest quarterbacks of all time, he didn't hesitate. The return of the scrambling Tarkenton, who had begun his career in Minnesota before spending the past 5 years as a New York Giant, gave real substance to the Super Bowl dreams of the Vikings and their fans.

Before Tarkenton's homecoming, Minnesota had

been forced to rely on its strong defense to stay atop the Central Division. Alan Page, the first defensive lineman to be named the NFL's Most Valuable Player, was the brightest star on a defensive unit that sported some of the most respected players in the game: Carl Eller, Jim Marshall, Wally Hilgenberg, Lonnie Warwick, Roy Winston, and Paul Krause. Known as the Purple Gang, the Vikings had surrendered only 133 points in 1969, 143 points in 1970, and 139 points in 1971—an average of less than 10 points per game. It was no exaggeration that the hard-hitting Vikings had earned their colorful nickname as much from the bruises they inflicted as from the color of their jerseys.

On the first Monday night of the 1972 season, Curt Knight teed up a Wilson "Pro" football and kicked it high into the warm September air of Bloomington, Minnesota—a simple act that the sell-out crowd at Metropolitan Stadium had impatiently awaited since Christmas Day, 1971. That was the day the Vikings had lost to Dallas, 20-12, in the first round of the playoffs, and only a new season with new victories could erase the ashen taste of that defeat.

Minnesota started from its 20. Three rushes fell inches short of a first down, and Mike Eischeid dropped back to punt. At the snap, Washington's Bill Malinchak dashed into the Vikings' backfield, aiming for the spot where the ball would leave Eischeid's foot. With impeccable timing, Malinchak's hand, Eischeid's foot, and the ball all met with a double thud at the 15. The ball ricocheted to the right, spinning crazily. Malinchak ran after it, scooped it into his arms, and raced into the end zone for a touchdown! Knight's conversion was good, and the excited Washington Redskins, most of whom were hugging and slapping hands on the sideline, broke on top, 7-0.

Eager to impress his former fans, Fran Tarkenton fired a 39-yard pass to Gene Washington, and Vikings rooters welcomed back their former star with a thunderous ovation. After a 9-yard pickup by fullback Oscar Reed, Tarkenton hit tight end John Beasley with a 14-yard strike at the Washington 13. However,

Minnesota was unable to get into the end zone, and Fred Cox came in to try a 22-yard field goal. Washington's Ted Vactor streaked in from the side and, even though he failed to get a hand on the ball, caused Cox to hurry his kick. He pulled it wide to the left, and the Redskins still led, 7-0.

At the start of the second quarter, the 'Skins nearly pulled off another big play, but Kilmer overthrew a wide-open Roy Jefferson at the goal line. Later in the period, the tide continued to turn in Minnesota's favor when Washington's Curt Knight, the NFC's leading scorer in 1971, missed a 51-yard field goal. After taking over at their 6, the Vikings marched 94 yards using a crafty blend of ten runs and seven passes. When halfback Clint Jones leapt into the end zone from a yard out, the game was deadlocked, 7-7.

With 1:35 left in the half, the Redskins switched to their hurry-up offense. After a few short passes, Kilmer surprised the Vikings by handing off to halfback Larry Brown, who broke loose on a 37-yard scamper to the Minnesota 25. But Washington could gain only 2 more yards on its next three plays, and Knight came in to attempt a 30-yard field goal. The league's highest paid holder, Sonny Jurgensen, deftly fielded a poor snap from center and placed the ball on its tip just in time for Knight to boot it through the uprights. With a minute remaining in the first half, Washington went back on top, 10-7.

Then the Redskins got greedy. Thinking they might get another quick score, the 'Skins called a time-out after Diron Talbert dumped John Gilliam for a big loss at the Minnesota 7. But halfback Clint Jones spoiled Washington's plans by exploding through the line for a 33-yard gain. Had the Redskins not called a time-out, the first half would have been over. But because they did, Minnesota still had 28 seconds in which to score. Tarkenton threw to halfback Bill Brown for 9 yards, then hit Gilliam for 10 more at the Redskins 41. After Brown positioned the ball in the center of the field with a 4-yard run, Fred Cox rushed in with 8 seconds left in the half. Mick Tingelhoff snapped the ball, Paul Krause spotted it, Cox kicked it, and—Ted Vactor blocked it! [Fig. 61] The gun sounded, and the relieved Redskins, led by their amazing special teams, ran to the locker room with their oddly earned 10-7 halftime lead intact.

Fig. 61   *Paul Fine Photo/Nate Fine Productions, Courtesy Washington Redskins*

The Washington Redskins got off to a bad start in the second half. On their first possession, Billy Kilmer threw an interception to Karl Kassulke, and Minnesota went to work at its 43. Fran Tarkenton threw to John Gilliam for one first down, scrambled for another, then tossed an 11-yard touchdown pass that Gilliam caught on his fingertips in the corner of the end zone. The efficient 57-yard drive restored the Vikings' confidence and put them in front for the first time, 14-10. The rest of the third period turned into a tense defensive struggle with neither side able to score. At one point, Minnesota made it as far as the Washington 20, but Oscar Reed fumbled and Jack Pardee recovered to end the threat.

At the start of the fourth quarter, Speedy Duncan, the NFL's leading punt returner in 1971, gave the 'Skins good field position with a clever return to the Washington 42. Two plays later, Billy Kilmer threw a wobbling, but accurate, 16-yard pass to Roy Jefferson at the Vikings 35. Then, on a crucial third-and-4, Larry Brown slashed through the middle of the line for a 14-yard gain and a first down at the Vikings 15. After a pass interference penalty moved the ball to the 3, Brown squeezed through a small opening and charged into the end zone for the go-ahead touchdown. Curt Knight hit the extra point, and Washington reclaimed the lead, 17-14.

Knight kicked off to Clint Jones, who ran it out to the 20 before he was clobbered by Bob Brunet. The violent tackle jarred the ball loose, and Bill Malinchak recovered for Washington at the Vikings 18! On first down, Larry Brown carried to the 9. Then fullback Charley Harraway turned the corner around left end and cruised into the end zone for a touchdown! [Fig. 62] With 9 minutes left in the game, the 'Skins appeared to be in control, 24-14.

Fig. 62   *Daniel Dmitruk/NFL Photos*

Ron McDole can't quite reach this pass by Fran Tarkenton   *Paul Fine Photo/Nate Fine Productions, Courtesy Washington Redskins*

Desperate measures were reluctantly incorporated into the Vikings' game plan as Tarkenton tried to jump-start the stalled Minnesota offense. After a long, long bomb to Gene Washington misfired, Coach Grant was forced to gamble on fourth and 1 at his 20. Clint Jones made the first down, but the drive soon fizzled and the Vikings had to punt. Minnesota quickly regained possession, though, and, with 5:08 left in the game, set out for the Washington goal line again. With Tarkenton completing five of ten passes, the Vikes marched from their 15 to the Washington 4. On fourth and 3, Tarkenton rolled out and threw a strike to Bill Brown, who lunged into the end zone for a touchdown. Fred Cox's extra point moved Minnesota to within a field goal, 24-21, but only 1 minute and 10 seconds remained in the game.

Both teams stocked their kickoff teams' front lines with experienced ball-handlers. As expected, Cox bunted an onside kick the necessary 10 yards, and a dozen players dove for the ball. It took the referee at least a minute to peel off all the bodies before he got to the bottom of the pile, where Washington's "King of the Special Teams," Rusty Tillman, lay clutching the ball to his chest. Unable to stop the clock, the Vikings could only swallow their disappointment and congratulate the Washington Redskins on their hard-fought 24-21 victory.

The Redskins special teams had scored one touchdown on a blocked punt, set up another with a fumble recovery, prevented two Minnesota field goals, and finally sealed the victory by recovering the desperate onside kick at the end of the game. Without those contributions, the 'Skins surely would have lost to a Vikings team that outgained them in total yardage, 382-203. However, thanks to the special performances of Malinchak, Vactor, Brunet, and Tillman, the Washington Redskins' 1972 season got off to a flying start.

CLOSE CALL

Washington Redskins vs. New England Patriots

October 1, 1972

After decades of backing losers, Washington Red-skins fans should have known better than to tempt Fate. In 1941, when the Redskins started out 5-1, a few unguarded remarks by some inexperienced fans snapped the spell and led directly to five losses in the next six games. Then in 1962, when the 'Skins broke on top of the Eastern Conference with a 4-0-2 record, Redskins Fever swept through Washington, causing a few delirious fans to link the words "championship" and "Redskins" in the same sentence. Naturally, the 'Skins dropped seven of their next eight games. So, when Washington opened the 1972 season with two victories, old-time fans could only shudder when brazen, band-wagon supporters began to predict not only that the 'Skins would still be undefeated when the Dallas Cowboys came to town in the sixth week of the season, but that Washington would waltz to the Eastern Division title.

Following the exhilarating opening-night victory over Minnesota, the Redskins had taken on the St. Louis Cardinals and, after building an early lead, coasted to a 24-10 victory with repetitive, but time-consuming, running plays. Bored by the endless line plunges, the customers at RFK Stadium demonstrated how quickly they had become jaded. Once grateful for any kind of victory, the restless fans began booing quarterback Billy Kilmer's monotonous play selec-

tion even though they knew he was simply protecting the 'Skins' big lead. Naturally, the Redskins resented being booed—especially while winning. "We're not paid to be fascinating," snapped linebacker Myron Pottios, "we're paid to win football games." Although it's hard to distinguish one boo from another, some of the jeering was undoubtedly directed at Coach Allen, who thus far had refused to play his flashiest and most popular trump card, quarterback Sonny Jurgensen.

Many Redskins fans were upset that Sonny was still on the bench, seeing action only when he held for Curt Knight's placekicks. Ironically, Sonny had performed that same duty in Philadelphia when Norm Van Brocklin led the Eagles to the NFL Championship in 1960. Trying to cover his disappointment with a joke, Jurgensen said, "Maybe that's my destiny, to hold for extra points on championship teams." Responding obliquely to the storm of criticism by saying, "Winning is the only thing that matters," Allen stuck with Kilmer. Whether he knew it or not, Allen was heeding the advice of former Redskins Coach Joe Kuharich, who once said, "You listen to the fans and you'll wind up in the stands with 'em."

Allen's unpopular decision to stay with Kilmer was made feasible only by the remarkable achievements of halfback Larry Brown. A relentless competitor who went for broke on every play, Brown had been the reliable workhorse on whose back the Redskins had ridden to the 1971 playoffs. Larry had started his NFL career in 1969 under Coach Vince Lombardi, who noticed that the hard-working halfback consistently missed signals and appeared to be out of sync with the rest of the offense. Finally, Lombardi discovered that Larry was partially deaf, and, after a hearing aid was implanted in his helmet, Brown blossomed into one of the most feared runners in the NFL. In 1970, he became the first Washington running back in history to crack the 1,000-yard barrier,

winning the NFL rushing title with 1,125 yards. Only in his fourth season, Larry was already the Redskins' all-time leading rusher with 3,214 yards.

Brown was once again pacing the league in 1972, but the rest of the offense was generating only middle-of-the-pack statistics. That was fine with Allen—as long as he had his opportunistic defense. While the offense sputtered in the first two games of 1972, Washington's defense and special teams had been magnificent, either scoring or setting up five of the club's six touchdowns with a blocked punt, a blocked field goal, two interceptions, and a fumble recovery. Al-

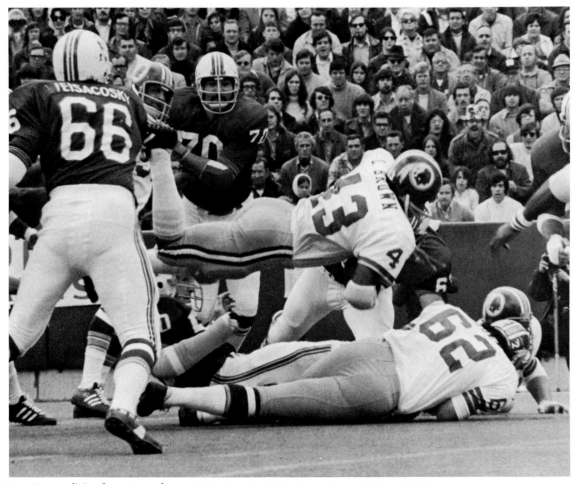

Larry Brown diving for extra yardage   *Paul Fine Photo/Nate Fine Productions, Courtesy Washington Redskins*

Fig. 65   *Paul Fine Photo/Nate Fine Productions, Courtesy Washington Redskins*

though the offense was not yet in top form, the Redskins were feeling confident about their upcoming game against the New England Patriots. "On paper we have the better team," drawled Diron Talbert, a popular defensive tackle from Texas. "[But] the players now are spoiled. I really believe that because we're only eighth in defense instead of first or second. But, if ¾ of the guys get up for the game, we should win it."

Predictions, however, are seldom treated kindly in football, especially when opponents like the inconsistent Patriots do such a good job of concealing their talents. The year before, New England had staggered to a 6-8 record, yet three of those victories had been against league superpowers: the Oakland Raiders, Miami Dolphins, and Baltimore Colts. Once again, the key to the Patriots' fortunes lay in the hands of quarterback Jim Plunkett, a Heisman Trophy-winning quarterback and AFC Rookie of the Year, and his favorite receiver, Randy Vataha. The two had been teammates at Stanford, and their years of practice together made them nearly telepathic. Although Plunkett and Vataha had made headlines throughout New England during 1971, their heroics had not been enough to redeem the club's otherwise disappointing season.

In the first two games of 1972, the erratic Patriots had been drubbed by the Cincinnati Bengals, 31-7, and had eked out a lucky victory over Atlanta when the Falcons placekicker blew a 10-yard field goal in the final minute. But now that New England's best runner, Carl Garrett, was out with an injury, the Redskins defensive line—Ron McDole, Manny Sistrunk, Diron Talbert, and Verlon Biggs—could dismiss the threat of the Patriots' ground attack and devote themselves to harassing Plunkett. With that in mind, bookies were giving 11 points to any sucker who thought the one-dimensional Patriots could even come close to the defensive demons of George Allen's Redskins. Typically, though, Coach Allen was worried that his team was ripe for an upset, telling reporters before the game, "I don't know whether we're ready for 'em. Yes, I'm serious. Everyone's taking them too lightly." The reporters dutifully wrote down Allen's words, but no one took them seriously.

In 1971, the Boston Patriots, hoping to widen their appeal and increase their profits, moved 32 miles from their birthplace to the bedroom community of Foxboro, Massachusetts, and changed their name to the New England Patriots. Their new address did not improve their performance, though, and the Patriots failed to reach .500 for the fifth year in a row. But even though the Pats were no better off in 1972, 60,999 gerrymandered fans packed Schaefer Stadium on a cool and breezy October afternoon to watch them take on the battle-hardened veterans of the Washington Redskins.

Both teams opened their attacks with long passes, and both gambits failed. Five successive punts in the first quarter eventually gave the Patriots an edge in field position, but Charley Gogolak, the ex-Redskins placekicker, squandered their only scoring opportunity when he bungled a 23-yard field goal. The first period ended in a scoreless tie.

After missing three of his first four passes, Redskins quarterback Billy Kilmer began to settle down in the second quarter. An 8-yard strike to Charley Taylor and a 36-yard pass to tight end Mack Alston advanced the ball to the Patriots 36. Larry Brown picked up 6, then Kilmer [Fig. 65] fired a 30-yard pass to Charley Taylor, who made a beautiful leaping grab in the end zone to stake the 'Skins to a 7-0 lead. On the Patriots' first play after the kickoff, halfback Jack Maitland fumbled, and Washington safety Richie Petitbon recovered at the New England 17. The Redskins quickly took advantage of the turnover as Larry Brown stabbed through the line for 11 yards and Charley Taylor caught another touchdown pass, putting Washington on top, 14-0. It was beginning to look like a blowout.

However, Jim Plunkett began to find the cracks in Washington's newly installed zone defense. Displaying remarkable composure in the face of the Redskins' strong pass rush, Plunkett mixed completions to Bob Windsor and Reggie Rucker with handoffs to rookie halfback Josh Ashton as the Patriots maneuvered from their 22 to the Redskins 15. On fourth and 1, New England Coach John Mazur disdained a field goal in order to go for the first down. The decision paid off handsomely as Ashton, a 6-foot 1-inch,

205-pounder from Tulsa, ripped through the Washington defense like an Oklahoma cyclone. Two plays later, Ashton dove into the end zone for New England's first touchdown, and, moments later, the first half ended with Washington ahead, 14-7.

Invigorated by its success at the end of the half, New England opened the third quarter with a long drive. A 22-yard pass to Randy Vataha and Ashton's 27-yard sweep were crowned by Reggie Rucker's 11-yard touchdown catch that tied the score, 14-14. A few minutes later, the Patriots proved it was possible to be both good and lucky when tight end Bob Windsor caught a 12-yard pass from Plunkett while lying flat on his back. Apparently believing that anything would work after that, New England tried a long option pass from halfback Bob Gladieux to Randy Vataha, but Redskins cornerback Mike Bass brought them back to reality with an interception. Weaving and dodging and doubling back, Bass covered nearly 90 yards on his return. Unfortunately, only 29 of them were in the direction of the New England goal line, and Washington took over at its 48.

Kilmer marched the Redskins down the field with the precision of a drillmaster, but Washington came up empty when he threw an interception at the goal line. Plunkett continued giving the ball to Ashton, who continued to gain 5 yards every time he touched it. Because of Ashton's success, the Redskins defensive line was forced to honor the run, and, given ample time to throw, Plunkett started making Washington's nickel defense look as if it were overcharging for its services. After reeling off four first downs, New England took the lead for the first time, 17-14, on a 42-yard field goal at the end of the third quarter.

Embarrassed to find themselves trailing, the Washington Redskins quickly retaliated. Kilmer completed three short passes, then slipped the ball to Larry Brown, who dodged 36 yards to the New England 20. After Brown plowed through center for another first down at the 10, Kilmer threw to Charley Taylor in the end zone. Charley caught it—barely out of bounds. On third down, Kilmer passed to tight end Jerry Smith, who latched onto it—in bounds—for a touchdown to put the Redskins back in front, 21-17.

Following the kickoff, Plunkett masterminded an 80-yard assault on the exasperated Washington defense. A sweep by Ashton picked up 14 yards. A pass to Vataha gained 15 more. Then two completions to Bob Windsor set up Plunkett's 24-yard touchdown pass to Ashton, and the Patriots forged ahead, 24-21, late in the fourth quarter.

Speedy Duncan returned Gogolak's kickoff to the 35, but two major penalties wedged the Redskins into a second-and-32 dilemma at their 13. Nevertheless, Kilmer surprised the Patriots with a 62-yard bomb to Charley Taylor, and the 'Skins were suddenly at the New England 25. Two minutes remained as Kilmer passed to Roy Jefferson deep in the end zone. Jefferson leapt—and caught it! On the way down, he was belted by cornerback Ron Bolton, and the force of the blow pushed his foot an inch beyond the boundary. Disregarding the effect of Bolton's push, the official ruled that Jefferson had simply landed out of bounds. The Redskins argued that Jefferson's feet would have come down in bounds had he not been driven out by Bolton, but the call stood and Washington had to settle for a field goal. Curt Knight came in for a 33-yarder and made it with ease, tying the game. But wait—a penalty! In his attempt to block the kick, Bolton had roughed the holder, Sonny Jurgensen, and now the Redskins had another opportunity to win the game outright.

George Allen faced a tricky decision. He could refuse the penalty and keep the 3 points, or accept the penalty and have a first down at the Patriots 21 with 1:39 left in the game. Of course, if he settled for the 24-24 tie, there was no guarantee the Redskins could keep the red-hot Patriots from scoring. Although conventional wisdom dictated: "Never take points off the board!," the thought of a tie against the lowly Patriots was so repugnant (overtime games didn't begin until 1974) that Allen decided to give back the 3 points, accept the penalty, and go for the victory. After all, Allen reasoned, if the offense couldn't score a touchdown, Knight, the most accurate kicker in the league in 1970 and its leading scorer in 1971, would only have to make a chip shot to regain the tie. And that scenario would give the Pats less time for retaliation.

On first down at the 21, Larry Brown was stopped

cold. On second down, Kilmer overthrew Jefferson. On third down, Kilmer spotted Jefferson open by a step—and overthrew him again! With 1:22 left on the clock, Curt Knight returned. The crowd held its breath. From 27 yards out, Knight booted it, and the ball spun past the goalpost—wide to the right by a foot! The Patriots still led, 24-21.

The embarrassed and angry Redskins vented their wrath on Josh Ashton, hammering him to the ground three straight times. The 'Skins took a time-out after each play, and, with 57 seconds remaining, Pat Studstill came in to punt from the Patriots 26. The ball was snapped, Studstill swung his leg and punted the ball right into the outstretched hand of the leaping Bill Malinchak! The ball ricocheted crazily toward the end zone, skittering on the hard artificial surface. Washington's Bob Brunet chased after it with Malinchak a step behind. The ball rolled into the end zone, and as it neared the end line, Brunet dove and slapped it back into play, right into the arms of the sliding Malinchak. Malinchak grabbed it and slid out

of the end zone in one motion. [Fig. 66] Was it a touchdown or a safety?

"It was as clean as it could be," said Malinchak. "There was no doubt in my mind that I had scored a touchdown. There was one official who wanted to call it a touchdown, but the other started waving his arms and saying 'Safety, Safety.' I looked at him, and he was just saying 'No, No, No.' I had the ball . . . I caught it clean. It was a touchdown." But after conferring in committee for several agonizing moments, the officials ruled that Malinchak had not had full control of the ball before going out of bounds. A safety was called, and the disappointed Redskins were awarded 2 points, which left the Patriots with a 24-23 lead. Although a field goal would now be enough to win the game, the Redskins had only 50 seconds (and no time-outs) to overcome their incredible string of misfortune.

From his 20, Studstill punted to Speedy Duncan, who returned it to the Patriots 48. On first down, Kilmer flared a pass to Larry Brown, but he was

Fig. 66   Was he out of bounds? *Paul Fine Photo/Nate Fine Productions, Courtesy Washington Redskins*

dragged down in bounds after a 6-yard gain. So to stop the clock, Kilmer had to waste a play by throwing the ball out of bounds. On third down, Kilmer aimed for Jefferson, but the ball was tipped away by cornerback Larry Carwell.

Fourth down. Twelve seconds remained in the game. Curt Knight returned to the field, seeking redemption and victory from 50 yards away. The snap and hold were perfect. Knight swung his leg and met the ball squarely. It took off like a shot toward the right goalpost. With distance to spare, the spinning ball sailed past the upright—three feet wide to the right! The sound of the gun was lost in the explosion of cheers. The Patriots had won, 24-23.

Everything had backfired for Washington in those final frantic minutes. Neither Larry Brown's third consecutive 100-yard game nor Billy Kilmer's three touchdown passes could compensate for Knight's two missed field goals and the questionable calls by the officials that had doomed the luckless Redskins. It was understandably difficult for the 'Skins to accept responsibility for the heartbreaking defeat; it was much easier to blame misfortune and the officials. But the harsh and unsettling truth was that the Patriots had deserved to win. Josh Ashton's extraordinary running (108 yards on 23 carries), Jim Plunkett's timely passing (17-33 and two TD's), and the offensive line's excellent blocking were clearly the overriding factors in New England's well-earned victory. When told of the Redskins' bitter protests, a Patriots official, well acquainted with the many excuses for losing, just smiled wickedly and said, "Let 'em bitch."

I LIKE SONNY

Dallas Cowboys vs. Washington Redskins

October 22, 1972

The major issue that polarized Washington area residents in 1972, setting brother against sister and Conservative against Liberal, was not whether President Nixon had ordered the break-in at the Watergate nor whether the United States should get out of Vietnam. No, what people really cared about in the Nation's Capital was whether Sonny Jurgensen or Billy Kilmer owned the Divine Right to quarterback the Washington Redskins. The Great Quarterback Controversy became the primary topic in Washington's newsrooms and barrooms, spawning heated debates and bumper sticker sales that were the envy of every politician in town. If you were a Redskins fan in 1972, chances are your car was labeled "I LIKE SONNY" or "I LIKE BILLY." There was no middle ground.

Now that Sonny Jurgensen, who had been injured during most of the '71 season, was healthy again, most fans felt that only his talented hand could guide the Redskins to football's Mount Olympus, the Super Bowl. Kilmer backers argued that Billy was a better leader and a "winner." Coach George Allen wrestled with the thorny problem for months before finally deciding that he liked Billy. Three weeks later, though, after the debacle in Foxboro, Coach Allen reluctantly decided to increase the Redskins' margin of error by replacing Kilmer with the 38-year-old

Jurgensen. Even though the embarrassing loss to the Patriots had not been Kilmer's fault, Allen figured a change in quarterbacks was the easiest way to cover up the team's problems. The real culprits had been the Redskins' porous zone defense, unfortunate tactics, two questionable calls by the officials, and two missed field goals at the end of the game. But Kilmer made a convenient scapegoat.

As soon as the switch was announced, more guesswork began. Had Allen started Kilmer in the first three games with the proviso that he would be replaced if he ever lost? Had Allen's desire to win finally conquered his desire to be the most celebrated sports figure in town? Or was Allen simply looking for more offensive punch to compensate for his defense's occasional off-day?

Whatever the reasons, by the sixth week of the season Allen could at least feel confident in his defense again. Playing man-to-man after scrapping its leaky zone defense, Washington redeemed itself by surrendering only 3 points over the course of the next two games. "[By playing a zone], we were trying to do the things other teams do," admitted linebacker Jack Pardee, "rather than what we do best."

Fortunately, the Redskins had also improved what they had done worst in their 25 years as league doormats: block. Doomed to failure for a quarter century because of lackluster offensive lines, Washington now fielded a solid line that could be counted on to protect the quarterback and open honest holes for the running backs. The synchronized teamwork of Paul Laaveg and Terry Hermeling on the left side complemented the savvy and skill of veterans Walter Rock and John Wilbur on the right. The keystone was center Len Hauss, a tough 9-year veteran from Georgia who was gunning for his sixth straight Pro Bowl appearance. "Lenny's having an absolutely fantastic year," declared Line Coach Mike McCormack. "From a leadership standpoint and [with his] blocking, he's holding everything together."

In the Fifties and Sixties, when everything was falling apart for Washington, the next best thing to a week off for other teams in the NFL was a game against the Redskins. Like their counterparts in baseball, the dreadful Washington Senators, the 'Skins had given the league a certain continuity with their longterm lease on the Eastern Conference cellar. In 1960, the Redskins' fortunes were at an all-time low when the Dallas Cowboys came into existence. Their arrival was well timed because they provided Washington with its only victory of the season, thereby saving the 1-9-2 'Skins the embarrassment of finishing lower than the 0-11-1 Cowboys. Since then, though, Dallas had achieved better records in every year except 1962 and 1964, and now led the series, 13-8-2.

Washington continued to founder in the Sixties, but its rivalry with the fast-lane Cowboys had grown hotter with every game as high-scoring passing duels between Don Meredith and Sonny Jurgensen routinely produced miraculous comebacks and last-second triumphs. "Our record seldom indicated we would play very well against Dallas," said Jurgensen, "but we always seemed to have good days, offensively and defensively, against them. For me, it's always been a challenge playing against Dallas."

And vice versa. In 14 games against the Cowboys, Jurgensen had burned Dallas for 3,536 yards and 26 touchdowns with teammates (other than his receivers) not known for their Hall of Fame credentials. Now that Sonny finally had a good team to play with, many observers around the league believed he soon would be wearing a Super Bowl ring. In fact,

Coach Vince Lombardi once said that if Green Bay had drafted Jurgensen, the Packers "never would have lost a game." Now, with the 1972 season nearly half over, Sonny finally was being given the opportunity he had waited 16 seasons for—the chance to play in an important game with talented teammates against the top team in the NFL, the World Champion Dallas Cowboys.

"Dallas is the best overall team in the league," said George Allen. "They've got experience, speed, and depth." The Super Bowl Champion Cowboys, who had made the playoffs six straight years, were coming to town tied with Washington for the lead in the NFC East. Led by veteran quarterback Craig Morton, who had reclaimed the starting position when Roger Staubach, the MVP of Super Bowl VI, separated his shoulder in the preseason, the 4-1 Cowboys were showing no signs of complacency or slippage.

Just emerging from the other end of the success scale, Washington had made the playoffs the year before for the first time since 1945. But with the deadliest passer in the game back in the lineup, the Redskins were raising their sights even higher. In a tuneup the week before, Jurgensen had been sharp, leading Washington to a 33-3 romp over the St. Louis Cardinals. The Redskins could do no wrong as NFL rushing leader Larry Brown racked up his fourth 100-yard game of the season and Curt Knight broke out of a kicking slump with a 4-for-4 performance. For the first time since 1960, the 'Skins appeared ready to stand toe to toe with the talented Cowboys.

Look at the similarities. Dallas' defense ranked first in the NFC against the rush, but the Redskins had given up only 1 yard more. Neither team had surrendered a single touchdown in their last two games, yet both were vulnerable to the pass. The Cowboys also led the NFC in total offense, but, with Jurgensen at quarterback, 4th-ranked Washington was now hitting on all cylinders. And, although the Redskins' "Over-the-Hill Gang" received a lot of publicity for having an average age of 29.3, the Cowboys, on average, were just a year younger.

There were some differences, too. Whereas Dallas used the draft to build its dynasty, George Allen had traded every draft pick he could (including one

Len Hauss
Copyright Washington Post; Reprinted by permission of the D.C. Public Library

that he traded twice) to stock the Redskins roster with proven veterans. Moreover, Dallas was essentially an offensive powerhouse that forced opponents to play catch-up, while George Allen's Redskins relied on defense to control games by setting up short scores with takeaways and blocked kicks.

During the week preceding the Cowboys game, Coach Allen did not have to contrive his usual puffery to motivate the Redskins; this time the truth would suffice. "We'll have a championship-type game against the Cowboys Sunday," proclaimed Allen. "The winner will be in the driver's seat. I only wish we had a 100,000 seat stadium this week." Even his usual incantation against unforeseen disaster—"We must play a top game and make no mistakes if we expect to win"—rang true. The Washington Redskins were confident; they truly expected to win. But so did the Dallas Cowboys.

53,039 crazed Redskins fans jammed into Robert F. Kennedy Stadium and shouted themselves hoarse before the game even began. Welcoming the 'Skins onto the field with a raucous standing ovation, the boisterous fans saved their loudest cheers for quarterback Sonny Jurgensen, who, for the first time in the George Allen era, was starting an important game in front of the home folks.

When the game got underway, though, the Cowboys quickly quieted the crowd. Starting at their 32, Dallas running backs Calvin Hill and Walt Garrison took turns gouging holes into the Redskins defensive line. Then Craig Morton completed a 21-yard pass to Bob Hayes and a 14-yarder to Garrison that gave the Cowboys a first down at the Washington 8. The Redskins defense stiffened, but Toni Fritsch kicked a 13-yard field goal and Dallas jumped out in front, 3-0.

On Washington's first possession, Jurgensen completed a pass to Charley Taylor for a 14-yard gain, but the cheers evaporated when Taylor fumbled and Cowboys linebacker Dave Edwards recovered at the Redskins 25. Led by linebackers Jack Pardee and Chris Hanburger, Washington's defense pushed Dallas back to the 39, but, on third and 24, Morton threw a touchdown pass to Ron Sellers and the Cowboys were cruising, 10-0.

The game nearly got out of hand on the first play of the second quarter when a Redskins lineman inadvertently barged into Jurgensen and knocked the ball out of his hands at the Washington 10. Although Larry Brown prevented an easy Dallas score by recovering at the 1, Mike Bragg had to punt from his end zone and the Cowboys inherited great field position at their 44. Dallas' well-oiled offensive machine hummed to perfection as it drove downfield, but it ran into a speed bump on third and 2 at the Redskins 5 when fullback Calvin Hill was stacked at the line. So Fritsch salvaged 3 points with a short field goal, inflating the Cowboys' lead to 13-0.

Because of Dallas' infuriating ability to run up a lead in the early stages of a game, opponents were generally forced to abandon rational game plans in favor of reckless long passes. Nevertheless, the Redskins refused to panic and stuck doggedly to their carefully wrought strategy of mixing short passes with probing runs. Their patience was rewarded as they began to move from their 26. Halfback Larry Brown broke through the line for 13 yards, Jurgensen hit Taylor for 12, and Brown swept right end for 15 more.

On the first critical play of the game, third and 10 at the Dallas 32, Jurgensen connected with Brown for a first down at the 17. Then, after a loss of 2 yards, Sonny recognized an incoming blitz and countered with an audible. Jurgensen took the snap and, while backpedaling, lobbed the ball over the blitzers' heads to Larry Brown, who had curled out of the backfield. The soft pass found Brown all alone in the Dallas secondary [Fig. 68], and Larry dashed into the end zone for a touchdown! With the addition of Knight's extra point, the Redskins climbed back into contention, 13-7. Seconds later, the first half ended.

The 19-yard touchdown pass to Brown was even

Fig. 68   *Paul Fine/NFL Photos*

more special because it gave Sonny Jurgensen a total of more than 30,000 yards passing in his career, a milestone that had been reached by only two other quarterbacks in history, John Brodie and Johnny Unitas. That Sonny had surpassed the mark while throwing a touchdown pass against the Dallas Cowboys seemed only natural.

Like Olympic sprinters, the Cowboys exploded out of the starting block as soon as the second half began. On Dallas' first play from scrimmage, Calvin Hill ripped through the line for 26 yards and a first down at the Washington 37. Then Walt Garrison broke off a 33-yard run to the Redskins 4. Two plays later, Garrison plunged into the end zone from the 1, and the Cowboys reclaimed their 13-point lead.

Trailing 20-7, Sonny Jurgensen finally took matters into his own hands. Unleashing the famous arm that Allen's ultraconservative game plan had stifled, Jurgensen retaliated with a 28-yard pitch to Jerry Smith near midfield. The Cowboys defense immediately spread out in anticipation of an all-out aerial assault. But Jurgy crossed them up by calling four consecutive running plays that gained a total of 18 yards. Then, with the Cowboys playing tight on second and 6 at their 34, Larry Brown took a pitchout and followed fullback Charley Harraway around left end. Harraway leveled an incoming Cowboy, springing Brown into the Dallas secondary. At the 15, Walter Rock annihilated the final Dallas defender, and Larry raced into the end zone while 53,000 fans roared their approval. Although still trailing, 20-14, the 'Skins were back within striking distance.

In an attempt to quickly regain the momentum, the Cowboys abandoned their successful running game. But three straight incompletions proved that strategy ill-advised, and Washington got the ball again at its 31. Because both Charley Taylor and Roy Jefferson were drawing double coverage, Jurgensen took what the Cowboys offered: Larry Brown. Sonny found Brown open twice, for 14 and 15 yards, and the 'Skins advanced to the Dallas 34. However, Jurgy missed connections with Charley Harraway on a third-down pass, and placekicker Curt Knight came in to attempt a 42-yard field goal. Knowing that Knight was as liable to kick the ball out of bounds as he was to kick it between the goal posts, the nervous crowd held its breath. Luckily for the Redskins, Knight's kick flew straight this time, reducing Washington's deficit to 3 points, 20-17. Fifteen minutes of football remained.

After the kickoff, the Dallas Cowboys began an erratic drive that eventually produced a third-and-6 at the Washington 43. At the snap, all three Redskins linebackers blitzed. Morton escaped and, with a wide-open field before him, could have easily run for the first down. But he hesitated as he neared the line of scrimmage, then pulled up and threw a terrible pass that sailed far over Walt Garrison's head. So, on fourth down, Fritsch tried a 50-yard field goal, but his kick sliced to the right and the relieved Redskins took over at their 20.

Given single coverage, Roy Jefferson finally got open, and Jurgensen hit him with a 26-yard strike at the 46. When the Cowboys went back to double-covering Washington's wide receivers, Sonny countered by passing to Brown underneath the Dallas zone for gains of 18 and 16 yards. On second and 6 at the Cowboys 13, Jurgy pitched out to Charley Harraway. Running to his left, Harraway feinted into the line, then sprinted to the outside, trying to get around the corner before safety Cornell Green could cut him off. [Fig. 69] Highly prized for his blocking ability but not known for raw speed, Charley suddenly became supercharged. He not only turned the corner and skirted past the diving Green, but kept accelerating right into the end zone! RFK Stadium was still quaking a moment later when Knight's PAT made the score: Washington 24, Dallas 20.

With 6:12 remaining in the game, it was now up to the Redskins defense to preserve the lead. With 53,000 rabid fans screaming at him, Craig Morton threw right into the teeth of the 'Skins' coverage. Cutting in front of Bob Hayes, cornerback Pat Fischer made a diving interception at the Washington 33, then scrambled to his feet and got back to midfield before Walt Garrison brought him down. Protecting their 4-point lead, the Redskins kept the ball on the ground and moved cautiously to the Cowboys 36. At the 2-minute warning, Curt Knight came in to try to

Fig. 69   *Gerald Martineau/Washington Post Photo*

add the points that would ensure a tie even if Dallas were to score another TD. But he missed, and the Cowboys took over at their 20.

53,000 nervous rooters were begging for "DE-fense, DE-fense, DE-fense" as Morton dropped back to pass again. He aimed for wide receiver Ron Sellers sprinting down the field, but the pass never got there. Jack Pardee tipped the ball into the air, and nickel back Speedy Duncan intercepted at the Cowboys 29, setting off an eruption of cheers that turned the stadium into a cauldron of sound. Desperate to get the ball back, Dallas smothered three straight Redskins rushes but used all of its time-outs in the process. On fourth down, Knight came in to ice the game with a 37-yard field goal—but choked again.

Still trailing, 24-20, the Cowboys had one final chance to win. Morton completed a 9-yard pass to Hill with 47 seconds remaining, but precious time was lost when he failed to get out of bounds. Unable to take a time-out, the Cowboys hurried to the line. Morton passed to Sellers on the sideline for a first down at the Cowboys 35, and the clock stopped with 30 seconds left in the game. Then Morton fired 16 yards to Lance Alworth, who stepped out of bounds at midfield. With 16 seconds left in the game, Morton threw to Bob Hayes in the hope that the former Olympian could use his incredible speed to break loose for a score. Hayes caught Morton's short pass at the Washington 38, but Pat Fischer and Mike Bass wrestled him to the ground before he could get out of bounds. With the crowd counting down the final seconds, the Cowboys rushed to get off one last play, but, before they could line up, they heard 53,000 voices yell, "THREE . . . TWO . . . ONE . . .," followed by a final explosion of cheers that told them the Washington Redskins had triumphed, 24-20.

After surviving a rocky start in the first quarter, the Redskins had rallied brilliantly and, unlike Washington teams of the past, had hung onto the lead at the end. "Time and again we've scored on them in the last minutes," said Sonny Jurgensen amid the joyous bedlam in the Washington locker room, "and time and again they've scored after us to beat us. After we got ahead today, we were aware this was a 60-minute game." The roaring crowd at RFK made sure the 'Skins didn't forget it. "We could feel the ground trembling down on the sidelines," exclaimed George Allen, who said the fans "were worth at least 3 points."

Jurgensen, normally the first to leave the dressing room to avoid reporters' questions, continued talking, his ruddy face shining with satisfaction. "I can't think of a more gratifying win than this one, I really can't. We finally got around to getting it together, and did what we started out to do. It's something we worked hard for." Then Sonny told the assembled sportswriters something he had never dared state in public before, something he had waited 16 years to say: "We're going to be champions."

He never said it again. The following week on his first pass of the game, Jurgensen somehow misstepped and tore his Achilles tendon to shreds. For Sonny Jurgensen, the quest for the 1972 championship was over.

Paul Fine Photo/Nate Fine Productions, Courtesy Washington Redskins

I LIKE BILLY

NFC Championship Game

Dallas Cowboys vs. Washington Redskins

December 31, 1972

5 3,129 excited fans arrived at RFK Stadium with one purpose in mind: to spur their beloved Washington Redskins to victory over the hated Dallas Cowboys in the 1972 NFC Championship game. After enduring 30 years of athletic mediocrity (and worse), Washington fans were determined to help the Redskins defeat the defending Super Bowl champions with the only weapon at their disposal—noise.

Before the kickoff, there was the usual amount of booing and cursing as the Cowboys were introduced. Then, as 53,000 anxious faces turned toward the Senators' old home dugout in search of a flash of Burgundy and Gold, the cheering began to build. When the clamor reached a roaring crescendo, Charley Taylor, the captain of the Redskins, bounded up the dugout steps and ran onto the field. Like a thunderclap, the pent-up frustrations from those 30 years of losing exploded from the throats of the crowd and rained down on the Washington Redskins as, one by one, they streamed to the center of the field.

Although it couldn't be heard above the incredible din, the last name called on the public address system belonged to Head Coach George Allen, the master motivator of the Redskins, who, for the past week, had been building a fire in his team's heart. With the tumultuous ovation acting like gasoline, that fire erupted into a full blaze. Not that he needed it, but quarterback Billy Kilmer had an extra source of inspiration. "Tom Landry said I was a good leader, but not a great quarterback," growled the husky-voiced Kilmer. "He said that I was not as good an athlete as Staubach. Dammit, that fired me up! I've been up all week."

George Allen, of course, had been fired up all season. Dedicated only to victory, Allen and his coaching staff had not taken a single day off since the beginning of training camp on July 5th. The Redskins had torn through their schedule, at one point winning nine in a row, and finished as Eastern Division champions with an 11-3 record. Having disposed of the Green Bay Packers, 16-3, in the first round of the playoffs, the Redskins were now only one victory away from Super Bowl VII. And because Washington's arch-enemy, the Dallas Cowboys, blocked its path to glory, this NFC Championship game had turned into a crusade. As he gathered his team around him, every fiber of George Allen's being resonated in harmony with the torrent of sound that cascaded from the heights of RFK Stadium. "Just remember this," shouted Allen, "forty men together can't lose!"

D allas' Toni Fritsch kicked off to the wild-eyed Washington Redskins. Like a boxer going for the midsection, Billy Kilmer struck first at the center

Billy Kilmer *Ron Ross/NFL Photos*

of the Cowboys' zone defense with a 15-yard pass to Roy Jefferson. Then Kilmer, by his own admission "the king of the wobbly passers," rifled a rare spiral to his other wide receiver, Charley Taylor, who caught it over the middle for another first down. The Redskins looked strong as they drove to the Cowboys 37, but Larry Brown fumbled a swing pass and Dallas took over at its 30.

The Cowboys offense trotted confidently onto the field, led once again by their great quarterback, Roger Staubach, who had missed the entire regular season with a shoulder injury. While Staubach was recuperating, veteran Craig Morton had guided the team to a 10-4 record. But, in the first round of the playoffs against the San Francisco 49ers, Morton had faltered. With the Cowboys trailing, 28-13, late in the fourth quarter, Dallas Coach Tom Landry sent in Staubach, and the former Heisman Trophy-winner from Navy reached into his deep bag of tricks and pulled out an amazing 30-28 Cowboys victory. After that performance, Landry had no choice but to start Staubach against the Redskins in the Championship game.

Normally, a crowd at a football game produces a drone that surges and planes in response to the action, never getting really loud until something exciting occurs. However, on that warm and cloudy afternoon on the last day of 1972, 53,000 crazed rooters at RFK Stadium took it upon themselves to play a leading, rather than supporting, role. Realizing the importance of preventing the Cowboys from jumping out to a quick lead, the fans turned up the volume right from the start. When Staubach was tackled a foot short of a first down on Dallas' first series, they screamed as if the Redskins had made a fourth-quarter goal-line stand with the outcome of the game on the line.

The Cowboys offense was clearly rattled, but their defense was just as dominating as Washington's, so several punts were exchanged. However, late in the first quarter, Kilmer began to solve the Dallas defensive puzzle. Starting at their 27, the Redskins controlled the ball for over 9 minutes while running on 13 of 17 plays. After giving up 62 yards, the Cowboys' Doomsday Defense finally stood its ground at the 11, and Washington placekicker Curt Knight ran onto the field. After leading the NFL in scoring the year before, Knight had stumbled badly in 1972, missing 16 of 30 field goals during the regular season. His problems had begun in the final moments of a wild early-season game against the New England Patriots in which he missed two field goals, allowing the lowly Patriots to upset the 'Skins, 24-23. Unforgiving Redskins fans booed Knight unmercifully on his subsequent failures, and Curt's confidence and success rate plummeted.

Ironically, the turning point for Knight came on another failure. Against the Green Bay Packers at home in the eleventh game, Curt tried a 51-yard field goal that hit the center of the crossbar and bounced back onto the field. Knight braced himself for the boos, but the fans at RFK recognized how well he had kicked the ball and gave him a heart-warming round of applause instead. From then on, Knight was a changed man, even tying a post-season record by kicking three field goals against those same Packers in the first round of the playoffs. So, midway through the second quarter of the Championship game, it was a mentally healthy Curt Knight who rammed his toe squarely into the ball at the 18 and sent it spinning through the uprights to give the Washington Redskins a 3-0 lead over the Dallas Cowboys. [Fig. 72]

Fig. 72   *Richard Darcey/Washington Post Photo*

Diron Talbert (72) pressuring Roger Staubach *Matthew Lewis/Washington Post Photo*

After the Cowboys failed to make a first down and punted back to the 'Skins, Billy Kilmer decided to break away from his conservative play-calling. "If I can get Charley Taylor, or anyone, one-on-one, I'll take it," said Kilmer. "They were giving me strong-side coverage [on Jefferson] and leaving Charley one-on-one. We felt we could throw that way. We wanted to pick on the weakest man. It's nothing against Waters so much as we didn't want to go to the other side against Mel Renfro. He can make the big play." So could Charley Taylor. On third and 10 from the Redskins 28, Taylor streaked by cornerback Charlie Waters and caught Kilmer's perfectly thrown 51-yard bomb over his shoulder at the Cowboys 21. "I had Taylor well-covered," said Waters, "but he just outran me . . . Taylor is just a great receiver, the best in the league, and it was a great pass by Kilmer." Three plays later, Billy led Taylor perfectly again on a 15-yard slant, and Charley grabbed the ball at the goal line for a touchdown! As 53,000 Redskins fans celebrated with a raucous rendition of *Hail to the Redskins*, Knight added the extra point to boost the Skins' lead to 10-0.

Finally, after 24 minutes of play, the Cowboys earned their initial first down of the game when Washington defensive tackle Diron Talbert sacked Roger Staubach a little too roughly. On the next play, "Roger the Dodger" hoodwinked the 'Skins with a naked reverse around right end that picked up 29 yards to the Washington 39. After another Dallas first down, fullback Calvin Hill, the finest practitioner of the option pass since Paul Hornung, spotted half-back Walt Garrison all alone in the end zone—but overthrew him. Had Hill completed that pass, Dallas would have been out of the hole; as it was, the Cowboys soon sputtered to a halt at the Washington 28. Toni Fritsch's 35-yard field goal attempt needed a friendly carom off the left upright, but it made it through and, with 2½ minutes remaining in the half, the Cowboys trailed, 10-3.

Four plays later, Dallas regained possession and moved quickly to the Washington 16. With 2 seconds on the clock, Fritsch blew a 23-yard field goal, the first time in his career that he had missed inside the 30. Buoyed by the unexpected gift, the Washington

Redskins clattered happily into their locker room with a 10-3 halftime lead and the complete approval of 53,000 True Believers.

The third quarter evolved into a test of wills similar to an arm wrestling contest between evenly matched opponents. Midway through the period, Dallas missed an opportunity to gain the upper hand when Redskins quarterback Billy Kilmer, on third and 1 at the Washington 31, fumbled as he was pulling away from center. Three Cowboys—Cornell Green, Charlie Waters, and Lee Roy Jordan—had chances to capture the squirming ball but failed. Finally, Washington tight end Jerry Smith recovered at the 18, and, on the next play, Mike Bragg punted out of danger.

Dallas Coach Tom Landry inserted Olympic sprint champion Bob Hayes to loosen up the pressing Washington defenders. The Cowboys sent Bullet Bob on a deep fly pattern, but Redskins cornerback Mike Bass blanketed him and tipped the pass away at the last moment. Having gained only 23 yards during the entire third quarter, the frustrated Cowboys punted back to Washington again.

Needing a replacement for cornerback Charlie Waters, who had injured his shoulder, Tom Landry passed over aging all-pro Herb Adderley in favor of 25-year-old Mark Washington. Kilmer immediately went to work on the new man in the Dallas secondary, completing three passes in a row. On third and 6 at the Washington 48, Kilmer drilled the ball to Taylor, who made a spectacular grab at the Dallas 45 to give the surging Redskins another first down. A moment later, the third period ended with Washington still in the lead, 10-3.

On the second play of the fourth quarter, Charley Taylor lined up on the right side of a spread formation. At the snap, Taylor exploded off the line, evaded linebacker D.D. Lewis, and sprinted down the sideline with a one-step lead on Mark Washington. His eyes riveted to the streaking Taylor, Billy Kilmer dropped behind his protective pocket and heaved the ball as far as he could. A beautiful spiral arced toward Taylor as he raced toward the goal line. From the stands, the pass appeared to have been overthrown, but Taylor turned on the afterburners, stretched out his arms, and grabbed the ball at the goal line as Mark Washington leapt at his heels in vain! Touchdown! [Fig. 74]

53,000 prayers had accompanied that pass, and 53,000 voices rang out in thanksgiving as it settled in Taylor's arms. When Charley slowly raised both arms over his head in his customary silent gesture ("I rest my case"), the roaring fans went completely berserk. Kilmer ran exuberantly off the field, both hands punching the air. With that pass, Billy had finally won the hearts of even the most devoted Jurgensen fans, who, until that moment, had withheld the affection and respect he had craved. And deserved.

Washington 17, Dallas 3.

Only 14 minutes remained for Roger Staubach to attempt another miraculous comeback. With the delirious mob at RFK howling full blast, Staubach tried to crank up the stalled Cowboys offense, but Washington's psyched-up defense was waiting for him. First, linebacker Chris Hanburger made an outstanding play by hurdling a blocker and sacking Staubach at the 23; then safety Rosie Taylor mugged fullback Calvin Hill, causing a fumble that Ron McDole pounced on at the Dallas 38. Pandemonium swept through the stands as the fans, like sharks in a feeding frenzy, smelled blood. A minute later, Knight solidified the Redskins' position with a 39-yard field goal, making the score 20-3, Washington.

Volley after volley of cheers rained down as the

Fig. 74   *Richard Darcey/Washington Post Photo*

Redskins defense kept the Cowboys bottled up deep in their territory on their next two possessions. Both times, Knight followed with a field goal (giving him a playoff-record four on the day) to drive the final nails into Dallas' coffin. On the Washington sideline, the two longest-serving Redskins, Len Hauss and Charley Taylor, stared intently into each other's eyes, not having to say a word to convey their feelings of pride and accomplishment. The exultant crowd counted off the final seconds, then poured onto the field to rejoice with their heroes, forming an impromptu cortege for George Allen as he was carried off the field in triumph.

Washington 26, Dallas 3.

The 30-year drought was over. The surprisingly one-sided victory gave Washington its first championship of any kind since 1942, when the Redskins defeated the Chicago Bears, 14-6. Former Redskins tackle Fran O'Brien spoke for millions of fans when he said, "I'm finally, finally in the right place after all these years!"

Just about everything had worked for the 'Skins, both on offense and defense. Dallas' perennial all-pro defensive tackle, Bob Lilly, graciously gave "credit to the Redskins; they did a hell of a job. A hell of a job!" Washington's defenders completely frustrated the Cowboys' rushing attack (just 37 yards between Garrison and Hill) while allowing Dallas to convert

Richard Darcey/Washington Post Photo

on only 3 of 12 third-down plays. In addition, Roger Staubach was sacked three times and harassed relentlessly while completing only 9 of 20 passes for 98 yards.

The Redskins offense finished with a flourish, scoring on six of its last nine possessions. Halfback Larry Brown contributed 104 yards on 30 carries and two pass receptions, while Charley Taylor, with seven catches for 146 yards and two TD's, enjoyed one of his best days ever. Billy Kilmer's success was reflected in his nearly perfect numbers—14 of 18 for 194 yards, two touchdowns, and no interceptions. Blackie Sherrod of the *Dallas Times Herald* saw it this way: "The Cowboys got Kilmer exactly where they wanted him, only to discover it was not Kilmer they were facing at all; it was Sammy Baugh in his golden prime. In all, Kilmer hit on 14 of his 18 passes. No hero in history, not Baugh, nor Unitas, nor Graham, nor Layne, has ever completed such a high percentage in a playoff game."

Above the pandemonium in the Redskins locker room, George Allen shouted, "Now we've got to have three cheers for the Redskins!," and his happy players responded unabashedly. Then Allen became serious as he pointed out that "winning in Washington means more than in other places . . . the fans have had enough losses."

As a light rain began to fall in the gathering darkness, the exhausted fans, reluctant to leave the site where their long-held dream of a championship had finally been fulfilled, shuffled slowly out of RFK Stadium. Trying to engrave the moment in their memories, they kept looking back to the field—and to the scoreboard. The evidence that their dream had become a reality was still there:

REDSKINS 26, COWBOYS 3

THE TACKLE

Dallas Cowboys vs. Washington Redskins

October 8, 1973

Two weeks after achieving their greatest victory in 30 years, the high-flying Washington Redskins crashed in Los Angeles on January 14, 1973. The Redskins went into Super Bowl VII so tightly wound they could only spin their wheels, and the undefeated Miami Dolphins swept past them for a lackluster 14-7 victory. One play typified the Redskins' frustration. Trailing 14-0, the 'Skins mounted an 83-yard drive to the Dolphins 6. On third and 2, tight end Jerry Smith got wide open in the Miami end zone, and quarterback Billy Kilmer threw him the ball. There was only one problem—the pass hit the goal post!

"Never saw anything like it in my career," said Kilmer. "I remember turning to [referee] Tommy Bell right after that happened and him saying: 'Not going real good, is it?' Then I come back and throw an interception to Jake Scott." Altogether, Kilmer threw three interceptions, and, with the Dolphins defense laying in wait for halfback Larry Brown, the Redskins offense was stymied all afternoon. The most honest assessment of Washington's performance came from offensive tackle Terry Hermeling, who simply said, "We laid an egg."

When the team reconvened for training camp in Carlisle in the summer of 1973, George Allen was again faced with the dilemma of who to pick as his starting quarterback. The people's choice, Sonny Jurgensen, was healthy again after working hard during the off-season to rehabilitate his Achilles tendon. He desperately wanted another shot at the championship, the only jewel missing from his crown of achievement. Coach Allen could not deny that the 39-year-old Jurgensen had the superior arm, but he also could not ignore the fact that Kilmer had led the Redskins to the Super Bowl and earned the respect of his teammates and opposing defenses. Just as he had done in 1972, Allen went with Billy at the start of the season, then switched to Jurgensen after the Redskins were upset by the St. Louis Cardinals in the second game of the year.

With Kilmer at quarterback in those first two games, the Redskins had rushed for 83 and 69 yards, meager sums for a team that lived by the run. Halfback Larry Brown, the NFC's leading rusher and Most Valuable Player in 1972, had been hampered by painful leg injuries yet continued to start despite the arrival of Duane Thomas. A standout halfback with the Cowboys who had starred in Super Bowl VI, the enigmatic Thomas was traded to San Diego after calling Coach Tom Landry a "plastic man." The Chargers were not able to motivate Thomas either, so they shipped him to Washington, where he had yet to show any sign of spirit or effort. Nevertheless, with

Jurgensen in the lineup, opposing defenses had to honor the Redskins' passing game to such an extent that Brown had regained the extra fraction of a second he needed to get around the corner.

In the off-season, George Allen had acquired two more veteran players, Dave Robinson and Ken Houston, to fill vacancies in Washington's solid, but aging, defense. Robinson, who took over for retired left linebacker Jack Pardee, had been a star on Vince Lombardi's legendary Packers teams. Now in the twilight of his outstanding career, Robinson was acquired as a stopgap measure, but Houston, who became the 'Skins' strong safety after Rosie Taylor retired, was in his prime. Otherwise, the Redskins were the same team that had demolished the Dallas Cowboys in the 1972 NFC Championship game.

Despite that embarrassing defeat, Cowboys Coach Tom Landry knew there was no need for a major overhaul of his veteran team. On offense, two rookies, fullback Robert Newhouse and tight end Billy Joe DuPree, had moved into starting positions and were adding extra punch to a strong Dallas attack led by quarterback Roger Staubach and the NFC's #1 rusher, Calvin Hill. The only change on defense was the promotion of D.D. Lewis to starting linebacker following the retirement of Chuck Howley. "The young guys have added a spark to this team," said cornerback Charlie Waters. "Maybe we're not as polished, but we are a lot closer."

More and more, games between the Redskins and Cowboys were taking on the tense atmosphere of Roman gladiator battles in which the losers REALLY lost. During Dallas Week, short tempers and long practices were the norm at Redskin Park. "I don't really like to talk to anybody the week before the Dallas game," admitted ex-Cowboys guard John Wilbur. "I even find it hard to communicate with my wife."

Obsession with victory was not limited to George Allen's Redskins. After their humiliating defeat in the NFC Championship game, the Cowboys had spent the entire off-season plotting their revenge. To goad his team, Coach Landry had hung a plaque in the Dallas locker room that featured a replica of a Redskins helmet and the inscription: "WASHINGTON REDSKINS, 1972 NFC CHAMPIONS." The 3-0 Cowboys knew that the only way to remove that plaque was to displace the 2-1 Redskins as NFC champs. "We think about the Redskins every day," said Rayfield Wright, Dallas' massive right offensive tackle. "I don't know if that's good or bad. But that's the way it is. The Redskins game is everything. We're on top now. We can't afford to go down."

Neither could the Washington Redskins.

Before the advent of ABC's Monday Night Football in 1970, bleary-eyed fans traditionally used Monday evenings to catch up on lost sleep. Now they were obliged to extend their bleariness until Tuesday. The popular prime-time show employed three announcers: steady Frank Gifford, humorous Don Meredith, and bombastic Howard Cosell. Although sports fans loved to hate Cosell & Co.—contest-winners in taverns across America got to throw bricks at Cosell's image on the screen—enough of them tuned in each week to make the show a bona fide hit. The main reason for the show's popularity, though, was the consistent quality of competition. ABC had been uncanny in its scheduling of matchups that always seemed to produce a thrilling finish. A Redskins-Cowboys game was a natural for Monday night.

Forced to wait an extra 30 hours for their football fix, 54,314 impatient fans at RFK Stadium vented their pent-up excitement as the Redskins were introduced. On Dallas' opening possession, special teams ace Bill Malinchak touched off an explosion of cheers when he blocked Marv Bateman's punt at the Cowboys 38. [Fig. 76] The excited crowd welcomed Sonny Jurgensen onto the field with urgent pleas for a quick touchdown, but Dallas was ready for him. Defensive end Pat Toomay sacked Jurgensen for an 11-yard loss, then, on fourth down, deflected Curt Knight's 53-yard field goal attempt.

The Cowboys took over at their 22 and, after three unproductive plays, got a break when Washington's Bob Brunet was called for roughing the punter. Given a second chance, Staubach fired a 21-yard pass to rookie tight end Billy Joe DuPree at the Washington 44. Then on third and 7, Staubach escaped the Red-

Fig. 76   *Matthew Lewis/Washington Post Photo*

skins' pass rush and scrambled for 9 yards. After full-back Calvin Hill rushed for another first down at the Washington 19, Redskins defensive tackle Bill Brundige chased down Staubach for an 11-yard loss, forcing the Cowboys to settle for a field goal attempt. Placekicker Toni Fritsch sank his foot into the ball at the 40, but Ron "Dancing Bear" McDole got a paw on the ball and, after Speedy Duncan recovered for

Washington at its 12, the Redskins' kick-coverage team ran off the field to an uproarious standing ovation.

Midway through the second quarter, Dallas began to march again. Calvin Hill galloped 31 yards on five carries, and wide receiver Otto Stowe caught two passes for 34 more. On the 19th play of the drive, Staubach went back to Stowe, who made a diving catch in the end zone for a 15-yard touchdown. Toni

Fritsch converted, and the Cowboys led, 7-0, with 49 seconds left in the half.

Speedy Duncan returned Fritsch's kickoff 38 yards to the Redskins 43, and Jurgensen quickly worked the ball to the Dallas 37. Unfortunately, Curt Knight pushed his 44-yard field goal attempt to the right (his ninth miss in his last twelve attempts), and the boo-birds at RFK serenaded him unmercifully as the first half came to an end. Dallas 7, Washington 0.

The Cowboys had dominated the first half, racking up thirteen first downs while limiting Washington to three, and the Redskins knew they were fortunate to be trailing by only a touchdown. As the second half got underway, it looked as if that pattern would continue. Fullback Calvin Hill, who had gained 62 yards in 12 carries in the first half, shredded the Redskins defense with runs of 18 and 8 yards as the Cowboys rolled to the Washington 16. However, two quarterback sacks ruined Dallas' plans for a touchdown, and Fritsch came in for a 38-yard field goal attempt. Amazingly, defensive end Verlon Biggs broke through the line and batted the ball away — the third blocked kick of the night for the 'Skins!

With 5 minutes left in the third quarter, Herb Mul-Key got the demoralized crowd re-excited with a 27-yard punt return to the Cowboys 40. Jurgensen passed for a first down. Then Brown and Harraway ran for another at the Dallas 19. But two plays later, Pat Toomay sacked Jurgensen for an 11-yard loss, and the Redskins had to call on Curt Knight to try a 30-yard field goal. He missed.

Although Washington's disgruntled fans were quickly losing faith, the Redskins defense never quit. On third and 3 at the Washington 27, Verlon Biggs and Bill Brundige sacked Staubach for the sixth time in the game, and Marv Bateman punted again. On the last play of the third quarter, Sonny Jurgensen unloaded a 36-yard bomb to Roy Jefferson at the Dallas 28. Then, with the help of a few penalties, the 'Skins moved to the Dallas 10, where they faced third and 1. Jurgy handed off to Brown. No gain. Fourth and 1. Unwilling to give Knight another chance to deflate the team's morale, Allen ordered Jurgensen to go for the first down. Fullback Charley Harraway

plowed into the Doomsday Defense, but was stopped short and the Redskins trudged off the field looking whipped.

Nine-year veteran Craig Morton took over for Roger Staubach, who had developed a severe charley horse in his leg. Continuing its heroic work, the Washington defense forced another punt, which Speedy Duncan returned 12 yards to the Redskins 43. Sonny Jurgensen then showed why he was still considered one of the most dangerous passers in the game. Two strikes to Charley Taylor gained 24 yards. Then Jurgy hit Larry Brown coming out of the backfield for 9 yards and Roy Jefferson for 3 more. From the Dallas 18, Sonny threw to Taylor in the end zone. The pass fell incomplete, but Charley drew an interference penalty, and the 'Skins had a first-and-goal at the 1! With the crowd on its feet, Larry Brown tried twice to squeeze into the end zone, but was nailed at the line both times. On third down, Jurgensen took one step back and lobbed the ball to Charley Taylor, who leapt and grabbed it in the corner of the end zone! Touchdown, Washington! Knight kicked the extra point, and, with 3:39 remaining on the clock, the score was deadlocked, 7-7.

After the kickoff, Craig Morton decided to take a chance. On third and 9 at his 19, Morton aimed a pass for Billy Joe DuPree in the right flat. Redskins defensive back Brig Owens, playing possum a few yards behind DuPree, made his move just as Morton released the ball. Cutting in front of DuPree, Owens intercepted the pass in full stride [Fig. 77] and dashed 26 yards into the end zone holding the ball aloft as 54,000 fans went crazy. Knight hit the extra point, and the Redskins went on top, 14-7!

Dallas returned the kickoff to its 27 with 2:30 left in the game. The Washington defense steeled itself for a furious onslaught by the Cowboys, but Morton was wild on three straight passes and Bateman had to punt again. Unable to field the punt safely, deep man Herb Mul-Key wisely backed away, content to let the ball roll dead. Suddenly, the ball took a crazy bounce and glanced off a Redskins blocker, making it a free ball, and Dallas' Mark Washington recovered on the Redskins 32! A stadium full of celebrating fans were stunned into silence.

Fig. 77   *Nate Fine Photo/Nate Fine Productions, Courtesy Washington Redskins*

After checking with Staubach to see if he could play, Landry reluctantly left Morton in the game. With the crowd shouting all around them, the exhausted Washington defenders braced themselves for one last effort. Two minutes remained as Morton passed to DuPree for a first down at the 21. The Cowboys netted only 1 yard on their next three plays, but, on fourth down, Morton nailed Walt Garrison with a 17-yard strike over the middle for a first down at the Washington 4. With 33 seconds remaining, the Cowboys took their final time-out. On first down, Morton misfired to Garrison, then couldn't connect with Stowe on his next two throws. That made it fourth and goal at the Washington 4 with 24 seconds left in the game.

Morton took the snap and rolled to his right. As defensive end Ron McDole charged toward him, Morton pumped once, then threw to Walt Garrison, who jumped slightly as he caught the ball at the goal line. In that same instant, strong safety Ken Houston rammed his right shoulder into Garrison's back, grabbed his waist, and whirled him around. [Fig. 78] As Garrison spun around, there was a critical moment when he could have reached out and broken the plane of the goal with the ball. Instead, he tried to bull his way in, churning his legs to get trac-

Fig. 78   Ken Houston and Walt Garrison fight it out at the goal line
Paul Fine Photo/Nate Fine Productions, Courtesy Washington Redskins

Fig. 79   *Copyright Washington Post; Reprinted by permission of the D.C. Public Library*

tion. [Fig. 79] With a final tug, Houston yanked him away from the goal line. In desperation, Garrison lateraled the ball as he was going down, but there was nobody there to catch it. The ball bounced around maddeningly, squirting through several Cowboys' hands before finally coming to rest under a pile of exultant Redskins. Final score: Washington 14, Dallas 7.

"I don't think we've ever had a team that showed more character than tonight," proclaimed Coach George Allen in Washington's boisterous locker room. "We're so proud of the Redskins. And what a game for the nation to see!" In truth, it was the defense's night, especially the secondary's, as they limited Staubach and Morton to just 13 completions in 31 attempts for 132 yards. Moreover, free safety Brig Owens scored the winning touchdown, and strong safety Ken Houston made the game-winning tackle. "That was the biggest tackle I've made in my life," acknowledged Houston. "I was looking for that play. They had been trying to hit that flare all night. I lined up on the goal line. Morton made a pump and I came up as soon as he threw it. I knew exactly where Garrison was and exactly where I was. As strong as Garrison is, I thought he would score, but I managed to keep him out."

Managed, indeed. More accurately, Ken Houston had just made the greatest tackle in the entire history of the Washington Redskins.

RETURN TO FORM

New York Giants vs. Washington Redskins

December 2, 1973

It took George Allen three years to utterly transform the Washington Redskins from a high-scoring loser into a low-scoring winner. Allen's game plans minimized the chance of mistakes but, unfortunately for fans, also minimized the chances of scoring and excitement. Instead of waging risky, crowd-pleasing passing shows, the Redskins tended to convert turnovers and field position into field goals and short-range touchdowns. But Allen could get away with his cautiousness on offense because his defense was the best in the conference. Leading the NFC in interceptions (23), sacks (48), touchdowns scored on turnovers (6), blocked punts (3), blocked field goals (3), and fewest points allowed per game (11.5), the Redskins defense deserved most of the credit for the team's division-leading 8-3 record.

With Ron McDole, Bill Brundige, Diron Talbert, and Verlon Biggs on the defensive line; Dave Robinson, Myron Pottios, and Chris Hanburger at linebacker; and Pat Fischer, Mike Bass, Brig Owens, and Ken Houston in the secondary, the Redskins defense smothered opponents with its combination of savvy, strength, and skill. One player simply looked so intimidating that his job was half done before he ever went out onto the field. "Through that face mask," said Billy Kilmer, "Verlon Biggs actually scared me. You can talk about Dick Butkus and some of the others all you want, but Biggs (6-foot-4 and 275 pounds) was the meanest-looking guy I'd ever seen. First time I saw him with the Redskins was in training camp, about midnight. He's coming down the hall with two Dobermans and two gals. I'm roomin' by myself, and peek out the door to see what all the commotion is about. There's Verlon. With those girls and those dogs. Taking up the entire hall. I slammed the door shut, locked it, and put some furniture in front of it. Scared me to death."

While Coach Allen encouraged his defense to play with aggressiveness and flair, he kept his offense under wraps. In fact, the strength of the Redskins defense camouflaged the weakness of the offense. With Sonny Jurgensen sidelined with bad knees, Billy Kilmer had once again taken over the quarterbacking duties. But Kilmer was far from healthy himself, suffering from an intestinal blockage that would put him into the hospital three times before the season was over. In addition, Billy was still hampered by chronic pain in his right ankle stemming from a car accident in 1962 that had nearly cost him his leg. But Billy Kilmer was a winner, a gritty leader whom hard men respected. Kilmer compensated for his imprecise passing with sure ball-handling, enthusiasm, clever play-calling, and courage. And a knack for victory, which was all that George Allen cared about.

Verlon Biggs (89), Diron Talbert, Bill Brundige (77), Pat Fischer (37), and Ron McDole (79)
Copyright Washington Post; Reprinted by permission of the D.C. Public Library

Even though the first-place Redskins were leading the Dallas Cowboys by one game as the 1973 season neared completion, there were signs of slippage from their Super Bowl form of the year before. In midseason, an embarrassing 19-3 defeat at the hands of the New Orleans Saints was followed by a 21-16 loss to the Pittsburgh Steelers. The 'Skins rebounded with three straight victories but, with only three games left, could not afford another letdown. "At this point in the season, every game is a must game for us," said Kilmer. "If we fail now, it's all over. It's a pressure situation, and we know it."

Based on past performance, it appeared that Washington's next opponent, the New York Giants, would be a pushover. Racked with dissension and injuries, New York's inconsistent play had produced a conference-following 2-8-1 record. The Giants were so laughably woebegone that even their home games were away games; while awaiting the completion of their new stadium in suburban New Jersey, the Giants were playing their "home" games at the Yale Bowl in New Haven, Connecticut.

Accordingly, the Redskins were made 14-point favorites to beat the New Yorkers for the ninth consecutive time. And, as usual, George Allen's biggest concern was that his team might be looking past the Giants to the critical rematch with the Cowboys a week later. "You'd think they wouldn't," fretted Allen. "You'd think they'd learned their lesson [in earlier losses to the Saints and Cardinals, both lightly regarded], but I'm worried they might be looking ahead."

Verlon Biggs sacking former teammate Joe Namath in critical 35-17 victory over Jets on Nov. 5, 1972
Paul Fine Photo/Nate Fine Productions, Courtesy Washington Redskins

Like middle-aged men trying to recapture their youth, the New York Giants and Washington Redskins renewed their 40-year-old rivalry at Robert F. Kennedy Stadium by trying to dazzle each other. The Redskins drew first blood. Billy Kilmer completed a 19-yard strike to Roy Jefferson and a 25-yarder to halfback Larry Brown as the 'Skins marched steadily to the New York 5. Unfortunately, Brown dropped a certain touchdown pass in the end zone, so Washington had to settle for Curt Knight's 12-yard field goal and a 3-0 lead. The Giants retaliated with a smooth, 80-yard excursion into the Redskins' end zone. Along the way, quarterback Randy Johnson completed five passes for 63 yards, and, on the sixteenth play of the drive, halfback Ron Johnson plunged into the end zone from the 3. Pete Gogolak's extra point gave the Giants a 7-3 lead.

On the ensuing kickoff, Speedy Duncan fumbled, and New York recovered at the 'Skins 28. Three plays later, Johnson fired a 12-yard touchdown pass to tight end Bob Tucker, and 53,590 Redskins fans squirmed in their seats as the scoreboard recorded the Giants' 14-3 advantage. Soon after the second quarter began, the crowd really got testy when Billy Kilmer threw an interception to linebacker Jim Files, who returned the ball to the Washington 23. On second and 12, Randy Johnson faked an end-around, then lobbed a short pass to Ron Johnson, who raced untouched into the end zone to inflate New York's lead to 21-3.

Washington continued to flounder but, near the end of the half, finally got a much-needed break when defensive tackle Bill Brundige recovered a Ron Johnson fumble at the New York 17. Halfback Larry Brown carried the ball five straight times and finally scored from the 3 to narrow the gap to 21-10. Brown's touchdown dispelled the team's mounting frustration, and Washington's defense quickly forced the Giants to punt. On first down from his 35, Kilmer threw deep to Charley Taylor, who caught the 53-yard bomb at the New York 12. The fans at RFK roared their approval, but the Redskins offense self-destructed and Curt Knight had to salvage 3 points with a 17-yard field goal. Trailing 21-13, the 'Skins headed for their dressing room with a smattering of boos echoing through the otherwise silent stadium.

Although his 4-for-12 passing had not been solely to blame for the Redskins' woeful performance in the first half, Billy Kilmer was the easiest target toward whom cranky (and fickle) fans could direct their displeasure. On Washington's first series of the third quarter, Kilmer silenced his critics by passing sharply to Charley Taylor for 15 yards and to Jerry Smith for 17 more. On the next play, a mixup in the backfield resulted in an unplanned quarterback draw. With no one to hand off to, Kilmer ran 5 yards upfield before two New York linebackers crashed into him. Billy limped back to the huddle with a sprained left ankle, but, although he tried to continue, the pain was too much. Recognizing his courage, the same fans who had booed Kilmer just minutes before now cheered him as he hobbled to the sideline. In his place, another gimpy-legged quarterback shuffled onto the field—Sonny Jurgensen.

A tremendous ovation greeted Jurgensen, who, because of knee problems, had sat out the last six games. Many fans assumed Sonny would step right in and immediately recapture the form that had made him the most feared passer in the National Football League. But at 39, out of practice and with a sore knee, the odds were stacked against Number 9. Not surprisingly, Sonny's first pass fell incomplete. And his second. Finally, with 2 minutes left in the third quarter, Jurgy got his first completion on a 5-yard pass to Jerry Smith, but the 'Skins still couldn't get past midfield.

At the start of the fourth quarter, the Giants recovered another fumble by punt-returner Speedy Duncan, and Pete Gogolak kicked a 22-yard field goal to increase their lead to 24-13. 12:42 remained in the game when the Redskins got the ball back at their 23. After a short pass and a holding penalty gave Washington a first down at its 35, Sonny Jurgensen stopped calling the safe, conservative plays that had taken the Redskins nowhere all afternoon and started winging it. A 5-yard pass to Charley Taylor was followed by a 14-yard strike to Smith and a 15-yard bullet to Jefferson at the Giants 31. The crowd started to come back to life as Jurgensen threw over the middle to Larry Brown, who broke four tackles on his way to a 20-yard gain to the Giants 9. Brown

Unable to move out of harm's way, Sonny Jurgensen uses his quick release to complete another pass
Paul Fine Photo/Nate Fine Productions, Courtesy Washington Redskins

limped back to the huddle but, one play later, sliced through the center of New York's defense to score from 6 yards out. The 77-yard touchdown drive, featuring five straight completions by Jurgensen, put the Redskins within striking distance of the Giants at 24-20.

With 53,000 Redskins fans lending vocal support, Washington's defense shut down New York's offense in three plays, and the 'Skins took over at their 34. In the Redskins' huddle, nobody said a word except Sonny Jurgensen. Given time to throw by his determined offensive line, Jurgensen continued his streak, completing passes to Roy Jefferson for 6 and 12 yards. However, rookie tackle George Starke got flagged for holding, and the Redskins faced a discouraging second-and-22 from their 45. Mindful of the Giants' deep coverage, Jurgensen threw short to fullback Charley Harraway, who charged up the middle for 21 yards. After Brown picked up the remaining yard on the next play, the 'Skins were back on track. On first and 10 at the Giants 33, Sonny hit Jefferson for 15 yards, then Harraway for 2 more. From his 16, Jurgensen dropped back and spotted Larry Brown getting open over the middle. Sonny zipped the ball to Brown at the 5, and Larry lunged into the end zone for his third touchdown of the day! [Fig. 83]

Now leading 27-24, Coach Allen entrusted his defense with the task of making the amazing comeback stick in the final 4 minutes. His trust was well placed. The Giants could not muster a single first down and punted back to Washington at the Redskins 3. Aware that a fumble could cost them the game, Charley Harraway and Larry Brown gained 9

Fig. 83   *Paul Fine/NFL Photos*

yards on two determined carries. After the Giants took their second time-out with 1:31 left in the game, Coach Alex Webster sent in his biggest defenders to stop what he assumed would be a running play on third and 1. Sure enough, after conferring with George Allen and offensive coordinator Ted Marchibroda on the sideline, Jurgensen called Larry Brown's number again. Needing a single yard to ice the game, the gallant halfback threw his exhausted body into the line once more. Brown, the eternal over-achiever, gained 7 yards, and the battered Redskins limped off the field, 27-24 winners.

"Every play was critical," said Charley Harraway in the locker room after the game. "Every man knew what he had to do. We were so keyed up, there were no mistakes to be made. No one had to say a thing." With the game on the line in the fourth quarter, Sonny Jurgensen had completed eleven straight passes as the 'Skins drove 77 yards and 66 yards for consecutive touchdowns. Sonny's accuracy (12-15 for 135 yards and one TD) was matched by Larry Brown's fortitude. "I was hurt before the game—a floating rib, ligaments, bruises," said Brown, who rushed 18 times for 71 yards and caught three passes for 61 more. "Every time I had contact it was painful. I was hurting considerably in the first half. But at some point in the game I just put it in the back of my mind and said 'The hell with it.' You have to play that way."

Men like Sonny Jurgensen, Billy Kilmer, and Larry Brown didn't know any other way to play.

SWAN SONG

Miami Dolphins vs. Washington Redskins

October 13, 1974

The long-awaited announcement came on Tuesday in the fifth week of the 1974 season. Sonny Jurgensen would start at quarterback against the Miami Dolphins! As the news rocketed around town, members of the "I Like Sonny" club rejoiced that Coach George Allen had finally concluded that the Washington Redskins simply were a more dangerous team with the 40-year-old Jurgensen at quarterback.

Billy Kilmer—despite the fact that he ranked first in the NFC in passing and had led Washington to playoff berths in 1971, '72, and '73—had played inconsistently in 1974. The 'Skins were having trouble moving the ball, and Billy's short passes, even when completed, were not distracting enough to keep opposing defenses from ganging up on all-pro halfback Larry Brown. With Kilmer at quarterback, the 2-2 Redskins had become too predictable with their unimaginative game plan of two rushes and a pass, two rushes and a pass, two rushes and a pass . . .

With the World Champion Miami Dolphins next on the schedule, Coach Allen knew he would need wider options and more firepower. So he turned to Sonny Jurgensen, an 18-year veteran with Hall of Fame credentials: 247 touchdown passes, twenty-four 300-yard games, and five 400-yard games. Sonny had also been the NFL's #1 passer twice, led the league in completions four times, and led the NFL in passing yardage five times. In addition, Jurgy had twice thrown five touchdown passes in a single game. Firepower he had. Although Jurgensen hadn't played a full season in three years due to a series of injuries (his latest was a knee problem requiring surgery in 1973), his relative inactivity had not produced dry-rot. As a relief pitcher for Kilmer in games against the Giants and Bengals earlier in the season, Sonny had completed 16 of 24 passes for 130 yards and two touchdowns with no interceptions.

Manny Fernandez, Miami's great defensive tackle, offered a unique opinion on the Redskins' Big Switch. "We heard about the Jurgensen thing on Tuesday, and we've been preparing for him," said Fernandez. "It kind of surprised us, especially after what Billy did against Denver." (Kilmer had had a big night in a 30-3 thrashing of the Broncos.) "Sonny's got that quick release like Namath," continued Fernandez, "but either one of those guys [Kilmer or Jurgensen] is no bargain. I'd rather see George Allen playing quarterback."

If it accomplished nothing else, at least Jurgensen's presence would shift Miami's focus away from Larry Brown, who, for the last three years, had been the workhorse in George Allen's ultraconservative ball-control offense. Excluding kickoffs and incomplete passes, the 5-foot-11, 195-pound Brown had handled the ball on 50% of all Redskins plays in 1972 and on 48% of all plays in '73. In his book, *Always on the Run*, Miami's Larry Csonka wrote: "Larry Brown is definitely a great back, but I think the Redskins use him too much. He's playing a rougher game than he's capable of. From what I've seen, he's really tearing himself down with all those carries. He gets hit awfully hard on his second effort. He's not that big a guy to hold up under all that pounding." Not surprisingly, Brown's career average of 250 carries a season (plus blocking and receiving duties) had led to injuries in both knees. Refusing to sit on the bench but unable to cut with the sharpness of former years, the NFL's Most Valuable Player of 1972 had been reduced to cannon fodder by 1974.

Another factor in Allen's decision to start Jurgensen may have been the memory of Kilmer's ineffectiveness against the Dolphins in Super Bore VII in January, 1973. For that game, which Miami won by the deceptively close score of 14-7, Dolphins defensive coordinator Bill Arnsparger had dared Kilmer to pass by devising a sliding defense to contain Larry Brown. Instead of penetrating, the Miami defensive linemen just slid down the line and waited for Brown to come to them. With Brown unable to break through and with Kilmer having an off-day, the Washington offense fizzled badly.

Arnsparger had also installed Miami's current 53 Defense that had stifled every club in the NFL. Named after #53, linebacker Bob Matheson, Arnsparger's favorite defense was really just a 3-4, but, with Miami's outstanding personnel, it had paralyzed offenses from Pittsburgh to Oakland. Jurgensen knew there was only one way to beat the Dolphins. "Execution is the thing," said Sonny. "Even a tipped ball against that defense can be an interception. You have to be precise in what you're doing."

Although Miami had played in three consecutive Super Bowls (and won the last two), all was not well with the current team. Bill Arnsparger had been lured away to coach the New York Giants. Then a short-lived strike called by the NFL Players Association disrupted their training camp. And three of their biggest stars—fullback Larry Csonka, halfback Jim Kiick, and flanker Paul Warfield—were playing out their options, having already signed fat contracts to play in (and legitimize) the World Football League the following year.

On the plus side, all-pro quarterback Bob Griese was enjoying his usual steady success, hitting on 65% of his passes; tight end Jim Mandich was leading the AFC in receiving; Nat Moore was picking up 18 yards per punt return; and Csonka, the lame-duck fullback, was averaging 4.6 yards per carry. The swarming Miami defense was still intact. And, most importantly, Don Shula, the most respected and successful coach in the NFL, was at the height of his considerable powers. So, despite their problems, the Miami Dolphins were still a great team.

The Washington Redskins were no slouches either, especially on defense, where Allen's favorites ranked first overall in the NFC. All-pro left linebacker Dave Robinson, who was in his final season, commented, "Our defense is playing better now at this point than we were last year. This would be a nice time for the offense to catch up." With Sonny Jurgensen at quarterback, there was every reason to believe it would. "I'm looking forward to us having our best football game of the season," said Jurgensen, excitedly. "We need it, and we've had a good week of practice to prepare for it. We just have to go out and play over our heads."

On Sunday at RFK Stadium, 54,395 expectant fans stood and cheered as, one by one, the members of the Washington Redskins offense were introduced. As usual, it was so loud that the announcer's voice was drowned out. But when Sonny Jurgensen stepped onto the field, the tumultuous ovation turned into ground-shaking hysteria. Plainly said, pandemonium was pandemic.

After the opening kickoff, the Redskins and Dolphins took turns flexing their defensive muscles. However, the second time Washington got the ball, Jurgensen completed four passes, and the 'Skins moved to midfield. But linebacker Mike Kolen intercepted at his 42, and the Miami juggernaut, in the person of fullback Larry Csonka, began its crushing work. The Redskins defense thought it had stopped the Dolphins at midfield, but, on fourth and 1, Shula showed his confidence by letting Csonka carry for the first down. The Dolphins continued to drive in their typically relentless style—seven runs by Csonka, two short passes by Griese, and five runs by halfback Hubert Ginn—until Ginn sprinted the last 6 yards into the end zone for a touchdown. Garo Yepremian, Washington's passing star in Super Bowl VII, added the extra point, and Miami broke on top, 7-0.

The next time the Dolphins got the ball, Ginn reeled off a 21-yard gain, and it looked as if the Redskins were in for a long afternoon. But 5-time all-pro defensive end Deacon Jones sacked Griese for a 10-yard loss, and Miami was forced to punt. From his 19, Jurgensen threw to tight end Jerry Smith, who could only get a finger on the ball and deflected it to Mike Kolen, who picked it off at the Redskins 36. Fortunately for Washington, Miami returned the favor two plays later. On third and 17, Griese aimed a pass for wide receiver Nat Moore, but Redskins cornerback Pat Fischer batted the ball into the air and linebacker Chris Hanburger intercepted at the Washington 27.

With 2½ minutes remaining in the first half, Jurgensen and his receivers finally got in sync. Completions of 21 yards and 11 yards to Brown, 21 yards to Charley Taylor, and 9 yards to Roy Jefferson advanced the ball to Miami's 10. With a minute remaining in the period, Jurgensen rolled to his right, spotted Jefferson in the end zone, and fired—right into the arms of Dolphins cornerback Tim Foley. Jurgensen's third interception was a painful blow to the fans who remembered Sonny's former brilliance, and it produced a low, disgruntled murmur throughout the stadium as the Washington Redskins shuffled toward their locker room, trailing the Miami Dolphins, 7-0.

Washington's Larry Jones returned the second half kickoff to the 43, and the Redskins looked sharp as they drove to the Miami 29, where they faced fourth and 1. After considering the advice of his 54,000 assistants in the stands, Coach Allen ordered Jurgensen to go for the first down. That was a mistake; fullback Larry Smith was clobbered by defensive tackle Bob Heinz for no gain. Miami's offense took over and, for the next 8 minutes, marched steadily toward the Washington end zone. The Redskins defense finally stiffened at its 15, but Yepremian soccer-kicked a 32-yard field goal to increase Miami's lead to 10-0. It was beginning to look like a replay of Super Bowl VII.

After Miami's mesmerizing drive, return specialist Larry Jones brought the somber crowd back to life with a spectacular 57-yard kickoff return. Jurgensen followed with a 17-yard strike to Jefferson, but the Dolphins defense clamped down and forced the 'Skins to settle for a 40-yard field goal by Mark Moseley. The Redskins were finally on the board, 10-3. Moseley kicked off to the Miami 15, where Bob Matheson, a wedge blocker, fielded the ball and ran 18 yards upfield before Dennis Johnson smashed into him. The ball came loose, and Washington's Brad Dusek recovered at the 33. Suddenly, the Redskins had a chance to tie the game.

On the first play of the fourth quarter, Sonny Jurgensen dropped back into his pocket and, out of the corner of his eye, saw Miami safety Jake Scott slip as he turned to cover Roy Jefferson on a post pattern. Like a cobra, Jurgensen struck. His pass spiraled downfield accompanied by an ever-increasing roar from 54,000 Redskins fans. Jefferson and the ball converged at the goal line, and Roy high-stepped through the end zone holding the ball aloft as the fans gave him a thundering tribute. [Fig. 84] Nineteen seconds earlier, the Redskins had been scoreless; now Moseley was tying the game at 10 points apiece.

With the excited crowd cheering every play, the Washington Redskins smothered the Dolphins on their next series and got the ball back at midfield. On third and 4, Jurgensen passed to Larry Brown for 13 yards. Cornerback Henry Stuckey took a cheap shot at Brown, who had gotten out of bounds, and the Redskins halfback retaliated with his fists. Although Brown was ejected and the 'Skins were penalized 15 yards, the first down was allowed to stand. On second and 22 from the Miami 42, Jurgensen hit Jefferson for 19 yards. But his next pass was incomplete, and Moseley was called upon to kick a 41-yard field goal that gave the Redskins the lead for the first time in the game, 13-10.

Fig. 84   Roy Jefferson and friends have reason to celebrate   *Richard Darcey/Washington Post Photo*

The 'Skins and 'Phins swapped turnovers. Then, with 5 minutes remaining, Moseley missed a 45-yard field goal attempt that, had he made it, would have given Washington several strategic advantages. As it was, the Dolphins could still tie the Redskins with a field goal or go ahead by 4 with a touchdown. The Washington defense dug in. Ginn was stacked for no gain, then Griese misfired to Mandich. On third and 10, Griese passed to Nat Moore, who shook off Mike Bass' tackle and sprinted 48 yards to the Washington 24. Four plays later, on third and 11 at the 13, Redskins cornerback Mike Bass blitzed, but Griese got

rid of the ball just before Bass crashed into him. The pass found Howard Twilley all alone in the left corner of the end zone, where Bass normally would have been, and Miami reclaimed the lead, 17-13. The dispirited crowd was dumb-struck.

On the kickoff, Herb Mul-Key, a free-agent running back with the reflexes of a housefly, darted 32 yards to the Redskins 40. With 1:44 remaining in the game, Sonny Jurgensen returned to the field to attempt one of those miraculous finishes on which he had built his reputation. With the precision of a surgeon, Jurgensen began his dissection of the Miami defense with a 6-yard completion to fullback Moses Denson, then followed with a 10-yarder to Jerry Smith. Charley Taylor assisted with a catch at the Dolphins 40. Then, with 49 seconds remaining, Jurgensen fired over the middle to Taylor, who was blanketed by a Dolphins defender. The perfect pass hit Taylor's outstretched hand just as he was clobbered from behind, but Charley hung on to the ball for an 18-yard gain and a first down at the 22. Time-out, Washington, with 40 seconds left in the game.

Roy Jefferson was next on Sonny's agenda; the old master's 16-yard pass was impeccable again, and the Redskins moved to within 6 yards of victory with 28 seconds to go. After a time-out, Jurgensen dropped back to pass again as his intended receiver, fullback Larry Smith, charged past him toward the end zone.

Smith got a step on linebacker Doug Swift, who, rather than give up the score, tackled him while the ball was in the air. Somehow the officials missed the obvious interference call, and the Redskins had to try again. So Jurgensen called a variation of the same play. This time Smith got through the line unscathed, turned at the goal line, and caught Sonny's pass just as linebacker Nick Buoniconti slammed into him from the side. Smith strained desperately to get the ball across the goal line as Buoniconti lifted him into the air and threw him down. Was it a touchdown? "Sonny just made a great throw; he threw it perfectly," said Smith. "I had no doubt that I was in. The only doubt was what kind of call the official would make." The verdict came an instant later: Touchdown, Washington! [Fig. 86]

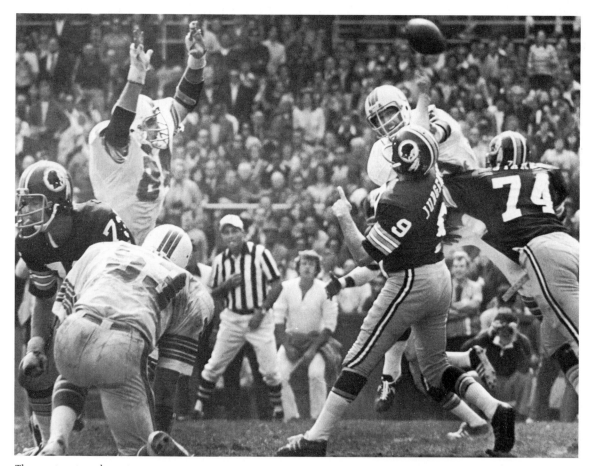

The master at work   *Richard Darcey/Washington Post Photo*

Fig. 86   *Paul Fine Photo/Nate Fine Productions, Courtesy Washington Redskins*

As 53,000 fans celebrated wildly, Sonny Jurgensen and his teammates ran off the field with one of the greatest victories in Washington Redskins history. Final score: Washington 20, Miami 17.

Even with Miami defenders covering his receivers like an extra uniform, Sonny Jurgensen had threaded the needle six out of seven times on the Redskins' game-winning, 60-yard touchdown drive. "What impressed me," said rookie quarterback Joe Theismann, "was his complete control over the whole situation. When he called time out prior to those last two or three plays, he came over to the sideline and said, 'These are the plays that I like,' and he named three of them. He knew what he wanted to do. Those are the three plays he called. It really was quite a thrill just to stand there and watch."

Altogether, Sonny completed 26 of his 39 passes for 303 yards and two touchdowns. When told that the 40-year-old Jurgensen had thrown for over 300 yards for the 25th time in his career, Miami defensive end Bill Stanfill muttered, "His arm didn't look 40."

Later, in the Washington locker room, former Redskins flanker Bobby Mitchell said, "They talk about Namath and all those other guys, but when it comes to throwing that ball, Sonny is the best, oh Lord, yes. He can put it where a guy doesn't even fight for the ball. All you do is run your pattern. The only guy who can get to that ball is you. And I'll tell you something else: he was just starting to get warmed up. If there had been a fifth quarter, hey, you really would have seen something."

Sadly, it was Sonny Jurgensen's last hurrah. Injuries would limit his playing time the rest of the season and Sonny would be unable to accomplish the final goal of his career: a Super Bowl victory. But Jurgensen's sterling performance on that October afternoon against the Dolphins provided a fitting climax to his career, a final gift to the millions of Washington Redskins fans he had thrilled for 11 remarkable years. One last time, the words on a hand-painted banner at RFK Stadium had been brought to life:

SONNY DAYS ARE HERE AGAIN!

HEARTBURN

Washington Redskins vs. Dallas Cowboys

November 28, 1974

"This team is going all the way," predicted Washington Redskins defensive end Deacon Jones. "That's right, all the way. I feel it. We all feel it. It's gonna happen." The surging Redskins, in second place in the NFC East with an 8-3 record, had won six of their last seven games and now needed only one more victory to clinch the wild-card spot in the playoffs. Naturally, they hoped that that victory would come at the expense of the Dallas Cowboys on Thanksgiving Day. "This is the year that will give us a character test," said offensive captain Charley Taylor. "A lot of guys are thinking about getting out of football. So this is the year to go all the way. Everyone has to evaluate himself and dedicate himself to the cause."

Midseason injuries to quarterback Sonny Jurgensen and to running backs Larry Brown and Larry Smith had cast doubt on the Redskins' chances of returning to the playoffs. But with Billy Kilmer in top form and fullback Moses Denson and former Cowboys halfback Duane Thomas running well, the 'Skins had won four in a row while averaging over 24 points a game. "We have problems," admitted cornerback Pat Fischer, "but we have all the ingredients to get to the playoffs and the Super Bowl."

Dallas was having problems, too, especially in its backfield. Fullback Calvin Hill, the Cowboys' leading rusher, was out with an injury, and reserve quarterback Craig Morton had just been traded to the New York Giants. Morton had forced the trade by staging a one-man strike to protest his lack of playing time in the Cowboys' first five games while Roger Staubach was giving up 10 interceptions. But when Staubach, famous for his timely scrambling and go-for-broke style, got back on track, the Cowboys recovered from their 1-4 start by winning five of their next six games.

Now in his sixth year, Staubach remained the Cowboys' only wild card in Tom Landry's complex but robotic offense. Dallas' penchant for cold, passionless precision was one of the reasons the Cowboys were contemptible to all right-thinking football fans. Although every Redskin hated every Cowboy on principle, one Washington player, defensive tackle Diron Talbert, was particularly hostile. A graduate of the University of Texas, Talbert was handsome, funny, and country-boy charming, but nothing invoked his contempt and anger like the Dallas Cowboys—especially Roger (The Dodger) Staubach. "If Staubach runs," said Talbert, "you like to get a good shot at him and knock him out of the game. You try to get a scrambling quarterback to scramble into the arms of somebody who's going to hurt him. If you knock him out, you got that rookie facing you. That's one of our goals. If we do that, it's great. He's all they have. They have no experienced backup."

After eight straight playoff appearances, it appeared that the Cowboys had grown complacent, that they had lost the edge that desperation gives a team. Despite having six all-pros on offense and six more on defense, Dallas had struggled to a 6-5 record and had been all but eliminated from playoff contention 11 days earlier by a loss in Washington. In that game, the Redskins had looked unbeatable as they ran up a 28-0 halftime lead. Dallas had stormed back in the second half, though, scoring three unanswered touchdowns. In the final minutes, the Cowboys were threatening again, but Washington's #1-ranked defense made a goal-line stand and saved the game, 28-21. Afterwards, Roger Staubach vowed that when the two teams met again in Dallas, "We'll kill 'em."

The Cowboys were 3-point favorites to defeat the Redskins in the rematch—a testimonial to the motivational impact of vengeance. "We owe them plenty," spat out Dallas defensive tackle Jethro Pugh. From the way he said it, it sounded as if he had been chewing on those words for a long time.

63,243 Cowboys fans filled Texas Stadium to celebrate one of the country's proudest traditions: football on Thanksgiving Day. As we all know, nothing quite stirs the heartstrings of honest-to-God Americans like home, hearth, and a vicious gang-tackle.

On the Cowboys' first possession, Dallas Coach Tom Landry showed why he is regarded as one of the shrewdest tacticians in the NFL when he ordered Duane Carrell to fake a punt on fourth and 7 at the Dallas 45. To the surprise of the Redskins and the delight of the crowd, Carrell completed a 37-yard pass to Benny Barnes for a first down at the Washington 18. Twelve penalty-laden plays later, the Redskins finally thwarted the Cowboys at the 7, but rookie placekicker Efren Herrera kicked a 24-yard field goal to stake Dallas to a 3-0 lead. Buoyed by its goal-line stand, Washington mounted a drive of its own that featured a 16-yard pass from Bill Kilmer to tight end Jerry Smith and an 11-yard ramble by fullback Moses Denson. On fourth and 4 at the Dallas 28, newcomer Mark Moseley booted a 45-yard field goal, and the first quarter ended in a 3-3 tie.

After the kickoff, the Cowboys marched to their 46, but linebacker Dave Robinson intercepted a Staubach pass and returned it to the Dallas 23. The Redskins failed to gain a first down with three running plays, so Moseley kicked a 34-yard field goal to give Washington a 6-3 lead. The rest of the second quarter lapsed into a punting contest until Dallas' Walt Garrison fumbled at his 33 with 17 seconds left in the half. Kilmer passed to Duane Thomas for 9 yards, and, on the last play of the half, Moseley booted a 39-yard field goal to boost the Redskins' lead to 9-3.

In the first half, the Washington defense had completely neutralized Roger Staubach, allowing him just two completions in eight attempts for 11 yards. Although Staubach had scrambled twice for 18 yards, he also was sacked twice by arch-rival Diron Talbert for losses amounting to 15 yards. The Redskins were practicing what Coach George Allen always preached: play mistake-free football and wait for a break.

As if on cue, Dallas fullback Walt Garrison fumbled on the first play of the second half, and, when Redskins linebacker Harold McLinton recovered at the Cowboys 39, Coach Allen went into a paroxysm of finger-licking, cap-pulling, and hand-clapping. Moses Denson ran for a first down at the Cowboys 28, then Kilmer rifled the ball to wide receiver Roy Jefferson at the 9. On first and goal, Billy hit Duane Thomas in the end zone for a touchdown, and the Redskins were in command, 16-3.

Roger Staubach began to rally the Cowboys with a 21-yard completion to Robert Newhouse. Then, two plays later, Staubach set sail on another scramble until Dave Robinson crashed into him at the Redskins 47. [Fig. 87] Staubach crumpled to the ground, unconscious. Diron Talbert's wish had come true; Coach Landry had no choice but to send in his completely inexperienced rookie quarterback, Clint Longley. After two warm-up plays, Longley completed his first professional pass—a flare to Garrison for 15 yards. Then, with the ball at the Washington 35, Longley lived up to his nickname, "The Mad Bomber," by throwing a long touchdown pass to tight end Billy Joe DuPree! The amazed Cowboys were back in the game, trailing 16-10.

Stunned by Longley's debut, the Redskins squandered their next possession and punted back to Dallas. Longley continued his magic act by passing to DuPree for 20 yards, wide receiver Drew Pearson for 9, and running back Charles Young for 14 more. On

Fig. 87 *UPI/The Bettmann Archive*

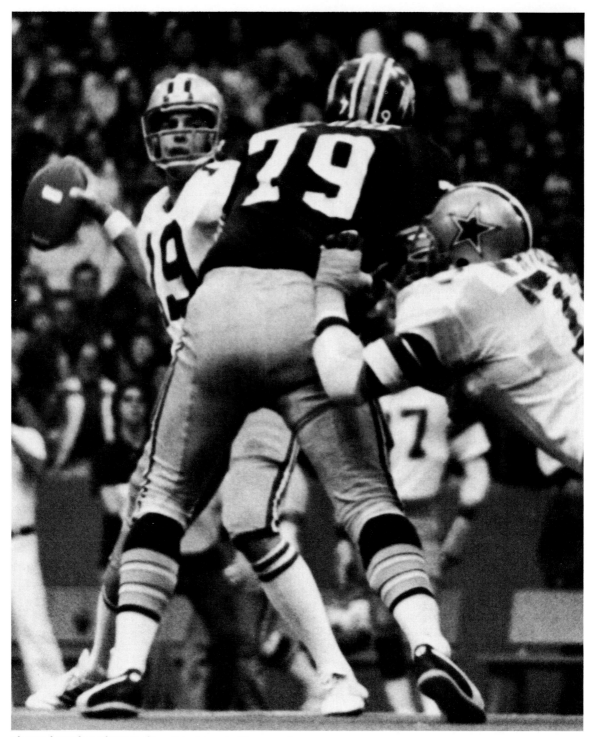

The Mad Bomber, Clint Longley   *Richard Darcey/Washington Post Photo*

second and 7 at the Redskins 12, Longley threw into the end zone for Robert Newhouse. The pass was broken up by cornerback Pat Fischer, but interference was called on Dave Robinson, giving the Cowboys a first down at the 1. On the next play, Garrison dove into the end zone for a touchdown, and Efren Herrera's point-after put the Cowboys back on top, 17-16.

On the first play of the fourth quarter, Billy Kilmer revived his shocked teammates with a 38-yard bomb to Roy Jefferson. On first down at the Dallas 22, Moses Denson plowed for 3 yards, then Duane Thomas cruised around left end for a 19-yard touchdown and the Redskins reclaimed the lead, 23-17. A minute later, running back Charles Young fumbled at his 16, giving Washington a terrific opportunity to put the game on ice. But Coach Allen ordered three straight line charges that left the 'Skins a yard short of a first down. Rather than risk losing momentum, Allen decided to take the 3 points. After all, he reasoned, a 9-point lead was nearly as good as a 13-point lead this late in the game. Mark Moseley lined up the 24-yard attempt and got the kick off, but Ed "Too Tall" Jones, Dallas' 6-foot 9-inch defensive end, blocked it! The Cowboys still trailed by 6 points.

After an exchange of punts, Dallas got the ball back at its 40 with 5 minutes left in the game. Charles Young swept left end for 14 yards; Robert Newhouse swept right end for 11; and Longley hit Pearson with a 10-yard pass at the Washington 30. On first down, Bill Brundige and Verlon Biggs nailed Longley for a 15-yard loss that moved the ball back to the 45. With 2½ minutes remaining, Longley completed a 20-yard pass to Drew Pearson, but cornerback Pat Fischer slammed into Pearson and caused a fumble, which Mike Bass recovered at the Redskins 31.

Washington needed to gain only one first down to wrap up the game. After two plunges by Denson netted only 4 yards, Allen still disdained the pass and ordered a sweep by Duane Thomas. The Cowboys were waiting for him and dumped their former teammate for a 6-yard loss. Mike Bragg punted, and Dallas took over at its 40 with 1:45 on the clock. With no time-outs left, the Cowboys had to hurry. An incompletion, a short pass to Garrison, and a scramble out

of bounds used 45 seconds. Faced with a critical fourth-and-6 at his 44, Longley threw to Bob Hayes at midfield. The ball arrived an instant before Hayes was tackled by safety Brig Owens. He appeared to be a yard short of the first down. But the official gave the Cowboys a favorable spot—just enough for a first down at midfield.

A pass to Pearson fell incomplete, leaving 35 seconds on the clock. In the Cowboys' huddle, wide receiver Drew Pearson told Longley that, despite double coverage, he could get open deep. Defying Coach Tom Landry's order to throw a medium-range pass over the middle, Longley called for the bomb. At the snap, Pearson ran 15 yards downfield, faked to the inside, and veered back to the left. Redskins nickel back Ken Stone bit hard on Pearson's fake, leaving the swift Dallas receiver open for a moment as cornerback Mike Bass and safety Brig Owens scrambled to catch up to him. Longley sidestepped the Redskins' all-out rush and, at the same instant that Pearson was throwing his fake, launched a 55-yard spiral toward the goal line. Running at full speed, Pearson caught up to the perfectly thrown pass at the 5 and ran triumphantly into the end zone! Touchdown, Dallas! The amazed fans at Texas Stadium stopped screaming only long enough for Efren Herrera to kick the tie-breaking extra point, then continued their wild celebration as the scoreboard registered the Cowboys' 1-point lead.

Twenty-eight seconds later, it was all over. Dallas 24, Washington 23.

Clint Longley's incredible touchdown pass had capped the most improbable comeback in the history of the NFL. That a rookie quarterback with no professional experience could lead the Cowboys back from a 16-3 deficit against the best defense in the conference and win on a last-gasp 50-yard touchdown pass against double coverage was not only amazing, but, according to guard Blaine Nye, "a triumph of the uncluttered mind."

In Washington, heartbreak turned into heartburn as a million warmed-over Thanksgiving dinners were eaten in glum silence. In Dallas, Cowboys fans were once again thanking their lucky stars.

SUDDEN DEATH

Dallas Cowboys vs. Washington Redskins

November 2, 1975

After being tackled 10,000 times (counting practices and games in high school, college, and the pros), and after playing hurt in virtually every game in the past 5 years, Larry Brown could no longer endure the constant pounding to his knees. "It's the football mentality," explained former Heisman Trophy-winner and all-pro halfback Mike Garrett. "You get hurt and you want to get back in there right away and prove you're better than anyone else. I was that way, too. It's what makes you good—and eventually it kills you. You don't give yourself a chance to heal, or you do suicidal things. It's that way from the day you start playing football."

With Brown reluctantly nursing his chronic wounds on the bench, Mike Thomas, a 5-foot-11, 195-pound rookie from Nevada-Las Vegas, had taken over at halfback and gained 124 yards as the Redskins improved their record to 4-2 with a 23-7 victory over the Cleveland Browns. Although Thomas resembled a healthy Brown in size, moves, and speed, he did not play with Brown's furious determination. Then again, neither did anyone else in the NFL.

Injuries to key players like Brown had taken an unusually heavy toll on the Redskins in 1975, endangering their chance of making the playoffs for a fifth straight year. In all, seven Washington starters, including wide receiver Roy Jefferson and guard Paul

Laaveg, were hurting as the team prepared for their first of two annual clashes with the Dallas Cowboys.

However, there was another, more subtle reason for Washington's inconsistent performance. Dissension was still in the air, both in the stands and in the locker room, over the forced retirement of quarterback Sonny Jurgensen. General Manager Allen had finally solved Head Coach Allen's thorniest problem by not renewing Jurgensen's $125,000 contract as an "economy measure." But the benefit of saving that $125,000 quickly paled in comparison to the damage done to public relations and team morale in the firing of one of the most popular and masterful players in Redskins history. At the very least, Allen could have used Jurgensen as a relief pitcher when the 'Skins were forced to play catch-up. But Allen, tired of the controversy and the undermining of his authority that the constant second-guessing still provoked, refused to let Sonny return. That may have been the biggest mistake in George Allen's career because it cost him the popular support of hundreds of thousands of fans who never forgave him for his ruthless treatment of the man they considered the best Redskins player in a generation.

Despite their physical and emotional wounds, the Redskins were rated as 3-point favorites over the Dallas Cowboys. In answer to reports that the 5-1 Cow-

Larry Brown cut a dashing figure in early 1973   *AP/Wide World Photos*

boys were not as awesome as they had once been, Allen scoffed, "That stuff about Dallas rebuilding this year—I never bought it in the first place. As far as I'm concerned, Dallas is the team to beat whether they're in first place, second place, or whatever. We have to play our best game of the year all the way around."

In a move to utilize quarterback Roger Staubach's ability to both run and pass, Cowboys Coach Tom Landry had resurrected the old shotgun formation. In addition to giving Staubach extra time to spot an open receiver, the new-old formation would help extend the former Heisman Trophy-winner's career, which had been shortened by 5 years of Naval service.

The Cowboys, ranked second on offense and fourth on defense in the NFC, were once again solid at every position. They even had two new stars with the same last name. Halfback Preston Pearson, who had replaced Calvin Hill after he defected to the now-defunct World Football League, was particularly effective on sweeps and screens while soft-handed wide receiver Drew Pearson was already confounding defensive backs with his meticulous sideline routes.

The Redskins needed this game badly; if they were to lose, they would be two games behind Dallas with only seven remaining. And with the 4-2 St. Louis Cardinals playing extremely well, the 'Skins would be hard-pressed to earn even a wild-card berth. "The games with Dallas the last four years have all been critical," said Allen. "We've got a great rivalry going. The stage is set for another one of the thrillers these teams always manage to come up with."

After 14 seasons in the NFL, quarterback Billy Kilmer knew precisely what it would take to reach the playoffs again. "We have to go out and play our hearts out every week. We're going for the championship and we can not let down. We have to play every play to the maximum. You do that and you'll win. The winners do it, and the losers don't. And it's like that every year."

5 5,004 nervous and excited customers squeezed into Robert F. Kennedy Stadium for the 31st renewal of the greatest rivalry in professional football: the Washington Redskins versus the Dallas Cowboys.

Overall in the series, Dallas owned a 16-12-2 advantage, but, since George Allen took over in 1971, the 'Skins had won five of the last nine. As usual, Allen had spurred his team to a frenzied peak of emotion, and the screaming crowd at RFK pushed the Redskins over the edge into just the right note of madness as Mark Moseley kicked off to open the game.

The Redskins defense kept the crowd cheering as it stopped the Cowboys on three plays and forced a punt, which Larry Jones returned 24 yards to the Dallas 41. Billy Kilmer opened with a 10-yard completion to Frank Grant at the 27 but misfired on two throws to Charley Taylor, so the Redskins had to settle for Mark Moseley's 43-yard field goal and a 3-0 lead. Moseley kicked off to rookie Roland Woolsey, who fumbled when John Pergine leveled him at the 25. 55,000 roaring fans jumped to their feet as Washington's Eddie Brown recovered on the Cowboys 27. However, four plays later, the Cowboys got off the hook when Moseley blew a 29-yard field goal attempt.

Moseley's shank broke the Redskins' spell of good fortune. On their next possession, Kilmer gave up an interception to cornerback Mark Washington at the Dallas 18, and the Cowboys offense suddenly came to life. Roger Staubach passed to Drew Pearson for 21 yards. Fullback Robert Newhouse ripped off two runs for 15 more. Continuing to mix their plays beautifully, the Cowboys marched to the Washington 27. On third and 4, Staubach tried to scramble for a first down but was caught by his old nemesis, Diron Talbert. Although Toni Fritsch missed a 43-yard field goal attempt, the momentum remained with Dallas. On the Redskins' next possession, Mike Thomas fumbled, and Mark Washington recovered for the Cowboys at the Washington 18. Three plays later, Staubach fired a 12-yard touchdown pass to Preston Pearson, and Dallas went on top, 7-3.

After missing connections on six of his first eight throws, it appeared that Kilmer had finally gotten his bearings when he completed two in a row early in the second quarter. However, Cliff Harris intercepted Billy's next pass at the Dallas 41 and returned it 27 yards to the Washington 32. The Cowboys worked the ball to the 10 in five plays, then Staubach whistled a pass to Drew Pearson, who was unattended in the end zone, and Dallas increased its lead to 14-3. Despite his poor start, Billy Kilmer didn't back off. He wobbled a 21-yard pass to Jerry Smith at midfield, then, one play later, hit Frank Grant with a beautiful 46-yard touchdown bomb. As he charged off the field, Kilmer shook his fist at the cheering fans who, moments before, had been booing him. Moseley kicked the point-after, and the 'Skins were back in the game, trailing 14-10.

The Cowboys retaliated with a crushing ground attack that chewed up 64 yards in 13 plays. Two passes to Preston Pearson fell incomplete, though, and Dallas had to settle for Fritsch's 33-yard field goal and a 17-10 lead. The Redskins began to stir again, but Mike Thomas' second fumble put the Cowboys back in business at the Washington 46 with 2 minutes left in the half. A 24-yard pass to tight end Jean Fugett and a 16-yarder to Preston Pearson moved Dallas to the Redskins 3. However, with 20 seconds remaining, defensive end Ron McDole pounced on a Staubach fumble, and Washington took over at its 24. Fullback Moses Denson carried for 10 yards, and the Cowboys contributed 15 more with a personal foul, giving the Redskins a first down at midfield. With 12 seconds left in the half, Kilmer fired to Charley Taylor for a 24-yard gain, and Moseley ran in for a 44-yard field goal attempt. To the dismay of the frustrated fans, he missed, and the first half ended with Dallas still on top, 17-10.

Although they had been handed four turnovers and completely shut down the Redskins' rushing attack in the first half (12 carries for 26 yards), the Cowboys, thanks to their own two fumbles, had been unable to put the game out of reach. History suggested that they would regret their generosity.

Washington opened the second half with a long, crisp drive. Mike Thomas rushed five times for 22 yards, and Billy Kilmer completed four out of five passes for 44 yards—the last one to Charley Taylor for a 2-yard touchdown. The 66-yard march reestablished the Redskins' confidence and tied the score, 17-17. After the 'Skins forced Dallas to punt on its next possession, Kilmer continued his hot streak

with completions to Frank Grant for 16 yards, Charley Taylor for 13, Mike Thomas for 20 yards, and Moses Denson for 7. Unfortunately, the end of the third quarter seemed to break Kilmer's charm. On first and 10 at the Cowboys 20, Billy gave up his third interception of the game (this one to linebacker Lee Roy Jordan at the 12), and the boo-birds began their dispiriting song.

The Washington defense held fast, though, and, on fourth and 20 at the Dallas 9, Mitch Hoopes prepared to punt. Only he didn't. With the Redskins trying to maximize their punt return, no one bothered to cover Bob Breunig, the Cowboys end. Daringly, Hoopes passed to Breunig, who ran to the 30, making the first down by a yard. The shocking play never paid off in the form of points for Dallas, but it certainly swung the momentum back to the Cowboys' side and prevented the Redskins from gaining excellent field position.

After an exchange of punts, Washington took over at its 20 with 5 minutes left in the game. On second and 10, Kilmer dropped back into his pocket and threw a wounded duck, "the worst pass I've made all year." Stepping in front of the intended receiver, Mike Thomas, Cowboys safety Cliff Harris picked it off and raced 27 yards into the end zone for a touchdown! Dallas 24, Washington 17.

With the unrestrained boos of the crowd burning his ears, Billy Kilmer, 0 for 6 in the fourth quarter (and with four interceptions overall), had to go back in to try to salvage the game. "I put us in a bad situation all day," admitted Kilmer, "and I had to pull us out. I had to keep on throwing." A 9-yard completion to Frank Grant calmed the crowd and got the 'Skins rolling. "It was very tense and very emotional in the huddle, but there wasn't any yelling," said Kilmer. "They were just very determined. I could see it in their faces." Mike Thomas carried for a first down, then Kilmer hit his rookie halfback with a short flare that Thomas turned into a 24-yard gain to the Dallas 21. After an incompletion, Thomas picked up 9 yards on a sweep but then lost a yard on third down. The outcome of the game now rested on one play: fourth and 2 at the Cowboys 13.

Trailing by a touchdown with only 2 minutes

Fig. 90   *Copyright Washington Post; Reprinted by permission of the D.C. Public Library*

remaining, the Redskins had no choice but to go for the first down. The nervous crowd rose to its feet as Kilmer handed off to Thomas, who headed for the sideline, found a hole, and cut upfield for 6 yards and a first down! Riding the crest of that emotional wave, Kilmer fired a 7-yard touchdown pass to Jerry Smith, and 55,000 fans roared with delight and relief. All that was needed now was the extra point. In a sudden hush that quickly became bedlam again, Moseley booted it through the uprights, and the game was deadlocked, 24-24.

Unfortunately, that left 1:47 on the clock, plenty of time for Roger Staubach to break Washington's hearts. A pass to Drew Pearson was on target for 21 yards. Then a 12-yard strike to Jean Fugett gave the Cowboys another first down at the Redskins 32. Two short tosses moved the ball to the Washington 22, and, with 13 seconds left, Toni Fritsch came in to try a game-winning 38-yard field goal. The Redskins called a time-out to unnerve the Austrian soccer-style kicker, and the screaming fans at RFK did their best to rattle him. As each tension-packed second ticked off, the roar of the crowd increased until it built to a thick, mind-numbing crescendo. Head bowed, Fritsch tried to concentrate as he waited to kick. The snap and hold were perfect. Fritsch swung his leg and connected solidly, lifting the ball above the desperate, outstretched hands of the Redskins. With plenty of distance to spare, the spinning football flew past the goal post—WIDE TO THE LEFT!

A few delirious seconds later, the fourth quarter ended with the score tied, 24-24, and, for the first time in their long rivalry, the Washington Redskins and Dallas Cowboys prepared to play an overtime period. Sudden death was waiting for one of them.

The Cowboys won the toss and elected to receive. After Preston Pearson returned Mark Moseley's deep kickoff to the 21, Roger Staubach pierced the Redskins secondary with a 32-yard pass to Drew Pearson. Two plays later, Staubach dropped back to pass again. Blitzing from the right side, all-pro linebacker Chris Hanburger charged into Staubach just as he threw. The ball fluttered aimlessly down the field to the 36, where Redskins safety Kenny Houston intercepted and returned it to midfield! During the runback, Staubach, in a rare display of anger, punched cornerback Pat Fischer, and 15 yards were tacked on, giving the 'Skins the ball at the Dallas 35.

Even though he needed only a field goal to win, Kilmer dared to throw two short passes to Charley Taylor, giving Washington a first down at the Dallas 11. After Mike Thomas carried for 2 yards, surehanded Larry Brown was sent in, and the former MVP responded by banging through the line for a 7-yard gain. On third and 1 at the 2, Brown knifed into the line again and picked up the first down. Only 1 yard away from victory, Kilmer decided not to risk another handoff. At the snap, Billy lunged over the back of right guard Walt Sweeney. [Fig. 90] He met a wall of Cowboys at the goal line, but kept his knees pumping and squeezed into the end zone for the winning touchdown! The Redskins had triumphed, 30-24!

The same fans who had booed Kilmer earlier now showered him with shouts of praise as he ran off the field with the game ball held aloft. Once more, victory had redeemed Billy Kilmer.

OFFICIAL VERSION

Washington Redskins vs. St. Louis Cardinals

November 16, 1975

If you think fanatical support for professional football teams began slowly and grew somewhat steadily to its present-day heights, then you don't know about a game in 1920 between the Decatur Staleys (soon to be the Chicago Bears) and the Racine (soon to be Chicago) Cardinals. Trailing 6-0 late in the game, Racine was threatening to score, but, just to make sure, a group of fans ran onto the field and helped the Cardinals linemen clear a path to the end zone for one of their running backs. Fearful for their health, the officials allowed the touchdown to stand, and Racine won the game, 7-6.

The Cardinals were charter members of the NFL (originally known as the American Professional Football Association), which at that time was a rag-tag collection of professional teams hailing mostly from small mill towns (Akron, Canton, Decatur, Hammond, Muncie, etc.) clustered around the Great Lakes. In 1922, the Cards changed their name (Racine was a street in Chicago) but not their reputation as zany losers. In one stretch between 1938 and 1945, they won only 12 games but, with their trick plays and multiple laterals, looked great doing it.

However, in 1947, with quarterback Paul Christman and halfback Charley Trippi leading the way, Chicago turned itself around and won the league Championship by defeating the Philadelphia Eagles, 28-21. In the Fifties, though, the Cardinals reverted to form, losing even more games (33-84-3) than the Redskins (47-70-3) despite the heroics of Hall of Fame halfback Ollie Matson. Then, in 1960, to prevent the fledgling AFL from entrenching itself in the choicest untapped market in the country, the Cardinals moved to St. Louis and began to build their offense and defense around the burgeoning passing game.

In the Sixties, the Cardinals offense featured quarterback Charley Johnson and receivers Bobby Joe Conrad, Sonny Randle, and Jackie Smith. On defense, St. Louis fielded the finest secondary in the league: Larry Wilson (the originator of the safety blitz), Pat Fischer, Abe Woodson (the father of the bump-and-run), and Jerry Stovall. Although the Cardinals became a highly respected team, they never reached the top of the standings.

That changed in 1974 when Don Coryell, in his second year as head coach, led St. Louis to the NFC Eastern Division Championship with a 10-4 record. The team became known as the "Cardiac Cards" for its uncanny ability to pull out heartstopping victories in the last few seconds. More often than not, the man responsible for those late-game heroics was halfback Terry Metcalf, who could not only run and catch and return kicks, but could also throw a deadly option pass. That may seem like a lot, but in college he also punted, placekicked, and played defensive back. A superb athlete who once long-jumped 25 feet 10 inches, Metcalf simply scared the hell out of everyone he faced.

But Metcalf was not the only Cardinal who could break open a game. Quarterback Jim Hart had developed into one of the most dangerous passers in the league; Jim Otis, a crushing fullback with speed, was leading the NFC in rushing; and wide receiver Mel Gray was pacing the conference in touchdown catches and yardage. St. Louis also featured a strong offensive line that had allowed only two sacks in eight games, and boasted among its members that rarest of NFL entities—an offensive guard with a recognizable name, Conrad Dobler.

Over the years, "Conrad the Barbarian" had gained a reputation as the league's dirtiest player and had even been accused of biting opponents. "What you need for Dobler," mused an old foe of the dark-eyed, swarthy, mustachioed lineman, "is a string of garlic buds around your neck and an iron stake. If the Cardinals played every game under a full moon, Dobler would make all-pro." But Dobler refuted that charge. Sort of. "I don't bite," said Conrad. "I believe in good hygiene, as a rule. Now, if a player sticks his finger inside my face cage, that's different. Then I'll bite—hard."

In 1975, the St. Louis Cardinals were at the height of their power, fighting for first place in the NFC Eastern Division with the Washington Redskins, who, because of injuries, were anything but at their height. Ten Redskins players were in various stages of infirmity; the latest casualties were cornerback Mike Bass, linebacker Brad Dusek, return specialist Larry Jones, quarterback Billy Kilmer, and placekicker Mark Moseley. When Don Coryell heard that Moseley was in the hospital with two abscesses in his right thigh, the Cardinals coach couldn't resist joking, "It's probably from the lead in his foot."

Kilmer had separated his right shoulder the week before when Giants defensive end Jack Gregory blind-sided him. In a valiant attempt to get ready for the Cardinals, Billy had tried everything to rehabilitate his shoulder—icepacks, whirlpools, deep heat, sonic stimulation, massages, and cortisone injections. But despite his heroics, Kilmer simply could not play, and the job of leading the 6-2 Redskins against the 6-2 Cardinals fell to Randy Johnson. A former New York Giant, Johnson had replaced Kilmer against his

Nate Fine Photo/Nate Fine Productions, Courtesy Washington Redskins

old team and led the 'Skins to a 21-13 victory by completing 11 of 16 passes. "If I can have the same kind of day against St. Louis," said Johnson, "there's no way we can lose with our defense."

The Redskins had already beaten the Cardinals, 27-17, earlier in the season to partially avenge the two defeats St. Louis had dealt them in 1974. That just served to whet Terry Metcalf's appetite for the clash that would determine which team would control the NFC East. "The Redskins have a lot of competitors who play you right down to the finish," said Metcalf. "That's the way I like it."

With 49,919 Cardinals fans looking on from the heights of Busch Memorial Stadium, Mark Moseley kicked off to renew the 44-year-old rivalry between the Washington Redskins and the St. Louis Cardinals. The Redskins defense, led by linebackers Chris Hanburger and Brad Dusek, was determined to shut down the Cardinals' running game. They succeeded on St. Louis' first two possessions, but, midway through the first quarter, halfback Terry Metcalf began to make his presence felt with consecutive runs of 8, 6, 5, and 6 yards. However, on second and 11 at the Washington 31, Metcalf fumbled after a 6-yard gain, and Hanburger recovered at the 25.

Two plays later, though, the Cards regained possession when Randy Johnson threw an interception to Clarence Duren, who returned the ball to the Redskins 22. St. Louis moved to the 3, but Jim Hart misfired on a pass to Mel Gray and the Cardinals had to settle for Jim Bakken's 20-yard field goal. Trailing 3-0 as the second quarter got underway, Washington shelved its ineffective running game and took to the air. Johnson hit Charley Taylor with a 9-yard pass at his 41, then followed with a 32-yarder to Frank Grant. Unfortunately, Grant fumbled when he hit the ground, and cornerback Norm Thompson recovered at the Cardinals 27.

St. Louis drove smartly down the field on the strength of Hart's passing and Jim Otis' running, yet came away with nothing when Bakken's 29-yard field goal attempt bounced off the upright. Buoyed by Bakken's miss, the Redskins began to click. Three rushes produced a first down; then Johnson connected with Mike Thomas for another 21 yards. At the Cardinals 48, Johnson hit Grant for a 12-yard gain before firing a perfect pass to Charley Taylor for a 36-yard touchdown! Moseley converted, and the Redskins led, 7-3.

An exchange of fumbles was followed by an exchange of punts, and, with 37 seconds left in the period, St. Louis set out to get one more score before halftime. Fullback Steve Jones rumbled up the middle for 14 yards, and Mel Gray caught a Hart pass for 29 more, giving the Cards a first down at the Washington 41 with 15 seconds remaining. St. Louis' next two plays produced only 3 yards, so, with 1 second left on the clock, Bakken came in to try a 55-yard field goal. It was a fake! Jim Hart, the holder, became Jim Hart, the quarterback. Before he could get his pass away, though, he was swarmed under by a host

of savvy Redskins, and the first half ended with Washington still ahead, 7-3.

It was hard to tell whether the low score reflected the domination of both defenses or the ineptitude of both offenses. Turnovers had played an unusually large role, spoiling scoring opportunities for both teams, and momentum had failed to bestow its fickle favor on either side. When the second half got underway, the frustrations continued. Washington's Larry Jones returned Jim Bakken's kickoff 44 yards to midfield, but quarterback Randy Johnson threw an interception on his first pass and St. Louis took over at its 42.

Jim Otis and Terry Metcalf took turns blasting through the Redskins defensive line, and the Cards marched unopposed to the Washington 15. On fourth and 1, Coach Coryell decided to send in Jim Bakken for a 32-yard field goal despite the obvious wishes of his 49,000 assistants in the stands. When Redskins defensive end Ron McDole blocked Bakken's kick, Coryell's acidic facial expression could have etched glass.

Starting at his 25, Johnson got the 'Skins rolling with a 14-yard completion to fullback Moses Denson. Halfback Mike Thomas reeled off 14 yards around right end, and Denson gained another 14 on a sweep to the St. Louis 29. On third and 12, Johnson fired a bullet to Roy Jefferson for 26 yards and a first down at the Cardinals 5. A sweep lost 4 yards, but, on the next play, Johnson finessed a pass to Mike Thomas for a 9-yard touchdown, and the 'Skins took a commanding 14-3 lead.

Jim Hart made the mistake of trying to catch up all at once, and his risky 50-yard bomb to Mel Gray was intercepted by safety Ken Houston at the Washington 25. Both teams grew conservative (probably because nobody wanted to add to the seven turnovers that had already been exchanged), and the result was four consecutive punts. Finally, with 12½ minutes remaining in the fourth quarter, St. Louis decided to take a chance. Hart threw deep for Mel Gray. The pass fell incomplete, but an interference penalty against safety Mike Bass produced the desired result—a first down at the Redskins 5. Two plays later, Hart gunned the ball to tight end J.V. Cain for the score, and the Cardinals were back within 4 points, 14-10.

After the kickoff, Randy Johnson decided it was time for a bomb of his own, but it blew up in his face when all-pro cornerback Roger Wehrli intercepted at the Cardinals 35. St. Louis failed to capitalize on Johnson's third interception, though, and Jeff West punted back to Washington after only three plays. Undaunted by his interceptions, Johnson fired a 22-yard strike to tight end Jerry Smith, then followed with a 19-yarder to Smith at the Cardinals 25. Although the St. Louis defense prevented the 'Skins from getting any closer, it could not keep Mark Moseley from kicking a 42-yard field goal that gave Washington a 17-10 lead.

After Terry Metcalf returned the kickoff to the 38, Mel Gray caught a 21-yard pass from Hart, and Otis bulled for 10 yards on a draw. On first and 10 at the Washington 31, Hart dropped back and looped a long pass to wide receiver Earl Thomas, but Pat Fischer, the former Cardinals cornerback, intercepted at the Redskins 3 and Washington took over with 3½ minutes remaining. Three straight running plays ate up nearly 2 minutes but did not produce a game-clinching first down. So, after Metcalf returned Mike Bragg's punt to the Redskins 39, 1 minute and 43 seconds remained for the Cardinals to try to catch the Redskins.

A pass from Hart to Ike Harris picked up 14 yards. Then, with Metcalf and Gray drawing double coverage, Hart threw to Earl Thomas for a 19-yard gain to the Washington 6 yard line. After three straight passes into the end zone fell incomplete, the outcome of the game rested on one final play. At the snap, wide receiver Mel Gray streaked into the end zone and cut sharply toward the middle on a path parallel to the goal line. Hart led him perfectly, but the pass was a little high. Leaping into the air, Gray caught the ball an instant before he was hit from behind by Pat Fischer. [Fig. 92] As Gray's left foot touched the ground, the ball slipped out of his arms. Was it a touchdown?

The officials huddled. The rule in question stated that in order to be a touchdown, a receiver must have possession with both feet on the ground. [Fig. 93] As the officials argued back and forth, replays on

Fig. 92   Mel Gray's right foot is clearly off the ground as the ball begins to slip out of his hands
Richard Darcey/Washington Post Photo

Fig. 93   By the time Gray's right foot lands, the ball is completely free. Notice referee's view is blocked
AP/Wide World Photos

television clearly showed that the ball had already come loose before Gray's second foot landed. However, the officials did not have access to those replays. Players from both sides indicated that the negotiations were favoring their team. Finally, after three tension-packed minutes, the referee made his decision — Touchdown, St. Louis!

Amid the Redskins' bitter protests, Bakken kicked the point-after-touchdown, tying the game at 17-17 with 11 seconds left in regulation. On the final play of the fourth quarter, Washington nearly produced a miracle of its own, but time ran out as Charley Taylor was tackled at the Cardinals 25 after catching a long pass from Johnson. For the second time in three weeks, the Redskins faced sudden death.

St. Louis won the crucial coin-toss and elected to receive. Terry Metcalf returned the kickoff to the Cardinals 25, and fullback Jim Otis went to work, carrying on eight of eleven plays as St. Louis swept downfield against the disheartened Redskins defenders. When the Cards finally stalled at the Washington 20, Jim Bakken ran onto the field to try a 37-yard field goal. Washington massed its best kick-blockers in the middle of the line. With 49,000 Cardinals fans holding their breath, Bakken stepped forward and booted the ball over the outstretched arms of the Washington defenders and through the uprights. The game was over. The Redskins had been scalped, 20-17.

"There is no doubt in my mind that pass was incomplete," fumed Coach George Allen after watching the replays of Mel Gray's "catch." "You have to have both feet down. He never does." Pointing out that Gray had hit himself in the helmet after the ball had come loose, Allen said, "That doesn't look like a guy who has scored a winning touchdown. Gray is dejected. He knows he dropped it. It's unfortunate, since this was a 'championship' game, it had to come down to this. I think there should be something in the rule book where, when a similar case like this comes up, when a bad decision has been made, a team doesn't have to suffer for it."

For the Washington Redskins, the use of instant replays to decide questionable calls would come eleven years too late.

LAST GASP

Minnesota Vikings vs. Washington Redskins

November 30, 1975

On Thanksgiving Day, 1975, Washington Redskins Coach George Allen was asked to list those things for which he was most thankful. "I've got a lot to be grateful for," replied Allen a bit hesitantly. "The team stayed together with more adversity than any team in football. Guys are playing on guts every week. And I have my health and my sanity. Of course, I'd rather have a two-game lead [in the NFC East]."

It's a wonder that Allen could claim even a fragment of sanity after Washington's last two games, in which back-to-back miscarriages of justice had deprived the Redskins of otherwise well-earned victories. Just one week after their bitter overtime loss to the Cardinals, the Redskins were burned by another dubious judgment call in the waning moments of a fierce battle with the Oakland Raiders. Trailing 23-16, the Raiders were given a first down at the 1 as a result of a questionable pass interference penalty in the end zone. After Oakland tied the game with a touchdown in the last few seconds, ageless George Blanda put the finishing touch on Washington's second scalping in a row by kicking the game-winning field goal in overtime.

That heartbreaker left the 6-4 Redskins one game behind both the Cardinals and Cowboys in the NFC Eastern Division race. What the 'Skins needed now

was an easy game to help steady themselves; instead, they faced the unpleasant task of battling the undefeated Minnesota Vikings. Led by quarterback Fran Tarkenton and halfback Chuck Foreman, the Vikings had already romped through 10 straight opponents and could afford to look upon the Washington game as a mere speed-bump on the way to their third straight Super Bowl appearance. "If they get by us, they've got a good chance to be 14-0," said Allen. "They can be loose and relaxed, and do the unorthodox."

When he first came into the league, Fran Tarkenton had been ridiculed for his ad-lib maneuvers by NFL traditionalists who predicted a short, unhappy career for the University of Georgia graduate. Fifteen years later, Tarkenton was leading the NFC in passing and had quarterbacked the Vikings to two consecutive Super Bowls while becoming the NFL's all-time leader in both career completions and rushing yards for a quarterback. In fact, Tarkenton's scrambling had made such a profound impact on the game that scouts began grading young quarterbacks as much for their mobility as for their passing. "There's nobody in the business any better at finding the open man," said Allen. "He's not scrambling to run; he scrambles to find an open man."

Tarkenton's favorite receiver, Chuck Foreman, doubled as the team's best running back. Leading the NFC in rushing (820 yards), receiving (50 catches), and touchdowns (14), Foreman was a graceful athlete with an amazing knack for slipping tackles. With Tarkenton and Foreman in the same backfield, the Vikings posed a problem that no defense in the NFL had been able to solve. Coach George Allen, who thrived on such challenges, decided to concentrate his manpower on stopping Foreman, reasoning that if Tarkenton was forced to pass out of necessity rather than choice, the Washington secondary would regain the crucial half-step that indecision takes away.

That half-step was especially important to aging veterans like cornerback Mike Bass, safety Ken Houston, and cornerback Pat Fischer. A master of the bump-and-run, Fischer was almost always assigned to cover an opponent's best receiver—Bob Hayes, Paul Warfield, Gene Washington, Otis Taylor, Harold Carmichael, or Mel Gray. However, now that he was 35, the 5-foot 9-inch, 170-pound Fischer was forced to rely more than ever on his savvy and experience to keep up with receivers who were getting bigger, stronger, and faster every year. Despite giving away as much as 50 pounds, Fischer never hesitated to stick his head into a ball-carrier's gut, earning him a well-deserved reputation as, pound for pound, the toughest player in the league.

"The only time you notice a cornerback is when he gets beat," lamented Fischer. "All a cornerback can do is lose a football game. He can't win them. If you blow it, it's 6 points. The fans, the newspapers, the commentators, everybody knows it immediately." In Fischer's case, though, the fans, who identified closely with his underdog status and appreciated his gritty tenacity, were willing to forgive his occasional misplay. After 15 seasons, Pat Fischer had earned the kind of respect that could not be rescinded.

For a cornerback, living with failure is part of the job. However, for teams that depend on enthusiasm to stay competitive, defeats like the ones the Redskins had suffered in the last two games sometimes have long-term effects. Knowing this, George Allen cajoled and prodded his downcast team into recapturing its feelings of pride and confidence. After the last two overtime disappointments, Allen knew another tough loss would be devastating.

Pat Fischer
Paul Fine Photo/Nate Fine Productions, Courtesy Washington Redskins

Pumped up by a standing ovation from the sellout crowd at RFK Stadium, the Washington Redskins came out firing on all cylinders. Larry Brown, starting at fullback in place of the injured Moses Denson, teamed with halfback Mike Thomas to establish Washington's ground game. On second and 8, Thomas got loose on a 34-yard sweep, giving the Redskins a first down at the Minnesota 24. Billy Kilmer hit Frank Grant with a 22-yard pass, then Brown turned the corner for a 2-yard touchdown. As 54,498 voices filled the air with cheers, Mark Moseley converted to give the Redskins a 7-0 lead.

Washington's defense kept the Vikings backed up in their own territory throughout the first quarter. On the first play of the second period, Larry Jones fielded Neil Clabo's short punt at the Vikings 45 and returned it 17 yards to the 28. Responding to the shouts of the crowd, Kilmer immediately went for the score, firing a 28-yard strike to Mike Thomas in the end zone. Touchdown, Washington!

Riding the emotional wave of their 14-0 lead, the charged-up Redskins stopped the Vikings twice more. Then, midway through the second quarter, Washington began another long drive from its 8. Ignoring the pain in his right shoulder, Kilmer completed five out of six passes for a total of 75 yards and capped his performance with a 27-yard scoring toss to wide receiver Frank Grant that increased Washington's lead to 21-0.

With 3 minutes left in the half, Tarkenton went to his hurry-up offense. Taking advantage of the Redskins' "prevent" defense, he completed five short passes to move the Vikings to the Washington 8. With 9 seconds remaining, Tarkenton fired into the end zone, and Chuck Foreman grabbed the ball for a touchdown to trim the 'Skins' lead to a more manageable 21-7. Nevertheless, as the Redskins headed for the clubhouse, the fans at RFK Stadium gave them a well-deserved standing ovation. If those fans had anything to do with it, Washington would not fall from grace for a third time.

Billy Kilmer's passing (8-10 for 139 yards and two TD's) and Mike Thomas' rushing (71 yards in 12 carries) had surprised and embarrassed the Vikings' famous Purple Gang defense. And, by keying on Chuck Foreman, the Redskins defense had successfully defused Minnesota's explosive ground attack. But that strategy began to blow up in their faces when the third quarter began. Forced to throw, Tarkenton completed six of seven passes (four of which went to Ed Marinaro for 47 yards) as the Vikings cruised to the Washington 3. On first and goal, Foreman dove into the end zone, and Minnesota climbed back into contention, 21-14.

The 'Skins responded with an impressive march of their own. Larry Brown tore off a 43-yard run, and Kilmer passed to Charley Taylor for 22 more. Although the drive stalled at the Vikings 15, Mark Moseley kicked a 32-yard field goal to increase Washington's advantage to 24-14. Minnesota countered with a copy-cat drive that ended with Fred Cox booting a 33-yard field goal that narrowed the score to 24-17.

When the fourth quarter got underway, the twice-burned fans at RFK started thinking incredulously about the possibility of yet another overtime debacle. That unsettling thought gained credence a few minutes later when Billy Kilmer limped off the field with an injured foot and Sam McCullum returned Bragg's 46-yard punt to the Minnesota 35. On first down, Tarkenton threw long to wide receiver John Gilliam, who caught the 46-yard bomb over his shoulder at the Washington 10. After a penalty moved the ball back to the 21, Tarkenton dropped back to pass. Finding no one open, Tarkenton took off running and, to the disgust of every Redskin on the field, made it to the end zone. Amazingly, Cox missed the conversion, and the Redskins still led, 24-23. After three overtime games in the last four weeks, apparently even God couldn't stand the agony of another sudden-death ordeal for Washington.

The ferocious Vikings defense poured in on the hobbling Kilmer three straight times. The results: a sack, a hurried incompletion, and an intentional grounding penalty that forced the Redskins to punt from their 15. Having completed 19 of his last 25 throws, Tarkenton saw no reason to abandon his short passing game when Minnesota took over at its 41. Two passes and two running plays worked the ball to the Washington 31. On third and 1, Chuck Foreman ripped through the line and raced into the end zone for a 31-yard touchdown, giving the Vikings the lead for the first time all day. Cox's point-after made the score Minnesota 30, Washington 24.

All eyes turned to Billy Kilmer. "If you opened up Kilmer's body," said linebacker Chris Hanburger, "all you'd find is guts." Unfortunately, Kilmer could not produce, and, while Mike Bragg punted to the Vikings, reserve quarterback Randy Johnson started limbering up behind the Redskins' bench. Six minutes

Mike Thomas   *Nate Fine Photo/Nate Fine Productions, Courtesy Washington Redskins*

remained when Minnesota took over at midfield. Seven plays consumed 27 yards, 4 minutes, and two of the Redskins' time-outs before Fred Cox came in for the coup de grace. But he missed the 40-yard field goal attempt, and, with 1:51 remaining in the game, the 'Skins still had one last chance to win.

Coach George Allen faced an excruciating decision: either stay with the injured Kilmer, who had completed only one of eight passes in the second half, or send in a healthy, but ice-cold, Johnson for the game's critical drive. Perhaps letting his heart get the better of his head, Allen stuck with Billy.

The Redskins started at their 23. The crowd groaned as Kilmer's first pass wobbled to the ground, a victim of a near-sack by all-pro defensive end Jim Marshall. However, his next pass landed in Frank

Grant's hands for a 21-yard gain and a first down at the Washington 44. One play later, Billy connected with Charley Taylor for another 21 yards. Then, with 1:04 remaining, Mike Thomas grabbed a flare and raced to the 15. On first down, Kilmer hobbled back into his pocket as Grant ran to the goal line. Billy threw as Grant cut sharply toward the middle, and the perfect pass met him 2 yards deep in the end zone. Touchdown! While the sellout crowd celebrated, Mark Moseley put Washington back in front, 31-30.

The game, however, was far from over. With 34 seconds and three time-outs left, the Vikings still had plenty of time to break 55,000 hearts. Tarkenton passed to Foreman for 20 yards. Time out, Minnesota. Tarkenton's next pass, to Brent McClanahan, gained 19 more. Time out, Minnesota. With 15 seconds left on the clock and the ball at the Washington 45, Tarkenton scrambled to his left and fired a 17-yard strike to Stu Voight at the Redskins 28. Only 5 seconds remained when the Vikings took their final time-out. Fred Cox came in again, determined to make up for his two earlier misses. Tarkenton spotted the ball at the 35, and Cox swung his leg, connecting solidly. The ball jumped off his foot and headed for the goalposts 45 yards away, but Ron McDole charged in and deflected it! [Fig. 96] While the football fluttered harmlessly to the ground, the gun sounded and the stadium rocked to the tune of the Redskins' 31-30 triumph!

"Ron Yary had been doing a pretty good job blocking down on me all afternoon," explained Ron "Dancing Bear" McDole in the exuberant Redskins locker room. "So Bill Brundige and I switched positions, and I came in from the outside. I actually turned sideways. I can't jump very high; you'd have to say I reached for it. It hit me in the left hand. I hit the ball real good, but I knew it traveled on. As I rolled over, though, I heard the crowd. Then I knew what happened."

By the width of Ron McDole's hand, the Redskins had survived one of the greatest rallies of all time. Fran Tarkenton overcame a 21-0 deficit by completing 27 of 37 passes for 357 yards and a touchdown without giving up an interception. At one point, Tarkenton, who would be named MVP at the end of the season, completed 18 of 20 passes for 282 yards. Although Billy Kilmer's stats were not nearly as impressive (13-25 for 233 yards), his gutsy performance on the 'Skins' game-winning drive was close to perfection. With the game on the line, Billy ignored the pain in his sprained ankle and completed four passes against a Vikings defense stacked with six defensive backs. According to Bud Grant, Minnesota's plain-spoken coach, that last drive was simply another "Kilmer masterpiece."

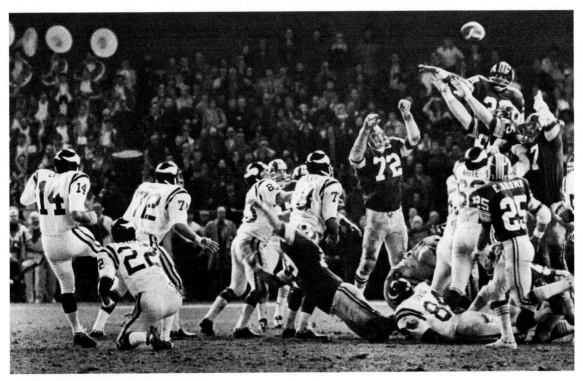

Fig. 96   *Richard Darcey/Washington Post Photo*

DE-FENSE, DE-FENSE

Washington Redskins vs. Dallas Cowboys

December 12, 1976

The Washington Redskins faced an unambiguous challenge in their final regular season game of 1976: defeat the Dallas Cowboys or miss the playoffs for the second year in a row. The Cowboys, who had wrapped up the Eastern Division Championship with an insurmountable 11-2 record, were already in the playoffs, but Washington, at 9-4, still needed one more victory to earn a wild-card berth. "It's all in our hands; we're in charge of our own destiny," said Billy Kilmer. "It's a matter of who wants it the most in Dallas. If we want it as a team, we'll get it. If we don't, we won't make the playoffs."

Victories in Dallas never came easily for the Washington Redskins. In fact, the Redskins had lost eight of their last nine games in Big D and had yet to win under Texas Stadium's truncated roof. But would the Cowboys, with their playoff spot already assured, have any incentive to win this game? "I don't buy that," said Dallas middle linebacker Lee Roy Jordan, who was about to play in his final regular season game. "If we win this game, we've got both our playoff games at home. That's plenty of incentive. Any time the Redskins and Cowboys go on the field, we kill each other. I don't expect it to be any different on Sunday. I know they're coming down here with fire in their eyes. We'll be ready for them."

By winning four of their last five games, the Redskins had escaped almost certain elimination from the playoffs and now were clearly at the top of their game. After missing the playoffs in 1975 with an 8-6 record, the 'Skins were determined to regain the respect of their peers and the adoration of their fans. "People have been cool to us all year," grumbled Washington middle linebacker Harold McLinton. "They wrote us off. I just want to show people that we're a playoff team. It's beyond the financial thing. This game won't be for money. It's one you have to play for your heart." Head Coach George Allen preached that "anyone who isn't ready now, whether he's a new man or a veteran, will never be ready for anything." And Billy Kilmer, who had survived a challenge from Joe Theismann for the starting quarterback job, simply said, "We have to win this week. Everybody knows it. It's our season."

The Redskins had added some new faces. Because he had long ago traded away his first five draft choices, the only way George Allen could upgrade the team significantly was through the newly created (and quickly dismantled) free agent market. With a flourish, Allen opened Jack Kent Cooke's checkbook and signed three top players: John Riggins, Calvin Hill, and Jean Fugett. Riggins, a free-spirited fullback who had rushed for over 1,000 yards while playing out his option with the New York Jets, and Hill, a

Yale graduate who had jumped to the now-defunct World Football League after five excellent seasons with the Cowboys, were brought in to bolster the 'Skins' running attack. Even though he had gained 919 yards and was voted Rookie of the Year in 1975, halfback Mike Thomas simply did not have enough bulk to absorb beatings on every play. Without reinforcements, Thomas would wear out as quickly as Larry Brown, who had hobbled valiantly through most of the last four seasons.

Jean Fugett, another ex-Cowboy, added a measure of versatility to the position he shared with veteran tight end Jerry Smith. "I can play inside or out," said Fugett when he first arrived in Washington. "The Ditka days of brute strength and sheer aggression are over. Sure, you have to be a good blocker, and I'm at least average. But I'm also quick and, I hope, fairly intelligent. I can wait a step to see where a cornerback or linebacker is heading and still get over there and cut him down, or break past him and fly if it's a pass play."

As if by magic, Allen also managed to acquire safety Jake Scott, guard Ron Saul, and cornerback Joe Lavender despite his depleted stock of tradable players. Saul, a 6-year veteran from the Oilers, quickly became a starter on an offensive line that now bore little resemblance to the unit that had played in Super Bowl VII just four years before. Of the five starters in 1976—Tim Stokes, Saul, Len Hauss, Dan Nugent, and George Starke—only Hauss had been on the Redskins' roster in '72.

On defense, six of Washington's starters were over 30 years old—McDole, Talbert, Hanburger, Fischer, Scott, and Houston—and when the Redskins were floundering in midseason, that seemed to be a problem. But after posting impressive wins over the Cardinals, Eagles, and Jets, Washington climbed back into the postseason hunt, thanks in large part to the outstanding play of its aging defensive secondary. Over the course of the season, 36-year-old Pat Fischer, 31-year-old Ken Houston, 30-year-old Jake Scott, and 25-year-old Joe Lavender had allowed opponents to complete only 42% of their passes and could take credit for most of the team's 24 interceptions and 19 fumble recoveries.

Only one obstacle blocked the Redskins' return to the playoffs: the Dallas Cowboys, who had whipped them, 20-7, earlier in the season. The outcome of the game would hinge on whether the 'Skins could maintain both their poise and their aggressiveness. "The Cowboys show you a lot of motion, a lot of different sets, mostly to confuse you," warned Washington's secondary coach, Ralph Hawkins. "You have to realize what formation they're in after they've finished all that running around." George Allen kept it simple: "To win, we just have to go out there and out-hit them."

On Saturday, 2,500 fans showed up at Redskin Park to give the team a rousing sendoff to Dallas. Coach Allen, delighted with the size and enthusiasm of the crowd, thanked the noisy well-wishers and declared, "This support reminds me of 1972 [the year the Redskins won the NFC Championship]. I hope we can reach the same heights!"

When the nationally-televised game got underway at Texas Stadium, the Cowboys and Redskins struggled like Olympic wrestlers to gain a slight advantage in leverage. Finally, after 13 unflinching minutes in which neither side yielded to the pressure, Washington took a chance. Bill Malinchak, the Redskins' masterful kick-blocker who had been lured out of retirement only two weeks before, charged in and dove for Danny White's foot as he punted from the Cowboys goal line. Stretched out parallel to the ground, Malinchak deflected the kick with his right hand, and the ball fluttered to the Dallas 18, where Washington took over.

A holding penalty pushed the Redskins back to the 26, but Billy Kilmer overcame that with a 17-yard completion to Frank Grant. Three plays later, though, the 'Skins were stopped at the 7 and had to settle for Mark Moseley's 25-yard field goal at the beginning of the second quarter. Trailing 3-0, the Cowboys finally got on track, but only after a roughing-the-punter penalty gave them a first down at midfield. Alternating rushes by Doug Dennison and Robert Newhouse, Dallas marched deep into Washington territory. Finally, Dennison skirted left end for a 12-yard touchdown, and the Cowboys led, 7-3.

After an exchange of punts, the 'Skins regained possession at midfield with 1:42 left in the first half. Kilmer began with a 15-yard pass to Mike Thomas, then hit Frank Grant at the Dallas 23. With a minute remaining, Jean Fugett grabbed Kilmer's next toss for a first down at the Dallas 6. After an incompletion, Kilmer fired to Fugett in the end zone for a touchdown, and the Redskins went back on top, 10-7.

A few seconds later, the first half ended, and the two teams repaired to their dressing rooms accompanied by the grumbling of 60,000 Cowboys fans. To the Redskins, it sounded like a symphony.

True to form, Washington's excellent defensive secondary had limited Roger Staubach to just two completions for 7 yards. However, the Cowboys' ground game had compensated by netting 94 yards on 24 carries. For the Redskins, Billy Kilmer had fared reasonably well (8-17 for 95 yards and a touchdown) while Mike Thomas and John Riggins combined for 55 yards in 16 running plays. The difference in the game remained Malinchak's blocked punt that had led to Moseley's field goal.

In the first series of the second half, Billy Kilmer threw an interception to Cowboys cornerback Mark Washington at the Redskins 44. Two plays later, Roger Staubach launched a deep pass to Butch Johnson, and the rookie receiver made a spectacular catch in the end zone to put the Cowboys ahead, 14-10. Kilmer tried to atone for his mistake with a spectacular play of his own, but his long pass was picked off. This time, however, the Cowboys were stymied by Washington's aroused defense, and White punted to Eddie Brown, who returned it 25 yards to the Redskins 45.

A 17-yard pass to fullback John Riggins [Fig. 97] and a 20-yard strike to Fugett advanced the ball to the Cowboys 10. On third down, Kilmer threw to Mike Thomas in the right flat. Linebacker Thomas "Hollywood" Henderson cut in front of Thomas and —with no one between him and the goal line 90 yards away—dropped the ball! On the next play, Moseley salvaged 3 points by kicking a 27-yard field goal, which narrowed the score to Dallas 14, Washington 13.

A promising drive by the Cowboys came to an abrupt halt when Jake Scott recovered a fumble at the Washington 9. [Fig. 98] Both defenses continued to dominate, and, with 7:24 left in the game, the Redskins took over at midfield. A pass to Mike Thomas and a handoff to John Riggins produced a first down at the Dallas 38. On third and 10, Kilmer spotted an incoming Cowboys blitz and called an audible. Avoiding the Dallas rush by sprinting out to his right, Billy looped a pass to Thomas, who grabbed it at the 20 and raced to the Cowboys 4 yard line before being caught from behind on a desperate shoestring tackle by safety Randy Hughes.

Thomas' big play carried a high price; he limped off the field with a twisted ankle and had to be replaced by former Cowboys fullback Calvin Hill. Two penalties moved the Redskins back to the 15. On second and goal, Hill took a pitchout and cruised around right end in the wake of a devastating block by Larry Brown. Once past the line, Hill broke two tackles and raced into the end zone for a touchdown! [Fig. 99] With 4½ minutes remaining, the 'Skins forged ahead, 20-14.

A 6-point lead late in the fourth quarter against the Dallas Cowboys was always an invitation to heartbreak. But Washington's veteran defense had other plans. On first down at his 21, Staubach was sacked by Ron McDole for a loss of 12. Then, on second down, defensive tackle Diron Talbert tipped Staubach's pass straight up in the air. When it came down, the ball was batted back and forth between several Redskins and Cowboys in a desperate game of volleyball before Washington's Dennis Johnson finally grabbed it at the Dallas 3! On first down, John Riggins swept around left end and charged into the end zone for a touchdown to give the Redskins a comfortable 27-14 lead.

3:30 remained. Staubach threw a scare into the 'Skins by quickly moving his team to the Washington 36. But after two incompletions, defensive end Ron McDole sacked Roger for a 5-yard loss. Then, on fourth and 15, McDole got to Staubach again and swatted away the Cowboys' last chance for a miracle finish.

Or so everyone thought until John Riggins fum-

Fig. 97 *Richard Darcey/Washington Post Photo*

Fig. 98 *Washington Post Photo*

Fig. 99   *UPI/The Bettmann Archive*

bled at midfield with 2 minutes left in the game, giving Staubach one more chance to be a hero. Fortunately, cornerback Joe Lavender quashed Dallas' very last hope with an interception, and the Redskins ran out the clock to preserve their 27-14 victory. The Washington Redskins were back in the playoffs.

"We were written off, pronounced dead and buried, but we've got some gutsy guys who just kept coming back," rasped a hoarse George Allen after the game. The Washington defense had played superbly, sacking Staubach five times and hurrying him so often that he could complete only 5 of 22 passes for 54 yards. When combined with two fumbles and eight punts, that had spelled doom for the favored Cowboys.

The old men of the Washington Redskins, considered over the hill for 6 years now, had lived to fight another day. "We overcame so much today," said Allen. "So many times it looked like we'd score, and we couldn't. It would have been easy to give up. But time after time we came back. That is what winning is really all about. We were down [earlier in the season]. The Giants game [a 12-9 loss] really hurt us. But the last month, I could feel us coming together. I like the feeling on this team. I like what I see. I see a lot of good things, and that's what makes a champion."

CHANGING OF THE GUARD

Philadelphia Eagles vs. Washington Redskins

September 10, 1978

On January 18, 1978, time ran out on George Allen. After seven successful years as head coach and general manager of the Washington Redskins, Allen must have realized that his continuing policy of mortgaging the future had finally caught up to him. Having traded away Washington's first five picks in the 1978 draft, and with most of his trusted veterans on the verge of retirement, Allen was looking down the maw of years of rebuilding. Although he had verbally agreed to a contract offer by Redskins President Edward Bennett Williams in the summer of 1977, the written version had remained unsigned on his desk for six months. Apparently, Allen (67-30-1 in the regular season with the Redskins and 2-5 in the playoffs) was waiting to see if his old job with the Los Angeles Rams would be offered to him. Fed up with Allen's procrastination, Williams announced that he had rescinded his offer, saying, "I gave George Allen unlimited patience, and he exhausted it."

When Allen first came to Washington in 1971, Redskins fans had just suffered through a quarter century of mediocrity and disappointment. So when Allen started preaching "The Future Is Now," everyone joined hands and shouted, "Hallelujah!" By trading future draft choices for aging stars, Allen succeeded in building an immediate winner, but, seven

years later, the team was still paying for those past triumphs and Allen's slogan had become a bitter joke. "You must have young players coming in all the time to develop consistency over the years," said Al Davis, the shrewd owner of the Oakland Raiders. "I think with George Allen's system, you eventually ruin the team."

Indeed, the signs of the Redskins' impending collapse had been accumulating for several years. After losing to the Minnesota Vikings, 35-20, in the first round of the 1976 playoffs, the 'Skins fell to 9-5 in 1977 and missed the playoffs for the second time in three years. By 1978, Allen had painted himself into a corner with his win-now-pay-later philosophy and could either stand pat and take his lumps or fold. Addicted to success, Allen froze when confronted with such a distasteful choice. Finally, after 6 months, Williams chose for him.

Five days later, Jack Pardee, a former all-pro linebacker with the Redskins and Rams, became the team's sixteenth head coach. Besides being extremely popular with the fans in Washington, Pardee had earned Coach of the Year honors in two different leagues — once in the defunct World Football League for leading the bankrupt Florida Blazers to the Championship game, and then in the NFL for taking the Bears from the cellar to the playoffs in three years.

Coach Jack Pardee

Copyright Washington Post; Reprinted by permission of the D.C. Public Library

One month later, Bobby Beathard, who had spent six years as Director of Player Personnel with the Miami Dolphins, became the team's general manager. Ironically, Beathard was drafted by the Redskins as a quarterback in 1959 but did not make the team. After a short (5-game) career with the Los Angeles Chargers of the fledgling American Football League, Beathard went into scouting. He worked for the Kansas City Chiefs and Atlanta Falcons until Miami hired him in 1972, the year the Dolphins went 17-0 and beat the Redskins in Super Bowl VII. In his six seasons with the Dolphins, Beathard demonstrated his eye for talent by drafting such players as Kim Bokamper, A.J. Duhe, Larry Gordon, Duriel Harris, Benny Malone, Freddie Solomon, and Ernie Rhone. Unlike George Allen (who did, in fact, become head coach of the Rams only to be fired in preseason), Beathard believed in using the draft to build a team.

Unfortunately, Beathard was missing his first five draft picks in 1978 and had to scramble to patch together a respectable team from the shambles that Allen left behind. Most of the "Over-the-Hill Gang" had fought their last battle. During the off-season, Charley Taylor, Len Hauss, Pat Fischer, Bill Brundige, Brig Owens, Rusty Tillman, Bob Brunet, Calvin Hill, and Jerry Smith retired with honors, joining Larry Brown and Roy Jefferson, who had bowed out the year before. Only six players from the Redskins' 1972 NFC Championship team remained: Billy Kilmer, Chris Hanburger, Harold McLinton, Ron McDole, Diron Talbert, and Terry Hermeling. Beathard did his best to plug the gaps by obtaining Coy Bacon, Perry Brooks, Fred Dean, Lemar Parrish, Ricky Thompson, and Tony Green. But former Redskins Coach Bill McPeak predicted that such stop-gap measures would eventually fail, saying, "You can only patch that dike so often. Then it's all patches—and it crumbles."

Allen's departure had its greatest impact at quarterback, where Joe Theismann, in his fifth year as a Redskin, finally beat out 39-year-old Billy Kilmer. Cocky and brash, but as nimble on his feet as he was with a quote, Joe had paid a full measure of dues. After being drafted out of Notre Dame by the Dolphins in 1971, Theismann resolved a contract dispute with Joe Robbie by jumping to the Canadian Football League, where he served three years with the Toronto Argonauts. In 1974, when the Dolphins traded his rights to the Redskins, Joe headed south. Not content to sit on the bench and watch Kilmer and Sonny Jurgensen take all the snaps from center, Theismann volunteered to run back punts, which he did for an impressive 10.5-yard average. Over the next three years, Theismann started 12 games as Kilmer's backup but always had to relinquish the reins when Billy was healthy enough to play. Under Jack Pardee, though, Joe was finally getting a chance to prove himself.

Fortunately for Theismann, Joe Walton, one of Allen's assistant coaches, had been retained and put in charge of the offense. "Joe took me as a personal challenge," said Theismann. "He took me under his wing and tutored me. He was very, very strict and disciplined. I owe the man everything. He was the first guy here to decide to go with me 100%. He was the first one to put faith in me." After seven years of working his way to the top, Joe Theismann began his 8-year reign as the Washington Redskins' starting quarterback on Opening Day against the New England Patriots. Although he performed adequately, Joe did not have the kind of game he had dreamed of, and the Redskins fell behind, 14-9. With 2½ minutes left in the game, the Patriots were killing the clock with running plays when, suddenly, defensive tackle Dave Butz smeared halfback Horace Ivory, causing a fumble, which linebacker Brad Dusek scooped up at the 31 and carried into the end zone for the game-winning touchdown!

The Redskins' next opponent, the Philadelphia Eagles, hadn't been as fortunate in their opening game, losing to the Los Angeles Rams on a last-second 46-yard field goal. After five years of trying but failing to reproduce George Allen's formula for instant success, the Eagles were just starting to get off the ground. While Washington's costly trades had produced an NFC Championship and five trips to the playoffs, Philadelphia's equally costly trades had built teams that had suffered through seasons of 5-8-1, 7-7, 4-10, 4-10, and 5-9.

Nevertheless, the Eagles, coached by Dick Vermeil, had finally formed a solid nucleus of players who would take them to Super Bowl XV two years hence. Ron Jaworski, in his second year as quarterback, spearheaded a dangerous offense that also featured halfback Wilbert Montgomery and an unstoppable 6-foot 8-inch receiver named Harold Carmichael. In addition, left linebacker Bill Bergey anchored an aggressive Philadelphia defense that soon would be called the best in the NFL. "We're all expecting it to be another dogfight," predicted Redskins linebacker Pete Wysocki. "Against these guys, it always is."

When the game began, the Redskins appeared to be outclassed. The first three times Joe Theismann dropped back to pass, he was dropped for losses. On offense, Philadelphia looked just as overwhelming: Mike Hogan carried for 15 yards, then Jaworski passed to Carmichael for 18 more, and Wilbert Montgomery bolted into the end zone from 34 yards out to stake the Eagles to an early 7-0 lead.

Tony Green, Washington's rookie kick returner, gave the 'Skins a much-needed boost by running the kickoff back to the 40 yard line. Halfback Mike Thomas skirted left end for 13 yards, then, a few plays later, Theismann connected with fullback John Riggins on a 16-yard pass to the Eagles 30. Two penalties and a short flare to Thomas worked the ball to the 4. On first and goal, Theismann rolled to his right, darted through an opening, and slid feet first into the end zone to tie the game, 7-7. [Fig. 101]

Fig. 101   *Richard Darcey/Washington Post Photo*

Philadelphia responded by driving the length of the field. The 'Skins defense stiffened at its 15, but Nick Mike-Mayer kicked a 32-yard field goal and the Eagles went up, 10-7. Tony Green's 41-yard kickoff return gave the Redskins excellent field position at the Philadelphia 38, but Washington frittered away its opportunity to pull even when placekicker Mark Moseley pushed his 35-yard field goal attempt to the right.

After forcing the Eagles to punt from deep in their territory, the Redskins geared up again at midfield. On first down, tight end Jean Fugett, seeing his first action of the year after hurting his knee in preseason, angled to the sideline, cut straight downfield, and ran under Theismann's deep pass at the 15. As Eagles safety Randy Logan slammed into him, Fugett was juggling the ball, but he finally latched on to it, spun out of Logan's grip, and charged across the goal line! Touchdown, Washington! Moseley's point-after was good, and the Redskins took the lead for the first time, 14-10.

Late in the second quarter, the Redskins took possession at their 26. A 23-yard pass to wide receiver Frank Grant, an 8-yard completion to John McDaniel, and four runs by Riggins advanced the ball to the Eagles 19. On second and 10, Jean Fugett ran a post pattern along the seam in Philadelphia's zone, and Theismann hit him between two defenders at the goal line. [Fig. 102] Touchdown! 54,380 Redskins fans at RFK Stadium whooped it up as the scoreboard changed to: Washington 21, Philadelphia 10.

For the first time in years, it seemed, the Redskins offense was hitting on all cylinders. Theismann, Thomas, Riggins, and Fugett were executing Joe Walton's progressive game plan with a flair unseen since the days of Sonny Jurgensen and Bobby Mitchell. At

Fig. 102   *Nate Fine/NFL Photos*

the end of the first half, the sellout crowd, happy to be watching a winning brand of football that was also entertaining, bellowed their appreciation and lifted their paper cups in tribute to the born-again Washington Redskins.

When the second half began, the Redskins defense kept the crowd cheering by forcing the Eagles to kick from their 31. Rick Engles boomed his punt 49 yards to Tony Green, who fumbled but quickly recovered and dashed 80 yards for a touchdown! With Moseley's conversion, Washington took a commanding 28-10 lead. Then, after an exchange of punts, quarterback Ron Jaworski completed five short passes, including a 10-yard strike to Wilbert Montgomery for a touchdown. But Mike-Mayer missed the conversion, and Philadelphia still trailed by 12 points, 28-16.

As the fourth quarter began, the Redskins regained possession at midfield. A quick toss to wide receiver Danny Buggs moved the chains to the Eagles 37. Then Theismann handed off to Riggins, who whirled at the line of scrimmage and lateraled the ball back to Theismann. Meanwhile, Danny Buggs was speeding by his unsuspecting defender, and Joe hit him in the hands with a beautiful spiral just before he crossed the goal line. [Fig. 103] Installed just three days earlier, the crowd-pleasing "flea-flicker" gave Washington a comfortable 35-16 advantage.

A 19-point cushion in the fourth quarter has a way of relaxing a team, a way of lulling it into a false sense of security and tricking it into playing loose on defense. With the suddenness of their namesake, the Eagles pounced on the unwary Redskins. While the 'Skins continued to congratulate themselves, Jaworski fired a 50-yard pass to wide receiver Ken Payne, giving Philadelphia a first down at the Washington 14. Wilbert Montgomery needed only two plays—a 6-yard reception and an 8-yard run—to get the ball into the end zone from there, and the Eagles trailed, 35-23, with 13 minutes left in the game.

Coach Pardee ordered Theismann to keep the ball on the ground to eat up some time. Unfortunately, Mike Thomas fumbled, and Philadelphia linebacker Frank LeMaster recovered at the Washington 23. On

Fig. 103

Nate Fine Photo/Nate Fine Productions, Courtesy Washington Redskins

first down, Jaworski nailed Harold Carmichael with a bullet at the 5. Then Montgomery took a handoff and charged across the goal line—but the touchdown was nullified by a holding penalty. Two plays later, Jaworski threw into the end zone, and Redskins linebacker Mike Curtis intercepted.

Theismann squandered Curtis' timely gift by tossing an interception of his own at the Washington 16. A minute later, Ron Jaworski was shaken up while completing a short pass, and the inexperienced John Walton had to take over at quarterback. A 4-yard run by halfback Cleveland Franklin set up fourth and 1 at the Washington 7. Realizing that a field goal was meaningless at this point, Coach Vermeil ordered his team to go for the first down. Walton dove over the line and made it with ease. On the next play, Wilbert Montgomery slammed into the end zone from the 5, and Philadelphia trailed, 35-30. Seven minutes remained.

After Mike-Mayer's kickoff, the Redskins marched to their 40, but Mike Thomas fumbled again and the Eagles took over at the Washington 34. The game was now in the slippery hands of the Redskins defense. Jaworski returned to action, but his screen pass to Montgomery was stopped for no gain. On second down, Franklin lost a yard. On third down, Jaworski faded back again, but, before he could get his pass off, defensive tackle Karl Lorch broke through and sacked him for a 9-yard loss. With 2:38 left on the clock, Philadelphia had to give up the ball.

Engle's punt was downed at the 'Skins 1 yard line, where a fumble would cost the game. Surprisingly, Thomas got the call. Hugging the football with all his might, he bulled to the 6. John Riggins carried on the next four plays while the Eagles used up all of their time-outs. On fourth and 5, Bragg punted to midfield.

51 seconds remained as Jaworski completed a pass to Wilbert Montgomery, but Chris Hanburger tackled him in bounds after a 7-yard gain and the Eagles had to rush to get off their next play. With 24 seconds left, Jaworski rifled a 9-yard strike to Keith Krepfle, who stepped out of bounds at the 35. Then two incompletions used up 19 seconds. On the last play of the game, Jaworski dropped back into his pocket as six Washington pass defenders dropped back in a deep zone, prepared to give up anything short of a touchdown. Wilbert Montgomery drifted across the line of scrimmage, and, with lots of room to maneuver, looked back for the pass. Jaworski laid the ball in his hands, and Montgomery turned upfield—without the ball! The sound of the gun punctuated the joyous roar of the crowd, and the relieved Washington Redskins ran off the field with their 35-30 victory.

After years of conservative game plans, the Redskins were overjoyed to have won a game with exciting plays: Tony Green's 80-yard kickoff return, Jean Fugett's two touchdown catches, and the "flea-flicker" to Danny Buggs. "Joe Walton drew it up on the sideline, right there in the dirt before we ran it," joked wide receiver Frank Grant. "He told Buggs to 'Go behind the green car, run up on the bumper, and Theismann'll hit you on the hood.'" Suddenly, football was fun once again in the Nation's Capital. "I still remember George Allen saying, 'You don't win with gimmicks,'" said John Riggins. "It's a good thing we had it today, because we wouldn't have won without it. I'll take those kind of gimmicks every time."

The surprising Washington Redskins went on to win their first six games in 1978 but collapsed down the stretch, losing their final five to finish at 8-8. As the defeats piled up, Bill McPeak's words came back to mind: "You can only patch that dike so many times. Then it's all patches—and it crumbles."

HEARTSTOPPER

St. Louis Cardinals vs. Washington Redskins

November 11, 1979

"Jack Pardee expects to win," remarked an old friend of the Washington Redskins' head coach. "It's not an ego thing with him. He's never overbearing or superficial. There's nothing rah-rah about his approach and he never gives a win-one-for-the-Gipper locker room trick talk. He's always quiet. But he expects to win."

Pardee had developed his attitude of quiet confidence in part by whipping an opponent much fiercer than any football player—cancer. A black mole on his arm was determined to be malignant in 1965, forcing Pardee to retire from the Los Angeles Rams at the age of 29. After the tumor was removed, Pardee endured debilitating radiation treatments that caused most of the muscle in his upper body to atrophy. Nevertheless, three months after the operation, Jack Pardee was back playing football again.

Nicknamed "Captain Crunch," Pardee came to Washington in 1971 as a principal figure in the "Ramskins" trade that brought instant success to George Allen's new team. Playing left linebacker and calling the defensive signals for "The Over-the-Hill Gang," Pardee enjoyed the best season of his career, intercepting five passes and being named all-pro. "He was a stunning innovator on defense," recalled defensive tackle Bill Brundige. "He could constantly change us. His mind was so sharp that sometimes, to put us in the right position, he would call defenses

that we hadn't worked on in three years. He was preparing to be a head coach all the while he was a player."

Coach Jack Pardee and Defensive Coach Richie Petitbon plot strategy on sideline with Chris Hanburger (55), Pete Wysocki (50), and Jake Scott (13)

Nate Fine Photo/Nate Fine Productions, Courtesy Washington Redskins

209

Pardee retired in 1973 and the following year was named head coach of the underfinanced Florida Blazers in the new World Football League. Despite the fact that his players went unpaid for three months, Pardee led the Blazers to the WFL Championship game. They lost, 22-21, but Jack was named WFL Coach of the Year. Impressed by his ability to motivate an unpaid team, George Halas hired Pardee to coach the 4-10 Chicago Bears. It took Jack only three years to move the Bears from the cellar to the playoffs, and, for that, he was named NFL Coach of the Year in 1977. Despite his success in Chicago, Pardee jumped at the chance to coach his old team when the Redskins asked him to take over for George Allen.

"When George left," said Brundige, "we were glad to see Jack come in. We felt Jack was one of the few coaches who would understand this football team. Someone else might come in and screw it up." When the 'Skins jumped out to a 6-0 start in '78, Pardee was hailed as a genius. Even when the Redskins lost their last five games and ended up with an 8-8 record, nobody blamed the coach. Most fans felt the collapse had been predestined by George Allen's irresponsible policy of deficit spending.

In 1979, Pardee had to weather another batch of retirements when the last of "The Over-the-Hill Gang"—Billy Kilmer, Chris Hanburger, and Ron McDole—along with veterans Harold McLinton, Mike Curtis, Bill Brundige, and Jake Scott called it quits. "In years past," said a long-time Redskins observer, pointing to the field, "you could look out there and see enough familiar faces to know you could count on X number of wins. This year you can't tell." Also missing were halfback Mike Thomas, who had been traded to the San Diego Chargers, and return specialist Tony Green, who was cut after giving a listless performance in training camp.

The Redskins began to rebuild. Despite having to wait until the fourth round of the 1979 draft, General Manager Bobby Beathard picked some gems out of the rubble: linebackers Neal Olkewicz, Monte Coleman, and Rich Milot, strong safety Tony Peters, and tight end Don Warren. Because of Beathard's drafting acuity, the rebuilding process took far less time

than anyone had imagined. After a tough 29-27 loss to the Houston Oilers in the opener, Washington reeled off four straight victories.

With Billy Kilmer no longer looking over his shoulder, quarterback Joe Theismann could finally relax. "This is the first year I've felt totally confident coming to camp. The fact that Billy is gone shows the coaching staff believes in me. I guess you can say it's like a weight was lifted off my shoulder." In the off-season, Theismann had worked hard to improve his short passing game, and the payoff came when his completion rate rocketed from 47.8% to over 60%. No longer looking to scramble on every other play, Theismann was finally grasping the connection between patience and consistency.

Part of the credit for Joe's success belonged to his blocking back, Benny Malone. "It's no accident that Theismann is getting better protection with Benny back there," said offensive backfield coach Fred O'Connor. A former Miami Dolphin, Malone had been brought to Washington by the man who originally drafted him: Bobby Beathard. "I like it rough, the rougher the better," said Malone. "I have geared myself and my body to take hits. I figure if I see a guy coming and he is going to whack me, why not go after him? Let him absorb the punishment." Said Theismann: "Benny's entire style fits into what we are doing. We want a physical team, a punishing team, because that's how we think we can win."

After ten games, the 6-4 Redskins were beginning to visualize themselves as true championship contenders. "Our goal right along has been to make the playoffs," asserted Coach Pardee. "These last six games are when the playoff teams will be determined." Standing directly between the 'Skins and their goal were the St. Louis Cardinals, coached by Oklahoma University legend Bud Wilkinson. Though only 3-7, the "Cardiac Cards" were dangerous, especially in the fourth quarter. Fullback Ottis Anderson, St. Louis' #1 draft choice, had already rushed for over 1,000 yards and caught 31 passes from quarterback Jim Hart. Now in his 13th season, Hart was at the top of his game and had two other deadly weapons at his disposal: Pat Tilley and Mel Gray. As their

Benny Malone
Copyright Washington Post; Reprinted by permission of the D.C. Public Library

37-7 whipping of the Minnesota Vikings the previous week illustrated, the Cardinals could score almost at will.

"It's going to be a tough game against a good team," predicted Coach Jack Pardee. "It will tell us something about ourselves." Although Pardee's words were not flashy, they were genuine. Just like the man.

5 0,868 cold and wet Redskins fans at Robert F. Kennedy Stadium watched helplessly as the St. Louis Cardinals marched through a steady downpour toward the Washington goal line. Running the football on five of their first six plays, the Cards advanced from midfield to the Redskins 10, where they faced fourth and 1. Ottis Anderson took a handoff and ripped through a big hole in the Redskins line.

But just before he got to the goal line, middle linebacker Neal Olkewicz slammed into him and knocked the ball loose. The slippery ball skittered into the end zone, and, after a mad scramble, cornerback Lemar Parrish finally fell on it. Washington took over at its 20.

The Redskins proved that they, too, could move the ball. Quarterback Joe Theismann started with a 9-yard completion to tight end Don Warren, then handed off six times in a row as Washington surged into St. Louis territory. On first down at the Cardinals 40, Theismann fired a pass to wide receiver Ricky Thompson, who caught the ball at the 24 and ran to the St. Louis 7 before cornerback Roger Wehrli forced him out of bounds. On the next play, fullback John Riggins skirted left end and charged into the end zone for a touchdown. Mark Moseley added the extra point, and the Redskins led, 7-0.

Washington's defenders stopped the Cards on three plays, but, when Tony Peters fumbled Steve Little's punt at the Redskins 26, they had to go right back in. Five straight rushes by Ottis Anderson set up a fourth and goal at the Washington 1 yard line. Using Anderson as a decoy, Hart slipped the ball to Theotis Brown, who dove into the end zone for a touchdown. A minute later, the first quarter ended with the score tied, 7-7.

A long Redskins drive fizzled at the Cardinals 36, but Washington got the ball right back when cornerback Joe Lavender intercepted a Jim Hart pass and returned it to the St. Louis 25. Two plays later, though, Theismann was sacked for a 10-yard loss, and the 'Skins had to settle for a 46-yard field goal by Mark Moseley.

Leading 10-7, the Redskins stopped the Cardinals twice more. Then, with 3 minutes left in the half, Theismann tried to extend Washington's lead. A pass to Don Warren picked up 17 yards, then Danny Buggs caught a pair of 14-yard bullets to advance the ball to the Cardinals 11. Finally, with less than a minute on the clock, Theismann dropped back and hit Ricky Thompson in the end zone with an 8-yard touchdown pass, and Washington took a 17-7 lead to the locker room.

Dave Butz (65) and Brad Dusek (59) wrestle Ottis Anderson to the ground

Nate Fine Photo/Nate Fine Productions, Courtesy Washington Redskins

The Redskins, it seemed, were mudders. Washington's defenders had prevented St. Louis from converting seven straight third-downs in the first half, and limited Jim Hart to just 2 completions in 8 attempts. Conversely, Joe Theismann had connected on 8 of 11 for 103 yards and two TD's, while Redskins rushers, notably John Riggins and Benny Malone, contributed 105 yards.

The steady rain continued to make a mockery of any attempt at finesse, and the third quarter was notable only for two interceptions by Redskins cornerback Lemar Parrish. Washington capitalized once with a 27-yard field goal to extend its lead to 20-7, but that was all. However, as the fourth quarter began, the 'Skins started rolling. Keeping St. Louis' defenders back on their heels with a cunning mixture of short passes and runs, Washington drove from midfield to the Cardinals 4. On third and goal, Theismann rifled a pass to Riggins in the end zone, and the Redskins took a seemingly safe 27-7 lead.

St. Louis tricked Washington with a fake punt on its next series, but eventually had to give up the football at the Redskins 34 when Coy Bacon sacked Hart on fourth down. Washington couldn't muster a clock-killing drive, though, and the Cardinals got the ball back at their 29. A screen to Theotis Brown picked up 19 yards, then a 20-yard completion to wide receiver Mel Gray was augmented by a roughing-the-passer penalty. Two carries by Anderson worked the ball to the 2, and, on first and goal, halfback Wayne Morris squeezed through the line for a touchdown. With almost 10 minutes left in the game, St. Louis trailed, 27-14.

The Redskins grew conservative, calling three straight running plays, then punting. The Cardinals, playing with the abandon that desperation affords, charged 55 yards in eight plays and scored again. With 4:38 still remaining, Washington's 27-21 lead was starting to look extremely fragile. St. Louis' resurgent defense stopped the 'Skins again, and, after Mike Bragg's 41-yard punt, Hart & Co. took over at their 44. Two short completions to tight end Richard Osborne, a 24-yard pass to Pat Tilley, and a sweep by Ottis Anderson advanced the ball to the Washington 21. On second and 6, Jim Hart fired to Anderson in the middle of the end zone. The big fullback came down with the ball, and the game was tied. A moment later, Steve Little untied it with his perfect kick, and St. Louis climbed on top for the first time, 28-27.

With 1:43 left in the game, the Redskins went into their 2-minute drill. On first down, Joe Theismann was sacked, but Benny Malone recouped the yardage on the next play. On third and 10 at the 28, Theismann threw to tight end Don Warren over the middle. The pass was high, and Warren could only get a hand on the ball, tipping it straight up in the air. With two Cardinals defenders on his back, Warren went up for the rebound like a power forward. When he came down with the ball at the 39, the Redskins were still alive.

With 1:05 left in the game, Theismann zipped a low fastball to Clarence Harmon on a slant to the sideline. In full stride, Harmon made a shoestring catch and headed upfield. At the 50, a Cardinals linebacker lunged and missed, and Harmon broke free down the sideline for a 35-yard gain! [Fig. 107]

Fig. 107   *Nate Fine/NFL Photos*

Fig. 108   *Copyright Washington Post; Reprinted by permission of the D.C. Public Library*

After three more plays gained 4 yards, Mark Moseley came in for the game-winning field goal from 39 yards away. The snap from center Ted Fritsch was poor, and the ball skidded back to Theismann like a hot grounder. Nevertheless, Joe fielded the wet ball cleanly and set it on its nose for Moseley, who unhesitatingly booted it through the uprights 39 yards away! [Fig. 108] The jubilant Redskins were back on top, 30-28.

36 seconds remained. Moseley squibbed the kick-off to the Cardinals 26. Wedge man Calvin Favron corralled it and, after a 10-yard return, lateraled to Will Harrell, who raced to the Cardinals 48 before he was tackled. With the sellout crowd screaming for his head, Jim Hart returned to the field in quest of one final miracle. On first down, he completed an 8-yard pass to Anderson, but his next two throws fell incomplete. Fourth down. With 9 seconds left in the game, Hart faded back and fired again, but Dave Butz leapt into the air and batted the ball away, preserving Washington's shaky 30-28 victory!

"I t would have been a crushing loss," admitted Joe Theismann, who had watched helplessly as Jim Hart completed 11 of 12 passes during the Cardinals three touchdown drives in the fourth quarter. "Every quarterback gets that hot once or twice in his life," said defensive tackle Diron Talbert. "When Hart throws the ball like that, he's hard to stop."

After 59 minutes of a contest that had been even in every category except interceptions (the Redskins picked off 3 while the Cards were shut out), the game had come down to one play: Mark Moseley's 39-yard field goal with 40 seconds left on the clock. Ted Fritsch's low snap had nearly cost the Redskins the victory, but Theismann's graceful scoop put the play back on schedule. "I saw the ball hit the ground," said Moseley. "But you just have to keep coming. I have enough confidence in Joe [Theismann] to know he's going to get the ball up somehow. The ground was soggy. The whole field was a mess between the hashmarks. Joe never slowed down, and neither did I." Coach Pardee conceded, "It wasn't very graceful, but I'll take it. This shows me something about our team. These people never give up."

READUM WEEPUM

Washington Redskins vs. Dallas Cowboys

December 16, 1979

Dallas Week got off to a rousing start. It began in the final minutes of a 38-14 victory over the Cincinnati Bengals when the sellout crowd at RFK Stadium started chanting, "BEAT DALLAS! BEAT DALLAS! BEAT DALLAS!" Then, in the locker room shortly after the game, several Washington offensive linemen pitched in to send a funeral wreath to Cowboys star defensive end Harvey Martin. The countdown to Sunday had begun.

The outcome of the final game of the 1979 season was far more important to the Redskins than to the Cowboys. Although both teams had compiled 10-5 records, Dallas had already clinched a playoff spot by virtue of its unbeatable intraconference record. Washington was still in the hunt. With one week left in the 1979 season, 13 NFL teams were trying to break through the traffic jam blocking the 10 roads to Super Bowl XIV in Pasadena.

The heaviest congestion was in the NFC, where the Los Angeles Rams, champs in the West, the Dallas Cowboys, and the Philadelphia Eagles had already clinched spots. That left Chicago, Tampa Bay, and Washington in competition for the two remaining openings. The Redskins had the inside track; almost every combination of wins and losses would put them in the post-season tournament. For instance, if they beat the Cowboys in the final game of the season, the 'Skins would be Eastern Division

champs and not have to bother with the wild-card game the following week. Or if either Tampa Bay or Chicago lost its final game, the Redskins would advance to the playoffs no matter what happened in Dallas.

That wasn't all. Even if Washington were to lose to the Cowboys and both Tampa Bay and Chicago were to win (leaving all three teams with 10-6 records), the NFL's tie-breaking procedure would still favor the 'Skins. In case of a three-way tie, the pertinent category in the tie-breaking system would be point differential in conference games, where Washington owned a 33-point lead over the Bears. In other words, if the Redskins were to lose to the Cowboys by, say, 6 points, the Bears would have to beat their final opponent, the St. Louis Cardinals, by at least 28 points to get into the playoffs. Since the low-scoring Bears had managed a total of only 29 points in their last three games, the Redskins looked like shoo-ins. Nevertheless, the Washington Redskins knew that to be assured of a spot in the playoffs they couldn't rely on anyone but themselves. With a chance to earn the home-field advantage throughout the conference playoffs, the Redskins were wise enough to prepare for the Dallas game as if it were for the Championship.

Even though they were already in the playoffs, the Cowboys wanted to win this game for three reasons: to clinch the home-field advantage; to give quarterback Roger Staubach a victory in the final regular season game of his brilliant career; and to exact some revenge on the Redskins, who had embarrassed them by kicking a late field goal in a 34-20 victory at RFK Stadium earlier in the season. "When the Redskins come down here, we'll bite their heads off," promised Harvey Martin immediately after that game. Even Coach Tom Landry, normally as emotional as a shovel, got angry and fired Thomas "Hollywood" Henderson for clowning on the sideline while his teammates absorbed the beating.

What had happened to the cold, precise, unemotional Dallas Cowboys who, for years, had been criticized for playing like robots? Many Dallas fans believed that the Cowboys might have won some of those Championship games they had narrowly lost if the poker-faced Landry had been able to incite his team to play with more spirit. Others argued that if Landry relied on raw emotionalism (like George Allen) instead of polished execution of innovative plays, Dallas never would have advanced to all those Championship games in the first place. "The Cowboys have taken it upon themselves to be more emotional," said Redskins Coach Jack Pardee. "They've changed. This is a new kind of Cowboys team—one that has some fire." Unfortunately for the Redskins, one thing had not changed on the Dallas Cowboys: the number of players selected to the Pro Bowl. Eight Cowboys—Roger Staubach, Tony Hill, Pat Donovan, Herb Scott, Harvey Martin, Randy White, Bob Breunig, and Cliff Harris—would be going to Hawaii after the Super Bowl, the largest contingent from any club in the NFL.

Although not as famous as "America's Team," Washington had been the hottest club in the league for the last two weeks, ever since halftime of a game against the Green Bay Packers. Angered by the 'Skins' lackadaisical play in the first half of that game, the usually soft-spoken Pardee had stormed into the locker room and lambasted his startled players at maximum volume. The tongue-lashing worked; the Redskins scored 31 unanswered points and won, 38-21. The following week, Washington looked just as powerful as it tore apart the Bengals, 38-14. Pardee now faced the most important game in his two years

with the Redskins. He had already exceeded everyone's expectations by taking over a team that had been nearly bankrupted by George Allen's disregard for the future and leading it to the brink of the playoffs. Now all he needed was one more victory to make the metamorphosis complete.

How had Pardee molded a hodgepodge of free agents, rookies, and veterans into a 10-game winner? "It was the pride of the old guys (Talbert, Houston, Bacon, Riggins, Butz), and the intensity of the new guys, along with simple game plans by a great coaching staff," explained linebacker Pete Wysocki. "Also, our morale has been excellent—it has to be when you don't have 80 jillion superstars."

Nevertheless, a lot of the credit for Washington's rejuvenation was being given to fullback John Riggins and quarterback Joe Theismann. After rushing for 1,014 yards and being named Redskin of the Year in 1978, Riggins had gained over 1,100 yards in '79. Theismann's performance had finally matched his braggadocio, and his teammates elected him Redskin of the Year in 1979. "Joe's been great; we count on him," said Wysocki. "But we kid him about the way he is. When we voted him the MVP on the team the other day, Joe started making a speech about how there are 45 guys on the team. So we all yelled at him, 'Shut up, hot dog.'" Undaunted, Joe kept right on talking. In his sixth year with Washington, Theismann had emerged as a first-rate quarterback after abandoning the notion that he had to win every game by himself. Instead of always looking for a big play, Joe was now content to throw short passes as a complement to Riggins' line charges. As a result, Theismann was the second-ranked passer in the NFC —right behind Roger Staubach.

Like many excited Redskins fans in the Washington area, Coach Pardee believed the 'Skins were in perfect position to make a run at the Super Bowl. "To be in this position—to have the 16th week determine the division title—was beyond anyone's dreams before the season," admitted Pardee. "I thought we'd have a good shot at the playoffs, but with Dallas coming off the Super Bowl, I thought they'd have the division wrapped up by now. Now, everything is ours—if we are good enough."

Joe Theismann
Copyright Washington Post; Reprinted by permission of the D.C. Public Library

The fog blurring the NFC playoff picture cleared just moments before the Redskins and Cowboys faced off for the opening kickoff in Dallas. The news wasn't good for the Washington Redskins. The Chicago Bears, who hadn't scored over 40 points in a game in four years, had just beaten the St. Louis Cardinals, 42-6. And the Tampa Bay Buccaneers had shown their offensive prowess in a 3-0 drubbing of the Lions. That left Washington with only one way to avoid watching the playoffs on television: beat the Cowboys.

The first break of the game went to the Redskins when linebacker Brad Dusek recovered a Ron Springs fumble at the Cowboys 34. Washington carefully worked the ball to the 3, but Joe Theismann was sacked for a loss and Mark Moseley kicked a 24-yard field goal to give the Redskins a 3-point headstart. Moments later, Dallas coughed up the ball again, and Dusek recovered for the 'Skins at their 45. Looking for a quick 6 points, Theismann threw deep to wide receiver Danny Buggs, who pulled in the 39-yard strike at the 18. John Riggins turned the corner for 14 yards, then Theismann scored from the 1 on a bootleg and Washington went up, 10-0.

The second period opened with the Redskins beginning a new drive at their 20. A 10-yard pass to Buggs, a couple of runs by Riggins, and a 20-yard completion to Clarence Harmon advanced the ball to the Washington 45. On second down, halfback Benny Malone caught a short pass from Theismann, shook off a tackle, and raced 55 yards into the Dallas end zone for a touchdown! The football gods were obviously smiling on the Redskins as the scoreboard registered their 17-0 lead.

The Cowboys didn't panic, though. Dallas used 13 plays to move 70 yards into the Washington end zone, with Springs finally slanting in from the 1. As the 65,000 Cowboys fans at Texas Stadium cheered, Rafael Septien converted to make the score 17-7, in favor of the 'Skins. With 1:48 left in the half, Dallas regained possession at its 15. Passing on every down, Staubach shredded the Washington secondary with completions of 21, 9, 12, 13, and 20 yards. A holding penalty against the Cowboys put them in a third-and-20 hole at the Redskins 26, but, with 15 seconds left in the half, Staubach rifled a pass to Preston Pearson for a touchdown to tighten the score to Washington 17, Dallas 14.

Like the Redskins in the first period, the Cowboys had been unstoppable in the second quarter, scoring two touchdowns and converting all five of their third-down plays into first downs. The Redskins were still leading, but the way things were going, that soon would be only a memory.

Sure enough, on Dallas' first possession of the second half, fullback Robert Newhouse crowned a 52-yard drive by bursting into the end zone from 2 yards out. Having scored touchdowns on three consecutive possessions, the Cowboys now led, 21-17. Both teams' defenses regained control, though, and no more scoring occurred during the rest of the third quarter. Finally, the Redskins started to roll again as the fourth period got underway. With Theismann throwing short to keep Dallas on its heels, Riggins began to wear down the Cowboys with his powerful charges, and Washington marched to the Dallas 7. On fourth and inches, Coach Pardee opted for a field goal rather than risk losing his team's shaky momentum, and Moseley split the uprights to pull the 'Skins to within a point, 21-20.

Two plays later, Pardee looked like a genius when Redskins safety Mark Murphy intercepted a Staubach pass and returned it to the Dallas 25. Trying for an immediate score, Theismann threw to wide receiver Ricky Thompson in the end zone. The pass fell incomplete, but free safety Cliff Harris was called for interference and the 'Skins were awarded a first down at the Cowboys 1. Riggins powered in on the next play, and with 10 minutes remaining in the game Washington went back on top, 27-21.

The Redskins defense choked off Dallas' plans for quick retaliation, and Washington got the ball back at its 31. After a 3-yard gain, John Riggins took a handoff and swerved to the right, where he found some running room. Thanks to devastating blocks by Ron Saul, George Starke, and Jeff Williams, Riggins broke free and soon was at full speed, hugging the sideline as he raced toward the Cowboys goal line. At the 20, Dallas' Cliff Harris tried to push the big full-

back out of bounds, but failed. Then Cowboys safety Dennis Thurman dove for Riggins' feet at the 7. [Fig. 110] Big John stumbled but kept his balance long enough to dive into the end zone! Touchdown, Redskins! Riggins' 66-yard dash stretched Washington's lead to 34-21 with less than 7 minutes remaining in the game.

When the 'Skins stopped the Cowboys on their next three plays, many of the 65,000 disappointed Dallas fans headed home for supper, resigned to the fact that the Redskins would run out the clock and go back to Washington as Eastern Division champs. But when Redskins running back Clarence Harmon, the hero of several earlier victories, fumbled at the Dallas 42, the remaining fans rekindled their faith. Staubach quickly completed a 14-yard pass to Butch Johnson and a 26-yarder to Tony Hill. Then, from the Washington 26, Staubach fired a bullet to Ron Springs, who caught it at the 8 and darted into the end zone for a touchdown. With 2:20 left in the game, the Cowboys trailed, 34-28.

Needing only one or two first downs to clinch the game, the Redskins soon faced a critical third-and-2 at their 33. Riggins got the call, but defensive tackle Larry Cole nailed him in the backfield and Washington was forced to punt with 1:53 left on the clock.

Seventy-five yards from victory, Roger Staubach appealed once more to the god of miraculous comebacks. A pass to Hill gained 20 yards; then a bullet to Preston Pearson picked up 22 more. On first and 10 at the Redskins 33, Tony Hill got open in the end zone—but Staubach overthrew him. Undaunted, Roger's next pass was right on target, landing in Pearson's arms at the 8 with 42 seconds remaining in the game. Desperate for a big defensive play, Washington decided to risk an all-out blitz. Anticipating the extra pressure, Staubach took a short drop and lobbed a soft pass over a charging linebacker. Tony Hill took one step to the inside, then raced straight into the end zone, stretched out his arms, and caught Staubach's delicate pass on his fingertips. [Fig. 111] Touchdown, Dallas! Septien's crucial point-after was good, and the Cowboys climbed back into the lead, 35-34.

The Washington Redskins had 39 seconds left to salvage their season. A holding penalty, a tipped pass,

Fig. 110   *Richard Darcey/Washington Post Photo*

and a hurried incompletion produced a third-and-20 at the Washington 16. With 16 seconds left in the game, Theismann threw long for tight end Don Warren. The pass fell incomplete—but defensive back Aaron Mitchell was flagged for pass interference, giving the Redskins a first down at their 49!

Nine seconds remained. Forced to hurry, Theismann overthrew wide receiver John McDaniel. The clock stopped with 5 seconds left. On second down, Theismann hit Warren with a quick pass over the middle at the Dallas 42. As soon as Warren hit the ground, Theismann, along with every other Redskin on the field, signaled desperately for a time-out as the clock hovered at 00:01. Placekicker Mark Moseley

ran onto the field to try a 58-yard field goal—but the referee ruled that the game had ended before the time-out was called. The Washington Redskins' season was over. The goddam Cowboys had won, 35-34.

Perhaps no game in the history of the Washington Redskins produced such radical mood swings. Against a background of playoff-like tension, the Redskins' jubilation over their early 17-point lead turned into dismay as the Cowboys fought back to gain a 21-17 advantage. Later, Redskins spirits soared again when Riggins sprinted 66 yards for the touchdown that seemed to clinch the game. But those spirits soon plummeted, replaced by chagrin and dis-

Fig. 111   *Richard Darcey/Washington Post Photo*

belief, as Staubach passed for two touchdowns in the final 3 minutes. Finally, when the officials disallowed their last timeout, the Redskins were left clawing the air in frustration and rage. "Where is the justice in this world," said a bitter Joe Theismann. "This is a team that started from absolutely nowhere and accomplished a lot. But not nearly as much as we thought we should. Everyone wanted this so badly. I've never seen anyone play with such heart. Know what this is like? It's like when you fall in love . . . you fall hard when it's over."

Harvey Martin added the final indignity. Storming through the doors to Washington's locker room, Martin returned the week-old funeral wreath by hurling it at the feet of the crestfallen Redskins. Amid the tears and bitterness and grief, the only thing missing was a dirge.

SCALPING PARTY

Detroit Lions vs. Washington Redskins

November 8, 1981

The devastating loss to the Dallas Cowboys in the final game of the 1979 season not only cost the Washington Redskins a spot in the playoffs that year, it continued to haunt them throughout the following campaign. A general malaise carried over from that game, sapping the team's spirit. At crucial moments, Coach Jack Pardee seemed confused, and his unenthusiastic players looked as if they were just going through the motions. A four-game losing streak was followed by a five-game losing streak, and season-ticket holders began staying away by the thousands. When the frustrating season finally ended amid rumors of an impending coaching change, the Redskins had sunk to 6-10, their first losing record in a decade.

As the losses piled up, it became clear that the Redskins were being pulled in two different directions. General Manager Bobby Beathard wanted to break in young players while they were still healthy and hungry. He wanted a snazzy, high-scoring offense. Most of all, he wanted a progressive coach who could inspire and communicate with his players. Jack Pardee, a quiet, controlled, disciplined man who believed that hard work was the sole answer to every problem, wanted to use his veterans, and, like his mentor for 14 years, George Allen, preferred a conservative offense that minimized the chance of mistakes. Something had to give.

When the season ended, Redskins Owner Jack Kent Cooke met several times with Pardee and Beathard in an attempt to find a solution. Neither man was willing to compromise. Finally, Beathard issued an ultimatum: either he or Pardee would have to go. As a result, one year after being named NFC Coach of the Year, Jack Pardee was fired.

Cooke gave Beathard a free hand in the selection of a new head coach. Rather than hire a big name like John Robinson or John Madden, Beathard trusted his instincts and chose Joe Gibbs, the relatively unknown mastermind of the San Diego Chargers' "Air Coryell" offense. Beathard convinced Cooke that Gibbs, with 17 years experience assisting some of the top coaches in the country, was the right man for the job. On January 13, 1981, Joe Gibbs became the 17th head coach in the history of the Washington Redskins.

Realizing that the Redskins personnel was not suited to an all-out aerial attack like the one he had designed at San Diego, Gibbs, in one of his first acts as head coach, visited John Riggins at his home in Kansas to try to persuade the big fullback to come back to the team. Impressed by the new coach's sincerity, Riggins, who had retired at the beginning of the 1980 season when the Redskins would not renegotiate his contract, returned to Washington, saying, "I'm bored, I'm broke, I'm back."

More changes were in the works. For the first time in decades, the Redskins went to training camp

221

freshly stocked with plenty of high-quality draft choices. In perhaps the greatest one-day haul of talent in Washington Redskins history, Bobby Beathard drafted Russ Grimm, Mark May, Dexter Manley, Darryl Grant, Charlie Brown, and Clint Didier. Beathard also traded a second-round pick to the Baltimore Colts for all-purpose halfback Joe Washington, a nifty cut-back runner with good hands. And when Beathard signed tackle Joe Jacoby, linebacker Mel Kaufman, and running backs Otis Wonsley and Terry Metcalf as free agents after the draft, the final stones in the foundation of future championship teams were set in place.

With all the changes in coaches, players, and attitude, Washington fans became excited again. However, when Joe Gibbs' inaugural season got underway, a combination of turnovers, penalties, and injuries caused his frustrated team to lose its first five games. Although Gibbs maintained a public veneer of confidence and optimism, privately he was feeling the pressure. "It was about the worst situation in the world," remembered Gibbs. "My job is to win games, and I was losing. I felt like a guy who is part of a business that's going bankrupt—and it was my fault."

Neither too proud nor too stubborn to change, Gibbs completely abandoned his pass-first philosophy in favor of a more conservative ball-control offense that featured only one running back (either John Riggins or Joe Washington) and two tight ends. Critics complained that the one-back formation was as unsophisticated as the old flying wedge, but the Redskins would soon prove that proper execution is more important than subterfuge. Coach Gibbs also got on the same wave-length with 8-year veteran quarterback Joe Theismann, who had been feeling alienated and unappreciated. One night, Theismann drove to Gibbs' home, and the two men settled their differences. After that, the Redskins won three of their next four games, and displays of confidence were no longer a charade out at Redskin Park.

"We're just getting our feet on the ground after that start we had," said Gibbs. "We are seeing who the producers are: people like John Riggins, Joe Washington, and Mike Nelms. We're still juggling positions; we're still trying to discover ourselves. But we're making real progress." With a few victories under their belts, players like safety Mark Murphy were starting to enjoy being a Washington Redskin again. When the 'Skins were 0-5, Murphy recalled that "the kids in the neighborhood made fun of me, and the dogs barked at me. Now the kids want to play catch, and the dogs want to show me all their tricks." Hard work and discipline had solved the penalty and turnover problems, and, now that most of the team was reasonably healthy, the Redskins were eager to show their fans at Robert F. Kennedy Stadium that they could beat a playoff contender.

Although only 4-5, the Detroit Lions, Washington's next opponent, were just a game out of first place in the evenly-matched NFC Central Division and were capable of beating any team in the NFL. After four coaches in 6 years had failed to lift the Lions out of their doldrums, Monte Clark was hired as head coach in 1978. In his first season, Clark led the Lions to a 7-9 record, but, after quarterback Gary Danielson injured his knee, Detroit's record plummeted to 2-14 in 1979. The Lions' fall from grace was cushioned, however, by the receipt of the #1 pick in the 1980 draft, with which they chose Oklahoma's Heisman Trophy-winner, Billy Sims.

After rushing for 1,303 yards, catching 51 passes, scoring 16 touchdowns, and being named NFC Rookie of the Year in 1980, Sims was being compared to NFL Hall of Famers Gale Sayers, Lenny Moore, and Elroy "Crazylegs" Hirsch. The Lions improved dramatically in 1980, finishing at 9-7, but, in 1981, ran into problems when Danielson went out again, this time with a dislocated wrist. After Jeff Komlo started and lost two games, Eric Hipple took over at quarterback and led the Lions to two victories in their next three games. With Sims in top form, averaging 4.6 yards a carry, Detroit was once again setting its sights on the playoffs.

Curiously, in eight games dating back to 1939, the Lions had never beaten the Redskins in Washington, and the oddsmakers predicted the 'Skins would continue that unusual streak by a margin of 2 points. "We're going to begin a stretch now against teams that are challenging for playoff berths," said Coach Gibbs. "That will tell us how good we are."

At 1:00 p.m. on November 8, 1981, Mark Moseley kicked off into the unseasonably warm air of RFK Stadium to begin the game between the Washington Redskins and the Detroit Lions. To the delight of the 52,000 fans in the stands, Detroit's rookie kick returner Robbie Martin was clobbered at the 21 by a pack of head-hunting Redskins. The force of their gang tackle dislodged the ball, and Jeris White recovered for Washington at the Lions 22.

It took the Redskins 25 seconds to score: halfback Joe Washington bolted into the end zone from the 7, and Washington jumped out to a 7-0 lead. Five minutes later, the 'Skins got another break when defensive end Mat Mendenhall recovered Eric Hipple's fumble at the Detroit 10. Unfortunately, the Redskins had to settle for Mark Moseley's 21-yard field goal and a 10-0 lead. Incredibly, Detroit turned over the football again on its next possession when Hipple tossed an interception to cornerback Lemar Parrish. This time, however, Washington could not capitalize at all, and Mike Connell punted back to the Lions.

Detroit finally started playing keep-away and marched easily down the field as Hipple and Sims took turns shredding the Washington defense. On the eighth play of the drive, Hipple threw deep to wide receiver Fred Scott, who hauled in the 36-yard strike in the end zone. So, despite three crippling turnovers, the Lions trailed by only 3 points, 10-7. Then on Detroit's first possession of the second quarter, Billy Sims zig-zagged for 29 yards. Two plays later, Hipple crashed into the end zone from 2 yards out to put the Lions ahead, 14-10.

After the kickoff, Joe Theismann awakened the slumbering Redskins with a 60-yard bomb to Virgil Seay at the Detroit 11. However, the Lions spoiled Washington's plans for a touchdown, so Moseley booted another short field goal to narrow the score to Lions 14, Redskins 13. On the ensuing kickoff, Detroit's slippery-fingered Rob Martin muffed the catch in the end zone, and two Redskins dove on the football. Somehow, though, the ball squirted free, and the Lions' Alvin Hall recovered for a touchback. Hipple capitalized on Detroit's good fortune by completing two passes to Fred Scott for 43 yards. When the Redskins started double-covering Scott, Hipple

countered by flipping an outlet pass to Sims, who raced 18 yards to the Washington 9. From there, it was simply a matter of letting Sims carry the ball three straight times for the Lions to chalk up another touchdown and forge a 21-13 lead. [Fig. 112]

Fig. 112   *UPI/The Bettmann Archive*

With 3 minutes left in the first half, Theismann finally took the wraps off wide receiver Art Monk, hitting him with a 30-yard pass at the Detroit 41. An 11-yard completion to Seay and a darting 11-yard run by Joe Washington advanced the ball to the Lions 18 with 1:44 remaining in the half. Two plays later, with the Redskins facing a critical third-and-1 at the 9, John Riggins bulled through the line for a first down. Then Monk ran under Theismann's lob pass in the corner of the end zone, and the 'Skins climbed back to within a point, 21-20.

Detroit's hurried bid for a final score before halftime ended with Redskins safety Mark Murphy intercepting Hipple's long pass at the 35. By taking the ball away from the Lions four times in the first half, Washington had reversed its early-season tendency

Art Monk   *Copyright Washington Post; Reprinted by permission of the D.C. Public Library*

to give away points on penalties and turnovers. But if the Redskins, trailing 21-20, were to win this free-for-all, Defensive Coach Richie Petitbon would occasionally need to find a less thrilling method of stopping the hard-charging Lions.

Washington Redskins quarterback Joe Theismann opened the second half by tossing a screen pass to Terry Metcalf, who snaked his way to a 23-yard gain. Strong runs by Riggins and short passes by Theismann kept the chains moving to the Detroit 11. But, for the fourth time in the game, the Lions squelched Washington's plans for a touchdown, and the 'Skins had to be satisfied with another short-range field goal and a 23-21 lead. Although Mark Moseley had now made field goals of 21, 33, and 28 yards, the Redskins knew they needed to score touchdowns to keep the pressure off their 33-year-old place-kicker, who was playing despite three pulled muscles in his kicking leg.

On Detroit's first possession of the second half, Billy Sims cut around right end and broke into the clear for a dazzling 51-yard gain to the Washington 15. Like the Redskins, though, the Lions couldn't cash in. Two plays later, Washington defensive end Mat Mendenhall crashed into fullback Dexter Bussey, knocking the ball loose at the 3, where Mark Murphy recovered for the Redskins. The 'Skins returned the favor a few minutes later, though, when Theismann's long pass to Monk was intercepted at the Detroit 4. On that disappointing note, the third quarter ended, and the teams switched goals with Washington barely ahead, 23-21.

It didn't stay that way long. A 14-yard gallop by Sims and a 43-yard pass-interference penalty gave the Lions a first down at the Redskins 39. Fullback Dexter Bussey blasted 23 yards through the disarrayed Washington defense, then Billy Sims ran into the end zone from the 13 to give Detroit a 28-23 lead. Twelve seconds later, the Lions were back in business on the Washington 44, thanks to another interception. But Tony Peters saved the Redskins from going down by two scores when he picked off a Hipple pass in the end zone.

Coach Gibbs replaced Riggins with Joe Washing-

ton. The former all-America halfback from Oklahoma revived the Redskins' dormant offense by snaring a 13-yard pass, then taking off on 7- and 14-yard runs. After Theismann hit Metcalf for 9 more, he handed off to Washington for gains of 13, 4, and 5 yards. Finally, Washington zipped into the end zone from the 12, and the 'Skins went back on top, 30-28, midway through the final period.

Joe Washington
Nate Fine Photo/Nate Fine Productions, Courtesy Washington Redskins

Inspired by Little Joe's performance (55 yards rushing and 13 yards receiving in the 80-yard drive), the Redskins defense finally forced the Lions to punt, and Washington took over at its 27 with less than 5 minutes remaining. With victory only one sustained march away, Coach Gibbs decided to keep the ball on the ground to eat up as much time as possible. Unfortunately, Joe Washington fumbled on first down, and Detroit linebacker Ken Fantetti recovered at the Redskins 29. The Lions were still alive.

Wise to Detroit's plans, Washington's defenders keyed on Billy Sims, allowing him only 1 yard on two carries. On third down, Hipple dropped back but never got his pass off as Dave Butz engulfed him at the Washington 33. On fourth down, with 52,000 screaming fans doing their best to rattle him, Lions placekicker Ed Murray calmly drilled a 50-yard field goal. Just under 3 minutes remained as the scorekeeper posted the new total: Detroit 31, Washington 30.

Mike Nelms returned Murray's kickoff to the 31, and the crowd welcomed the offense back onto the field with raucous shouts of encouragement. On first down, Joe Theismann dropped back to pass, eluded a couple of onrushing Lions, and took off on a 20-yard scramble. Aware that Detroit was clogging the passing lanes with extra defensive backs, Theismann handed the ball to Joe Washington on two successive misdirection plays that gained 6 and 14 yards. Then two more runs by Washington advanced the ball to the Detroit 24—just close enough for Mark Moseley to have a chance at a game-winning, 41-yard field goal. (In recent weeks, the injured Moseley had missed his last five field goal attempts from over 40 yards away.) Trying to get the ball a little closer, Theismann handed off to Washington once more. This time, though, the Lions were not fooled, and they pounced on Little Joe for an important 3-yard loss. Then, to ensure having enough time for retaliation in case Moseley was successful, Detroit took its next-to-last time-out.

Forty-four yards away from the bright yellow goalposts, Mark Moseley took a deep breath and waited for the snap from center Jeff Bostic. When Joe Theismann placed the ball on its point, Moseley disregarded the pain in his injured right leg and swung —hard. The ball jumped off Moseley's square-toed shoe, cleared the outstretched hands of the Detroit linemen, and headed for the back of the end zone. With each revolution of the spinning ball, the roar of the crowd grew louder. Finally, the ball descended

—and cleared the crossbar with several yards to spare! As tumultuous cheers poured down from the stands, Moseley's excited teammates jumped all over him, pounding his back, then ushered him to the sideline with a series of bearhugs. The Redskins were back on top, 33-31.

The see-saw game wasn't over, though; in fact, 45 seconds remained. After the kickoff, Hipple completed two passes, then called his final time-out at midfield. There was only enough time for one desperate play. Having sent all his receivers deep, Hipple aimed a towering pass toward a mass of bodies converging at the goal line. When the ball arrived, Lions receivers and Redskins defenders grappled for possession. As time expired, Mark Nichols, a rookie receiver for the Lions, outjumped everyone and caught the ball—at the 2 yard line! But before Nichols could take a step, Joe Lavender and Mark Murphy threw him to the ground, and the game was over. By a single stride, the Washington Redskins had escaped the Lions, 33-31!

"You just figured whoever got the last chance would win it," said Coach Gibbs. "I figured two or three times the game was over, that they would win. They were making yards so easy I couldn't believe it." Darrell Royal would have believed it. When he was head coach at the University of Texas, Royal had endured seven games against Oklahoma teams spearheaded first by Joe Washington, then by Billy Sims. Almost every time his Longhorns team played against Washington or Sims, Royal had resorted to the same rueful comment: "He makes you awfully disappointed in your tacklin'." Facing each other for the first time, Sims and Washington performed like identical twins—Sims rushed 21 times for 159 yards and two touchdowns while Washington racked up 144 yards and two TD's on 27 carries for the Redskins. Most remarkable was the fact that Joe Washington gained 79 of those yards in the fourth quarter when the Redskins were trailing, a time when most teams discard their running game in favor of passes.

"The start was unbelievable," said Detroit's disappointed head coach, Monte Clark. "The worst I can remember. It was ridiculous." By the end of the game, though, the breaks had evened out. After an exchange of nine turnovers, seven touchdowns, five field goals, and 963 yards, Detroit linebacker Stan White couldn't believe what he had just seen. "I don't see how we lost it. It just seemed like we moved the ball all day, did a lot of good things, and, when it was over, we still lost."

In the closing moments, Redskins defensive tackle Dave Butz had had only one concern. "The thing that got me," said Butz, "was how long it took for the referee to shoot off that little gun of his. All I saw on the last play was one of their guys coming down with the ball, and that guy not shooting off his little gun." He finally did, though, and the victorious Washington Redskins ran off the field to the exultant cheers of 52,000 exhausted fans.

BEAT THE CLOCK

Washington Redskins vs. New York Giants

November 15, 1981

Lawrence Taylor, the New York Giants' hotshot rookie linebacker, needed to be taught a lesson. Two months earlier, the Giants had forged ahead of the Washington Redskins in the fourth quarter on their way to a 17-7 victory. After the game, Taylor had gloated, saying, "I knew they would start folding." Naturally, Taylor's insult galled the 0-2 Redskins, and, even though there appeared to be some validity to his assessment, they vowed to make him eat his words when the two teams met again in midseason. However, when Washington lost its next three games, the chances of that happening seemed remote.

The player most frequently criticized for those early-season losses was quarterback Joe Theismann. Playing with a sprained thumb on his throwing hand, Theismann had gotten off to a rocky start, throwing 9 interceptions in those first five losses. However, since his late-night, heart-to-heart talk with Coach Gibbs (and the switch to the one-back set), Joe had led the 'Skins to four victories in their last five games while completing 62% of his passes for 900 yards and five TD's. "For the first five weeks we were changing everything every week—calls, formations, players, what have you," explained Theismann. "Now we are doing the things that we feel comfortable with. It shows. We are executing better and the mental mistakes have been reduced. We are doing things we should have been doing earlier, but maybe you have to go through growing pains with a new coach and new players before you can settle in."

Those new players, including a bumper crop of rookies—Mark May, Russ Grimm, Dexter Manley, Larry Kubin, Charlie Brown, Darryl Grant, Clint Didier, Joe Jacoby, Otis Wonsley, and Mel Kaufman—were being hailed as the foundation for an entirely new kind of team. But the first two stones of that foundation had been laid the year before when General Manager Bobby Beathard acquired free-agent center Jeff Bostic and wide receiver Art Monk. As the 'Skins' first #1 draft choice since 1968, Monk made an immediate impact in his first season, catching 58 passes and being named to the league's all-rookie team. Combining excellent hands with speed, fluid grace, and power, the 6-foot-2, 209-pound Monk reminded fans of Redskins Hall of Famer Charley Taylor (whom Gibbs had just hired to coach the receivers). Jeff Bostic, a star on the Redskins special teams in 1980, took over as the starting center in '81. With rookies Joe Jacoby and Russ Grimm on his left, and veterans Ron Saul and George Starke on his right, Bostic became the fulcrum of a huge offensive line that would transform Washington into an NFL powerhouse.

Another player making a sudden impact was defensive end Dexter Manley. Unabashedly talkative and friendly off the field, Dexter was plainly dangerous when he got his body (6-foot-3, 250 pounds) up to speed (4.6 in the 40). After watching Manley lead the special teams in tackles, Coach Gibbs decided he could not afford to keep his most exuberant player out of the starting lineup. Even though he sometimes ignored the possibility of a running play in his zeal to get to the quarterback, Manley brought an intensity and zest to the field that could not be replaced. "You've got to be one way or no way," explained Manley. "I can excite people and the people can excite me." Sometimes his enthusiasm was not appreciated by his teammates, who, unlike Manley, did not wear their game-faces to every practice. "Dexter does a lot of things that irritate you, but he's also refreshing," said middle linebacker Neal Olkewicz. "I don't know if he can tone it down. He plays with an intensity you rarely see."

Now that the team was finally in synch, the Redskins were looking forward to a little revenge at the expense of the Giants, especially Joe Theismann, who had never performed well as a pro in his home state of New Jersey. As the Redskins traveled to Giants Stadium in East Rutherford, N.J., Theismann promised to redeem himself—and give Lawrence Taylor a lesson in NFL etiquette.

The Washington Redskins received the opening kickoff and went to work at their 20. Joe Theismann completed a 9-yard flare to halfback Terry Metcalf for a first down, but his next pass was picked off by linebacker Brian Kelly, who returned it 27 yards to the Washington 12. Before the 63,133 customers at Giants Stadium warmed their seats on the blustery 50-degree afternoon, quarterback Phil Simms nailed wide receiver Johnny Perkins with a touchdown pass over the middle, and New York jumped on top, 7-0. Undaunted by the interception, Theismann went right back to the air, passing to tight end Rick Walker for a 24-yard gain. After Theismann scrambled for another first down, fullback John Riggins plowed for 5, then 4, then 3, then 16 yards. From the Giants 9, Theismann rolled to his right, putting pressure on linebacker Brad Van Pelt, who

didn't know whether to cover the run or the pass. Van Pelt's momentary hesitation allowed wide receiver Ricky Thompson to get open in the right corner of the end zone, and Theismann laid the ball in his hands for 6 points. Mark Moseley converted, and the game was tied, 7-7.

Ricky Thompson
Nate Fine Photo/Nate Fine Productions, Courtesy Washington Redskins

Danny Pittman returned Moseley's kickoff to midfield. Although Phil Simms had been sidelined for several weeks with leg injuries, his timing was impeccable as he drove his team to the Redskins 24. But a little rust finally showed on a pass to Perkins. The ball ticked off the wide receiver's fingertips and caromed into the arms of free safety Mark Murphy, who was playing centerfield at the 7. Three plays later, though, the Redskins had to punt, and the Giants regained possession at their 38 as the second quarter began.

Simms led off with a 19-yard pass to halfback Lou Jackson, then let fullback Leon Perry and Jackson run through the line six consecutive times for a total of 31 yards. On the twelfth play of the drive, Jackson slanted into the end zone from the 4, but the Giants had to be satisfied with a 13-7 lead when Scott Brunner bobbled the snap on the extra-point attempt.

After the kickoff, the Redskins managed two first downs, but a deep pass to Thompson fell incomplete and Mike Connell had to punt. On the Giants' first play, Lou Jackson fumbled, and Washington linebacker Monte Coleman recovered at the New York 22. The Giants' 3-4 defense rose to the occasion, though, pushing the 'Skins back to the 32 and forcing Mark Moseley, who was recovering from three separate muscle pulls in his kicking leg, to try a 49-yard field goal. Although long enough, the kick sailed wide to the right, and the Giants kept their 13-7 lead.

A sack by defensive tackle Dave Butz squelched New York's next drive, and Washington took over at its 26 with 3:44 left in the first half. Theismann threw to Metcalf for 18 yards; Riggins bulled for 8 more on two carries; then Theismann completed four straight passes to set up second and 1 at the Giants 21. With 50 seconds remaining in the half, Joe Washington darted 7 yards on a draw. But the 'Skins were stopped at the New York 8, and Moseley kicked a 25-yard field goal to draw Washington to within 3 points, 13-10.

Although trailing, the Redskins had dominated the first half, gaining 200 yards while limiting the Giants to 86. Joe Theismann had been particularly effective, completing 14 of his first 19 throws, while John Riggins was averaging 4 yards per carry on his 12 charges. The Giants were clearly in trouble.

New York's Alvin Garrett opened the second half by returning Mark Moseley's kickoff to the 40. Two plays later, Phil Simms overthrew a long pass

that, nevertheless, stuck to the outstretched fingertips of wide receiver Earnest Gray at the Redskins 15. From there, five dives into the line produced a Giants touchdown, and New York led, 20-10. The 'Skins retaliated by putting together a long drive that began with a 14-yard completion to John Riggins. A Theismann scramble (plus 15 yards for unnecessary roughness), a 17-yard pass to tight end Don Warren, and a defensive pass interference penalty in the end zone gave Washington the ball at the 1. Taking advantage of his massive offensive line, John Riggins broke through the middle for a touchdown, and the 'Skins were back in the game, 20-17.

After stopping the Giants cold, the Redskins marched to the New York 20, where they faced fourth and 1. Rather than risk losing the team's tenuous momentum, Coach Gibbs decided to go for the field goal. But Moseley missed from 37 yards, and the Giants took over at their 20. Under similar circumstances earlier in the season, the frustrated Redskins might have unraveled. But the team had matured tremendously during the past two months under Gibbs' patient leadership. Instead of knuckling under, they dug in and forced the Giants to punt. Two plays later, on third and 15 at his 37, Theismann threw a 29-yard strike to Terry Metcalf for a first down at the New York 34. Then Theismann bootlegged the ball for another 14 yards, and Riggins caught an 11-yard pass at the 3. Seconds later, Don Warren grabbed Theismann's short pass for a touchdown, and, for the first time in the game, the Redskins led, 24-20.

Realizing there were only 6½ minutes remaining in the fourth quarter, the Giants' rooters came alive. Fullback Leon Perry responded to their pleas with a clever 23-yard sweep around left end, but, on third and 8, linebacker Monte Coleman sacked Simms for a 9-yard loss and New York had to punt again. Too much time remained for the Redskins to simply sit on the ball. Facing second and 15 at his own 35, Theismann stepped back into his pocket and fired —straight into the outstretched hand of Giants defensive end Curtis McGriff. The ball ricocheted straight up in the air, but McGriff couldn't quite reach it when it fluttered back to earth. Two plays later, the relieved Redskins punted out of danger.

John Riggins   *AP/Wide World Photos*

After a quick exchange of punts, New York had one more shot from its 41. On first down, Simms went back to pass but was leveled by 300 pounds of Dave Butz and 250 pounds of Dexter Manley. The crushing tackle knocked Simms out of the game, replaced, to the quiet delight of the Redskins, by ice-cold Scott Brunner. However, Brunner surprised everyone by passing to Perkins for 22 yards, then hitting Earnest Gray for 20 more to give the Giants a first down at the Washington 27. His next three attempts fell incomplete, but, on fourth and 10, Brunner dropped back, avoided the Redskins' furious rush, and pegged the ball to wide receiver John Mistler,

who caught it in the center of the end zone 27 yards away. Touchdown, New York! To the disgust of the Redskins, the celebrating Giants led, 27-24, with only 45 seconds remaining in regulation.

Placekicker Joe Danelo, who had been booming his kickoffs deep into the end zone all afternoon, was surprised when his coaches ordered him to squib-kick to avoid a long runback by Mike Nelms, the NFC's leading kickoff returner. Nevertheless, Danelo obeyed, and he kicked a squirmer down to rookie Darryl Grant, a 275-pound wedge man. Grant fielded the spinning ball at the 26 and stormed upfield like a runaway bulldozer for 20 important yards. Only 38 seconds remained, but at least Washington was starting from its 46. After a short completion to Joe Washington and a near-interception by Giants linebacker Harry Carson, Theismann, finding all his receivers covered, scrambled up the middle for 10 yards and a critical first down. Washington took its second time-out.

Only 16 seconds remained as Theismann tossed a perfect screen to Joe Washington, who—dropped it. Little Joe made amends on the next play, though, by catching an 8-yard flare to advance the ball to the Giants 32. With 5 seconds left, the Redskins called their final time-out, and Mark Moseley trotted onto the field in quest of a tie. Bostic's snap was perfect. As Theismann spotted the ball on the 39, Moseley stepped forward and swung his injured leg. The line judge fired his gun just as the end-over-end kick sailed through the uprights, tying the game at 27-27 and giving Washington a chance to win in sudden-death overtime.

The resurgent Redskins lost the coin-toss and kicked off to the Giants. Determined to give Theismann & Co. a chance to win, Washington's defense forced New York to punt from its 26. Dave Jennings' 47-yard punt outsailed its coverage. Justifying the Giants' fear of him, Nelms backpedaled to his 27, then raced 26 yards to the New York 47. Even though the Giants defense had contained Joe Washington's draws all afternoon, Coach Gibbs called the play once more, and the shifty halfback from Oklahoma darted 12 yards to the Giants 35. After three conservative plays inched the ball to the 32, Moseley went back in for the coup de grace.

Mark rammed his square-toed kicking shoe into the football at the 48 and sent it spinning end-over-end toward the goalposts. 63,000 spellbound fans at Giants Stadium followed the ball as it climbed and descended, then finally dropped over the crossbar! It was good! Moseley and Theismann threw their arms around each other in a jubilant hug as the big scoreboard added the 3 points and flashed the final score: Washington 30, New York 27!

Coach Joe Gibbs beamed amid the pandemonium in the locker room and said, "I don't know how much prouder I can be of this team. To be where we are, after the start we had—it's a testimony to these guys never quitting." After his finest game to date as a Redskins quarterback (25 of 38 for 242 yards and two touchdowns, plus 49 yards rushing), Joe Theismann said, "What you're seeing is the development of character. Our young guys are seeing that, no matter what the odds, no matter what the circumstances, nobody on this football team is going to quit. We did not fold up our tent after they scored at the end today. What's happening . . . is that winning is becoming contagious."

In the Giants locker room, Lawrence Taylor was silent.

HOG WILD

Washington Redskins vs. Philadelphia Eagles

September 12, 1982

"Football," somebody once said, "combines the two worst aspects of American life—violence and committee meetings." If that is true, then football-mad Americans must have an insatiable appetite for committee meetings because most of the violence in the modern game has been muzzled by rule changes. Today, it's hard to imagine that as late as 1942 players were not required to wear helmets; in 1947 tacklers could punch at the football; as late as 1955 a ball-carrier could continue to run until he was pinned to the ground; in 1961 it was still legal to tackle a ball-carrier by the facemask; as late as 1973 receivers could deliver crackback blocks at the line; in 1975 spearing was still allowed; and as late as 1976 it was perfectly legal to clothesline a ballcarrier. Now that rules protect players from outright barbarism, most of the remaining violence is confined to the line of scrimmage, where it is hidden amid the chaos.

In olden days, when the bloated shape of the football dictated a high percentage of running plays, blocking and tackling were considered art forms even among the glamour boys. "Four yards and a cloud of dust" was not a putdown denoting an unimaginative offense; it described the game plan of almost every successful team in history. Even in the modern era, great teams like the Green Bay Packers, Miami Dolphins, and Pittsburgh Steelers staked their fortunes on a strong ground attack. In fact, there has never been an NFL champion that passed more often than it ran.

From the birth of the league in 1920 to the present day, the key to a productive rushing attack has remained constant: a dominant offensive line. That was precisely the ingredient the Washington Redskins had lacked during the Fifties and Sixties, when they were muddling through 15 losing seasons. In those days, it seemed the only time Washington could squeeze out 4 yards on a running play was when it faced a fourth-and-5. Memories of running backs Johnny Olszewski, Don Bosseler, Billy Barnes, A.D. Whitfield, and Gerry Allen (each of whom led the team in rushing in various years) ramming into a pile of defenders a yard behind the line of scrimmage come to mind much too readily. A rueful comment by former New York Giants Coach Steve Owen could have been applied to the mid-century Redskins. "My line is so tough," said Owen, "that my own backs can't even get through it."

Although the linework improved greatly in the Seventies, it took a quantum leap in 1981 when Coach Joe Bugel assembled the biggest offensive line in the history of the NFL. Averaging 6-foot-5 and 280 pounds, tackle to tackle, Washington's line became known as "The Hogs." From left to right: Joe Jacoby,

Russ Grimm, Jeff Bostic, George Starke, and Fred Dean/Mark May—the Hogs were the first offensive line in the NFL to gain fame as a group. Over the years, many defensive lines, like the Fearsome Foursome of the Rams and the Steel Curtain of Pittsburgh, had captured the attention of fans, but, until the Hogs arrived, offensive linemen in the NFL could count on only two things: jammed necks and complete anonymity. A matched set of tight ends, Don Warren and Rick Walker—both 6-foot-4 and 245 pounds—were also invited to join the exclusive club that began one day at practice when Coach Bugel told his men: "Okay you hogs, let's go down in the bullpen and hit those sleds." "Some guys might have resented it," said Bugel, "but these guys loved it."

To counteract the strength of the popular 3-4 defense, Coach Gibbs, who had made his reputation designing creative pass plays, installed a one-back offense featuring 240-pound fullback John Riggins. With the Hogs clearing the way, the Redskins' running game became as effective as a stiff left jab. "The one-back is a heck of an innovation," admitted George Young, general manager of the New York Giants. "Instead of having a small halfback trying to block on sweeps, the Redskins now have a tight end on either side doing the blocking. And with all that motion, it creates mistakes; they are always trying to get a speed guy on a slow guy or a big guy on a little guy. And with four receivers on every play, it messes up your run support."

"John Riggins is going to have to carry a big load," said Coach Gibbs. "We're going to lean heavily on him." One year after returning out of shape from his year-long sabbatical, Riggins, now in his 11th season, was delighting the coaches with his new commitment to fitness. "Last season, John was affected by the year's layoff," continued Gibbs. "He's like a different runner this season. He was sluggish; now he's strong. But it's more than that. He looks quick, the quickest I've ever seen him." Backfield coach Don Breaux marveled at the way Riggins made "so many yards after the initial contact. He does that because he initiates the hit. He's constantly falling forward for another yard." "The thing about John," added quarterback Joe Theismann, "is that he gets better as the game goes on. You never know how far John is going

to go because he comes out of pile after pile after pile. He's so strong in his legs. He'll give you a shoulder and [with] those legs, you're talking about tackling a mass. He's invaluable."

There was another 11-year veteran on the team, placekicker Mark Moseley. But, unlike Riggins, Moseley had barely survived training camp. The year before, Mark had suffered a series of pulled muscles in his kicking leg, yet was very effective inside the 40, making 14 of 17 attempts. But from further out, he had succeeded on only 5 of 13. Figuring Moseley was washed up, the 'Skins drafted Dan Miller out of the University of Miami and all but handed him the kicking job while General Manager Bobby Beathard tried to trade Moseley for a defensive end. But, in the final preseason game, Miller bungled two field goals, and Moseley was reluctantly retained. Although keeping the 34-year-old Moseley would prove to be the most fortuitous choice in recent club history, the Redskins were so unsure of him at the time that they decided to keep Miller on the taxi squad.

Mark Moseley was thoroughly familiar with the uncertain nature of life in the NFL. In 1972, he was just starting his second season with the Houston Oilers. The day after the first game, Oilers Coach Bill Peterson stunned Moseley by revealing, "I had a dream that you were on waivers. So I waived you." After spending a year building septic tanks in Texas, Moseley signed with George Allen's Redskins in 1974 and beat out Curt Knight for the kicking job. Over the next 8 years, Mark had fulfilled his own dreams by leading the NFL in field goals three times while rewriting nearly every placekicking entry in the team's record book.

The Washington Redskins' first test of the 1982 season came against the Philadelphia Eagles, a powerful team whose key players had taken them to the playoffs four consecutive years and to Super Bowl XV in January, 1981. Quarterback Ron Jaworski, halfback Wilbert Montgomery, and wide receiver Harold Carmichael gave the Eagles a first-rate offense, but it was Philadelphia's league-leading defense that made them so hard to beat. "This is a really tough, tough opener for us," said Washington Coach Joe Gibbs.

When the Eagles marched 67 yards on their first

possession, the Redskins looked as though they could have benefited from a few extra weeks in training camp. Ron Jaworski accounted for 48 of those yards with four sharp passes; fullback Perry Harrington shot through the line for an 18-yard gain; and Wilbert Montgomery scored from the 4. Tony Franklin converted, and the 68,885 fans at Veterans Stadium cheered as the scorekeeper posted the Eagles' 7-0 lead. Following the kickoff, Philadelphia stopped the Redskins after a couple of first downs and took over at its 36. Jaworski immediately burned the Washington secondary with a 34-yard bulls-eye to Montgomery at the 30. Three plays later, Franklin split the uprights with a 44-yard field goal, and Philadelphia led, 10-0.

When Mike Nelms fumbled the ensuing kickoff at the Redskins 18, the hot and sunny afternoon turned bleak for Washington. The 'Skins escaped an early grave, though, when Wilbert Montgomery coughed up the ball and cornerback Joe Lavender recovered at the 15. Joe Theismann passed to Don Warren for one first down, then scrambled for another as the first quarter came to an end. After switching goals, the 'Skins marched steadily to the Philadelphia 27. Unfortunately, on the twelfth play of the drive, Theismann fumbled while being sacked, and Carl Hairston recovered for the Eagles at their 36.

Washington's defense stood its ground and forced Philly to punt. With the Hogs clearing the way, John Riggins accounted for three straight first downs as the 'Skins surged to midfield. Noticing that Philadelphia's safeties were starting to crowd the line to defend against Riggins, Theismann countered with a deep pass to wide receiver Art Monk, who grabbed it at the Eagles 7. Two plays later, Theismann laid a 5-yard touchdown pass in Monk's hands, and the Redskins were back in contention, 10-7.

After the Eagles were forced to punt from their end zone, Washington took over at the Philadelphia 46 with 1:38 left in the first half. A 19-yard pass to Warren, a 10-yard run by all-purpose back Clarence Harmon, and an unsportsmanlike conduct penalty against Philadelphia advanced the ball to the Eagles 8. On second and goal, Theismann dropped back and fired a touchdown pass to rookie receiver Charlie Brown, and the Redskins took the lead, 14-10.

Only 35 seconds remained in the half, but that was enough time for Ron Jaworski to complete three passes, including a 32-yarder to Ron Smith at the Redskins 27. With 1 second showing on the clock, Tony Franklin came through with a 44-yard field goal, narrowing the score to Washington 14, Philadelphia 13.

After a horrible beginning, the 'Skins had regained their composure and fought back to take the lead. Displaying patience and maturity, Joe Theismann (13-19 for 132 yards, two TD's, and no interceptions) had almost single-handedly rallied the Redskins from the brink of disaster. And he would have to do it all over again in the second half.

On the first play of the third quarter, Philadelphia halfback Wilbert Montgomery took a handoff from Ron Jaworski and cruised around right end. Suddenly, Montgomery broke through a hole and dashed 86 yards into the end zone! Luckily for Washington, an official ruled Montgomery had stepped out of bounds after only an 8-yard gain. It didn't really matter, though. Jaworski proceeded to complete four consecutive passes, including a 26-yarder to Montgomery and a 46-yard bomb to Harold Carmichael, and Montgomery burst into the end zone from the 2 to put the Eagles back on top, 20-14.

On Philadelphia's next possession, Jaworski continued to feast on the Washington secondary as he hit Montgomery for a 42-yard touchdown. It was Wilbert's third touchdown of the day, and it gave Philadelphia a 27-14 lead. Then, at the beginning of the fourth quarter, the Eagles were threatening to turn the game into a rout as they drove into Redskins territory again. However, two quarterback sacks—the first by linebacker Neal Olkewicz and the second by defensive end Tony McGee—forced Philadelphia to punt.

The Redskins started at their 22. Trailing by 13 points, Washington could no longer afford to punch the ball downfield with time-consuming running plays. On first down, Theismann launched a deep pass to Charlie Brown streaking down the sideline on a fly pattern. Brown caught up to the long pass at the Eagles 35 and raced untouched into the end zone for a 78-yard touchdown! With just under 11 minutes left in the fourth quarter, Moseley's PAT shortened Philadelphia's lead to 27-21.

Dave Butz and Tony McGee wrecked the Eagles' plans for rapid retaliation by sacking Jaworski on third down. Max Runager punted 48 yards to Mike Nelms, who fielded it at the 24 and dodged his way to the Philadelphia 48. Nelms's inspirational 28-yard return was matched by Theismann's 28-yard strike to Don Warren on first down. Then Theismann picked up 9 more yards on a deftly thrown pass to Wilbur Jackson at the 10. It took John Riggins only two carries to score from there, and Washington reclaimed the lead, 28-27.

After the kickoff, three plays left the Eagles just shy of a first down at their 23. Coach Dick Vermeil decided to gamble. From punt formation, the center snapped the ball to the blocking back, Frank LeMaster, who tried to vault the line for the first down. The Redskins weren't fooled, though, and LeMaster was tackled for a 1-yard loss. While the disgruntled fans at Veterans Stadium booed, Washington took over at the Philadelphia 22 and gained 9 yards in three plays. Rather than risk coming away empty-handed with just 3 minutes left in the game, Coach Gibbs ordered a field goal attempt. Moseley made the 30-yarder with ease, increasing the Redskins' lead to 31-27 and forcing the Eagles to score a touchdown in order to win.

Philadelphia added to its dilemma by failing to return the kickoff beyond its 10. Using a hurry-up offense, Jaworski threw on every down, content to take the short gains that the Redskins were conceding. Four completions and an interference penalty moved the ball to the Washington 38. At the 2-minute warning, defensive end Dexter Manley sacked Jaworski for a 10-yard loss, but two passes recouped the lost yardage and gave the Eagles another first down at the Redskins 24. With 1:39 remaining, Billy Campfield caught a 20-yard pass at the 4 amid six defenders. Two throws into the end zone fell incomplete. Then, with just over a minute left in the fourth quarter, 6-foot 8-inch wide receiver Harold Carmichael caught Jaworski's perfect lob in the end zone, and the Eagles surged back in front, 34-31.

Fifty-eight seconds remained as Mike Nelms re-turned a short kickoff to the Redskins 37. Joe Theismann went to work, completing three quick passes that advanced the ball into Philadelphia territory. After a 6-yard toss to Clarence Harmon, the Redskins hurried to get off their next play, and an overanxious Eagle jumped offside, giving Washington a first down at the Philadelphia 35. With 23 seconds left, Theismann dropped back to pass again, but couldn't find a receiver and had to scramble for 4 yards. With 0:06 left on the clock, Joe Gibbs had no choice but to call his last time-out and send in Mark Moseley for a 48-yard field goal attempt. 68,000 hecklers did their best to distract him, but Moseley boomed his kick right down the middle and the game was deadlocked, 34-34! After five lead changes, three of which had occurred in the final 6 minutes, a sudden-death overtime period was needed to decide this topsy-turvy game.

Washington won the important coin-toss, and Mike Nelms returned the kickoff to the 29. On first down, Theismann passed to Charlie Brown, who caught the ball at the 33—then fumbled. Fortunately for Washington, the ball took a friendly bounce, and Brown recovered. One play later, on third and 5 at the 34, Coach Gibbs fooled the Eagles by calling a draw play, and Clarence Harmon gained 6 yards to keep the drive alive. After a holding penalty subtracted 10 yards, Art Monk slanted across the field and grabbed a 28-yard pass at the 42. Two plays later, Theismann went back to Monk on a button-hook. Catching the ball at the 24, Monk side-stepped his lunging defender and ran to the Philadelphia 9. That was close enough for Coach Gibbs, who ordered a field goal on first down. Mark Moseley came through like a champ. His 26-yard field goal was perfect, and the Washington Redskins claimed their first victory of the 1982 season, 37-34.

"I don't think anything will replace that kind of excitement," said a happy Mark Moseley in the Redskins' boisterous locker room after the game. Later, in a more pensive mood, Moseley said, "I thought I had been traded to about 27 teams this time two weeks ago. I can't believe the coaches ever doubted

Coach Joe Gibbs and Joe Theismann celebrate   *Richard Darcey/Washington Post Photo*

my ability." Was the pressure off now that he had gone 3 for 3? "There'll always be pressure," answered Moseley. "But if you've worked hard enough and been around long enough, the pressure becomes a positive pressure. You work so hard everything comes naturally. It's like walking. You don't trip when you walk because you've practiced it so much."

Joe Theismann's arm had been as effective as Moseley's foot. "This is the best game I've had," said Theismann, who completed 28 of 39 passes for 382 yards and three touchdowns. "It's the sweetest because we won here [in Philadelphia] against a great team. I wanted to show maturity this year, and I hope this is a good start toward that goal." Coach Gibbs agreed, saying, "Joe was a little shaky last year early, but he asked us to stick with him and today was the best I've seen him play. This was the Joe Theismann we were hoping to see."

PERFECTION

New York Giants vs. Washington Redskins

December 19, 1982

The 1982 NFL season came within 24 hours of being cancelled. On September 20, 1982, the NFL Players Association called a strike, and the union's members—Bears, Raiders, and Redskins alike—walked out. Over the course of the next 57 days, the players' initial demand for a 55% share of the owners' gross revenue was modified to a demand for half of the television revenue. When the owners balked at that, the players tried to negotiate a wage scale based on length of service that would have been the envy of the Royal Family. Finally realizing the owners would never hand over a duplicate key to their private bank vault, the players cut their losses and settled on November 16, the last day that a total cancellation of the 1982 season could have been avoided. A make-shift, 9-game schedule was salvaged, to be followed by a playoff tournament reminiscent of the NBA's in which 16 of the league's 28 teams would compete to see who would play in Super Bowl XVII in Pasadena.

Under the terms of the new agreement, only about 20% of the players, mostly older ones, made any gains from the new minimum wage scale. Severance benefits would begin for players after 4 years of service, but, since that was the length of an average career in the NFL, many players would never get an extra dime when they left the game. Bonuses were awarded to the players to make up for past inequities,

but that money merely cancelled out their losses in salary during the 8-week strike. Most observers felt the owners had won, if not by a knockout, then by a TKO. But Redskins quarterback Joe Theismann claimed, "No one won; not the players, not the owners and especially not the fans. I just hope we can produce the kind of product for them that we had before the strike."

The Redskins had been 2-0 at the time of the walkout, and Head Coach Joe Gibbs' main concern was that his players maintain their unity while on strike so that divisiveness would not tear the team apart. "The clubs that come out ahead when this strike ends," said Gibbs at the beginning of the walkout, "will be the ones that stick together." To that end, Joe Theismann organized unofficial practices, and, when the players returned, the Redskins looked noticeably sharper than their opponents as they won three of their next four games to move to 5-1.

"Defensive improvement is the biggest change in this team," said Gibbs. "I don't feel helpless anymore when the other team has the ball. They are able to stop people now." With three games left in the "regular" season, Washington sat atop the NFC's non-divisional leader board, needing only one more victory to be assured of a spot in the playoffs for the first time in 6 years.

The Redskins' next opponent, the New York

Giants, were fighting for one of the last playoff spots. After an 0-3 start, New York had won its last three games, repeating a pattern that had worked well for them in 1981 when they made the playoffs for the first time in 18 years. The heart of the Giants was their defense, and the heart of their defense was the best set of linebackers in the game: Lawrence Taylor, Brad Van Pelt, Brian Kelley, and Harry Carson. A game with the New York Giants was like going 15 rounds with Joe Frazier; you might win, but you wouldn't want a rematch. However, the same could be said of the Washington Redskins. ''We're a bunch of blue-collar workers who don't mind slugging it out every week,'' said offensive line coach Joe Bugel. ''We expect a very physical, probably low-scoring game,'' cautioned Coach Gibbs. ''The Giants are going to come gunning for us. We'd better be ready.''

The Washington Redskins appeared devastatingly ready as they drove from their 27 to the New York 34 on their first possession of the game. Another noisy sellout crowd at RFK Stadium watched with accumulating pleasure as fullback John Riggins plowed through the Giants line and Joe Theismann completed four straight passes. However, Brian Kelley intercepted Theismann's next pass and returned it to the New York 46. Trying to capitalize on the break, Giants quarterback Scott Brunner threw three straight times. The first two passes gained 11 yards each; the third one landed in wide receiver Johnny Perkins' hands in the end zone for a 28-yard touchdown. Joe Danelo converted, and the Giants led, 7-0.

Furious with himself, Theismann returned to the field vowing to make amends for his costly interception. A 26-yard completion to wide receiver Charley Brown gave the Redskins some breathing room at their 38. Theismann followed with a 17-yard bullet to Brown, who was brought down at the New York 45. After a scramble picked up 7 yards, Joe fired a strike to Art Monk at the 12. Cornerback Terry Jackson slammed into Monk, and the ball popped loose. Giants safety Beasley Reece recovered at the 3, and the frustrated Redskins offense came away empty-handed again.

The 'Skins defense, led by middle linebacker Neal

Olkewicz, stopped the Giants in three plays and forced a punt that Mike Nelms returned to the New York 47. Realizing the importance of getting on the scoreboard, Theismann called three conservative plays, then hit Monk with a 26-yard pass at the Giants 8. After the teams switched goals at the end of the first quarter, Theismann tried to run it in himself on third and goal at the 7, but was stopped at the 4. On fourth down, Mark Moseley was greeted by a thunderous ovation. Moseley, who had accounted for the winning points in four of the Redskins' five victories in 1982, had made 18 straight field goals and was taking dead aim at Garo Yepremian's NFL record of 20 consecutive field goals. The crowd quieted momentarily as Mark lined up the 20-yarder, then exploded with cheers as the ball split the uprights for the 19th time in a row. Though still trailing, 7-3, the Redskins felt they had broken their jinx.

The second quarter evolved into a defensive struggle with neither team able to mount a serious threat. Then, with 1 minute left in the half, Giants cornerback Terry Jackson intercepted a pass from Theismann, and New York found itself only 25 yards from paydirt. Fullback Rob Carpenter carried for 6 yards, then Brunner passed to Floyd Eddings at the 5. On second and goal, cornerback Jeris White was called for pass interference in the end zone, giving the Giants a first down at the 1, and, with 18 seconds remaining, Butch Woolfolk blasted through the middle for the touchdown that put the Giants ahead, 14-3.

The Redskins returned to a reception that was rather pointed in its lack of enthusiasm from the 50,000 patrons in the chilly stands. The finger of blame was being aimed directly at Joe Theismann, whose four interceptions in the first half had ruined two scoring opportunities and set up both Giants touchdowns. But Joe Gibbs remained positive. During intermission, Gibbs told his players in the dressing room that they ''were fortunate not to be further behind. If we can put together one pounding, sustained drive with a lot of plays and score a touchdown, we'll be right back in the game.''

That's exactly what the Redskins did. Theismann passed to halfback Joe Washington for 6 yards and to wide receiver Alvin Garrett for 7. Two 17-yard completions, one to Warren and the other to Brown, gave the 'Skins a first down at the New York 22. When the Redskins braintrust figured the Giants were ripe for a little chicanery, Joe Washington took a pitchout and headed to his right with the intention of throwing a halfback pass to Art Monk. But Monk was covered. With a gang of Giants defenders converging on him, Washington reversed his direction and high-tailed it back to the left. Little Joe had only one teammate on the left side of the field: Joe Theismann. Seeing Washington heading back his way, Theismann ran down-

field and looked like a Single Wing tailback as he threw an honest-to-God rolling body block on Terry Jackson, the only Giant obstructing Washington's path to the end zone. [Fig. 118] Thanks to Theismann's pluck, Little Joe scored. Then the improbable occurred; Mark Moseley blew the extra point. Still, the 'Skins were back in the game, trailing, 14-9.

Both defenses dominated the rest of the period, and neither team was able to get beyond midfield. With the temperature dropping to the freezing point, passing became increasingly difficult as the fourth quarter got underway. That's when Big John Riggins

Fig. 118   Joe Theismann (on ground) wanted to be made an honorary member of the Hogs after this block on Terry Jackson   *Gary A. Cameron/Washington Post Photo*

took over, carrying on seven of the next eight plays for gains of 5, 10, 7, 6, 2, 10, and 4 yards. When New York finally stopped Washington at the 14, Mark Moseley entered the game to try for his record-tying 20th consecutive field goal. From 31 yards away, Moseley's aim was true, and the Redskins crept to within 2 points of New York, 14–12.

The 'Skins stopped the Giants again, but, a few minutes later, Riggins was swarmed under on a chancy fourth-and-1 at the Washington 40. Nevertheless, timely sacks by linebackers Neal Olkewicz and Mel Kaufman kept New York from capitalizing on that tactical error, and the Redskins got the ball back at their 29 with 3:28 left on the clock. Snow

began to fall. Taking advantage of an accommodating alignment by the Giants defense, Theismann passed to tight end Rick Walker for 20 yards. Then, three plays later, Theismann hit Charlie Brown for 14 yards and a first down at the New York 25. Riggins banged for 6, but a holding penalty on the next play moved the 'Skins back to the 29. After Riggins regained 5 critical yards, the Giants called their final time-out with 45 seconds remaining.

Riggins tried the line once more, but was tackled at the 25 for a loss of 1. Fourth down. The Redskins let the clock run down to 11 seconds before calling a time-out. Mark Moseley came in, patted his holder, Joe Theismann, on the rear, and simply said, "Let's

Fig. 119   It's all on the line for Mark Moseley   *Nate Fine/NFL Photos*

get it, Joe." Forty-two yards separated the Redskins from the playoffs and Moseley from the most coveted record in kicking. The snow was starting to stick to the frozen field. Just as they had practiced it a thousand times, center Jeff Bostic snapped the ball to Theismann, who set it down smoothly on its point and rotated the laces out of harm's way. Moseley stepped forward and imbedded his right foot into the ball. [Fig. 119] A moment after it left his foot, Mark heard the disheartening sound of the ball grazing an

outstretched hand. A voice cried out, "I tipped it! I tipped it!"

But Moseley's kick was so strong, so centered, so perfect that the slight deflection didn't matter. The spinning ball kept to its path and cleared the snow-topped crossbar connecting the goalposts! Mark Moseley's dream had come true. With a grand smile lighting his face, Moseley punched the air and whirled to embrace Theismann. [Fig. 120] A moment later, Jeff Bostic hoisted him into the air, and,

A moment later, Moseley and Theismann rejoice   *Gary A. Cameron/Washington Post Photo*

as his fellow Redskins pounded him on the back and shouted their congratulations, the scorekeeper acknowledged Mark Moseley's 21st consecutive field goal with quiet eloquence: Redskins 15, Giants 14.

"It was like a Hollywood script. You couldn't have written it any better," crowed safety Mark Murphy. "We knew Mark was going to make it. I've seen him do it in that situation so many times. It was just unbelievable!" Everything about that record-setting kick had contributed to its glory: that it was good from 42 yards in snowy conditions despite being tipped, and that it won a tough game in the last seconds to catapult the Redskins into the playoffs for the first time in 6 years. It was the kind of scenario that kids fantasize about, where every circumstance imaginable collaborates perfectly to set up the ultimate in last-second heroics. For one dazzling moment in the life of Mark Moseley, reality was as perfect as the dream.

WE WANT DALLAS

NFC Championship Game

Dallas Cowboys vs. Washington Redskins

January 22, 1983

Just before the playoffs began, 33-year-old John Riggins went to Coach Joe Gibbs and, in a manner as straightforward as his running style, announced, "I'm really getting down the road and don't have many of these playoffs left. I've rested two weeks and I'm ready. Give me the ball." Fortunately for the Washington Redskins, Gibbs complied with his big fullback's wish. When the top-seeded Redskins faced Detroit in the first round of the 1982 playoffs, Riggins hit the line like a piledriver, gaining 119 yards on 25 carries as the Redskins annihilated the Lions, 31-7, for their first playoff victory in a decade.

A week later, Riggins did even more damage, bowling over the Minnesota Vikings 38 times for a record-setting 185 yards. In the fading moments of that 21-7 triumph, Gibbs motioned Riggins to the sideline to give the fans at Robert F. Kennedy Stadium a chance to salute him. With diesel horns blasting and raucous cheers raining down on him, Big John stopped at midfield and bowed from the waist —first to the north, then to the south—as an impish grin spread across his rugged face. The fans, of course, went nuts.

Those two playoff victories catapulted the Washington Redskins, winners of six in a row and thirteen of their last fourteen games, into the NFC Championship game against their old rivals, the Dallas Cow-

boys. The accursed Cowboys were riding a 6-game winning streak of their own—that's how many consecutive times Dallas had beaten the Redskins, starting with that 35-34 disaster on the last day of the 1979 season that had cost the 'Skins a spot in the playoffs.

The latest revival of that ongoing tragedy, a 24-10 shellacking, had been enacted at RFK Stadium only 6 short weeks before. In that game (the Redskins' only setback of the strike-shortened season), the Cowboys had sacked quarterback Joe Theismann seven times and intercepted three passes. Six weeks later, the Redskins were impatient for revenge—and itching for nationwide respect. "Everyone says we haven't beaten anyone, that we've been lucky," said left guard Russ Grimm. "They point to the fact that we lost to Dallas the last time. That's why we wanted the Cowboys again this season. If we beat Dallas, what are they going to say? It'll prove what we already know, that we are a good team."

"They've been a thorn in our side since I've been here," continued Grimm, "and we'd like to do something about it. We don't like them, and they don't like us." Defensive end Dexter Manley chimed in, saying, "I respect them, but I don't like them. We need to win this game to get the respect we deserve." Playing in their third consecutive NFC Champion-

John Riggins
Nate Fine Photo/Nate Fine Productions, Courtesy Washington Redskins

ship game, the 8-3 Cowboys were favored by 2½ points, due, in part, to their impressive record over the past two decades. Since their birth in 1960, the Dallas Cowboys had compiled the best record in the NFL (202-115-6), made the playoffs 16 of the previous 17 seasons, advanced to the NFC Championship game 10 times, played in 5 Super Bowls, and were crowned World Champions twice.

The Washington Redskins, on the other hand, had earned just one NFC Championship in the past 40 years. But the 'Skins, winners of their last four games by an aggregate score of 107-24, were currently the hottest team in the league. The keys to Washington's success—a powerful ball-control offense, an opportunistic defense, and devastatingly efficient special teams—had been forged by two men, General Manager Bobby Beathard and Head Coach

Joe Gibbs. After taking over for George (The Future Was Then) Allen in 1978, Beathard had restocked the Redskins' depleted roster by consistently finding overlooked pearls in the murky waters of the draft's late rounds and in the picked-over free-agent market. "Lots of people around the league know personnel," said Assistant General Manager Bobby Mitchell. "He knows what players will help the Redskins. That's the edge he gives our coaches." In recognition of the fact that 26 of the 49 Washington players who were suiting up for the Championship game had been free agents and 11 more were drafted in the fifth round or below, Beathard was chosen the NFL's 1982 Executive of the Year.

Beathard engineered his greatest coup in 1981 when he hired a head coach as obscure as some of his players. In only his second year with the Redskins, Joe Gibbs earned consensus Coach of the Year honors by molding Beathard's ragamuffin crew into a powerful team with no apparent weakness. A dedicated worker, Gibbs often toiled well past midnight before falling asleep on a couch in his office. His habits were infectious; the Redskins became the hardest-working team in football.

The foundation of Gibbs' ball-control offense was a huge line known affectionately as the Hogs. Whether power-blocking for Riggins or pass-blocking for quarterback Joe Theismann, the Hogs—Jacoby, Grimm, Bostic, May, and Starke—were indisputably the best offensive line in the NFL. There was only one Hog who wasn't a lineman: John Riggins, whose size and fun-loving nature made him one of the guys. Although a bit eccentric off the field, Riggins was a paragon of reliability on it. In 1982, he lost only one fumble in 240 carries while registering his 2,000th NFL carry and his 8,000th career rushing yard.

Washington's precise passing game provided the perfect counterpoint to Riggins' old-fashioned charges. Joe Theismann, the newly crowned passing champ of the NFC, had been particularly accurate in the playoffs, completing 73% of his throws despite the loss of wide receiver Art Monk, who had broken his foot during the last game of the regular season. Alvin Garrett, one of three diminutive wide receivers known as the Smurfs, compensated for Monk's absence in the playoffs by catching three touchdown passes against the Lions and one against the Vikings.

Although it wasn't receiving an equal share of publicity, Washington's defense was just as effective as its offense. The defensive line, anchored by tackles Dave Butz and Darryl Grant, specialized in repelling running backs and was reinforced by a matched set of tough linebackers: Mel Kaufman, Neal Olkewicz, and Rich Milot. All-pro strong safety Tony Peters headed a resourceful squad of defensive backs, the brains of which belonged to defensive signal-caller Mark Murphy.

The Redskins special teams had done their part, too, especially placekicker Mark Moseley, whose record-setting 23 consecutive field goals had played a crucial role in Washington's 8-1 regular season. For his efforts, Moseley was named the NFL's Player of the Year by both the Associated Press and *The Sporting News* and the NFC's Player of the Year by UPI —the first time a placekicker had been so honored.

Joe Theismann provided the crucial element of leadership. "The thing about Joe that impresses me is his heart," said wide receiver Charlie Brown. "You see that he never quits, so you can't quit either. He breathes fire." Indeed, Theismann had become nearly messianic during the playoffs. "The most important thing now is to win Saturday and get to the Super Bowl," preached Theismann. "Nothing is more important. Nothing."

Perhaps overlooked by the oddsmakers when they made the Cowboys the favorites was the stunning effect the crowd at RFK Stadium could exert. "Our fans are unique," said Gibbs. "I think the emotional lift our fans give us is a very important part of our team. I remember we had to struggle in some games early in the season. Without our fans, the outcome of those games would have been different." The Cowboys certainly knew what to expect at RFK on Saturday. After Dallas had defeated the Green Bay Packers, 37-26, to earn its berth in the Championship game, Head Coach Tom Landry noted, "Now we have to go to Washington and play before their crowd. Up there, you just hope you can hear the signal count." Tony Dorsett, the Cowboys' star tailback, who had run for 110 and 99 yards in Dallas' first two playoff victories,

admitted, "RFK's a place you don't want to go play, because of the fans. They don't like us. They're the kind of fans everybody ought to have. They're boisterous up there. It's rough, it's so loud. It's like it's the last day of your life."

"WE WANT DALLAS! WE WANT DALLAS!" taunted 55,045 crazed Redskins lovers in perfect unison as the two bitter rivals faced off in cloudy, 38-degree weather. Occasionally the menacing chant would die down, and the fans, many of whom wore buttons emblazoned with "Dallas Sucks," were left on their own to beseech and curse as they saw fit. Soon, however, the mighty chorus would swell to life again and fill the air with "WE WANT DALLAS! WE WANT DALLAS! WE WANT DALLAS!"

On their first possession of the game, the Cowboys did their best to dampen the fans' enthusiasm by driving 70 yards in ten plays. When the Redskins finally stopped the Cowboys at the Washington 15, Coach Landry decided to go for 3 points, and Rafael Septien made the 32-yard kick (his 15th consecutive playoff field goal) to put Dallas on top, 3-0. The Redskins looked equally sharp when they got their first shot with the ball. With the Hogs blowing the Cowboys off the line, Riggins appeared unstoppable as he bulled for 7 yards on the first play, then 5, then 3, then 17 more. Theismann completed his first four passes, including a 19-yard beauty to wide receiver Charlie Brown for a touchdown that set off an explosion of cheers and a rousing chorus of *Hail to the Redskins*.

The entire receiving corps, nicknamed the Fun Bunch, gathered in the end zone to celebrate Brown's touchdown. Pumping their arms twice, then jumping in unison, they shared a communal high-five to acknowledge each other's role in the 6-point play. Brown then took the ball to the sideline and presented it to Art Monk in a touching tribute to the injured player's contributions all season. As the two men hugged, Moseley kicked the extra point, and the Redskins led, 7-3.

When the second quarter began, John Riggins continued to pulverize the Cowboys, but, after a long drive, Washington came away empty-handed when

Moseley's 27-yard field goal attempt hit the top of the left upright. Several minutes later, a Redskins punt produced the first break of the game. Aware that Washington's Monte Coleman was about to decapitate him, Dallas' Tony Hill muffed the catch. The ball ricocheted into the end zone, where it was recovered by Coleman for an apparent touchdown. However, since a muff can not be advanced, the ball was awarded to Washington at the 11. Riggins pounded to the 5 on his first carry and to the 3 on his second. After Joe Washington hurdled the line for a first down at the 1, Riggins dove into the end zone for a touchdown! [Fig. 122] The 55,045 highly partial witnesses at RFK reveled in their good fortune as the scorekeeper posted the new numbers: Washington 14, Dallas 3.

In the waning moments of the first half, Dallas went to its hurry-up offense. In quick succession, quarterback Danny White completed a 25-yard pass to Dorsett, a 16-yarder to Robert Newhouse, and a 12-yarder to Butch Johnson that gave the Cowboys a first down at Washington's 32. With 23 seconds left in the half, White took the hike in shotgun formation and dropped back to pass again. As he started to throw, Dexter Manley smashed into him at full speed. [Fig. 123] The ball fell harmlessly to the ground.

Fig. 122   *UPI/The Bettmann Archive*

Fig. 123   Dexter Manley rings Danny White's clock   *AP/Wide World Photos*

White fell too, but not without harm as his head cracked into the nearly frozen soil with Manley's 250 pounds squarely on top of it. At first the fans cheered Dexter's big play, but they grew silent as they watched Dallas' medical personnel work on the motionless White. A few minutes later, as the nearly unconscious quarterback was helped from the field, the crowd, torn between relief and ambition, disavowed their earlier curses by applauding the fallen Cowboy.

Without White at quarterback, the visitors appeared to be doomed, especially when White's understudy, Gary Hogeboom, was greeted by thundering choruses of "WE WANT DALLAS" and the disconcerting sound of 55,000 fans smacking their lips. There was only enough time for Hogeboom to throw one short pass (his ninth of the season) before the half expired with the Cowboys trying unsuccessfully to get their field goal team on the field. Leading

14-3, the confident Redskins headed for the dressing room as the fans repeated their three favorite words: "WE WANT DALLAS!"

Washington return specialist Mike Nelms fumbled the second-half kickoff at the Redskins 7. Luckily, two Cowboys failed to recover the loose ball, and Washington's Nick Giaquinto fell on it for a touchback to avert an easy Dallas score. Nevertheless, a few minutes later, the Cowboys got the ball in excellent field position when Jeff Hayes' short punt was returned to the Washington 38. The Redskins defense figured an inexperienced quarterback like Gary Hogeboom would first get the feel of the game by handing off a few times. Instead, Hogeboom boldly threw to Rod Hill for 15 yards and to Butch Johnson for 15 more. One play later, all-pro wide receiver Drew Pearson got open just in front of the end zone, and Hogeboom nailed him with a 6-yard touchdown pass to bring the Cowboys back to 14-10. All of a sudden, Redskins fans began hoping Danny White would make a miraculous recovery.

Determined to make up for his earlier bobble, Mike Nelms fielded the ensuing kickoff at the 4 and headed for the right sideline. Slipping through a wave of tacklers [Fig. 124], Nelms followed his blockers and broke into the clear near midfield, then raced to the Cowboys 20 before Dennis Thurman finally brought him down. The record-setting 76-yard return shifted the momentum back to the Redskins. After quieting the excited crowd so his teammates could hear the signals, Joe Theismann rolled to his right and fired a bullet to Charlie Brown, who made a diving catch at the Cowboys 6. Then, with air horns blasting all over the stadium, John (The Diesel) Riggins rammed into the end zone for his second touchdown, and the 'Skins were back in control, 21-10.

The Washington Redskins have a woeful history of losing games to untested quarterbacks who somehow inflict more damage than the stars they replace. Looking suspiciously like Clint Longley, a poised Gary Hogeboom marched the Cowboys down the field with the precision of a drillmaster. On the 14th play of the drive, Hogeboom connected with Butch Johnson on

Fig. 124
Nate Fine Photo/Nate Fine Productions, Courtesy Washington Redskins

a perfect 23-yard touchdown pass, and, after Johnson finished his ridiculous posturing in the end zone, Septien tacked on the PAT, once again drawing the Cowboys to within 4 points, 21-17.

At the beginning of the fourth quarter, the Redskins managed to keep their shaky lead intact when Septien missed a 42-yard field goal attempt. A few minutes later, though, Dallas appeared ready to forge ahead as they moved crisply down the field. Fortunately, Hogeboom tossed an interception to Washington linebacker Rich Milot, who made a graceful, spinning, over-the-shoulder grab at the Redskins 40.

Washington's offense trotted onto the field, hoping to put the game out of reach with a steady drive into the Cowboys end zone. A 26-yard pass from Theismann to Brown and five charges by Riggo advanced the ball to the 12, leaving Joe Gibbs with a tough choice on fourth and 1. Closing his ears to the

Fig. 125   *Richard Darcey/Washington Post Photo*

pleas of the 55,000 "coaches" in the stands, Gibbs opted for a field goal, and Moseley came through from the 29 to give Washington a 24-17 advantage midway through the fourth quarter.

Dallas took over at its 20. On first down, defensive end Dexter Manley bore down on the back-pedaling Hogeboom as he prepared to throw a screen pass. Hogeboom tried to lob the ball over Manley, but Dexter leaped and tipped the pass high into the air. [Fig. 125] Defensive tackle Darryl Grant lumbered under the ball and intercepted it at the 10, sloughed off a tackler at the 5, and barged into the end zone!

[Fig. 126] The stunning touchdown detonated a burst of cheering that literally shook the stadium as the fans celebrated the 'Skins' nearly insurmountable 31-17 lead.

With 7 minutes left in the game, Hogeboom tried desperately to recoup those points, but he overthrew a fourth-down pass to Hill and Washington took over at the Dallas 38. 4:26 remained. Even though the Cowboys knew he would carry on every play, John Riggins was unstoppable. As the clock ticked down toward zero, it was Riggins for 2 yards, then 8, then 4; then 12, 5, and 6 more; finally for 1 and 3 yards before the Cowboys took their last time-out with 1:05 remaining.

After one final assault by Riggo, Joe Theismann dropped to one knee, and thousands of screaming fans stormed the field as the Dallas players trudged dejectedly to their locker room. The celebration turned out to be slightly premature, however; one more play had to be run. After enough reluctant Cowboys were rounded up from their dressing room, Drew Pearson (who had played quarterback at Joe Theismann's old high school) took Dallas' final snap and downed the ball to officially end the game.

By the hallowed score of 31-17, the Washington Redskins were crowned NFC Champions! The moment the game ended, snow began to fall, and, as Coach Joe Gibbs was carried off the field in triumph, a fan looked up at the sky and shouted happily, "Look! Even the angels are throwing confetti!"

Fig. 126   *Ron Ross/NFL Photos*

The victory was truly a team effort. John Riggins produced 140 yards and two touchdowns in 36 carries (the first time a running back had ever strung together three 100-yard games in the playoffs). Joe Theismann deftly completed 12 of his 20 passes for 150 yards and a touchdown. In addition, Mike Nelms' 76-yard kickoff return, Dexter Manley's constant pressure on the quarterbacks, and Darryl Grant's timely interception combined to bring Washington its first football championship since the glory days of the "Over-the-Hill Gang." With champagne dripping off his head, an ecstatic Joe Theismann summed up the feelings of every Redskin: "Gotta tell you, this one makes up for it all. I'm the happiest man in the world. I never thought this would happen to us or to me. This is the greatest moment of my life. We beat the Cowboys! We're going to the Super Bowl! What else could you want?"

Just one more thing, Joe. Just one more thing.

THE POWER AND THE GLORY

Super Bowl XVII

Miami Dolphins vs. Washington Redskins

January 30, 1983

Destiny was working overtime, arranging coincidences between Super Bowl VII and Super Bowl XVII. In 1972, after compiling a 12-2 record, the Washington Redskins had thrashed the Dallas Cowboys, 26-3, in the NFC Championship game. But in Super Bowl VII against Don Shula's Miami Dolphins, the 'Skins had lost, 14-7. Ten years later, the Redskins had once again earned the best record in the NFC and whipped the Cowboys, 31-17, in the Championship game to gain a spot in Super Bowl XVII against those same Miami Dolphins, still coached by Don Shula. This time, the Redskins hoped that Destiny had a different outcome in store for them.

The similarities went deeper. The Redskins and Dolphins were both well-coached, conservative teams with a remarkable talent for exploiting turnovers. Both clubs preferred rushing to passing, and both counted on smart defenses to confuse rather than overpower their enemies. Both teams also prided themselves on excellent special teams play. Yet, because neither club had won a playoff game since 1974, the 'Skins and 'Phins were usually overlooked by the national media. "We're what the Redskins are to the NFC, the Rodney Dangerfields of football," declared Bob Baumhower, the Dolphins all-pro nose guard. "We don't seem to get any respect." Although the Dolphins defense had allowed the fewest yards in

the NFL (while the Redskins were surrendering the fewest points in the league), it had remained anonymous until somebody started calling them "The Killer Bees."

Six of the Dolphins defensive starters' last names began with the letter "B," but the nickname applied not only to Bob Baumhower, Doug Betters, Glenn Blackwood, Kim Bokamper, Lyle Blackwood, and Bob Brudzinski but to the rest of the stingy Miami defense as well. In the Dolphins' three playoff victories leading to the Super Bowl, their aggressive 3-4 Killer Bee defense had shut down the New England Patriots, 28-13; the high-powered San Diego Chargers, 34-13; and the New York Jets, 14-0. When asked if he thought the Dolphins could stop Washington's powerful one-back offense (which was designed specifically to overpower the 3-4), defensive end Kim Bokamper replied, "A lot of people thought there wasn't a crack in the Jets' offense; a lot of people thought there wasn't a crack in the San Diego offense. But we managed to find them."

"Defense is really very basic," added Bob Baumhower. "It's a question of whipping the man in front of you and getting to the man with the ball." The leading practitioner of that simple truth was Miami's roving linebacker, A.J. Duhe, who had terrorized the Jets in the AFC Championship game and intercepted three passes, one of which he returned for a touchdown. Altogether, in the last two playoff games, the Dolphins had intercepted 10 passes while limiting the best receivers in the AFC—Kellen Winslow, Wes Chandler, Charlie Joiner, and Wesley Walker—to a grand total of five catches.

In the beginning of the season, Miami had experienced similar problems with their own passing attack. Starting quarterback David Woodley was replaced by Don Strock so many times that fans began calling whoever was playing quarterback "Woodstrock." Suddenly, though, in the first two rounds of the playoffs, Woodley caught fire, completing 33 passes in 41 attempts. If he could keep that up, Washington would be in for a very long afternoon. "Miami has a great scheme and they are well-prepared," observed Redskins Coach Joe Gibbs. "We couldn't beat them last year or in preseason this year. They have good offensive balance and very good speed, and their receivers gave us an awful lot of trouble. They seem to have that toughness about them that makes them hard to beat."

The Washington Redskins were equally hard to beat, having won six in a row and 18 of their last 21 games. Redskins General Manager Bobby Beathard, the former personnel director for the Dolphins who had drafted many of the Miami players including A.J. Duhe (and, ironically, Joe Theismann, who later was traded to Washington), attributed the Redskins' newfound success to second-year Coach Joe Gibbs. "Joe will hate me for saying this," said Beathard, "but he will go down as one of the great coaches because he can do everything they can: the X's and O's, being able to motivate players, getting along with players and—Shula is great at this—getting players to have pride in themselves." Selected as Coach of the Year in every poll in 1982, Gibbs decided to let his players enjoy the festivities of Super Bowl Week without a curfew.

That philosophy was in direct contrast to the way George Allen had handled his 1972 Redskins team before Super Bowl VII. Coach Allen was so obsessed with avoiding distractions during the hullabaloo of Super Bowl Week that his constant griping turned out to be the biggest distraction of all. The Redskins were so tightly wound in that January, 1973, game that they could never uncoil, and the Dolphins beat them, 14-7, in the lowest-scoring game in Super Bowl history.

Perhaps mindful of Allen's overreaction, Gibbs soft-pedaled everything, including the incessant queries about whether the Redskins had already shot their entire supply of emotional ammunition in the furious NFC Championship game against Dallas the week before. Hundreds of reporters covering the game kept asking Gibbs' players the same question. "There still is talk about the Dallas game, and there should be because we should remember that game for a long time," replied halfback Joe Washington. "But this game is more important by five times over. We just need to stay at the same level that we had for Dallas, and even make it better." Tackle George Starke was more succinct: "Beating Dallas was Super Bowl I. Now we play Super Bowl II."

The Redskins offensive game plan was simple —give the ball to fullback John Riggins at least 30 times. In 21 of the last 23 games in which Riggins had carried over 30 times, the Redskins had won. Conversely, they had lost all seven of the games in which he had carried fewer than 30 times. In Washington's three playoff victories preceding the Super Bowl, Big John had gained a total of 444 yards on 98 rushes while carrying on over 50% of the Redskins' plays. "John Riggins hitched us to a wagon," said Boss Hog Joe Bugel, "and pulled us along." When Washington's most quotable and exuberant defensive end was asked how he would stop Riggins if he was an opponent, deputy sheriff Dexter Manley grinned wickedly and said, "I'd handcuff him."

Riggins was not the only Redskin at the top of his game. Throughout the playoffs, quarterback Joe Theismann had passed both accurately and judiciously, compiling an incredible 124 rating based on a 69% completion average. In his first years in Washington, Theismann had languished on the bench as George Allen wrung a few extra seasons out of Billy Kilmer. Frustrated, Theismann asked to be traded many times, but Allen, who prized experience over potential, refused. Half-jokingly, Theismann even suggested that Allen "trade me now, and then bring me back when I'm 30." Now 33, Joe had obviously paid attention while watching former Redskins quarterback Sonny Jurgensen (who, along with Bobby Mitchell, had just been voted into the NFL Hall of Fame) and Kilmer win big games against top opponents. "You can't be impatient against Miami," said Theismann. "They won't let big plays beat them. You need to execute and not get flustered. Mistakes will kill you." George Allen never said it better.

Embarrassed by the players' strike, the NFL did not celebrate Super Bowl XVII with the same excessive overindulgence that it usually musters. When the league (lamely pleading lack of time) failed to host its annual party, Redskins Owner Jack Kent Cooke opened his wallet and invited 500 camp-followers to a little impromptu wing-ding of his own. George Preston Marshall, the flamboyant original owner of the Redskins, would have been proud of his successor's sense of occasion. The party was a hit, and the hit of the party was John Riggins, who traded his camouflage pants for white tie, tails, gloves, top hat, and a cane. Swaggering through the ballroom, Riggins provided the perfect comic relief for his teammates, who were already feeling jittery two days before The Game. Like an emperor at an ancient orgy, Riggins threw back his head and shouted, "Let the show begin!"

On Super Sunday, 1983, after the Golden Knights Parachute team, trailing the colors of the NFL, the AFC, the NFC, the Miami Dolphins, and the Washington Redskins, dropped into the Rose Bowl brimming with 103,667 anointed fans; after the introduction of the players; after the introduction of the officials; after a moment of silence in honor of Alabama Coach Paul "Bear" Bryant; after the National Anthem; after thousands of balloons soared into the California sky; after Elroy "Crazylegs" Hirsch flipped the specially minted Super Bowl coin that the three Dolphins co-captains called correctly; after the eight Washington co-captains chose to defend the south goal; and after Joe Theismann's last-second

pep talk that reminded his Redskins teammates that the winners would each get "$70,000 and a big ring," Washington's Jeff Hayes kicked off into the sunshine-soaked Pasadena air to launch Super Bowl XVII.

Miami started badly. Quarterback David Woodley almost had his first pass intercepted. Then he misjudged how much yardage he needed on a third-down scramble and slid to a halt a yard short of the first down. The Dolphins punted, and Washington took over at its 29. The Redskins opened predictably by sending fullback John Riggins straight up the middle behind the Hogs, who immediately established their territorial rights by pushing the entire Dolphins defensive line backwards 5 yards. After Riggins picked up a first down with two more carries, Joe Theismann decided to test the Miami secondary. A flanker screen to Charlie Brown worked for 11 yards, but Washington could get no closer than the Dolphins 48 and Hayes punted to Miami at its 20.

On second down and 6 at his 24, Woodley looped a pass to wide receiver Jimmy Cefalo, who was completely uncovered on the right sideline near midfield. The ball arrived before Washington's badly beaten defenders could recover, and Cefalo raced untouched into the end zone for a shocking 76-yard touchdown! Placekicker Uwe von Schamann added the conversion, and the excited Miami Dolphins led the embarrassed Washington Redskins, 7-0.

Washington's kick-return specialist, Mike Nelms, pumped some air into his deflated teammates with a strong runback of the ensuing kickoff. But a penalty brought the ball back to the 25, and the Killer Bees stopped the Redskins without a first down. Taking over at their 38, the Dolphins looked unstoppable as they gained 25 yards on three consecutive running plays. On first and 10 at the Redskins 37, Woodley dropped back to pass again, but, just as he cocked his arm to throw, defensive end Dexter Manley crashed into his left side and jarred the football loose. [Fig. 127] The ball skittered 25 yards toward the Washington bench and nearly went out of bounds, but Redskins defensive tackle Dave Butz gingerly corralled it at the Miami 46.

Hoping to catch the Dolphins off guard, Theis-

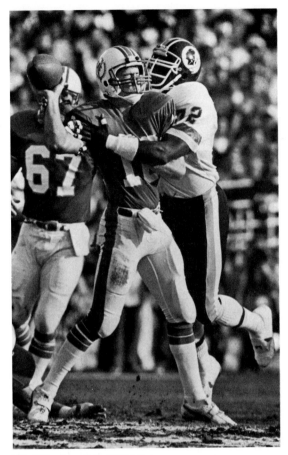

Fig. 127   *George Gojkovich/NFL Photos*

and von Schamann booted a 20-yard field goal to increase Miami's lead to 10-3.

The Redskins took over at their 20. A short outlet pass from Theismann to Rick **Walker** turned into a 27-yard gain thanks to Walker's **determined running.** Then a 15-yard screen pass to Riggins, a scramble by Joe Theismann, and two more runs by Riggo advanced the ball to the Miami 4, where the Redskins faced a critical third-and-1. With the Dolphins bracing themselves for another charge by Riggins, Coach Joe Gibbs reopened his bag of tricks and pulled out a confusing new maneuver called the Explode Package. Just before the snap, all five Washington receivers shifted in unison to the right, and center Jeff Bostic hiked the ball while Miami's pass defenders were still trying to realign themselves. The Dolphins' momentary indecision allowed wide receiver Alvin Garrett to gain a one-step advantage on his defender, and he caught Joe Theismann's perfectly timed lob in the end zone for Washington's first touchdown! [Fig. 128] The Fun Bunch gathered and high-thirtied, and Moseley kicked the point-after to tie the score at 10 apiece.

The tie lasted 13 seconds—the time it took Fulton Walker to dash 98 yards with Jeff Hayes' kickoff. With 1:34 remaining in the half, the Dolphins zipped back in front, 17-10.

Although stunned by the record-setting runback, the 'Skins regrouped and went into their 2-minute drill. A 30-yard pickup on a pass interference penalty and a 26-yard completion to Charlie Brown gave Washington a first down at the Miami 16. With 14 seconds left in the half, the Redskins took their final time-out. Coach Gibbs decided to try one more play, figuring that if his team couldn't score a touchdown they could at least get the ball out of bounds and kick a field goal. With everyone in the Rose Bowl standing and yelling, Theismann rolled left and hit Alvin Garrett at the 7, but Garrett was so far from the sideline that he couldn't get out of bounds. The first half ended with the Redskins field goal unit futilely trying to get on the field. Theismann's gaffe had almost certainly cost the 'Skins 3 points—points the Redskins could ill afford to squander while trailing the Dolphins, 17-10.

mann tried a flea-flicker off a reverse that barely missed picking up big yardage when flanker Charlie Brown landed out of bounds after the catch. Shelving the gadget plays for a while, the 'Skins returned to their ground attack. The change in tactics paid off as Washington moved steadily to the Miami 14 at the end of the first quarter. On fourth down, Mark Moseley kicked a dead-center, 31-yard field goal, and the Redskins were on the board, 7-3.

But Miami quickly reclaimed the momentum when Fulton Walker returned the kickoff to midfield. Copying Washington's successful ball-control tactics, the Dolphins marched steadily to the Redskins 3. Washington's defense finally drew the line, though,

Fig. 128   *Peter Read Miller/NFL Photos*

In his first-half summary, NBC's Merlin Olsen observed, "Joe Gibbs has done a masterful job of devising counters to [Dolphins defensive coordinator] Bill Arnsparger's defense. And even though Miami's ahead, we've seen signs that Washington can move the ball successfully against their defense. We'll see more of it in the second half." What the nationwide audience of 80-100 million people had already seen (between $800,000-per-minute commercials) was Joe Theismann completing 9 of his 11 passes for 103 yards plus a touchdown, and John Riggins meeting his first-half quota of 17 carries for 58 yards. But Washington's statistical superiority had been overshadowed by Miami's two big plays—Cefalo's 76-yard touchdown reception and Walker's 98-yard kickoff return—that had given the Dolphins a one-touchdown lead.

Would the Redskins' patient grind-it-out strategy

eventually pay off? Would the 'Skins bounce back from the frustration they were feeling at the end of the half when they came away empty-handed? Would the disappointment of Super Bowl VII be repeated? Would the KaleidoSuperScope halftime show ever end?

The Washington Redskins appeared sluggish as the third quarter opened, but, on their second possession, got a big boost from wide receiver Alvin Garrett, who took a handoff from John Riggins on a reverse and dashed 44 yards against the grain to the Miami 9. Two plays later, on third and goal at the 3, Coach Joe Gibbs called for the Explode Package again. This time, however, Theismann's pass into the end zone sailed beyond his target, and Washington had to settle for Mark Moseley's 20-yard field goal, which cut Miami's lead to 17-13.

The Dolphins were stymied on their next two possessions as Redskins defensive backs Jeris White and Tony Peters broke up third-down passes with bone-jarring tackles. But when Joe Theismann threw an interception to Miami's A.J. Duhe at the Washington 47, the immediate future looked bleak for the Burgundy and Gold. Fortunately, Washington's pass defenders kept coming up with big plays. Woodley tried another bomb to Cefalo, but cornerback Vernon Dean deflected the ball to safety Mark Murphy, who made a sensational juggling interception at the 5.

The Redskins offense took over, and Riggins powered out to the 18 on two carries. Then Theismann, under a heavy rush by Kim Bokamper, threw a pass that the Miami linebacker batted straight up into the air. Keeping his eye on the ball, Bokamper was about to intercept when Theismann lunged and slapped the ball out of his hands at the 3 yard line. [Fig. 129] Theismann's heads-up play saved a touchdown—and possibly the game.

As the fourth quarter began, the Redskins were advancing steadily on the Dolphins again. After reaching the Miami 43, Washington tried a flea-flicker (a handoff from Theismann to Riggins, a lateral back to Theismann, followed by a long pass to Charlie Brown), but it was picked off by Miami's Lyle Black-

Fig. 129   *Rob Brown/NFL Photos*

wood at the 1. The 'Skins defense kept the Dolphins bottled up inside the 5, and Miami punted back to Washington just beyond midfield. Riggins charged for 7 yards (giving him 100 yards on the day), but two more plunges brought up fourth down and a foot. Deciding it was time to take another chance, Coach Gibbs ordered his offense to go for the first down. In the Redskins huddle, Joe Theismann called the play this way: "Let's go. Goal line, goal line. Eye left, tight wing, 70 Chip on 1. Ready?" The Redskins broke the huddle with a shout and lined up in a compact, short-yardage formation across from the tightly-bunched Dolphins.

103,000 anxious spectators rose to their feet to watch the crucial play. As Theismann began calling the signals, tight end Clint Didier went into motion from left to right, then reversed his direction. Don McNeal, the Dolphins cornerback mirroring Didier's moves across the line, slipped when Clint turned. Bostic snapped the ball, and Theismann handed it to John Riggins, who shot through a big hole off left tackle. With the first down already in hand, Riggins had only one man between him and the goal line — Don McNeal, who, because of his slip, was late getting back to the corner. McNeal hit Riggins high and hard, but Big John absorbed the blow and kept running. [Fig. 130] Clawing at Riggins' jersey for a better

Fig. 130   The moment of truth   *Dave Cross/NFL Photos*

grip, McNeal hung on for a couple of steps, but the big fullback sloughed him off and broke into the clear down the left sideline. Forty years of frustration melted away from the hearts of millions of Redskins fans as John Riggins sprinted toward the Miami end zone. Lyle Blackwood gave chase for a while, but Riggins turned on his afterburners and scored! The Washington Redskins were finally ahead, 20-17.

The Hogs had opened the gate to victory with six excellent blocks. Jeff Bostic, Joe Jacoby, and Rick Walker smothered Baumhower, Bokamper, and Gordon at the line of scrimmage. Russ Grimm dove through the line and got a piece of inside linebacker Earnie Rhone, and Clint Didier stuffed Blackwood at

the corner. Leading Riggins through the hole, blocking back Clarence Harmon finished off Rhone to put Riggo one-on-one with McNeal. For Big John, those were perfect odds.

Now it was up to the Redskins defense to preserve the fragile lead. Thanks to a string of perfectly-timed collisions in the Washington secondary, Miami quarterback David Woodley had not completed a single pass since early in the second quarter, missing his last nine in a row. On third and 11 at his 26, Woodley tried once more, but his long bomb to Duriel Harris fell incomplete and Miami had to punt once again.

With 8:49 left in the game (and while reserve quarterback Don Strock warmed up behind the

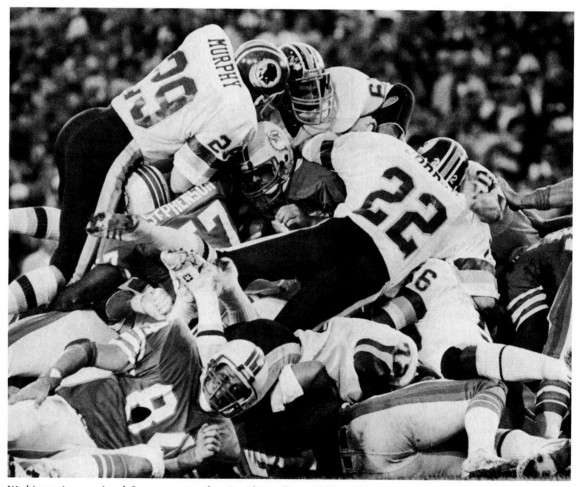

Washington's swarming defense was more than David Woodley could handle   *AP/Wide World Photos*

Dolphins bench), the Redskins began a long, time-consuming drive. Riggins gained 18 yards on five straight rushes, surpassing Franco Harris' Super Bowl rushing record of 158 yards. A few plays later, on third and 9 at the Miami 18, Joe Theismann rolled to his left and threw a short pass to Charlie Brown, who struggled heroically to get a first down at the 9. Riggins returned for the coup de grace, but fumbled at the 6 just as his knee hit the ground. A Dolphin recovered, but the officials ruled that the play had ended before the fumble occurred and Washington retained possession.

With exactly 2 minutes remaining, the Redskins faced another crucial play: third and goal at the 6. If the Dolphins could limit Washington to a field goal, they would then trail by only 6 points with plenty of time left for a game-winning drive. Coach Joe Gibbs called for the Explode Package again. Immediately after all five receivers shifted to their new positions, Theismann took the snap, rolled to his right, and threw on the dead run to Charlie Brown at the right edge of the end zone. Arriving at the same instant as the ball, Dolphins cornerback Gerald Small slammed into Brown, who somehow caught the bullet pass as he was being knocked out of bounds. The official on the spot started to call it incomplete, then, realizing that Brown's feet probably would have come down in bounds had he not been forced out, thrust his arms into the air to signal a touchdown!

That did it. Super Bowl XVII was clinched. Once more the Fun Bunch jumped for joy, just like the millions of Redskins fans all around the country who were celebrating Washington's 27-17 lead. There was only enough time for mopping-up exercises. Miami's reserve quarterback Don Strock came in and, after trying an end-around, misfired on three straight passes to end the Dolphins' quest. All-purpose running back Clarence Harmon received the honor of gaining the Redskins' final first down before Theismann dropped to one knee to kill the last seconds of the game. With the 27-17 victory secured, Joe Theismann fulfilled his long-held dream of running off the field after a Super Bowl triumph with both arms held aloft—one hand holding the game ball, the other hand signaling, "We're number one!"

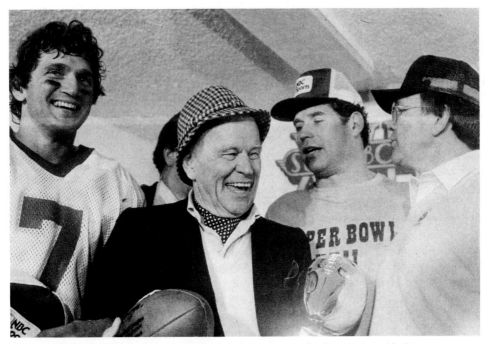

Owner Jack Kent Cooke, Coach Joe Gibbs, Joe Theismann, and John Riggins with the Vince Lombardi Trophy   *AP/Wide World Photos*

In the champagne-spraying pandemonium of the Washington locker room, Redskins Owner Jack Kent Cooke proudly accepted the Vincent T. Lombardi Trophy from NFL Commissioner Pete Rozelle. After President Ronald Reagan congratulated Coach Gibbs on the telephone, Most Valuable Player John Riggins was asked what the victory and his 166-yard performance had meant to him. "Well, I'm very happy," answered Riggins, smiling mischievously. "And, at least for tonight, Ron's the president, but I'm the king."

Other heroes were easy to find. Every man on the Redskins defense had played superbly, especially in the second half when they prevented Miami from completing a single pass while allowing only two first downs. Joe Theismann's 15 completions in 23 attempts for two touchdowns had meshed perfectly with Riggins' fourth consecutive 100-yard game. The gigantic Hogs had dominated the line of scrimmage all afternoon, and the tiny Smurfs grabbed every pass within their considerable reach.

Back in Washington, long-reserved bottles of vintage champagne were uncorked to toast the new Super Bowl champions, and several hundred thousand ecstatic Redskins lovers poured into the streets of Georgetown to party with their fellow fanatics. No one who wore Burgundy and Gold remained a stranger that night as the crowd of revelers celebrated the Washington Redskins' first World Championship in 40 years. Destiny had finally evened the score.

WASHINGTON XXVII MIAMI XVII

WAR DANCE

Los Angeles Raiders vs. Washington Redskins

October 2, 1983

Steve Owen, the former New York Giants coach now in the Hall of Fame, was once asked what could be done to reduce violence in the National Football League. Owen snorted derisively, then explained that "football was invented by a mean son of a bitch, and that's the way the game is supposed to be played." Forty years later on a warm October afternoon in 1983, the Washington Redskins and the Los Angeles Raiders would demonstrate that, despite changes in rules and equipment, the brutal core of the game remained intact. "It's going to be two physical teams going toe-to-toe," predicted Boss Hog Joe Bugel a few days before the big game. "It will be like the heavyweight championship of the world."

Over the years, football has become cleaner and safer, but it will always be populated by players who love nothing better than to turn out somebody's lights—legally, of course. Chief among NFL headhunters in the late Seventies was Raiders free safety Jack Tatum, who almost single-handedly brought about the banishment of the clothesline tackle: a dangerous technique in which a defender's extended arm creates the same problem for a ballcarrier that a low-lying tree limb poses for an unwary horseback rider. In a 1978 exhibition game against the New England Patriots, Tatum nearly decapitated wide receiver Darryl Stingley by clotheslining him as both

men collided at top speed. Stingley suffered a broken neck and has been paralyzed ever since.

The Raiders' reputation for playing dirty served them well. Opponents would spend so much time worrying about how to deal with Los Angeles' underhanded tactics that they neglected to prepare properly for the Raiders' legitimate strengths. That was fine with Al Davis, the team's managing partner and spiritual leader, who had whittled his philosophy of life down to one motto: "Just win, baby!" And that is precisely what the Raiders did. Owners of the highest winning percentage in the NFL since 1960, the Raiders had already taken home two Super Bowl trophies and were the current favorites to win Super Bowl XVIII.

Like the Redskins, Los Angeles was a rugged, no-nonsense team that relied on pure physical strength to dominate the other teams in the NFL. Offensive stars like quarterback Jim Plunkett, tight end Todd Christensen, wide receiver Cliff Branch, and tailback Marcus Allen were continuing the Raiders' high-scoring tradition that had helped them earn playoff berths in 10 of the last 15 seasons. Defensively, though, Los Angeles was even scarier. With defensive ends Howie Long and Lyle Alzado bracketing nose guard Reggie Kinlaw on the line, and with linebackers Ted Hendricks, Rod Martin, Bill Pickel, and Matt

Millen plugging the gaps, opponents were usually forced to give up any notion of running the ball. That usually proved fatal because the Raiders secondary —Lester Hayes, Ted Watts, Mike Davis, and Vann McElroy—were the best in the league at man-to-man coverage.

Los Angeles held one more distinction: it was the only team in the NFL that the Washington Redskins had never defeated. The Raiders had won all three meetings, the last two by field goals in the last few seconds. However, those Redskins teams were not the defending Super Bowl champions, a fact that oddsmakers recognized by installing Washington as 2-point favorites. Although the Redskins remained essentially intact from the year before, Coach Joe Gibbs could attest that the Super Bowl victory had created as many problems as it solved. Cornerback Jeris White quit after a contract dispute, quarterback Joe Theismann started griping about being underpaid, and two players, safety Tony Peters and running back Clarence Harmon, were arrested in separate incidents for possession of cocaine. In addition, defensive end Mat Mendenhall wandered away from training camp without explanation.

There was some happy news, too. Fullback John Riggins, after signing a two-year, $1,500,000 contract, was back in uniform for his 11th season, as was all-pro wide receiver Art Monk, who had missed the 1982 playoffs and Super Bowl with an ankle injury. The Redskins had upgraded their defense by drafting cornerback Darrell Green and defensive tackle Charles Mann.

Following a summer of high expectations graced by the inductions of quarterback Sonny Jurgensen and flanker-halfback Bobby Mitchell into the Pro Football Hall of Fame in Canton, Ohio, the Redskins' bubble burst in their season opener at RFK Stadium when they blew a 20-point lead to the Dallas Cowboys and lost, 31-30. After that disappointing debut, the vengeful Redskins ran over their next three opponents with their straightforward ball-control attack. Some of the fans were still not satisfied, though, grumbling that the offense lacked imagination and, like George Allen's teams, had become predictable and boring. However, with 23 victories in their last

28 games, the Redskins were not about to change their winning formula.

Unless they had to.

The opening series for both the Washington Redskins and Los Angeles Raiders revealed their respective game plans. Washington started with three carries by fullback John Riggins. L.A. began with three passes by Jim Plunkett, two of which fell incomplete. When his third attempt was picked off by safety Curtis Jordan, 55,045 fans at RFK Stadium roared their approval as he returned it to the Raiders 11. Riggins plunged through the line for 9 yards on two carries. On third and 1 at the 2, Riggo was stopped cold but kept churning his legs and finally squeezed into the end zone for a touchdown! Mark Moseley tacked on the extra point, and Washington led, 7-0.

Forced to hurry by the Redskins' furious pass rush, Plunkett threw another interception, this one to nickel back Ken Coffey at the Washington 33. [Fig. 133] Los Angeles swarmed after Joe Theismann, sacking him once and blocking a pass to force the 'Skins to punt on fourth and 28. Then the Raiders turned the ball over again—this time on a Kenny King fumble that Darrell Green recovered at midfield. John Riggins carried for one first down, and Rick Walker picked up another with a 17-yard reception. On second and 7 at the 10, Howie Long dumped Theismann in the backfield, and, after an incompletion to Monk, Mark Moseley came in for a 36-yard field goal attempt. He missed.

Los Angeles continued to play giveaway as Jim Plunkett threw his third interception of the first quarter to linebacker Mel Kaufman, who returned it 23 yards to the Raiders 23. This time the Redskins made it as far as the 7 before Howie Long and Bill Pickel sacked Theismann for the fourth time in the game. Two minutes into the second period, Washington had to settle for Mark Moseley's 28-yard field goal and a 10-0 lead.

An exchange of punts pinned the Raiders at their 1 yard line. Undismayed by his horrendous start (1 for 8 with three interceptions and two sacks), Jim Plunkett lofted a deep pass to Cliff Branch, who grabbed it at the 44 and sprinted into the end zone

Fig. 133   *Heinz Kluetmeier/Sports Illustrated © Time Inc.*

for a 99-yard touchdown! The Raiders were back in the game, trailing 10-7.

Coach Joe Gibbs decided to take his foot off the brake. Theismann passed to Art Monk for 18 yards, then followed with an 11-yarder to Charlie Brown. After 15 yards were tacked on for a personal foul by Lester Hayes, Theismann fired a 23-yard strike to Monk at the Los Angeles 11. Riggins plowed for 6 yards on two carries. On third down, halfback Joe Washington found an open spot in the end zone and grabbed Theismann's 5-yard pass for a touchdown! As the crowd celebrated, Moseley's kick increased

the Redskins' lead to 17-7. Washington was back in control.

With Marcus Allen unable to play due to a badly bruised hip, running backs Frank Hawkins and Kenny King took turns carrying the ball, and the Raiders finally started to hit on all cylinders. Plunkett completed three straight passes, including a 39-yard bomb to Malcolm Barnwell, as Los Angeles moved from its 18 to the Washington 10. However, defensive end Dexter Manley thwarted L.A.'s plans for a touchdown by sacking Plunkett for a 13-yard loss. The sellout crowd at RFK continued to howl when placekicker Chris

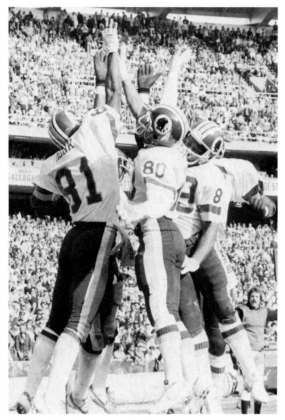

The Fun Bunch
Nate Fine Photo/Nate Fine Productions, Courtesy Washington Redskins

Bahr came up short on a 41-yard field goal attempt, and the first half ended with Washington on top, 17-7.

Thanks mainly to Howie Long's three sacks of Joe Theismann, the Raiders were still in the game. Otherwise, Los Angeles, which had handed out three interceptions and a fumble in the first quarter, would have been trailing by far more than 10 points. Like a heavyweight champion who had survived a furious pounding in the first few rounds, the Raiders had kept their feet and were now ready to deal out some punishment of their own in the second half.

Washington, however, drew first blood. John Riggins ran for a first down at the Raiders 47, then

Theismann passed to tight end Don Warren, who caught the ball at the 32 and barreled to the 14. [Fig. 135] Once again the Raiders' defense stiffened inside its 20, but Moseley salvaged 3 points with a 29-yard field goal, boosting Washington's advantage to 20-7.

Midway through the third quarter, Jim Plunkett suddenly recaptured his passing touch. On first down at his 17, he arched a long spiral to Todd Christensen for a 41-yard gain, then followed with a 17-yard strike to Frank Hawkins. From the 25, Plunkett dropped back again, avoided the Redskins pass rush, and hit wide receiver Calvin Muhammad in the end zone for a touchdown. Los Angeles was back within striking distance, 20-14. The Raiders continued to roll, stuffing the 'Skins inside their 15 and taking over at midfield. Seven plays later, Plunkett rifled a 22-yard touchdown pass to Calvin Muhammad, and L.A. surged ahead for the first time, 21-20.

Joe Theismann responded with a 33-yard heave to wide receiver Charlie Brown, but the third quarter ended on a low note for the Redskins when Riggins fumbled at the Los Angeles 35. The Raiders breezed downfield again. When Plunkett capped the 65-yard drive with a 2-yard touchdown pass to Todd Christensen, the Raiders extended their lead to 28-20.

With the stunned crowd urging them on, the Redskins began to regroup. Joe Theismann completed two passes to Charlie Brown for 25 yards, then hit Art Monk at the Raiders 32. Unfortunately, a holding penalty negated Monk's reception, and the 'Skins had to punt from their 43. Jeff Hayes got off a booming spiral that sent Greg Pruitt back-pedaling to his 3. Thirteen seconds later, Pruitt was spiking the ball in the Redskins' end zone, punctuating a dazzling 97-yard touchdown run! With 7:31 left in the game, the Raiders appeared to be in total command, 35-20.

A penalty on the ensuing kickoff saddled the 'Skins with terrible field position at their 13. On first down, Theismann backpedaled and dumped a screen pass to Joe Washington, who broke free and raced 67 yards to the L.A. 20! Hurrying to conserve time, Theismann fired a 10-yard completion to Donny Warren, then looped a touchdown pass to Charlie Brown in the end zone to bring the 'Skins back to 35-27.

Jeff Hayes kicked off—a perfect onsides squirmer

Fig. 135   *Heinz Kluetmeier/Sports Illustrated © Time Inc.*

that eluded two Raiders and landed in the arms of Washington's Greg Williams at the Los Angeles 32! Theismann passed to Warren for 19 yards, but, one play later, Howie Long stifled the excited fans by sacking Theismann for an 18-yard loss. A pass to Joe Washington recouped 14 yards, but the Redskins had to settle for Mark Moseley's 34-yard field goal on fourth down. With 4½ minutes remaining in the game, the Raiders' lead had been whittled to 5 points, 35-30.

Roaring encouragement on every play, the crowd rejoiced as L.A.'s Frank Hawkins was tackled twice in a row for losses. On third and 15, Plunkett connected with Todd Christensen, but Ken Coffey dragged him down after a gain of 9 yards and the Raiders were forced to punt at the 2-minute warning. Joe Theismann went to work at his 31. A 9-yard pass to Charlie Brown used 30 seconds. Unperturbed, Theismann unleashed a 26-yard strike to Brown at the Los Angeles 34 and called his second time-out. After consulting with Coach Gibbs on the sideline, Theismann again picked on cornerback James Davis, who was substituting for the injured Ted Watts. Charlie Brown got a step on the flustered Davis and grabbed Theismann's 28-yard toss at the 6 as the cheers of 54,000 Redskins fans filled the air. With 43 seconds left in

the game, Los Angeles called a time-out to give themselves a chance to retaliate in case Washington scored.

On first and goal, Theismann looked for Brown in the end zone but had to throw the ball away. On second down, he dropped back in his pocket as Joe Washington slipped through the middle of the line. Theismann planted his leg and threw—hard. At the goal line, Washington turned and dove for the ball, plucking it out of the air as he tumbled into the end zone! Touchdown! [Fig. 136] The jubilant Redskins were back on top, 37-35.

In the last 30 seconds, Jim Plunkett tried to con-

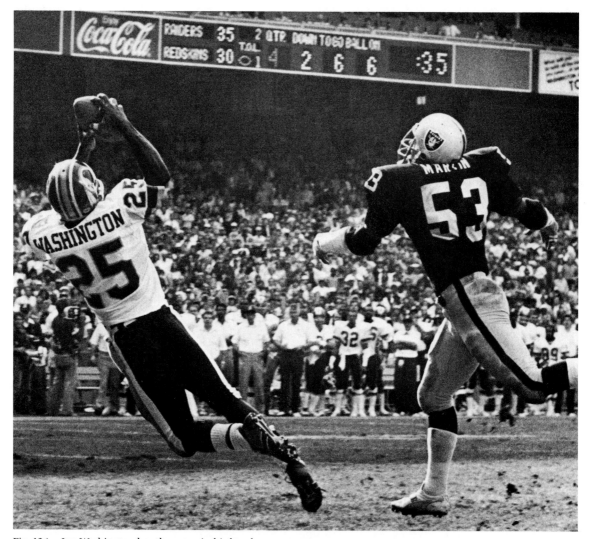

Fig. 136   Joe Washington has the game in his hands   *Gary A. Cameron/Washington Post Photo*

jure up a miracle finish of his own, but cornerback Vernon Dean intercepted a desperate 50-yard heave to clinch the game. By scoring 17 unanswered points in the last 7 minutes and 31 seconds, the Washington Redskins had pulled off one of the most amazing comeback victories in NFL history. Washington 37, Los Angeles 35.

I t took every one of Charlie Brown's 11 receptions (for 180 yards), John Riggins' 91 yards rushing, and Joe Washington's five clutch catches to defeat the powerful Raiders. The star of the game, however, was quarterback Joe Theismann, who was magnificent, especially down the stretch when he completed 9 of his last 12 throws. In all, Joe hit on 23 of 39 passes for three touchdowns and a career-best 417 yards—against the toughest defense in the league.

"The Raiders tried to come in here and intimidate us," declared Dexter Manley. "But they were totally shocked. We intimidated them." Howie Long, the Raiders unrelenting defensive end who sacked Theismann four times, confessed "it was the longest, hardest football game I've ever played in." One of the men who had double-teamed Long was frank in his admiration for his all-pro opponent. "Howie Long was great," said Redskins tackle George Starke. "He was fighting; spitting at people. But after the game, he came over to me and said, 'You guys were great.'"

As Steve Owen had said 40 years earlier: "That's the way the game is supposed to be played."

DESTRUCTION CREW

Washington Redskins vs. Dallas Cowboys

December 11, 1983

In baseball, it's the Yankees and Dodgers; in basketball, it's the Celtics and Lakers; in football, it's the Redskins and Cowboys. Those are the rivalries that define each sport. When adversaries like these go at it, there is always more at stake than conference standings, playoff berths, and championship rings. Honor, pride, and glory ride on each pitch, each basket, each tackle. No matter what their records, Army and Navy, Harvard and Yale, Alabama and Auburn, Oklahoma and Nebraska, USC and UCLA play as if the national championship was at stake. But when, in fact, there is that added stake, when both teams share the same record and are competing for the same prize, rivalries like those can produce the kind of intensity that turns games into wars.

Such a game would be played at Texas Stadium in the next to last week of the 1983 season between the Dallas Cowboys and the Washington Redskins, both of whom had already clinched playoff berths with identical 12-2 records. The prize: home-field advantage throughout the playoffs. In the past, the site of playoff games had proved especially crucial to the Redskins. Since 1970, when the current playoff system went into effect, Washington had made the playoffs six times. In five post-season games at RFK Stadium, the 'Skins were undefeated. On enemy fields, they were 0-4.

Over the years, the Redskins and Cowboys had tangled 47 times. Although Dallas had gotten the better of Washington in match play, compiling a 28-17-2 advantage, many of those victories had been registered in the Sixties against inconsistent Redskins teams that were long on offense but short on defense. That was no longer the case. "Football is a game of consistency," declared Dallas Coach Tom Landry, "and that's what Washington has more than anyone else. They do the same thing every week, and they do it against everybody."

The 1983 Redskins specialized in jumping off to quick leads using the legs of John Riggins, the blocks of the Hogs, the arm of Joe Theismann, and the heads-up play of their ball-hawking defense and special teams. Once in front, the 'Skins would pound their opponents into pulp with their unrelenting ground attack. "The Redskins, all of a sudden, are the best team," continued Landry. "They are playing better than anyone else. Whether they are better than we are is what we'll find out Sunday."

In September, the Cowboys had stolen the opening game of the season from Washington by roaring back from a 23-3 halftime deficit to win, 31-30. Since then, though, the Redskins had lost only once: a 48-47 free-for-all at Green Bay. Having won 27 of its last 30 games, Washington was now the dominant team in the NFL. With two games to go, the Redskins had scored a league-high 479 points and created a remarkable plus-40 turnover ratio. Placekicker Mark Moseley had already set an NFL record with his 147 points, wide receiver Charlie Brown was leading the conference with 71 catches, and quarterback Joe Theismann was gunning for the NFL's Most Valuable Player award with his accurate passing and enthusiastic leadership.

Yet the Cowboys were favored by 2½ points. Was it because Dallas had a history of cooling off hot teams when it really counted? Or was it because the Redskins secondary, nicknamed "The Pearl Harbor Crew" after it was bombarded so often, appeared vulnerable to Danny White's passes? Perhaps it was because Tony Dorsett had been the only running back in 1983 to gain over 100 yards against the Washington front four—and, when Dorsett got 100, the Cowboys always won. Or was it because the Redskins had lost nine times in their last ten appearances at Texas Stadium?

"It's not a coincidence that the Cowboys have been in the playoffs 16 of the last 17 years," said Washington defensive coordinator Richie Petitbon. A true dynasty, the Cowboys had parlayed excellent coaching, a multi-faceted offense, and a grudging defense into the best record in the NFL over the past two decades. Fourteen of their current starters had played in at least one Pro Bowl: defensive tackles Randy White and John Dutton, defensive ends Harvey Martin and Ed "Too Tall" Jones, linebacker Bob Breunig, cornerback Everson Walls, quarterback Danny White, halfback Tony Dorsett, wide receivers Tony Hill and Drew Pearson, tackle Pat Donovan, tight end Billy Joe DuPree, guard Herbert Scott, and placekicker Rafael Septien.

While the Redskins relied mostly on brute force, the Cowboys generally won with finesse. Their constant shifting was designed to confuse rather than overpower their opponents. Tom Landry's reputation as a coaching genius was well-deserved, especially for his ability to direct Dallas' intricate offense from the sideline. "Landry is such a great signal caller," marveled Petitbon. "I remember a few years ago when Roger Staubach wanted to call the plays. Those quar-

terbacks don't realize what a favor Landry does for them." Redskins safety and defensive signal-caller Mark Murphy (who had challenged the 60-year-old Landry to a footrace after the Dallas coach had said, "I can outrun Murphy") likened a game against the Cowboys to "trying to beat a computer at chess."

"I don't know what Dallas will do this game," admitted Redskins linebacker Rich Milot, "but I do know what we have to do: play aggressive and make bodies fly."

Dressed in camouflage and combat boots, the grim-faced Washington Redskins filed out of their chartered jet in Dallas ready for war. In comparison, the silk-shirted, Gucci-shod Dallas Cowboys looked like a bunch of big sissies when they reported to work on game day. Round 1 to the Redskins. The game, however, would not be decided in the dressing room; it would be won on the hard plastic carpet of Texas Stadium, a half-domed arena perched on the mall-studded prairie midway between Dallas and Fort Worth.

Over 65,000 Cowboys fans cheered with uncharacteristic passion as Dallas' Rafael Septien kicked off to Mike Nelms, who returned the ball 18 yards to the 25. On the first play of the game, John Riggins demonstrated the Redskins' intentions by charging through the Dallas Flex defense for 11 yards. Riggins crashed for 7 more, then, to keep the Cowboys back on their heels, Joe Theismann hit Charlie Brown over the middle with a perfectly-timed pass good for 22 yards and another first down at midfield. After Theismann escaped a big rush and scrambled up the middle for 17 yards, the Redskins picked up 27 more on a pass interference penalty. While the crowd booed, Riggins plowed to the 3. On second and goal, Big John used his surprising speed to get outside and dashed untouched into the left corner of the end zone! The 'Skins had accomplished their first mission by breaking on top, 7-0.

The Cowboys quickly discovered that the Washington defense was as well-prepared as the Washington offense. Defensive tackle Dave Butz sacked quarterback Danny White, then Dexter Manley turned a lateral to fullback Ron Springs into a 7-yard loss, forcing White to punt back to the ball-hungry Redskins. Mike Nelms, who never called for a fair catch in his career, fielded the 48-yard punt at his 19, somehow absorbed an immediate head-on collision with Rod Hill, and cut to the sideline. At the 30, Nelms tried to hurdle a Cowboy but was somersaulted onto his head. Despite the one-point crash landing, Nelms held onto the ball.

Two charges by Riggins picked up 8 yards, then Theismann fired a strike to Art Monk for 22 more. Given plenty of time to wait for tight end Clint Didier to break free on a post pattern, Theismann sailed the ball into Didier's hands at the 25, and Clint sprinted into the end zone for the Redskins' second touchdown! [Fig. 137] Moseley converted, and, after only 9 minutes, Washington was ahead, 14-0.

Big Dave Butz ended Dallas' hope of putting together a nerve-settling drive when he sacked Danny White at the Cowboys 34. Dallas punted, and Washington took over with good field position at its 39. Three rushing plays left the Redskins a foot short of a first down. Coach Gibbs, hoping for a quick knockout, ordered his team to go for it on fourth down, but Riggins was stopped cold and Dallas took over at the Redskins 48 with rekindled enthusiasm. White wasted no time. First, he threw to Dorsett in the flat for 19 yards, then he passed to tight end Doug Cosbie, who made a sensational diving catch as he tumbled into the front of the end zone. The resurrected Cowboys trailed by only a touchdown, 14-7, as the first quarter came to an end.

Alternating Joe Washington and John Riggins in the backfield, the Redskins moved steadily from their 22 to the Cowboys 24 in 11 plays. However, a penalty and two sacks by linebacker Anthony Dickerson pushed the 'Skins back to midfield, and, after Jeff Hayes' short punt, the Cowboys got the ball at their 33. For the next 6 minutes, Dallas pieced together a disjointed drive that eventually fell apart at the Washington 18 when wide receiver Tony Hill dropped a pass in the end zone. The Cowboys salvaged 3 points, though, on Rafael Septien's 35-yard field goal, and Washington had to be satisfied with a 14-10 lead at halftime.

After a torrid start, the Redskins had allowed the

Fig. 137   *Richard Darcey/Washington Post Photo*

Cowboys to creep back into the game. The turnaround began when Coach Gibbs, holding a 14-point lead, got greedy and went for the Cowboys' jugular vein on fourth and a foot. The moment Riggins was tackled, the momentum of the game switched to the Cowboys.

Since taking over in Washington, Coach Joe Gibbs had exhibited an uncanny knack for tinkering with game plans during intermission. However, this was one time that Gibbs could stand pat. The Redskins had accomplished their first objective by establishing their running game. To prevent Dallas' strong safety from helping out on the run, Gibbs had started three wide receivers, and the Redskins' rotating tandem of Joe Washington and John Riggins had gained 86 yards in 21 carries. Washington had also accomplished its primary defensive goal by limiting Tony Dorsett and Ron Springs to a total of 31 yards on the ground. All the Redskins needed to do now was lure the momentum back to their side.

The Cowboys received the second-half kickoff and

advanced to midfield, where they faced fourth and 1. The Cowboys lined up as if they were going to run a play, but it soon became apparent that they were really just trying to pull the Redskins offside. Somehow, though, Danny White got his wires crossed and audibled to a real play. With Coach Landry screaming at him to abort the play, White continued his count. Even his center, Tom Rafferty, yelled, "No! No! No! Don't run that play!," but White insisted, and, finally, Rafferty had no choice but to snap the ball. White handed off to Ron Springs, who headed to his left but was immediately swarmed under by three Washington defenders: Charles Mann, Larry Kubin, and Greg Williams. The ill-fated play lost 2 yards, and the jubilant Redskins took over at the Dallas 47.

On the sideline, the normally impassive Landry was having a fit.

Momentum rarely keeps company with stupidity, so it was no surprise that it turned its back on the Cowboys. However, it also shunned the Redskins, and the two teams traded punts. Virgil Seay returned Dallas' punt 41 yards to the Cowboys 7, but Theismann squandered Washington's golden opportunity by throwing an interception to Michael Downs. Two plays later, Danny White passed to Doug Cosbie. The ball slipped through Cosbie's hands and caromed to teammate Drew Pearson. Just as Pearson was gaining control, cornerback Vernon Dean smashed into him from behind. The ball popped into the air again, right into the arms of cornerback Darrell Green, who

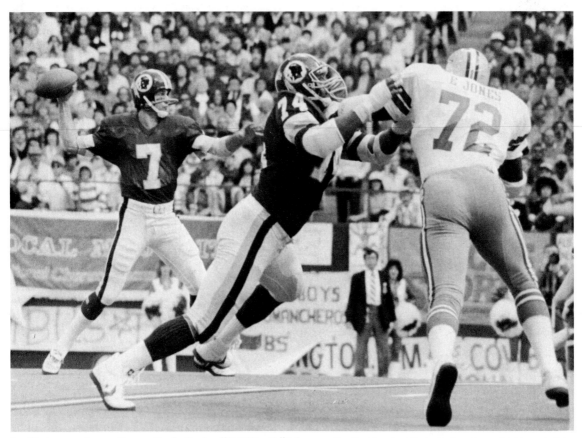

Joe Theismann fires as George Starke fends off Ed "Too Tall" Jones   *Nate Fine Photo/Nate Fine Productions, Courtesy Washington Redskins*

had just arrived on the scene. Green tumbled to the ground, then scrambled to his feet and ran into the end zone. But, even though no one had touched him, the play was whistled dead at the Dallas 43, the spot where Green had fallen. It was the final twist to a play that looked more like the work of clumsy jugglers than that of highly skilled athletes.

Theismann struck. Sprinting to his left, Joe lofted a wobbly but accurate pass to Art Monk, who had shed his defender with an abrupt stop-and-go maneuver. Monk caught the ball in full stride at the 10 and continued right into the end zone! Touchdown, Washington! Six members of the Fun Bunch gathered to celebrate in their usual communal fashion, but Michael Downs and Dennis Thurman were in no mood to allow any festivities in their end zone. The two spoilsport Cowboys did their best to disrupt the party, but the Redskins receivers jumped and high-fived above them anyway.

Intent on protecting their 21-10 lead, the fired-up Redskins defense quickly forced another Dallas punt. Washington drove unmercifully from its 29 to the Cowboys 32, but, at the beginning of the fourth quarter, Mark Moseley missed a 49-yard field goal attempt. With plenty of time left for a comeback, the Cowboys offense started to click, then self-destructed with two personal foul penalties—the last one by Tony Dorsett, who stupidly threw the ball at a tackler, nullifying a 13-yard gain. On first and 27 at his 44, Danny White waited too long to pass and threw an interception to Redskins safety Greg Williams, who returned the ball 25 yards to the Cowboys 38. [Fig. 139] Ol' Man Momentum had finally made up his mind.

Fig. 139   Drew Pearson (88) and Darrell Green (28) go airborne as Greg Williams (47) intercepts   *UPI/The Bettmann Archive*

One play later, Joe Theismann sent Charlie Brown on a deep fly pattern. Brown got a step on young cornerback Rod Hill, but stumbled at the last moment and couldn't reach the ball. It was a close decision, but the official on the scene called pass interference against Hill, giving the 'Skins a first down at the Cowboys 4. Dallas' defense held the line for three plays—barely. Facing fourth and a foot, Coach Gibbs decided to go for it. Theismann took the snap from Jeff Bostic, whirled, and handed the ball to Riggins, who dove over the blocks of Jacoby and Grimm. A wall of Cowboys met him at the goal line, but Riggins shoved his way into the end zone and the Redskins appeared to be in complete control, 28-10.

Mindful of the Cowboys' big comeback in the first game of the season, Washington refused to relax. Trailing by 18 points with 11 minutes remaining, Danny White was forced to throw on every down. After picking up two first downs, White overthrew Tony Hill, who had gotten wide open over the middle. On the next play, White forced a pass that ended up in the hands of Redskins safety Greg Williams.

John Riggins and the magnificent Hogs returned to the groans of the crowd and rammed the ball down the Cowboys' throats for nine time-consuming plays. With 2:37 remaining in the game, Mark Moseley put the final stroke on the Washington Redskins' masterpiece by kicking a 38-yard field goal to make the final score: Washington 31, Dallas 10.

"In big games, defense will win it for you," said Joe Theismann, "and our defense won it today." By giving up only 205 total yards, intercepting three passes, and limiting Tony Dorsett to a paltry 34 yards rushing, the Redskins defense not only shut down the Cowboys' vaunted offense, they embarrassed it. "I guess we invaded Dallas today," laughed linebacker Rich Milot as he and the rest of the Washington Redskins pulled on their cammies, laced up their combat boots, and headed home to RFK Stadium, where they would enjoy the spoils of victory throughout the 1983 playoffs.

RESURRECTION

Washington Redskins vs. Dallas Cowboys

December 9, 1984

For the Los Angeles Raiders, Super Bowl XVIII was a dream come true. For the Washington Redskins, it was a living nightmare. Until then, everything about Washington's 1983 season had been successful. Led by Joe Theismann, the NFL's Most Valuable Player, the Redskins set a new scoring record of 541 points and won the NFC Eastern Division title with a 14-2 record. Then, in the playoffs, Washington destroyed the Los Angeles Rams, 51-7, and outlasted the San Francisco 49ers, 24-21, to set the stage for what everyone thought would be a rematch of the titans in Super Bowl XVIII. Earlier in the year, the Redskins and the Raiders had played a thrilling game, which the 'Skins had won in the last minute, 37-35. But in the Super Bowl, the Raiders' tough man-to-man coverage completely shut down Washington's passing attack, and the favored Redskins were blown out, 38-9.

Nine months later, the 'Skins looked as if they still had not recovered from that awful beating when they lost their first two games of the 1984 season. A 5-game winning streak proved to be an excellent tonic, though, and as the season neared completion, the NFC East leaderboard had become as congested as a Metro train on game day. Going into the next to last weekend, three teams—the Cowboys, the Giants,

and the Redskins—were tied for first place with 9-5 records. And lurking one game behind were the St. Louis Cardinals at 8-6. With the Redskins playing the Cowboys and the Giants taking on the Cardinals, there was only one way a team could break out of the pack and assure itself of a spot in the playoffs: win both of its final two games.

The first game was crucial. "For the Redskins, it's cut and dried," said Coach Joe Gibbs. "It's simply a matter of Washington versus Dallas. The winner will be in the playoffs and the loser will probably be out of it. That's the way it's supposed to be." Redskins halfback Joe Washington explained it a little more vividly: "We know that if we lose this sucker then we might as well put our season in mothballs."

Injuries to Joe Theismann, who had sprained the thumb on his throwing hand in November, and to fullback John Riggins, who missed several games with persistent back spasms, had hampered the Washington offense all season. Even so, Big John had gained over 1,000 yards for the fifth time in his career. Now, for the first time in 10 weeks, Riggins, halfback Joe Washington, and wide receiver Charlie Brown would suit up for the same game. "You always feel better when your guns are completely loaded," said all-pro kick returner Mike Nelms. "Of course, we've had to operate before with only five bullets in the gun." The only "bullet" still missing was center Jeff Bostic, the keystone of the offensive line, who was out for the rest of the season with a knee injury. "I think you'll see the old Redskins this week, the team that everybody expected us to be, the team that we were last year," predicted 14-year veteran placekicker Mark Moseley.

Having beaten the Cowboys, 34-14, earlier in the year at RFK Stadium, the Redskins had a chance to become the first Washington team ever to defeat Dallas twice in the same regular season. Although tied for the division lead, the Cowboys had played spottily due to troubles in their offensive line and at quarterback, where Coach Tom Landry was once again faced with a dilemma that had dogged him throughout his career: which of two good quarterbacks should start? Tired of being Danny White's understudy, Gary Hogeboom bellyached in the preseason that he never had been given an honest shot at the first-string job. Updating an idea from the early Sixties when he alternated quarterbacks Eddie LeBaron and Don Meredith on every play, Landry rotated his two quarterbacks on a game-to-game basis. Not surprisingly, that arrangement satisfied no one, serving only to divide the team into two camps. Realizing the Cowboys were floundering without consistent leadership, Landry finally chose the more experienced White, leaving Hogeboom to stew on the bench.

The Cowboys had also been touched by scandal. Several members of "America's Team" had been accused of using cocaine, leading one wag to rename them "South America's Team." Still, with all their problems, the Cowboys were muddling through. Riding the back of its defense, which was ranked second in the NFC, Dallas had worked itself into position to make the playoffs for the 19th time in 20 years. Like the Redskins, all they had to do was win their final two games. "I absolutely love being the underdog," said Dallas linebacker Jeff Rohrer when he learned Washington was favored by 2 points. "We have been on top so long that now it's kind of neat that we can turn the tables a little. Now we can stick it to the Redskins the way they've stuck it to us."

The last time the outcome of a regular season game between the Dallas Cowboys and Washington Redskins had been this crucial was in 1979 when Dallas' Roger Staubach pulled off a miraculous 35-34 comeback victory to deprive Washington of a spot in the playoffs. Five years later, the Redskins, especially Joe Theismann and John Riggins, still remembered. So did the Cowboys, who appointed the retired Staubach as honorary captain for this game.

As usual, Dallas started in high gear, particularly Danny White, who connected on six of his first seven passes. Having to face a third down only once in their first ten plays, the Cowboys marched 80 yards and scored on a 6-yard pass from White to Doug Donley. Rafael Septien converted, and the Cowboys broke on top, 7-0.

Dallas' first play on defense—a sack of quarterback Joe Theismann—was just as effective as its offensive efforts. Theismann recovered with a 22-yard completion to Clint Didier and a 13-yard quarterback draw, but Washington ran out of gas just past midfield. The Cowboys continued to dominate throughout the first quarter, keeping the ball 11½ minutes, yet couldn't improve their lead.

As the second period began, the Redskins started to do what they did best—run the football. John Riggins bulled through the line four times for 24 yards. Then, after Theismann hit three short passes, Riggo blasted for 21 more on three carries as Washington surged to the Cowboys 10. On third and 9, though, Theismann was sacked, and Mark Moseley was called on to salvage the drive. His dead-center, 31-yard field goal put Washington on the board, 7-3.

Following the kickoff, the Cowboys regrouped at their 23. A screen pass to Tony Dorsett clicked for 39 yards. Then fullback Timmy Newsome caught the Redskins out of position and reeled off 30 yards on a draw. After Dorsett picked up 6 more over right tackle, White faked to his tailback, rolled to his right, and hit Doug Cosbie with a 2-yard scoring pass. Dallas was firmly in control, leading 14-3.

Joe Theismann retaliated with a 30-yard pass completion to Art Monk, the league-leading receiver's 91st catch of the year. A 14-yard scramble, a

9-yard strike to Charlie Brown, and a pass interference penalty gave the Redskins a first down at the Cowboys 15. Once again, though, Washington could not get into the end zone, and Mark Moseley's 34-yard field goal gave little solace to his teammates, who still trailed, 14-6.

Dallas continued to apply pressure. From his 40, White threw deep to wide receiver Mike Renfro, who caught the bomb at the Redskins 25, avoided Darrell Green's diving tackle, zig-zagged past Curtis Jordan, and ran into the end zone for a 60-yard touchdown! Leading 21-6 and having scored three touchdowns in four possessions, the Cowboys clearly had Washington on the ropes. Although they had successfully moved the football, the Redskins were scoring only on field goals while the Cowboys were scoring touchdowns—a tradeoff that could not continue if the 'Skins hoped to stay in the game. At the end of the first half, the normally blasé Texas Stadium crowd of 64,286 roared its approval as the Cowboys, leading 21-6, swaggered to their dressing room.

Fig. 140   *John McDonnell/Washington Post Photo*

The Redskins desperately needed a break, and, 2 minutes into the second half, they got it. On Dallas' first possession, Danny White, who had completed 13 of 18 passes for 198 yards in the first half, threw to wide receiver Doug Donley on a slant pattern. Timing his move perfectly, cornerback Darrell Green cut in front of Donley, intercepted at the 32, and, with a phalanx of Redskins clearing the way, jogged into the end zone for a touchdown! [Fig. 140] Although trailing, 21-13, the 'Skins were back in the game.

Jeff Hayes kicked off to Chuck McSwain, who charged straight upfield. Otis Wonsley smashed into him at the 20, the ball squirted free, and Anthony Washington recovered for the Redskins at the Cowboys 31! Two short passes moved the ball to the 15, but a sack by safety Dennis Thurman pushed Washington back to the Dallas 22. On third and 17, Theismann dropped back and pegged the ball to Calvin Muhammad, who put on the afterburners and caught up to the pass in the corner of the end zone for a touchdown! In less than 4 minutes, the Redskins had recouped two touchdowns and now trailed

by only a point, 21-20. Except for a few blasphemous Redskins fans, the crowd at Texas Stadium was dead silent.

Danny White settled down, and the Cowboys moved 43 yards in nine plays. On second and 10 at the Washington 37, White rolled to his right and fired to Cosbie. The pass never reached him. Redskins safety Ken Coffey tipped the ball into the air, and Darrell Green grabbed it for his second interception. Although Washington couldn't capitalize, the turnover was important because it foiled Dallas just as it was recapturing the momentum.

After several punts were exchanged, the Cowboys took over at their 21 late in the third quarter. On first down, fullback Timmy Newsome tried the middle but ran into Washington defensive tackle Darryl Grant, who stripped the ball from his grasp. As the crowd groaned, linebacker Mel Kaufman fell on it at the Dallas 23. It was the Cowboys' fourth turnover of the third quarter, and it gave Washington a handsome opportunity to take the lead. John Riggins

Mel Kaufman wraps up Danny White as Charles Mann (71) prepares to lend a hand   *John McDonnell/Washington Post Photo*

pounded for 15 yards on three carries, and Theismann passed to Art Monk for 4 more. But on third and 3, the Dallas Flex stiffened, and Washington had to settle for a 21-yard field goal by Mark Moseley. Once down by 15 points, the Redskins had climbed into the lead, 23-21. Now, it was Dallas that was reeling.

Danny White revived the struggling Cowboys with a 26-yard pass to Tony Hill, who made a leaping catch along the sideline. Then a 13-yard strike to Ron Springs gave Dallas another first down at the Wash-

ington 43. On the first play of the fourth quarter, White lofted a long spiral to Hill, who caught it at the 5 and ran into the end zone for a 43-yard touchdown! The Cowboys were back in front, 28-23.

After an exchange of punts, the Redskins took over at their 45 with 9:41 remaining in the game. Tight end Don Warren got the 'Skins rolling with a sideline catch for 9 yards. John Riggins burst through right tackle for 13 more, giving him over 100 yards rushing. Then, for the third time in the second half,

Joe Theismann called a time-out to correct a mix-up at the line of scrimmage, leaving the 'Skins without a time-out down the stretch.

When play resumed, Theismann handed off to Riggins, who transferred the ball to Art Monk on a reverse. Monk headed for the left sideline with only one man to beat: Dallas safety Michael Downs. Monk stutterstepped. Downs dove at his feet—and grabbed only his shadow. With a clear lane ahead of him, Monk hugged the sideline for 18 yards before he was brought down at the Cowboys 15. One play later, Theismann hit Monk with a bullet at the 1. It then took three tries, but John Riggins finally wedged into the end zone for a touchdown, and, with 6½ minutes left in the game, the Redskins reclaimed the lead, 30-28.

After surviving a scare when White overthrew a wide-open Tony Hill, Washington stopped the Cowboys at midfield. Unfortunately, the 'Skins were unable to sustain a clock-killing drive and had to punt back to Dallas with 1:58 left in the game. The Cowboys went into their hurry-up offense at their 29. After a 6-yard pass to Ron Springs, Washington cornerback Vernon Dean diagnosed a screen pass to Dorsett and dumped him for a 7-yard loss. A hurried incompletion set up fourth and 11—the most important play of the season. Danny White took the snap in shotgun formation and threw down the middle for Ron Springs, who had just started to cut to the inside. The ball, however, was thrown to the outside, and when it hit the ground, the Redskins clinched their 30-28 victory!

Guess who's going to get the ball?   *Nate Fine Photo/Nate Fine Productions, Courtesy Washington Redskins*

Led by their ecstatic coach, the triumphant Washington Redskins ran off the field whooping for joy, all alone in first place.

Coach Joe Gibbs called it "one of the all-time gut checks I've ever been a part of." By limiting the Cowboys to six first downs in the last half; by disrupting Danny White's timing so that he could complete only 9 of 24 second-half passes; by controlling Tony Dorsett all afternoon (15 carries for 42 yards); and by forcing four turnovers in the third quarter, the Redskins defense had kept the Cowboys at bay long enough for the Washington offense to overcome the 15-point deficit. "It was like we were an animal smelling blood," said Curtis Jordan in the jubilant Washington locker room. "It was almost like we could hear them in the third quarter saying, 'Oh my God, here they come again.'"

"This was like a high-stakes poker game," said an excited Joe Theismann. "They pushed all their chips in. Now, we're going on. And they are about gone." Sure enough, one week later, in the final game of the regular season, the Washington Redskins sewed up their second straight Eastern Division Championship by defeating the St. Louis Cardinals, 29-27. And, in a delicious reversal of what happened in 1979, the Cowboys were squeezed out at the finish line.

SLINGS AND ARROWS

New York Giants vs. Washington Redskins

November 18, 1985

Just two years after being named the NFL's Most Valuable Player, quarterback Joe Theismann had become the league's Most Criticized Player for his part in the Washington Redskins' puzzling slide into mediocrity. Spoiled by the success of Washington's two Super Bowl seasons, the fans and media came down hard on the 12-year veteran after the 'Skins lost to the Chicago Bears, 23-19, in the first round of the 1984 playoffs and struggled to a 5-5 record in 1985. Not that their criticism was totally unjustified. Theismann had slipped to 13th place (out of 14) in the NFC quarterback rankings, and was dead last in yards passing per game (148) and yards per attempt (4.41). Unable to escape pressure with the nimbleness of his youth, the 36-year-old Theismann had fallen victim to sacks, hurried passes, and, worst of all, 16 interceptions in the first ten games of the season.

Even so, Coach Joe Gibbs remained loyal to Theismann, who had started 120 of the last 123 Redskins games and led the team to a league-best 39-10 record over the past three years. But did Gibbs really have a choice, given the fact that Theismann's substitute, Jay Schroeder, was an ex-baseball player with almost no college football experience and with just eight NFL passes under his belt? To be fair, Theismann's passing was not the only reason the Redskins were struggling. Widespread injuries, especially to the Hogs, Washington's famous offensive line, and to fullback John Riggins, had necessitated a constant shuffling of personnel which put the Redskins' once-powerful running game out of kilter.

In anticipation of such problems, and to fill the void the 36-year-old Riggins would create when he retired, General Manager Bobby Beathard had traded a first-round draft pick to the New Orleans Saints for their all-time leading rusher, fullback George Rogers. A 6-foot-2, 230-pound Heisman Trophy-winner from the University of South Carolina, Rogers was a bruising inside runner with straight-ahead speed. In an effort to keep both of his big fullbacks reasonably healthy (and to massage both of their egos), Gibbs alternated Riggins and Rogers on a quarter-by-quarter basis. However, because of differences in timing and because neither player stayed in the lineup long enough to get into the flow of the game, the Redskins' running attack started slumping. Although the 'Skins were the only team in the NFL to have gained more yards rushing than passing, many believed that this statistic referred more to the ineptitude of Washington's passing attack than to the strength of its running game.

At Redskin Park, frustration was mounting at the same rate that time was slipping away. "We're hang-

George Rogers
Nate Fine Photo/Nate Fine Productions, Courtesy Washington Redskins

ing on the edge now," admitted safety Curtis Jordan. But the ever-positive Gibbs kept insisting that his team, although mired in fourth place in the NFC Eastern Division, still had a chance to salvage the season. "We have to find a way to get into the playoffs," said the Redskins coach. "It's going to take [a victory in] just about every game." That wouldn't be easy, especially since Washington's next opponent was the division-leading New York Giants, who had already beaten the Redskins, 17-3, earlier in the season.

Coached by Bill Parcells, the Giants had shed their two-decade-old reputation as losers and were currently on a 4-game winning streak. "Coach Parcells has molded a team of fighters," said Giants defensive end Casey Merrill. "Now we expect to win." On offense, New York was conservative but effective, rank-

ing third in the conference. Six-year veteran quarterback Phil Simms was the #3 passer in the NFC, typical of a troubled career in which his performance always exceeded his popularity. Halfback Joe Morris, an undersized over-achiever cut from the same cloth as Dick James, Mike Garrett, and Floyd Little, was as dangerous as any back in the NFL. But the Giants were clearly in their element when they were on defense. Led by linebackers Harry Carson and Lawrence Taylor and defensive end Leonard Marshall, New York's conference-leading defense could crush any offense in the league, as it had demonstrated a month earlier when it held the Redskins to just 69 yards of total offense.

Washington had only one advantage on its side —the element of desperation. "We're about reaching the end of the road here," said Joe Gibbs. "We either get things turned around or we're going to lose this year." By making the Washington Redskins 1-point favorites for this Monday night clash, the odds-makers reconfirmed that desperation is the strongest motivator and that motivation is the key to winning in the NFL. "Somehow, some way," said Joe Theismann, "we've got to make it happen."

When the nationally televised Monday night game got underway at RFK Stadium, Joe Theismann's lack of confidence was evident in his first two passes; although both were completed, they were so short that the Redskins were left with fourth and 3. Punter Steve Cox, acquired after Jeff Hayes tore a thigh muscle in Chicago, short-hopped center Jeff Bostic's low snap and began his three-stride set-up. Instead of kicking the ball, though, Cox lobbed a surprise pass to teammate Raphel Cherry 11 yards downfield, and the Redskins were right back in business.

Theismann tried to capitalize on the Giants' temporary disarray by throwing deep to Art Monk, who had beaten cornerback Elvis Patterson by several yards. But Theismann's pass was so badly underthrown that Monk had to make a good play just to keep the ball from being intercepted. The boo-birds at RFK, jaded by the Redskins' record-setting production of 541 points in 1983, began to warm up.

Theismann's next pass, however, was reminiscent of his glory days: an 11-yard strike to Monk over the middle. Then, two plays later, Theismann kept the drive going with a 15-yard completion to wide receiver Gary Clark, a refugee from the floundering USFL. On first down at the Giants 10, Theismann flipped a short pass to tight end Don Warren, who headed toward the goal line on a collision course with all-pro linebacker Lawrence Taylor. Taylor sprang at the 3, but Warren hurdled over him and landed in the end zone. Touchdown, Redskins! Mark Moseley added the extra point, and 53,371 fans at RFK Stadium celebrated Washington's 7-0 lead. No one was happier than Joe Theismann, who had completed six of his first seven passes.

After an exchange of punts, the Giants picked up 24 yards on a pass interference penalty, and, on the following play, Simms handed off to halfback Joe Morris, who scooted through a small opening at left tackle, broke into the Washington secondary, and outran every Redskins defender to the end zone. The 56-yard touchdown run silenced the crowd and tied the game, 7-7.

The second quarter opened with the Redskins on the move. On first down at his 46, Coach Gibbs called a flea-flicker, one of Washington's favorite plays. Theismann handed off to Riggins, who whirled at the line and lateraled back to Theismann. Looking deep, Joe stepped up into the pocket to avoid the grasp of linebacker Harry Carson. At that moment, Lawrence Taylor leapt at Theismann from behind. Theismann fell forward, and all of Taylor's 240 pounds landed on Joe's right leg. It snapped like a brittle twig. Taylor jumped off Theismann and urgently called for medical help, but it was too late. Joe Theismann's career was over. As ABC-TV replayed the gruesome sequence over and over again, Theismann was strapped to a stretcher and taken by ambulance to Arlington Hospital, where later he would undergo surgery to set the compound fracture. As Joe Theismann left the field, not only the 53,000 fans but all the Giants and Redskins players gave him a standing ovation—an uncommon tribute to an uncommon man.

Reserve quarterback Jay Schroeder took over. In the broadcasting booth, Hall of Fame quarterback

Joe Namath said, "Schroeder's gonna have a tough time tonight. A backup quarterback in the NFL doesn't get much practice time during the week, so he's gonna be rusty and he's not gonna be on top of his game." So when Schroeder, on his second play, completed a beautiful 44-yard pass to Art Monk at the Giants 13 yard line, Namath laughed, "Hey, I wanna see him when he really gets on top of his game." Schroeder's startling pass awoke Redskins fans from the nightmare of Joe Theismann's injury, and they kept cheering as Washington advanced to the New York 4 on two running plays. However, on third and 1, John Riggins fumbled, and, when Lawrence Taylor recovered for the Giants, Jay Schroeder had his first taste of NFL disappointment.

There was no further scoring in the first half, and the two teams went to their locker rooms tied, 7-7. The Giants had played so conservatively that Phil Simms threw only one pass in the first 26 minutes. Conversely, with the amazingly composed Jay Schroeder at quarterback, the Redskins had transformed themselves into the swashbucklers of the NFC. Throughout the country, football fans were asking the same question: "Who is that guy?"

The Redskins had another surprise waiting for the Giants. Washington's Steve Cox kicked off to New York to open the second half, but the Giants never received it. Instead of kicking deep, Cox bunted the ball 10 yards, then fell on it himself before the retreating Giants linemen could double back. With the crowd still laughing, Schroeder faked a handoff and threw a long, arching pass to Art Monk, who leapt and caught the ball at the Giants 4. As Schroeder punched the air in triumph, the crowd roared in happy amazement. Three plays later, John Riggins dove into the end zone for the 103rd time in his career, and the 'Skins jumped back on top, 14-7.

Once again, though, Washington's lead was short-lived. Phil Simms connected on three straight passes, including a 29-yard screen to rookie tight end Mark Bavaro. Then, on first down at the Washington 41, Joe Morris duplicated his earlier touchdown by blasting through left tackle and racing into the end zone. Eric Schubert's PAT deadlocked the game, 14-14.

Suddenly, the Redskins developed a serious case

Jay Schroeder   *Nate Fine/NFL Photos*

of fumble-itis. First, John Riggins coughed up the ball. Then, after Washington's defense stopped Joe Morris on a fourth-and-1, George Rogers fumbled at the Redskins 24. Three plays later, the Giants surged into the lead when Morris ran 8 yards through left tackle for his third touchdown of the night. New York 21, Washington 14.

Coach Joe Gibbs benched both of his big, famous, fumbling fullbacks in favor of Keith Griffin, a much smaller halfback normally used only on passing downs. As the fourth quarter began, the Redskins started to move. Schroeder scrambled for 11 yards, then rifled a pass to Gary Clark at midfield for 17 more. After Griffin ran for another first down, Schroeder passed to Clark on a long, perfectly-timed button-hook at the Giants 17. The drive stalled at the 11, but Mark Moseley kicked a 28-yard field goal to whittle the Giants' lead to 21-17.

Cox kicked off—onsides, again! The spinning ball squirted past a New York lineman, and Washington's Greg Williams dove on it at the Giants 47. [Fig. 145] It was the third time that Cox had fooled the Giants —the perfect rebuttal to New York's three fumble recoveries. Jay Schroeder passed to Clint Didier for 9 yards. Then, after Griffin picked up the first down, Schroeder fired to Art Monk at the Giants 24 (giving Monk seven catches for 130 yards). A penalty moved the ball to the 14. On first down, Didier ran a quick post. Schroeder's perfect pass met him at the goal line, and Clint pulled it in for the score! Even Mark Moseley's badly shanked extra point attempt couldn't dampen the enthusiasm of the excited crowd as they cheered Washington's 23-21 lead.

After four punts were exchanged during the next 4 minutes, New York took over at its 17 with 1:33 remaining in the game. On first down, Simms es-

Fig. 145   *Gary A. Cameron/Washington Post Photo*

caped a big rush and passed to Tony Galbreath for 10 yards. Then, Washington got a break. Cornerback Darrell Green clearly interfered with Phil McConkey on the next play, but the officials didn't spot it and New York was left with a second-and-10 at its 27. 1:21 remained in the game. "Listen to this crowd," exclaimed announcer Frank Gifford as the Giants came to the line. "The stadium is rocking." Under heavy pressure from defensive tackle Dean Hamel, Simms tried to force a pass to wide receiver Bobby Johnson—and Redskins cornerback Vernon Dean intercepted at the 40! An explosion of cheers burst over the field, and the sellout crowd kept roaring as Jay Schroeder killed the clock and raised the ball over his head in triumph. The miracle was complete, 23-21.

In the bedlam of the Redskins locker room, sportswriters charged at Jay Schroeder like blitzing linebackers. Once again, the unflappable young quarterback made all the right moves. "I don't think I should've been playing any earlier," answered Schroeder earnestly. "There's no way you can pull a Joe Theismann. He's been MVP of the league; he's done everything you can possibly ask of him. But I knew all along, I just had to be ready all the time."

There was no doubt that all 45 Redskins players had rallied around their new quarterback, giving their utmost to ease his initiation. But the team had an even better reason to give their best. At halftime, the Washington Redskins had dedicated the game to Joe Theismann, who for 8 years was the team's starting quarterback and inspirational leader. Anything less than a courageous performance ending in victory wouldn't have been a fitting tribute to one of the best and most competitive players in the history of the game.

SECOND EFFORT

Washington Redskins vs.
San Diego Chargers

September 21, 1986

Sadly, great football players get old. The fastest legs slow down; the strongest arms weaken; the most flexible bodies grow stiff. Thousands of collisions finally take their merciless toll until only the fires of competitiveness retain their original brilliance. Few players can look objectively at themselves and admit they have lost the edge that made them great. Thirty-six-year-old John Riggins, the oldest running back in the NFL, was no exception.

Despite chronic back problems, Riggo refused to retire at the end of the 1985 season even though he had been relegated to a back-up position behind George Rogers. Wanting to avoid the furor that George Allen had created in 1975 with his insensitive and untimely dismissal of Sonny Jurgensen, Coach Joe Gibbs hoped that Big John would retire gracefully so that the Redskins could celebrate a "John Riggins Day" at RFK Stadium and everyone part on relatively happy terms. But the fierce pride that had motivated John Riggins to become one of the greatest running backs in NFL history would not let him admit that his career was finally over. So, at his insistence, the Redskins unceremoniously released the man most responsible for their recent success.

Not surprisingly, many of his teammates thought Riggo could still contribute. "At times in the past," said linebacker Mel Kaufman, "you'd think Riggins

was dead and couldn't do it anymore. Then he'd rise up and do incredible things." As the fourth leading all-time NFL rusher (11,352 yards), the #2 touchdown scorer (116), and the Most Valuable Player of Super Bowl XVII, John Riggins earned every dollar and every ovation that he was given in his 14-year career. "He's a local legend, a team legend, and he's got to be an NFL legend," eulogized defensive tackle Darryl Grant. "Guys will come and go, but you'll never forget John Riggins."

As famous for his Mohawk haircut, camouflage pants, and unbridled sense of humor (remember that white-tie dinner when he told his table-mate, Supreme Court Justice Sandra Day O'Connor, to "Loosen up, Sandy, baby") as he was for his game-winning 43-yard touchdown in Super Bowl XVII, John Riggins was relentlessly colorful and charismatic. Nicknamed "The Diesel" for his powerful, straight-ahead running style, Riggo will undoubtedly take his rightful place alongside such rugged players as Bronko Nagurski, Ollie Matson, and Marion Motley in the Pro Football Hall of Fame.

Coupled with Joe Theismann's career-ending injury, Riggins' release signaled a new era for the Washington Redskins. "It's going to be different around here without him," said Mel Kaufman. "Almost like a changing of the guard." Unknown quarterback Jay

Schroeder had taken over for Theismann in the middle of the 1985 season and surprised the nation by leading Washington to victories in five out of six games. Still, it was not enough. Even though their 10-6 record matched three playoff teams, the Redskins came up short in the tie-breakers and were excluded from post-season play for the first time since 1981.

Despite Schroeder's dazzling performance, there were some doubts that he could continue his success in 1986. Although he was far more accurate when he planted his right foot and stepped forward like a baseball catcher pegging to second, Schroeder had a tendency to desert the pocket and throw on the run. When the USFL folded in August, the Redskins jumped at the chance to sign Doug Williams, the former quarterback for the Tampa Bay Buccaneers, just in case Schroeder proved to be a flash in the pan.

The demise of the USFL bore other fruit for the Redskins. Halfback Kelvin Bryant, whimsically drafted in the sixth round in 1983 after already signing with the USFL (where he would become the league MVP), joined the team just before the season began. With visions of Larry Csonka and Mercury Morris dancing in their heads, sportswriters began lobbying for a return to the two-back system so that Bryant, a fast and shifty racer, could get enough playing time. Unfortunately, neither Bryant nor starting fullback George Rogers was a good blocker, a disadvantage that outweighed all other considerations in the coaches' minds. "To run our offense, we need at least one big back," maintained Joe Bugel, the assistant head coach in charge of the offense. "This is not a scatback offense. Everything starts with the off-tackle play, and we need a big mule back there. That's why Rogers is a first-down back, because we're an off-tackle team." Bryant became the third-down, long-yardage specialist.

In their first game of the season, the Redskins buried the Philadelphia Eagles, 41-14, with both Rogers and Bryant playing important, but separate, roles. Then, in the next game, the second-guessing ended when Kelvin suffered a knee injury that would sideline him for 6 weeks. In that same game, a hard-fought 10-6 victory over the Los Angeles Raiders, the

Kelvin Bryant
Nate Fine Photo/Nate Fine Productions, Courtesy Washington Redskins

Redskins also lost linebacker Mel Kaufman for the season with a torn Achilles tendon.

In those first two victories, Schroeder dismissed any doubts about his ability by completing 31 of his 57 passes for 502 yards. With every game, he was getting closer to becoming a first-rate quarterback in the fabled tradition of Sammy Baugh, Eddie LeBaron, Sonny Jurgensen, Billy Kilmer, and Joe Theismann. He just needed a little experience to polish the rough edges.

Schroeder's counterpart in the upcoming game against the San Diego Chargers was Dan Fouts, the most dangerous quarterback in the league for over a decade. Known as "Top Gun," Fouts had passed for over 300 yards 47 times in his 14-year career and had surpassed the 400-yard mark six times. "When you play a team like San Diego," said Richie Petitbon, Washington's assistant head coach in charge of defense, "they're going to make a lot of yards, but hopefully not a lot of touchdowns. We're not naive enough to think that we're going to go out there and shut this team out. This is a legit, high-powered offense."

The Chargers had opened the season with a 50-28 trouncing of the Miami Dolphins, a reminder of how tough they were in San Diego Jack Murphy Stadium, where they had won seven consecutive games while averaging 38 points. Nevertheless, the Chargers, coached by Joe Gibbs' former mentor, Don Coryell, could also play giveaway and self-destruct. The week before, against the New York Giants, San Diego had turned the ball over seven times and lost, 20-7. So the question was which Chargers team would show up to play against the Redskins: the unstoppable scoring machine or the self-destructive bumblers?

Unfortunately for the Washington Redskins, it was the unstoppable scoring machine.

In front of an enthusiastic sellout crowd basking in the California sunshine, the Redskins surprised the Chargers by opening the game with a reverse to Art Monk that picked up 21 yards. Four runs by George Rogers and a 13-yard pass to Clint Didier moved the ball to the San Diego 12. However, the 'Skins blew an opportunity to get an easy touchdown when Schroeder overthrew a wide-open Gary Clark in the end zone, and Washington had to settle for Mark Moseley's 29-yard field goal and a 3-0 lead.

San Diego began at its 20. Dan Fouts passed to Trumaine Johnson for 21 yards. First down. Lionel James swept left end for 11 yards. First down. After a 15-yard penalty against defensive end Dexter Manley, Gary Anderson slipped through the middle for 17 more. First down at the Washington 15. Then a reverse to Anderson picked up another 10. Four plays, four first downs. After a penalty moved the ball back

to the 13, Fouts screened to Anderson, who faked Rich Milot out of his chin strap, zig-zagged past Darrell Green, and dove into the end zone. The stunning 80-yard drive put the Chargers ahead, 7-3, and gave a chilling indication of what was yet to come.

San Diego's swarming defense forced a punt, which Steve Cox shanked, giving the Chargers excellent field position at the Washington 47. On third and 18, Fouts avoided a blitz and fired to wide receiver Wes Chandler for 19 yards. Then Fouts connected with Buford McGee for 18 more and a first down at the Washington 18. Three plays later, McGee squeezed into the end zone from the 1, and Rolf Benirschke's PAT boosted San Diego's advantage to 14-3.

It got worse. At the beginning of the second quarter, the Redskins drove to San Diego's 24, mainly on a 51-yard bomb from Schroeder to Clark, but Moseley's 41-yard field goal attempt bounced off the left upright. Then, for the third straight time, the Chargers drove the length of the field. Subsidized by a 36-yard pass interference penalty, San Diego marched 76 yards in nine plays. Buford McGee sliced into the end zone from the 1 for his second touchdown, and the Chargers were in total command, 21-3.

Return specialist Ken Jenkins resuscitated the comatose Redskins with a splendid 37-yard kickoff return. Starting at his 47, Schroeder completed two passes to Art Monk for a total of 17 yards, but a penalty moved the ball back to the San Diego 41. On third and 10, Schroeder threw deep to Monk, who was blanketed by cornerback Wayne Davis as he raced down the right sideline. When Schroeder's pass arrived, Davis tipped it away, but Monk stabbed at the ball and pulled it in with one hand! [Fig. 147] The sensational catch gave Washington a first down at the Chargers 3, and George Rogers did the rest, knifing through left tackle for a touchdown to re-establish the Redskins' dignity and cut San Diego's lead to 21-10.

After an exchange of punts, Fouts led the Chargers downfield again in the waning moments of the first half. A 24-yard draw play and three straight completions advanced the ball to the Washington 6. With 11 seconds left in the half, Fouts went for the

Fig. 147   *Stephen Dunn/Focus West/NFL Photos*

knock-out, but his pass was picked off by cornerback Vernon Dean in the end zone! Although trailing, 21-10, the Redskins left the field at intermission believing there still was room for hope.

While the Chargers offense had purred like a 12-cylinder Ferrari in the first half, Washington's offense performed like a hotrod missing second and third gears. With George Rogers averaging 2.4 yards on nine carries and Jay Schroeder hitting on 6 of 17 passes, the Redskins had found only one effective weapon—the bomb.

On the second play of the second half, Schroeder struck again with a 41-yard pass to Art Monk at the

San Diego 32. Two plays later, Jay counteracted a blitz with a quick toss to Gary Clark at the 17. Three determined charges by Rogers pushed the ball to the 3, but the Redskins then began to self-destruct. On second and goal, Schroeder tried to hand off to blocking back Don Warren, but he was not expecting it and the ball came loose. Schroeder recovered, but Washington now faced third and goal at the 7. Jay took a two-step drop and threw to Clark at the goal line. The pass was perfect, but Clark dropped it as he turned to step into the end zone. Once again, Mark Moseley was called into action, and his 24-yard field goal edged the Redskins closer, 21-13.

San Diego's next possession ended abruptly when Dexter Manley sacked Dan Fouts, and Washington got the ball back at its 42. Again the Redskins drove inside the Chargers 10, but had to be satisfied with Moseley's 26-yard field goal to make the score: San Diego 21, Washington 16. The Chargers retaliated with a 50-yard field goal by Rolf Benirschke that increased their advantage to 24-16. Realizing he could no longer afford to swap field goals or wage time-consuming drives, Jay Schroeder fired deep to Art Monk, who caught the perfectly thrown pass just past midfield and ran to the Chargers 16 for a 58-yard gain! A short completion to Warren and a 10-yard sweep by George Rogers finished the job, and, as the third quarter came to an end, Washington was breathing down San Diego's neck, 24-23.

Early in the fourth quarter, the Redskins lost a chance to forge ahead when Moseley's 47-yard field goal attempt was blocked. San Diego reclaimed the momentum by driving to Washington's 14, and, with 9 minutes left in the game, Rolf Benirschke booted a 31-yard field goal to extend the Chargers' lead to 27-23. After an exchange of punts, the Redskins stormed back with a 46-yard pick-up on a pass interference penalty at the San Diego 29. However, on the next play, Gary Clark fumbled after catching a 5-yard pass, and the Chargers took over with less than 4 minutes remaining.

Washington's defense gave up one first down, then forced the Chargers into a crucial situation: third and 10 at the San Diego 33. Fouts threw over the middle for Trumaine Johnson, who appeared to be open by

two steps, but cornerback Darrell Green, the fastest player in the NFL, put on a burst of speed and deflected the ball away! San Diego had to punt.

Exactly 2 minutes remained as Jay Schroeder surveyed the 70 yards the Redskins needed to cover in order to win the game. On first down, Schroeder arched a long spiral to Art Monk, but cornerback Wayne Davis batted the ball away. Disdaining short passes, Schroeder let fly with a spiral that traveled 60 yards in the air and landed safely in Gary Clark's hands at the San Diego 14! [Fig. 148] Because they had already used their three time-outs, the Redskins had to race downfield to set up the next play.

Over the din created by 57,853 screaming fans, Schroeder shouted an audible, but Clark, on the left side of the field, could not hear it. Although he figured Schroeder would toss the ball out of bounds to stop the clock, Gary improvised a route toward the end zone. At the snap, Schroeder dropped back four steps and fired. Clark split two Chargers defenders, looked back, and caught the low, hard pass as he slid into the end zone! "I just took an educated guess on my route," said Clark, "and I was right." Leading 30-27, the miracle comeback was nearly complete. But 1:16 remained—plenty of time for Dan Fouts to retaliate.

Steve Cox kicked off into the end zone, forcing the Chargers to start at their 20. A pass to Kellen Winslow was wide. A 20-yard pass to Wes Chandler was low. On third and 10, Fouts tripped as he started to back-pedal, and defensive end Charles Mann downed him at the 7. Facing fourth and 23, Fouts faded back into his end zone and threw long, but Redskins safety Curtis Jordan intercepted to seal the Chargers' fate. Washington 30, San Diego 27.

With a weary smile softening his weathered face, Curtis Jordan explained in his laziest Texas drawl how Jay Schroeder, a 25-year-old quarterback with a total of nine starts in his collegiate and professional career, could have pulled off such an improbable comeback: "You see him out there having a hard time early, and then you look at what he does when we really need it. When it's time to swell up and do something, he comes up with the big play. He's a winner—that's it."

Fig. 148   *Gary A. Cameron/Washington Post Photo*

Washington's other heroes were not hard to find. Art Monk's 174 yards on seven catches and Gary Clark's 144 yards on six receptions did the most damage, but George Rogers had kept the Chargers honest with 87 yards on the ground. And, after being pushed all over the field in the first half, the 'Skins defense had surrendered only 100 yards the rest of the way. "We're fighting and scratching, just like we did in 1982," said a happy Neal Olkewicz in the boisterous Redskins locker room. "This victory really reminds me a lot of the way that team was winning four years ago."

SHOOTOUT AT RFK

Minnesota Vikings vs. Washington Redskins

November 2, 1986

"For me, this is real difficult," said a tearful Mark Moseley, who earlier had missed a short field goal and an extra point at crucial times in the Washington Redskins' dispiriting 30-6 loss to the Dallas Cowboys. Moseley didn't try to blame anyone else; he didn't try to excuse his performance. There was only regret. "I've never let the team down before. But last week and this week something's happened. I've let the team down when it needed me . . . This might have been the last game of my career. It's not an easy thing to face . . . Maybe it's time to move on."

Ever since his long-time holder, Joe Theismann, had broken his leg in 1985, Moseley had struggled to recapture the consistent form that made him the best clutch kicker in the league. By missing 14 of his last 27 field goal attempts, though, the 16-year veteran had gradually lost the confidence of his teammates and finally his coach, Joe Gibbs. The day after the Dallas game, Mark Moseley—the sixth leading scorer of all time with 1,351 points, the NFL's Most Valuable Player in 1982, and the holder of 10 Redskins records and 3 league records (including 23 consecutive field goals)—was given his unconditional release.

It's a chilling testimony to the insecure nature of NFL careers that 4 years after Washington's victory in Super Bowl XVII, the three players most responsible for that great triumph—John Riggins, Joe Theis-mann, and Mark Moseley—were no longer on the Redskins roster. At Redskin Park, there was no time for sentimentality as General Manager Bobby Beathard quickly signed soccer-style kicker Max Zendejas to take over Moseley's job. Ironically, Max was a cousin of Tony Zendejas, whom Moseley had beaten out in 1985 before Tony was traded to the Houston Oilers—the same team that had released Moseley on a whim back in 1972.

Despite the kicking-game problems and several key injuries, the Redskins won six of their first eight games in 1986 and were tied with the New York Giants for the lead in the NFC East. "You like to coach teams that work hard, play hard, and get excited," said Coach Gibbs. "Nobody expected us to be 6-2. That's been fun." One of the reasons for Washington's surprising success was the play of ex-USFL wide receiver Gary Clark. After catching 72 passes in his rookie season, the 5-foot-9, 173-pound Clark was currently leading the conference with 44 receptions. In addition, Clark had just set a new club record the previous week, gaining 241 yards on 11 receptions against the Giants.

Clark, Art Monk, and Clint Didier gave quarterback Jay Schroeder three excellent targets, and, with designated receiver Kelvin Bryant in the backfield again after recovering from a knee injury, the Redskins' scoring prospects looked bright. However, the receiving corps couldn't take all the credit for Washington's 6-2 record. Fullback George Rogers was second in the NFC rushing derby with 702 yards; defensive end Dexter Manley was leading the league in quarterback sacks; and Steve Cox had the longest punting average in the NFC.

Unfortunately, the 'Skins rushing defense had been as effective as a picket fence in a flood. Running backs Curt Warner, Hershel Walker, Joe Morris, and Gary Anderson had shredded the once-stingy defense at will. "You can look at it and say, 'Well, they're great backs,'" reasoned Coach Gibbs, "or you can look at it and say, 'We're missing tackles.'" To Redskins fans, the latter theory appeared to be the more honest answer.

Coach Gibbs knew that their next opponent, the Minnesota Vikings, would give his defense plenty of practice at open-field tackling. The Vikings had already proven themselves to be a legitimate playoff contender with a 27-24 overtime victory over the powerful San Francisco 49ers and a 23-7 dismantling of the Super Bowl champion Chicago Bears. Elusive wide receivers Anthony Carter and Leo Lewis provided excellent targets for the #2-ranked quarterback in the NFC, Tommy Kramer, who had already thrown 16 touchdown passes in eight games. Head Coach Jerry Burns, in his first season at the helm after many years as an assistant to Bud Grant, had brought about the resurgence in the Vikings' fortunes by instilling an enthusiastic attitude in his young players and refurbishing Minnesota's tattered defense.

The 5-3 Vikes realized that this game would probably play a critical role in determining one of the wild-card berths at the end of the season. The Washington Redskins knew what was at stake, too. "A game in the conference like this is very important," said Coach Gibbs. "They are in the race with us. San Francisco was here last year in a similar situation and when we lost to them, it cost us. Everyone has a tendency to look at the end of the year. I'd rather start earning a spot early."

Sunshine and a light, balmy breeze greeted the 51,928 Redskins fans who filled Robert F. Kennedy Stadium for the 154th consecutive time, a continuing NFL record for sellouts that began in 1966.

During those 20 years, the temperamental make-up of the crowd had evolved from loyal discontent in the late Sixties to enthusiastic encouragement in the early Seventies to giddy celebration in the early Eighties when the Redskins drove to two straight Super Bowls. However, by 1986, the Redskins' Golden Anniversary season, complacency was muffling the voice of the crowd. Instead of the Redskins reacting to the pleas of their long-suffering and impassioned fans, the crowd was now sitting on its hands waiting for the team to do something exciting enough to warrant its applause.

This phenomenon was not limited to Washington, as Dallas Cowboys Coach Tom Landry knew only too well. "Fans mature with a team," explained Landry. "They watch you win year in and year out and become more subdued. It's not unique to Dallas. I think it's the same everywhere." Consequently, the ovation for the Redskins during the player introductions was nowhere near as earth-shaking as the ones in the "Over-the-Hill Gang's" glory days. In fact, as Steve Cox prepared to kick off to the Vikings, only half of the ticket-holders even bothered to stand up. Yet by the end of the afternoon, those same fans would be screaming themselves hoarse as they watched the Redskins and Vikings play one of the wildest and most exciting games in NFL history.

Quarterback Jay Schroeder got Washington off to a rousing start with a 40-yard pass to Don Warren. Then George Rogers burst through the middle for another first down. After Schroeder hit Clint Didier for a 14-yard gain at the Minnesota 8, Rogers did the rest, finally plowing into the end zone from 2 yards out. Max Zendejas kicked the extra point, and Washington led, 7-0.

Minnesota returned Cox's kickoff to its 26. On first down, defensive end Charles Mann stripped the ball out of Tommy Kramer's hands. Linebacker Neal Olkewicz fell on the fumble at the Vikings 34, and the Redskins had a chance to administer an early knockout. Schroeder fired to Gary Clark for 20 yards, but the 'Skins were thwarted at the Minnesota 8 and had to be satisfied with Zendejas' 25-yard field goal and a 10-0 lead.

After the kickoff, Tommy Kramer demonstrated his passing touch by delivering a 25-yard strike to tight end Steve Jordan, who caught it at midfield and ran to the Washington 29 for a 48-yard gain. Three plays later, Ted Brown punched into the end zone from a yard out, and Minnesota was back in the game, 10-7.

On the Redskins' next possession, Max Zendejas came up short on a 51-yard field goal try, and the Vikings took over at their 33. On first down, Kramer faded back, pumped once, and launched a bomb to Leo Lewis, who caught it over his shoulder at the 29 and dashed into the end zone for a spectacular 67-yard touchdown! The Vikings led the stunned Redskins, 14-10.

Midway through the second quarter, Dexter Manley had a defensive end's dream come true. Minnesota center Dennis Swilley hiked the ball over the head of Tommy Kramer, who was in shotgun formation, and Dexter, rushing in from the right side, had an unobstructed path to the ball. Manley breezed by Kramer, caught the ball on the first bounce, and raced into the Minnesota end zone 26 yards away! However, the unusual touchdown was not punctuated with the usual extra point; Zendejas' kick was blocked, and Washington led by only 2 points, 16-14.

Near the end of the half, the Vikings drove from their 14 to the Redskins 12 as Kramer completed four out of five passes against the harried Washington secondary. On third and 2, halfback Darrin Nelson bolted through left guard to score an apparent touchdown, but a holding penalty against the Vikes moved the ball back to the 22. After Kramer overthrew Lewis in the end zone, Chuck Nelson kicked a 39-yard field goal to put Minnesota back on top, 17-16, as the first half came to an end.

Having given up almost 400 yards of total offense in the first half, the Redskins and Vikings retired to their respective dressing rooms to install a defensive tactic that somehow had been omitted from both teams' game plans: the open-field tackle.

Apparently, the Redskins did not pay attention. On the Vikings' first possession of the second half, tight end Steve Jordan grabbed a medium-range pass from Tommy Kramer at the Washington 45 and sprinted into the end zone to complete a 68-yard

touchdown play. The murmuring spectators at RFK could only watch and shake their heads as the Vikings celebrated their 24-16 lead.

The Redskins retaliated with a 39-yard pass from Schroeder to Art Monk, but, when the drive bogged down at the Minnesota 25, Washington had to settle for a 42-yard field goal by Zendejas. Trailing 24-19, the 'Skins defense finally forced the Vikings to punt, and the offense regrouped at its 25. On second and 13, Schroeder was flushed from the pocket. He retreated to his goal line to avoid a sack by defensive tackle Keith Millard, then threw clear across the field to Gary Clark, who spun out of the grasp of several tacklers and ended up with a spectacular 27-yard gain. It was a school-yard play, but it ignited the fans. Not wanting to waste the momentum, Coach Gibbs let his offense go for a first down a few minutes later on fourth and 2 at the Vikings 40. George Rogers not only got the first down, he blasted through a huge hole created by R.C. Thielemann and Jeff Bostic and raced 40 yards into the end zone! That put the Redskins back on top, 26-24.

Washington's lead lasted three plays. On third and 5 from his 24, Kramer lofted another deep pass to Leo Lewis, who caught it at the Redskins 38, sidestepped cornerback Vernon Dean, and outraced everyone to the end zone. The stunning 76-yard touchdown vaulted the Vikings back into the lead, 31-26, as the third period ended.

Early in the fourth quarter, Minnesota took advantage of two pass interference penalties and drove 75 yards in 11 plays. Darrin Nelson scored on a 1-yard pass from Kramer, and the Vikes appeared to be in control, 38-26. Six minutes remained when Jay Schroeder hit Clint Didier with a 30-yard pass at the Minnesota 34. On the next play, Schroeder threw deep again, and Art Monk came down with it in the end zone for a 34-yard touchdown! The fans' cheers melted into groans, though, when Zendejas blew his second extra-point attempt. If it's true that kickers have educated toes, then Max had either developed amnesia or forged his transcript. But at least the 'Skins were within striking distance, 38-32.

Thanks to their defense, the Redskins got the ball back at their 46 only a minute and a half later. On first down, Schroeder threw into tight coverage, and cornerback Carl Lee made a diving interception. Or so it seemed. Joe Gibbs thought Lee might have dropped it, so he called a time-out to give the replay official enough time to carefully review the tape. Gibbs was vindicated when playback official Nick Skorich ruled that the ball had been trapped, and the Redskins retained possession. Not that it did them much good; two more incompletions brought out the punting team. But at least Steve Cox pinned Minnesota back at its 12.

With the crowd roaring on every play, Washington's defense stuffed the Vikes on three consecutive running plays, and, with exactly 2 minutes left, Ken Jenkins returned Greg Coleman's punt to the Minnesota 46. On first down, Schroeder went deep to Clint Didier, who made a brilliant sliding catch just before the ball hit the ground at the 2. But it was close enough for a check of the instant replay. As the replay officials reviewed the tape over and over again, the screaming crowd at RFK worked itself into a frenzy. Unable to find a replay that clearly showed whether Didier had trapped the ball or not, Skorich finally let the play stand. First and goal at the 2!

At Jay Schroeder's request, 52,000 shouting fans quieted themselves, but when George Rogers burst into the end zone [Fig. 149], a thunderclap of cheers exploded from the stands. With the score tied, 38-38,

Fig. 149   *John Doman/St. Paul Pioneer Press Dispatch*

Max Zendejas came in for the game-winning extra point, but, incredibly, his conversion attempt was blocked! It was Zendejas's third extra-point miss of the day, and murderous curses rained down on him as the resurrected Vikings celebrated their good fortune.

And so to overtime. Washington won the important coin-toss and chose to receive the kickoff. Clarence Verdin returned the ball to the 22, and a face-mask penalty added 15 yards, allowing the 'Skins to begin at their 37. Short completions to Monk and Didier moved the ball to the Vikings 44. Then Kelvin Bryant carried for 6. On second and 4 at the 38, Jay Schroeder took a short drop and threw to Gary Clark near the left sideline. Clark caught the quick-out at the 34, faked to the inside, and whirled to the outside, a lightning-fast maneuver that left cornerback Carl Lee grasping at air. Clark raced down the sideline, eluded a final desperate tackle by safety John Harris at the 15, and ran triumphantly into the end zone! Final score: Washington 44, Minnesota, 38.

Gary Clark celebrates his winning touchdown on the shoulders of his jubilant teammates
AP/Wide World Photos

"I feel like we just played five games," said an exhausted Coach Joe Gibbs in the Redskins' boisterous locker room. "We won it, lost it, won it, lost it, and won it. I have to give a lot of the credit to the crowd. They deserve a game ball for all the noise they made. I don't know if you can get more exciting." By giving up 490 yards through the air to Tommy Kramer, missing three PATs, and converting on only 3 of 15 third-down opportunities, the Washington Redskins had certainly done their utmost to keep the game exciting. In the end, though, the Redskins had come up with every critical play when they needed it. Washington's ability to turn pressure situations into great plays was a testament to its character. "If I had to pick one thing for a team to have," said Gibbs admiringly, "I would pick guts."

As long as men like Gary Clark, Jay Schroeder, and Clint Didier were on the team, the Washington Redskins would always have an ample supply.

TO 'SKIN A BEAR

NFC Divisional Playoff Game

Washington Redskins vs. Chicago Bears

January 3, 1987

"I've never seen a man that mad," stated Washington Redskins offensive guard R.C. Thielemann. "I never thought a man could say that many things without using one curse word. We all were waiting for that one word." "The pitch was so high," said another surprised player, "I thought it was some kind of bird." Orange sections, water cups, and chairs flew through the air. Linebacker Rich Milot called it "the most emotion I've ever seen from a coach. Ever. By a long shot."

The star of that impromptu halftime show was none other than Redskins Coach Joe Gibbs, normally a mild-mannered advocate of the Dale Carnegie Method of Positive Feedback. "He's not the type of coach to jump on the team [at halftime]," said center Jeff Bostic. "He usually comes in and explains what went right and what went wrong. Mostly in a very logical manner." But after watching his Redskins sleep-walk to a 14-0 halftime deficit against the lowly Philadelphia Eagles in the final game of the season, Gibbs finally blew up.

Startled by their coach's ferocity, the chagrined Washington players sought absolution in the second half by scoring three unanswered touchdowns to win, 21-14. Gibbs' explosion had a nice carry-over effect, too. The following week, in the first (wild-card) round of the NFC playoffs, the 12-4 Redskins defeated the Los Angeles Rams, 19-7, to earn a matchup against the defending Super Bowl Champion Bears in Chicago.

The Bears were aptly named; they were big, rough, and dangerous. With players like halfback Walter Payton, the NFL's all-time leading ground-gainer, linebackers Mike Singletary and Wilber Marshall, and defensive ends Dan Hampton and Richard Dent, Chicago could rip a team to shreds, as it had demonstrated in a 45-10 mauling of the Redskins one year before.

But the Bears were missing one of their sharpest claws: quarterback Jim McMahon, who had dislocated his right shoulder on a blatantly late body-slam by Charles Martin in a game against the Green Bay Packers. With reserves Steve Fuller and Mike Tomczak filling in for McMahon, Chicago's powerful offense became pedestrian, yet the Bears continued to win due to their strong defense and weak schedule. By the end of the season, the 14-2 Bears had set an NFL record by surrendering only 187 points in 16 games, and, in 13 of those games, had limited their opponent to fewer than 15 points. However, a few detractors were quick to point out that Chicago hadn't beaten a playoff team since the first week of the season.

Just before the final game of the regular season,

Bears Coach Mike Ditka decided to gamble on the high-risk, high-dividend talents of a rookie quarterback who had joined the team in midseason: Doug Flutie. When he first arrived, the Heisman Trophy-winning, millionaire refugee from the defunct USFL's New Jersey Generals was given a cold reception by his new teammates, who figured Ditka was simply trying to gain the upper hand in his ongoing power struggle with the rebellious and free-spirited McMahon. But Ditka insisted that he had signed Flutie to insure against the loss of the injury-plagued McMahon. When McMahon went out for the season a few weeks later, Ditka looked pretty smart, especially when Flutie completed 8 of 14 passes in the Bears' season-ending 24-10 victory over the Dallas Cowboys. "The little guy is pretty special," said the vindicated coach. "He makes things happen. He's a winner."

The Washington Redskins had a winner of their own. Jay Schroeder, in his first full season as the starting quarterback, had set a new Redskins record by passing for 4,199 yards. More importantly, with 17 victories in his 22 starts, Schroeder had established himself as a consistent winner and a resourceful leader with a flair for the big play. Under Schroeder, the Redskins, who were supposed to be rebuilding after the retirements of John Riggins and Joe Theismann, had fought their way to 13 victories by making a habit of coming from behind. Only once, though, in an emotional 41-14 thumping of the Dallas Cowboys at RFK Stadium, had the 'Skins displayed the kind of dominance that had taken them to Super Bowls XVII and XVIII.

Overall, Washington's offense had performed surprisingly well in 1986: receivers Art Monk, Gary Clark, Clint Didier, Don Warren, and Kelvin Bryant had combined for 232 catches while fullback George Rogers balanced the attack by rushing for 1,318 yards and 18 touchdowns. But could the Redskins score against the powerful Bears defense? With a 32-3 record over the past two seasons, the World Champion Chicago Bears were once again the Monsters of the Midway. No wonder the *Chicago Tribune* headlined its game-day story: "Bears Ready—If Redskins Show Up."

Jay Schroeder and Coach Joe Gibbs
Nate Fine Photo/Nate Fine Productions, Courtesy Washington Redskins

65,141 Bears fans jammed Soldier Field on a surprisingly mild afternoon for Chicago in January. With light winds failing to stir up trouble, the 40-degree temperature was a godsend to a team wanting to pass.

Steve Cox kicked off. Chicago's Dennis Gentry caught the ball at the 5, broke through a big hole at the 20, and raced 60 yards before the NFL's Fastest Man, Darrell Green, finally hauled him down at the Washington 35. The fans at the old stadium roared their approval and assumed the rout was on. Quarterback Doug Flutie faced a 5-man Redskins defensive line whose primary goal was to control the dangerous Walter Payton. To counteract that strategy, Flutie tried to hit champion sprinter Willie Gault in the end zone for a quick touchdown, but Green tipped the pass away at the last instant. Then, on fourth down, Chicago's frustration became complete when placekicker Kevin Butler hooked a 49-yard field goal attempt to the left. Round 1 to the Redskins.

Taking over at the Chicago 32, Jay Schroeder opened with three straight passes and completed two for a first down near midfield. When three more plays left the 'Skins an inch short of another first down, Coach Gibbs decided to punt rather than risk giving the ball to the Bears in such convenient field position. Cox's kick pinned Chicago at its 10. The Bears managed two first downs on the ground, but the short drive fizzled when Flutie fumbled as he was rolling to his left. Although he scooped it up and managed to get the pass away just before Dexter Manley crashed into him, it fell incomplete (for the fifth time in six attempts) and the Bears had to punt.

George Rogers ignited the Redskins offense with a 9-yard burst up the middle, then both Kelvin Bryant and Gary Clark caught passes for first downs. At the Chicago 28, Jay Schroeder diagnosed an incoming blitz and changed the play at the line of scrimmage. With defensive tackle Steve McMichael charging uncontestedly at him, Schroeder released the ball while backpedaling away from the line. Running straight downfield in tandem with teammate Gary Clark, Art Monk caught the perfectly thrown pass at the Bears 5 and tumbled into the end zone for a touchdown! Former Maryland placekicker Jess Atkinson, who had replaced the erratic Max Zendejas before the last game of the season, booted the extra point, and Washington jumped out in front, 7-0.

Early in the second quarter, the Bears offense got on track. From midfield, Flutie launched a deep pass to Willie Gault, who caught the ball at the 20, do-si-doed around safety Curtis Jordan, and loped into the end zone to complete a 50-yard touchdown play. The excited crowd at Soldier Field kept right on cheering as Kevin Butler's extra point tied the game, 7-7.

Four plays later, the Chicago fans rejoiced again when Bears cornerback Mike Richardson intercepted a Schroeder pass and returned it 43 yards down the sideline to the Washington 4. Two plunges into the line advanced the ball to the 2 yard line, setting up another important test of the Washington defense. On third down, Walter Payton took a pitchout and headed to his left, but, before he could get up to speed, Dexter Manley broke through and nailed him in the backfield for a 3-yard loss. As the Redskins

congratulated each other for their spirited goal line stand, the Bears settled for Butler's 23-yard field goal and a 10-7 lead.

Rookie Dwight Garner fumbled the ensuing kickoff, but the 'Skins escaped disaster when fellow deep man Eric Yarber recovered for Washington in the end zone. It proved to be only a temporary reprieve, though, as the Bears stopped the Redskins on three plays, then quickly drove to the Washington 23. The 'Skins defense stiffened, but Butler's 41-yard field goal gave Chicago a 13-7 lead.

With less than a minute left in the half, the Bears got the ball again and went into their hurry-up offense. However, linebacker Monte Coleman deflected a Flutie pass to Vernon Dean, who intercepted and returned it to the Washington 43. Trying for one last score before halftime, Jay Schroeder connected with Kelvin Bryant for a 24-yard gain, and, on the last play of the half, Steve Cox attempted a 50-yard field goal. It fell short, and the Bears kept their 13-7 lead.

As expected, both defenses had dominated, especially Chicago's, which had completely shut down Washington's attack in the second quarter. Even with their promising start, the Redskins had averaged a mere 1.9 yards on their infrequent first-down plays, and in the second period moved the chains just twice. Washington's defense had kept the 'Skins close by limiting Walter Payton to 29 yards rushing and restricting Doug Flutie to 6 completions in 16 hurried attempts. However, if the Bears had fully capitalized on all their scoring opportunities, the Redskins would have been trailing, 28-7.

On the second play of the second half, disaster nearly struck the Washington Redskins again. From his 39, Jay Schroeder stepped back and threw a pass into the right flat. Chicago linebacker Wilber Marshall stuck up a paw and swatted it down, but failed to latch onto it for an interception—the fifth time that the Bears had just missed coming up with a game-breaking play.

Midway through the third quarter, Doug Flutie wasn't as lucky. Cornerback Darrell Green intercepted one of his passes and returned it 17 yards to the Chicago 26. Two plays later, on third and 7, Washing-

Jay Schroeder unloads the ball before Steve McMichael (76) and Richard Dent (95) unload on him
UPI/The Bettmann Archive

ton's offensive line held off another all-out blitz long enough for Schroeder to get off a pass to Art Monk, who made a tumbling catch in the end zone. Touchdown, Washington! Jess Atkinson converted, and the opportunistic 'Skins climbed back on top, 14-13.

Chicago's Dennis Gentry did it again, returning Steve Cox's kickoff 48 yards to the Washington 42. Halfback Neal Anderson swept left end for 11 yards, and fullback Calvin Thomas barged through the middle for 13 more. On first down at the Washington 18, Walter Payton tried the same play but ran smack-dab into massive defensive tackle Darryl Grant. Payton went backward, the football went forward, and Washington safety Alvin Walton fell on it at the 17.

From that moment on, the Washington Redskins took control of the game. They drove down the field like a gathering storm on an 18-yard pass to Art Monk, a 10-yard scamper by Kelvin Bryant [Fig. 153], a 9-yard completion to Monk, and an 8-yard run by George Rogers. Everything worked, including a quarterback keeper by Jay Schroeder for another first down. On the first play of the fourth quarter, Rogers crashed into the end zone from a yard out, and the Redskins took a 21-13 lead. 65,000 Bears fans were speechless.

Chicago continued to struggle against Washington's pass defense, and, after two Flutie floaters were nearly intercepted, the Bears had to punt again. The

Fig. 153　Kelvin Bryant takes advantage of Joe Jacoby's strong-arm tactics on Dan Hampton (99)

Lucian Perkins/Washington Post Photo

'Skins kept the pressure on with a 46-yard drive capped by Jess Atkinson's 35-yard field goal, and, midway through the fourth period, Chicago was looking down the muzzle of a 24-13 *Redskins Special*. A few minutes later, after failing to convert on third down for the ninth time in ten tries, the Bears punted, then forced the Redskins to do the same. Washington's punt bounced twice before Chicago's Lew Barnes fielded it at the 10. With five Redskins bearing down on him, Barnes' hands turned into bricks, and Washington's Monte Coleman grabbed the fumbled ball at the Chicago 4.

Although the 'Skins didn't get a touchdown, they did get another field goal from Jess Atkinson, his sixth consecutive 3-pointer in the playoffs, to forge a solid 27-13 lead. With 2 minutes remaining in the game, Washington softened its coverage to prevent the bomb, and Flutie used short passes to drive the Bears to the Redskins 5. But wide receiver Willie Gault dropped a pass in the end zone, and Chicago's last chance at a miracle finish evaporated like the frozen breath of all those disappointed Bears fans shuffling slowly toward the exits of Soldier Field.

When the scoreboard clock reached 0:00, the upset was official: Washington Redskins 27, Chicago Bears 13.

"We were juiced!" exclaimed Curtis Jordan after being asked how the Redskins had managed to play such an inspired game against such a fierce opponent. "We didn't feel like anybody respected us. We were ticked off at the way we were viewed by everybody, including the Bears. That makes for a dangerous team." Art Monk, smiling serenely after his two-touchdown performance, agreed. "The Bears overlooked us. Everybody told them they were going to kick our butts. And they believed it."

The Redskins won thanks to three second-half turnovers that had led to 17 points; a pass defense that limited Doug Flutie to only 11 completions in 31 attempts; and Jay Schroeder's quick thinking that turned two Chicago blitzes into Washington touchdowns. "It's a great feeling, being the underdog and winning," crowed Joe Jacoby. "It's sweet. It's satisfaction."

HAIL TO THE REDSKINS

Super Bowl XXII

Washington Redskins vs. Denver Broncos

January 31, 1988

"Joe Gibbs has gone to his knees," intoned CBS announcer Pat Summerall.

"One play," said his partner, John Madden.

"One play," confirmed Summerall.

Thirty-seven seconds remained in the 1987 NFC Championship game as the Minnesota Vikings, trailing 17-10, lined up at the Washington Redskins 6 yard line. It was fourth and 4. Minnesota quarterback Wade Wilson shouted his signals into the deafening roar of RFK Stadium, backpedaled eight steps, and fired a perfect pass to halfback Darrin Nelson at the goal line.

"Nelson!" exclaimed Summerall. "Through his hands! And the Redskins will go to the Super Bowl!"

Darrell Green, who had just laid a hard shoulder into Nelson's back, raced upfield pointing to heaven. In the owner's box, Jack Kent Cooke hugged Leslie Stahl. On the sideline, a dazed Joe Gibbs was pummeled by his ecstatic players. In the stands, 55,000 delirious Redskins fans hollered and hugged and high-fived as millions of home viewers clapped and yelled and gave thanks.

The Washington Redskins were on their way to Super Bowl XXII!

AP/Wide World Photos

Earlier in the year, few people were giving the Washington Redskins much of a chance to make it to the Super Bowl. The 1987 season was filled with doubts and disappointments, controversies and questions. In fact, no other Super Bowl team was ever plagued by so many questions. They had begun in January, right after the New York Giants blew away the Redskins, 17-10, in the 1986 NFC Championship game: How could the 'Skins improve enough to overtake an awesome Giants team that had beaten them three straight times in 1986?

Joe Bugel, Assistant Head Coach in charge of the offense, believed the answer lay in building a bigger line to offset the Giants' giants. Bugel decided that 260-pound center Jeff Bostic, a starter for 6 years, was too small to handle nose tackles like New York's Jim Burt. So, on the first day of training camp, Bostic was replaced by 275-pound all-pro left guard Russ Grimm, whose spot was taken over by 275-pound Raleigh McKenzie, giving the Redskins a net gain of 15 pounds. "I think we can definitely be better than the offensive line we had in the '82 Super Bowl," said Grimm, who, along with Bostic, was one of the original Hogs. "But I don't think size means everything. It's still a game of leverage, it's still a game of feet, and it's still a game of assignments."

Later in the season Grimm was injured, and Bostic was passed over again. "I asked myself how I was good enough to snap every snap in 1986, then be moved to back-up center in 1987, and, when the center's hurt, still not be able to play?" said the frustrated veteran after McKenzie was moved to center and 6-foot-5, 305-pound rookie Ed Simmons went in at guard. "In training camp, they said it was my size. Now I'm not so sure." Two weeks later, after every other backup lineman had been injured, Bostic was finally given an opportunity to play. Suddenly, with Bostic at center, Joe Jacoby and Mark May at tackles, and "Wide Base" McKenzie and R.C. Thielemann at guards, the Redskins offensive line jelled into a synchronized unit that truly rivaled the Hogs of '82 and '83. In fact, Bostic played so well that when Grimm returned to the active list, he could not crack the lineup. Size, it turned out, was not the answer.

But what was the matter with the Washington running game? Except in a 27-7 victory over the Buffalo Bills in November and a 34-17 win over St. Louis in December, the Redskins did not control any game with their running attack. No longer could Washington depend on picking up crucial first downs on fourth and 1. No longer could the 'Skins run out the clock with the Riggo Drill, an unstoppable barrage of Counter-Trey plays. Part of the problem was attributable to a series of injuries to fullback George Rogers, who had hobbled through training camp with a sprained big toe, then dislocated his shoulder on Opening Day, pulled a groin muscle in midseason, and sprained an ankle in the NFC Championship game. Slowed by his nagging injuries, Rogers struggled to gain 613 yards, an average of only 3.8 yards per carry. Kelvin Bryant, who was too light and injury-prone to shoulder the entire load, had to be saved for passing situations. Nevertheless, he contributed 406 yards on 77 carries and caught 43 passes for 490 more.

Waiting in the wings, though, was rookie halfback Timmy Smith, a 5-foot-11, 216-pound sleeper from Texas Tech who, because of leg injuries, had missed most of his junior and senior years in college. As the season progressed, Coach Gibbs started working Smith into the lineup more and more, bringing him along slowly like a young boxer. A workable pattern emerged at the end of the season: Rogers would start, then give way to Smith in the second quarter. In the playoffs, Smith blossomed, gaining 66 yards against the Chicago Bears and 72 more against the Vikings. "I think it's working good now," said Kelvin Bryant, who still came in on passing downs. "We're always fresh and all three can get the job done." Had Coach Gibbs finally found the solution?

The big question, of course, was who should start at quarterback: Jay Schroeder, the ninth man in history to pass for over 4,000 yards in a season, the man who had won 75% of his games as a Redskin, the man who was worth close to a million dollars a season in his new 3-year contract; or Doug Williams, a 32-year-old journeyman with gimpy knees, a man no other NFL team had wanted when the USFL folded, a man who threw only one pass in 1986?

Nearly traded to the Los Angeles Raiders during the preseason, Williams finally got a chance to demonstrate his wares when Schroeder dislocated his shoulder on Opening Day. Williams played superbly, completing 17 of 27 passes for 272 yards and two touchdowns as Washington defeated the Philadelphia Eagles, 34-24. A week later in his first start as a Redskin, Williams looked good again, but the Atlanta Falcons eked out a 21-20 victory when two bad snaps cost the 'Skins a field goal and an extra point. The following week . . .

STRIKE. After failing to reach a collective bargaining agreement with the owners' Management Council, nearly every member of the NFL Players Association walked out on September 21. The sticking point in the negotiations was free agency. The players believed free agency had been guaranteed by the Emancipation Proclamation; the owners likened it to making kidnapping legal. In an attempt to bring the union to its knees, the owners voted to continue the season with teams made up of non-union players—scabs. When notified that the replacement games would count, General Manager Bobby Beathard and Joe Gibbs went into overdrive to field and train a competitive team.

Ten days later, the "Redscabs" gave a surprisingly professional performance, upsetting the St. Louis Cardinals, 28-21, despite the efforts of St. Louis' non-striking quarterback Neil Lomax and wide receiver Roy Green. Washington's Anthony Allen even set a record of 255 yards receiving and caught three touchdown passes from quarterback Ed Ruppert, who had learned the Redskins' system in training camp. The following week the "Redscabs" routed the New York "Giants," 38-12.

Thanks to the growing acceptance of the replacement teams, the strike was also turning into a rout. Realizing they had been outflanked by the owners, hundreds of union members crossed the picket lines and went back to work. The only team that remained 100% loyal to the union was the Washington Redskins. On Thursday, October 15, the strike ended, and the Redskins reported to work as a unit only to be told they had missed the Wednesday deadline and would have to sit out one more game.

The players felt they were getting their noses rubbed in it. "They came in for the first meeting and wanted to do the following things and I had to explain to them that they missed the deadline and couldn't play," recalled Gibbs. "At that point it was very heated. I think it was good, but it was heated." Disturbed by the bad blood in the room when the stormy meeting broke up, Coach Gibbs called a second meeting for later that afternoon. "About 80 to 85 per cent of our guys came back. At that point everybody had vented their frustrations and we were able to just sit and say 'What is the best way to handle this? . . . How can we do this as a team?' When we left I felt so much better about it." Player representative Neal Olkewicz acknowledged that Gibbs "did a good job of not alienating us. That's when guys were at their worst. It helped."

Heavily laden with non-striking veterans like quarterback Danny White, tailback Tony Dorsett, and defensive tackle Randy White, the Dallas Cowboys figured to cream the "Redscabs" in the final replacement game on Monday Night Football. Amazingly, Gibbs' replacement players, led by quarterback Tony Robinson, who was on work-release from prison, made a heroic effort and came away with a heartstopping 13-7 victory. "I think people will always remember the scabs," said safety Skip Lane. "It was history in the making, if for nothing else than how quickly they fielded teams. To be able to do that in two weeks was incredible, and, with the Redskins, a real tribute to their organization and to their people. I think it showed that there really isn't that large of a difference in the level of play . . . it showed that the bottom 50% of them and the top 50% of us are pretty interchangeable."

Although they had lost three weeks' pay and every bit of their bargaining leverage, the real Redskins found it hard to stay mad at their replacements. After all, they had won three straight games and handed the 'Skins a 4-game lead over the Giants, who lost all three of their strike games. "If you left 1-1 and came back 1-4," said Anthony Allen, who was retained after the striking players returned, "you would have to feel down as a team. You'd be a lot more angry than if you came back 4-1. Anytime you're winning, that's got to put you in a positive frame of mind. I'm sure that had to help the team a lot."

The month-long strike produced another benefit: it gave injured Redskins like George Rogers, Dexter Manley, Neal Olkewicz, Clint Didier, and Mark May a chance to heal. Jay Schroeder, too. Although pleased with Williams' performance, Coach Gibbs gave Schroeder his starting job back, and Washington fans settled down to watch the 4-1 Redskins drive to the playoffs. In their first game back, the 'Skins played listlessly for the first three periods against the New York Jets, dropping pass after pass and falling behind, 16-7. Frustrated and angered by the strike and disappointed in Washington's lackluster performance, the brooding fans at RFK Stadium booed every time the offense bogged down. Even though Schroeder and Kelvin Bryant finally pulled out a 17-16 victory in the last few minutes, it was clear that the Redskins would have to play much better to win back their fans.

The 'Skins finally put it all together against Buffalo. With Schroeder passing to Bryant for two touchdowns and George Rogers racking up 125 yards in 30 carries, Washington destroyed the Bills, 27-7. However, the following week in Philadelphia, quarterback Randall Cunningham scrambled and passed the Eagles to a come-from-behind 31-27 victory. Although he passed for 265 yards and two TD's, Schroeder had been way off, overthrowing open receivers 9 times and finishing with only 16 completions in 46 attempts.

When Schroeder started overthrowing his receivers again the next week against the Detroit Lions, Gibbs benched him in the second quarter, the first time in 7 years that the coach had pulled a starting quarterback. Doug Williams replaced the shocked and angry Schroeder and threw two touchdown passes in 7 minutes. Immediately after the 20-13 victory, Coach Gibbs attempted to ward off a guessing frenzy in the media by naming Williams as the starter for the upcoming Rams game. Schroeder, feeling betrayed that he was not told of his demotion personally, left the dressing room in a huff.

On Monday night, the 7-2 Redskins fell behind the Los Angeles Rams, 30-9, before Williams spearheaded a Washington counterattack that produced 17 unanswered points. Trailing 30-26 in the final minute of the game, the Redskins drove to the L.A. 14. Williams fired a bullet into the end zone, hitting Art Monk on the numbers—but Monk dropped it. On the next play, Williams gunned another pass to Monk, who missed again, deflecting the ball into the hands of Rams cornerback LeRoy Irvin to end the game. Through no fault of his own, Doug Williams was 0 for 2 as a starter.

On Thanksgiving Day, Williams suffered a painful back spasm during practice. Rather than play at half speed (and under the false impression that a starter could not lose his job through injury), Williams stepped aside for Schroeder. It was a typically unselfish move for Williams, who knew that a victory over the New York Giants would be an important confidence-builder for the struggling Redskins. On Sunday, the Giants played like champions as they jumped out to a 16-0 halftime lead. But in the second half, Schroeder caught fire, and the 'Skins overcame New York, 23-19.

Now Joe Gibbs had to make another tough decision. Should he stick with Schroeder, a hot quarterback (28 of 46 for 331 yards and three touchdowns) under whose leadership the Redskins offense had finally jelled? Or should he give the job back to the more consistent Williams, who had played well in every game but had not been able to win? When Gibbs chose Schroeder, Doug Williams had to choke back tears that had been welling in his eyes for 10 years.

The following week against St. Louis, the Redskins repeated their pattern of falling behind, then rallying with one or two quarters of superior play. Trailing 17-10, Washington blew out the Cardinals by scoring 21 points in 6 minutes. The 34-17 victory gave the Redskins a 9-3 record and clinched the Eastern Division Championship with three games left in the regular season.

Washington split its next two games—a 24-20 win over Dallas and a 23-21 loss to the Miami Dolphins—then traveled to Minnesota for the final game of the season. The 'Skins needed a victory to keep alive their slim chance of hosting a playoff game at RFK Stadium, but the 8-6 Vikings had far greater incentive: a victory would assure them of a wild-card berth in the playoffs. Minnesota controlled the first half, but, thanks to a 100-yard interception return by Washington cornerback Barry Wilburn, the game was deadlocked, 7-7, at halftime. Midway through the third quarter, Coach Gibbs grew frustrated with the sputtering Redskins offense and yanked Schroeder, who had thrown two interceptions while completing 9 of 17 passes for only 85 yards.

Williams came in cold, but, three plays later, pinpointed a 46-yard touchdown pass to Ricky Sanders. Unfortunately, two interceptions allowed the Vikings to score 17 unanswered points, and, with 9½ minutes remaining in the fourth quarter, Minnesota led, 24-14. Williams settled down and led the 'Skins on a long drive that culminated in a 37-yard field goal by Ali Haji-Sheikh. Now trailing by a touchdown, the Redskins defense clamped down, and, with 2:21 left, Washington took over at its 40. After a 9-yard completion to Gary Clark, Williams hit Sanders on a crossing pattern over the middle, and Ricky raced into the end zone for a 51-yard touchdown! A minute later, with the score tied, 24-24, safety Alvin Walton intercepted a Wade Wilson pass and returned it to the Minnesota 22, giving Washington a chance to win in regulation. Unfortunately, Haji-Sheikh missed a 33-yard field goal attempt, and the game went into overtime.

The 'Skins won the coin-flip, and Ricky Sanders returned the kickoff to the Washington 47. Two more completions to Sanders (giving him 8 catches for 164 yards) and an 11-yard burst by George Rogers set up a 26-yard field goal attempt by Haji-Sheikh. This time his aim was true, and Washington won, 27-24, to finish the regular season at 11-4.

Coach Gibbs now faced his toughest decision: Which quarterback should lead the Redskins into the playoffs? More often than not, the 'Skins had looked smoother with Williams at the controls. His 10 years of experience showed in his ability to stay in the pocket, calmly looking for secondary receivers while side-stepping 300-pound rushers. In comparison, Schroeder appeared skittish, abandoning the pocket whenever he felt pressure and throwing off-balance. Williams had certainly been more con-

sistent, completing 58% of his passes to Schroeder's 48%. But Gibbs could not ignore the fact that Schroeder had a knack for winning and, when his arm was healthy, could throw as well as anyone in the league. On the other hand, Williams was more adept at keeping long drives alive with his accurate short passes. Washington waited three days for the decision. On Wednesday, Joe Gibbs announced his choice: Doug Williams.

Former Redskins quarterback Joe Theismann believed that Gibbs chose Williams because he was tired of depending on Schroeder's last-minute heroics to pull out games that could have been won easily with a more consistent attack. "A pattern has developed over the last two years of living off the big pass," said Theismann. "Then you start to ignore the short possession-type game. [But] to me, Joe Gibbs is more comfortable in a controlled passing game. Then, by choice, take your big shots." Although the coach had faith in both men, Williams' consistency and ability to handle pressure apparently tipped the scales in his favor. Gibbs knew that, no matter what happened, he could count on Doug Williams to overcome any adversity.

Even during the lowest moments of his roller-coaster career—he had led the Tampa Bay Buccaneers to the playoffs only to be vilified for his race, starred in the USFL only to be injured, signed with the Washington Redskins only to sit on the bench for an entire season, played well in relief only to relinquish the reins when Schroeder recovered, won the starting assignment only to hurt his back, then recovered from the back spasm only to be told he had lost his job—Doug Williams had never given up on himself. "The diamonds," said Williams, "are still out there for me."

As soon as the regular season ended, things started to fall into place for the Redskins. Washington became the beneficiary of two upset victories by the Minnesota Vikings, who had backed into the playoffs when the St. Louis Cardinals lost their final game of the season. In the wild-card round of the playoffs, the Vikings destroyed the favored New Orleans Saints, 44-10, then, one week later, knocked off the San

Francisco 49ers, 36-24. That meant the Redskins did not have to travel to San Francisco to play the red-hot 49ers. It also meant that the winner of their divisional playoff game with the Chicago Bears would get to host the NFC Championship game against Minnesota.

But first Washington had to get by the Bears. In Chicago. With Jim McMahon at quarterback. With a wind-chill factor of minus 23 degrees. And with all-time leading rusher Walter Payton determined to end his matchless career in a blaze of glory. Moreover, Coach Mike Ditka's team was anxious to avenge the 27-13 defeat at the hands of the Redskins in the 1986 playoffs.

When Chicago took a quick 14-0 lead, it looked as if it was all over for Washington. But Doug Williams pulled the team together. A 32-yard strike to Ricky Sanders set up George Rogers' 3-yard touchdown run, then, a few minutes later, Williams grooved a pass to Clint Didier for an 18-yard touchdown that tied the game, 14-14, at the half.

Three minutes into the third quarter, Darrell Green made the play of the game when he caught a Bears punt at the Redskins 48, dashed down the right sideline, hurdled a tackler at the 35, cut to his left to avoid another Bear, and ran into the end zone for a spectacular 52-yard touchdown! [Fig. 155] Unfortunately for Washington, Green paid a high price for

Fig. 155   *UPI/The Bettmann Archive*

his high hurdle: sprained rib cartilage. "He just jumped out of his ribs," said trainer Bubba Tyer. With Green unable to return to his cornerback spot except for one play, the Redskins defense rose to the challenge, intercepting three passes and sacking Jim McMahon five times. On Chicago's last play, Walter Payton was shoved out of bounds a yard short of a first down, and Washington celebrated its hard-earned 21-17 victory. "We're taking the Championship game back to our fans," exulted Clint Didier. "Who would have thought that a couple days ago?"

The comeback victory over the Bears was achieved in typical fashion by the Redskins, who had been toughened by close games all year. In fact, throughout the 1987 season, Washington seemed to thrive on adversity, winning 6 of its 9 games that had gone down to the wire. Had it not been for their outstanding defense, the Redskins could easily have finished below .500. Somewhat overlooked in the constant search for the right mix on offense were these exceptional defensive performances: strong safety Alvin Walton's 104 tackles, defensive end Charles Mann's 13 sacks, and cornerback Barry Wilburn's league-leading 10 interceptions. Of course, being overlooked was nothing new to four Redskins linebackers who, between them, had put in 34 years of first-class service with the team: Neal Olkewicz, Rich Milot, Monte Coleman, and Mel Kaufman.

The Redskins defense saved some of its most heroic work for the NFC Championship game against the Vikings at RFK Stadium before a capacity crowd of 55,212 roaring fans. Early in the third quarter with the score tied, 7-7, defensive tackle Dave Butz, a 15-year veteran of NFL wars, tipped a Wade Wilson pass to linebacker Mel Kaufman, who intercepted and returned the ball to the Minnesota 17. Three plays later, Ali Haji-Sheikh split the uprights with a 28-yard field goal, and the 'Skins forged ahead, 10-7. In the middle of the fourth quarter, the Vikings drove to the Washington 3 yard line. On first down, fullback Rick Fenney gained 2 yards. On second down, he was stopped for no gain. On third and goal at the 1, D.J. Dozier tried to vault the line, but middle linebacker Neal Olkewicz dove into the backfield and grabbed his ankle before he could get off the ground. No gain!

Instead of taking the lead, the Vikings had to settle for a field goal and a 10-10 tie. Despite an injured shoulder, Redskins quarterback Doug Williams, who earlier had missed enough passes for Coach Gibbs to consider replacing him, finally connected with wide receiver Gary Clark on a 43-yard bomb. Two plays later, Williams threaded the needle with a perfect throw to Clark in the end zone, and the 'Skins climbed back on top, 17-10. When the Vikings marched to the Washington 6 in the waning moments, it looked as if the two teams would have to play an overtime period for the third game in a row. That's when Joe Gibbs dropped to his knees.

"One down to the Super Bowl," announced Frank Herzog in the WMAL radio booth. "From the 6 yard line, it's fourth down and 4. Wilson takes the snap . . . Looking left . . . Throws it into the end zone . . . Batted away—incomplete! The Redskins are going to the Super Bowl!"

Like children waiting for Christmas, Washington Redskins fans impatiently counted down the 14 days to Super Bowl Sunday. Each morning in the newspapers and each evening on the local news, the story grew larger as the great day approached. Instead of the usual one or two columns on the 'Skins, *The Washington Post* started churning out ten or twelve articles per day. And given a chance to moonlight as sportscasters, news anchors from every Washington TV station traveled to San Diego with an entourage of six dozen writers, reporters, producers, technicians, and camera operators for a week of unabashed ballyhooing. Redskins Fever had struck again.

In the midst of all the festivities, questions over personnel continued to dog Coach Joe Gibbs. Who would start Super Bowl XXII: George Rogers, who had a newly sprained ankle, or Timmy Smith? Ricky Sanders, who had caught six passes for 92 yards against the Bears, or Art Monk, whose injured knee had finally healed? Ali Haji-Sheikh or Jess Atkinson? Gibbs played his cards carefully, saying Rogers and Sanders would start, but that Smith and Monk would see action. When it turned out he could not re-activate the steady and popular Atkinson, whose left ankle had been dislocated on Opening Day, Gibbs must have felt relieved that he did not have to make

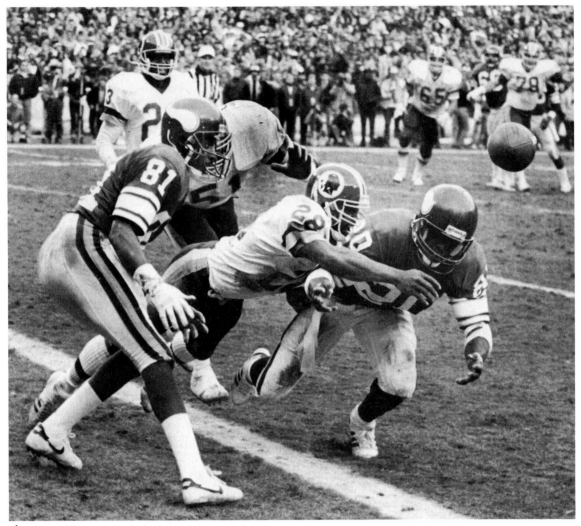

The answer to a prayer   *Lucian Perkins/Washington Post Photo*

his most ticklish choice. Because he wanted to use his last roster move to re-activate Monk, Gibbs was forced to stick with Haji-Sheikh, who had made 13 of 19 field goals attempts during the regular season but missed two out of three in the NFC Championship game.

Even with 2,000 reporters searching for controversial stories, Super Bowl Week proceeded without major incident. Much was made over Doug Williams being the first black to quarterback a Super Bowl team, but the former Grambling star withstood the media blitz by patiently explaining that he was playing because of his skill, not his color. Former Redskins quarterback Sonny Jurgensen put the whole issue into perspective when he sought out former Green Bay Packers quarterback Bart Starr to ask him how it had felt in 1967 to be the first white quarterback to win the Super Bowl.

In contrast, most of the questions directed at Denver Broncos quarterback John Elway centered on how it felt to be the brightest star in the NFL firmament. It was a logical question for the man who had taken an otherwise average team to two Super Bowls in a row. If ever there was a one-man team, the Denver Broncos were it. Elway's receivers, Vance Johnson, Mark Jackson, and Ricky Nattiel—the Three Amigos—were, in truth, better at grabbing publicity than they were at grabbing passes. The Broncos' running attack was strictly diversionary. But with Elway throwing for 24 touchdowns and 3,738 yards and scrambling for 348 more, the 12-4-1 Broncos had managed to win eight out of their last nine games, including a 34-10 pasting of the Houston Oilers in a divisional playoff game and a 38-33 free-for-all against the Cleveland Browns in the AFC Championship.

"Elway's developed to a point where he's like a Larry Bird or a Wayne Gretzky," noted Seattle Seahawks defensive backs coach Ralph Hawkins. "Elway makes the average player good and the very good player extremely good." San Diego Chargers defensive coordinator Ron Lynn, whose team also had to face Elway twice a year, said, "He was always blessed with the wealth of talent, the fine body, the good, quick feet, the arm, and that almost mystical escapability . . . [Now] he's completely under control. He still avoids the rush, of course, but now he looks to throw the ball upfield instead of just taking off. He's more adept at understanding the total structure of a defense."

Could Elway put enough points on the board to outscore a balanced team like the Redskins? Or would Washington keep him off the field with its ball-control running game? Would the Redskins' front four be able to contain Elway? Or would the Three Amigos turn the Washington secondary into desperados? Would Doug Williams have the kind of game he was capable of? Would Washington's huge offensive line overpower the smaller but quicker Broncos? Would the Redskins finally peak? Or would they succumb to the pressure and fall on their faces? At long last, the Washington Redskins were ready to give some answers.

73,302 anointed fans who had paid between $100 and $2,500 per ticket squeezed into San Diego Jack Murphy Stadium to participate directly in the pageantry of Super Bowl XXII. No longer a grudge match between two competing leagues, the Super Bowl had evolved over 22 years into an unofficial national holiday, a celebration of American values: competitiveness, teamwork, and excellence. A global audience, including 105 million Americans and 1.5 million Washington area viewers, tuned in to witness the battle between the Broncos and the Redskins, a match that, when whittled down to its core, pitted Denver's artistry against Washington's strength.

First, the Redskins offense was introduced. With deadly purpose knifing out of their glazed eyes, Ricky Sanders, Don Warren, Joe Jacoby, Raleigh McKenzie, Jeff Bostic, R.C. Thielemann, Mark May, Clint Didier, Gary Clark, Doug Williams, George Rogers, and their head coach, Joe Gibbs, emerged from a 50-foot cocoon of blue balloons and ran onto the sun-splashed green field. The Broncos offense, looking far more relaxed, followed with Head Coach Dan Reeves bringing up the rear.

At the center of the field in front of an American flag that sprawled for 40 yards, Herb Alpert trumpeted the National Anthem. As the crowd cheered the final notes, six Blue Angels roared overhead and the flag, made up of thousands of red, white, and blue balloons, rose skyward, unraveling like a gigantic DNA molecule. Six Redskins co-captains—Charles Mann, Dave Butz, Mark May, Joe Jacoby, Reggie Branch, and Dean Hamel—met the Broncos' four co-captains at midfield. Dave Butz called "Heads" as Hall of Fame receiver Don Hutson flipped the specially-minted coin into the cool, dry air. "It is a head," announced the referee, Bob McElwee. "Washington has won the toss and will receive at this end. Good luck, men."

The game began like an instant replay of Washington's catastrophic experience in Super Bowl XVIII. A nervous Gary Clark bobbled a third-down lob from Doug Williams, and the Broncos took over at their 44. On Denver's first play, John Elway lined up in shotgun formation. At the snap, wide receiver Ricky Nattiel sprinted straight down the right sideline past cornerback Barry Wilburn. Elway fired, and his long, arching pass dropped into Nattiel's arms at the 5.

Wilburn's tackle came too late, and Nattiel fell into the end zone for a 56-yard touchdown! Rich Karlis converted, and the excited Broncos led the deflated Redskins, 7-0.

After Gary Clark dropped another third-down pass, Denver got the ball back at its 31. On first down, John Elway tried the bomb again, but Darrell Green blanketed Mark Jackson and the ball fell incomplete. However, Elway came right back with a strike to Jackson, who broke free across the middle for a 32-yard gain. Coach Reeves further embarrassed the Redskins defense with one of his favorite trick plays: Elway handed off to Steve Sewell, who headed to his left, stopped, and threw a pass back across the field to the unattended quarterback for a 23-yard pickup. Two plays later, on third and 3 at the Washington 6, Elway tried a quarterback draw, but 15-year veteran Dave Butz wasn't fooled and the Broncos had to settle for a field goal and a 10-0 lead.

When Ricky Sanders fumbled the ensuing kickoff at the Washington 16, Redskins fans who had draped themselves in lucky shirts, hats, socks, and hog snouts and who had made sure to sit in their lucky chairs while drinking their lucky beverages, started shifting positions, changing drinks, and removing any article of clothing that they suspected might be offending Lady Luck. Apparently it worked because Terry Orr dove into the pile and wrestled the ball away from three Broncos, depriving Denver of a chance to go up 17-0.

Art Monk, seeing his first action since injuring his knee in early December, pulled the Redskins out of a deep hole with a 40-yard catch and run. But the Broncos defense clamped down, and Washington had to punt again. With the Redskins now keying on the pass, Denver Coach Dan Reeves switched to his running attack, and the Broncos marched from their 28 to the Washington 30 in four plays. The drive ended, though, when safety Alvin Walton nailed Elway for an 18-yard loss, and Denver was forced to punt.

For the fourth time in a row, the Redskins started from inside their 20. And for the fourth time in a row, they self-destructed. A 25-yard run by Timmy Smith, who had started in place of George Rogers, was nullified by a holding penalty. When Williams connected with Kelvin Bryant for 20 yards, it seemed that the 'Skins had finally broken their jinx. But on the next play, Doug slipped on the unstable sod and twisted his left knee, tearing loose scar tissue from a previous injury. [Fig. 157] Jay Schroeder replaced Williams, but the switch didn't change the Redskins' fortunes as Bryant dropped a perfect pass—the fourth drop by a Washington receiver in the first quarter. Considering the number of things that had gone wrong, the Redskins were extremely fortunate to be trailing by only 10 points as the two teams switched goals.

When Doug Williams limped back onto the field for Washington's first possession of the second quarter, the Broncos figured he would be reluctant to expose himself to a pass rush. They were wrong. On first down at the 20, Williams took a short drop and sailed a perfect spiral to Ricky Sanders, who caught the ball in stride at midfield [Fig. 158] and outraced two Denver defenders to the end zone for a stunning 80-yard touchdown! Ali Haji-Sheikh's point-after was good, and Washington suddenly was back in the game, 10-7.

Invigorated by the record-tying touchdown pass, the Redskins defense forced two more incompletions by Elway (making it six misses in a row), and Washington took over at its 36. With their nerves finally under control, the Redskins put together a masterful drive that began with an 8-yard pass to Don Warren. Timmy Smith blasted up the middle for 19 yards on a perfectly executed trap play, and Kelvin Bryant got outside for 7 more. On third and 1 at the Denver 27, Clark ran a corner pattern, and Williams threw a feather-soft pass that Gary caught in mid-air as he dove over the goal line. Touchdown, Washington!

Trailing 14-10, Denver continued its trickery, getting 25 yards on a shovel pass to Sammy Winder. Two plays later, Elway sidestepped Dexter Manley and scrambled for 21 more. But that was all Washington would surrender, and, when Rich Karlis hooked a 43-yard field goal attempt, the 'Skins kept their 4-point lead. Despite difficulty in transferring his weight to his aching left leg, Doug Williams continued to throw, hitting Gary Clark with a 17-yard strike at the Washington 42. On first down, Coach

Fig. 157   *James A. Parcell/Washington Post Photo*

Fig. 158   *UPI/The Bettmann Archive*

Gibbs called the counter-gap play, and the Redskins offensive line executed it perfectly. Timmy Smith took a handoff from Williams, broke through a huge hole over right tackle [Fig. 159], and veered to the right sideline. Forty yards later, free safety Tony Lilly angled in for the tackle, but Smith fended him off with a straight-arm and tightroped the final few steps into the end zone! Touchdown! Redskins 21, Broncos 10!

The charged-up Washington defense stopped Denver without a first down, and Doug Williams & Co. went back to work. On first and 10 at midfield, Ricky Sanders went into motion to his left, cut downfield at the snap, and angled toward the right corner of the end zone. Given plenty of time to spot the wide-open Sanders, Williams lofted another perfect spiral that Ricky caught over his right shoulder at the 10 and carried into the end zone for Washington's fourth touchdown of the quarter! Haji-Sheikh added the extra point, and the jubilant Redskins stretched their lead to 28-10.

Fig. 159 *Lucian Perkins/Washington Post Photo*

Fig. 160   *UPI/The Bettmann Archive*

After the kickoff, John Elway tried to duplicate his first pass of the game, but, this time, cornerback Barry Wilburn matched Ricky Nattiel stride for stride, then outfought him for the ball and intercepted at the Washington 21. One play later, Smith burst through the middle for another big gain, finally being pushed out of bounds 43 yards downfield. After an incompletion, Ricky Sanders caught a short pass at the 30, ducked under a high tackle, and streaked to the Denver 13. On third and 5 at the 8, Williams looped a pass into the corner of the end zone, and Clint Didier pulled it in, giving Doug Williams four touchdown passes in one quarter and the Washington Redskins an insurmountable 35-10 lead.

Just seconds before halftime, cornerback Brian Davis intercepted another Elway pass to crown the greatest quarter in Redskins history. The numbers tell the story: 35 points in five possessions, the most points ever scored in one period in 222 NFL postseason games. Doug Williams: 9 of 11 for 228 yards and four touchdowns, tying Terry Bradshaw's four-touchdown performance in Super Bowl XIII. Ricky Sanders: 5 receptions for 169 yards and two touchdowns, eclipsing Lynn Swann's record of 161 yards in Super Bowl X. Timmy Smith: 5 carries for 122 yards and one touchdown. All in just one quarter.

Washington 35, Denver 10.

In the second half, Timmy Smith continued to shred the Broncos defense and ended up scoring another touchdown on his way to setting a Super Bowl rushing record of 204 yards. Not bad for a rookie starting his first NFL game. The coaches had waited until just before the opening kickoff to tell Smith he was starting. "We just didn't want to rattle him," said Joe Bugel. "We wanted him to enjoy the trip over and think he'd get in for five or six plays." Smith gave the credit for his outstanding performance to the offensive line, which had opened gaping holes even when the Broncos knew what was coming. "Those holes were pretty darn big," said Smith. "I just had to hit them at full speed and I was guaranteed 10 yards."

In all, the Redskins set or tied 14 Super Bowl records, including yards passing (340), yards rushing (280), total yards (602), and touchdowns (6). The 42-10 final score also reflected Washington's complete containment of John Elway, who was sacked five times, intercepted three times, and limited to only 66 yards passing in the second half. "We wanted to put a lot of pressure on Elway," said Assistant Head Coach Richie Petitbon. "We basically went at him with five guys, and the fifth man was a different guy almost every time." By the end of the game, the Redskins defense had bathed itself in glory. Alvin Walton: 7 tackles and 2 sacks. Dave Butz: 2 tackles and 2 blocked passes. Barry Wilburn: 3 tackles and 2 interceptions. Dexter Manley: 4 tackles and 1½ sacks. Charles Mann: 3 tackles and a sack. Todd Bowles: 5 tackles. Darryl Grant: 2 tackles and a tipped pass. "We beat the best there was," said Butz. "That's all you can ask."

"The first quarter, they totally dominated and we were not able to make a play," said Coach Joe Gibbs, his face shining with his second Super Bowl victory. "Once we made a big play, then everything went our way." Actually, it took several big plays to turn the momentum in Washington's favor: Art Monk's first-quarter catch, Terry Orr's recovery of Ricky Sanders' fumble on the kickoff, and, strangely enough, Doug Williams' injury. Like Sammy Baugh in the 1937 NFL Championship game, Williams could not transfer his weight to his aching left leg when he threw. So, like his predecessor a half century earlier, Williams was forced to arch soft passes instead of firing bullets, and, like Slingin' Sam, he couldn't miss. "All I can say is that was the greatest quarter of football I've ever been associated with," said Williams. "You don't see that kind of football every day. How do I explain it? I guess with a 'Wow' or an 'Awesome.' There's no other way to do it." Clint Didier gave it a good try: "In that second quarter, we were like a volcano that just erupted. Boom! We had 35 points on the board. I couldn't believe it."

When the game finally ended, Doug Williams limped slowly and triumphantly off the field, cradling a game ball under one arm while holding his helmet aloft amid a swarm of photographers. "The dream is over," thought Williams with satisfaction. "After all the ups and down in 10 years of professional football, there's nothing left." Nothing, that is, except receiving the Most Valuable Player award, parading down Pennsylvania Avenue in front of 650,000 grateful fans, meeting the President, and being the guest of honor at another, more personal, parade in his hometown of Zachary, Louisiana.

Looking out over the ocean of cheering admirers in front of the District Building on Wednesday, Doug Williams summed up his feelings: "I consider myself a real, real lucky person because, first of all, two years ago when I became a free agent there was only one team that gave me an opportunity to play, and that was the Washington Redskins. So no matter what success I've had, I have to credit a lot of people like Joe Gibbs, Bobby Beathard, and Mr. Cooke, who gave me the opportunity to play.

"And on winning that MVP award, you could have given it to a lot of people. You could have given it to the whole defense. You could have given it to Timmy Smith. You could have given it to Ricky Sanders. And, for sure, you could have given it to the offensive line because, at that particular time I was hurt, I could hardly move and those guys did things for me that the average quarterback doesn't get, and that's blocking. So all I'd like to say is that I'm just glad to be a part of the World Champion Washington Redskins and be a part of this city, Washington, D.C. Thank you."

For Doug Williams, it was a final touch of class.

Fig. 161   *Lucian Perkins/Washington Post Photo*

BRAVES ON THE WARPATH OFFICIAL TRIVIA QUIZ

1) How many head coaches have directed the Washington Redskins?
   a) 12   b) 17   c) 9   d) 21

2) Where did Manny Sistrunk go to college?

3) What was Dick James' jersey number?

4) Who was the only member of the 1972 Redskins who never attended college?

5) Five times in the Fifties, the Redskins drafted a quarterback with their #1 pick. Name two of them.

6) The Redskins drafted one player twice, using #1 picks in 1945 *and* 1946, yet he refused to play professional football. Name him.

7) Name the three linebackers that George Allen imported from the L.A. Rams in 1971.

8) What were Billy Kilmer's three nicknames?

9) Name two Redskins defensive linemen who later became famous with the Raiders.

10) Who punted for the 'Skins after Mike Bragg but before Jeff Hayes?

11) Who holds the Super Bowl record for most rushing yards?

12) Whom did the Redskins get in trade from the Minnesota Vikings for all-pro safety Paul Krause?

13) Whom did the Redskins get in trade for Dick James and Andy Stynchula?

14) Who was the original owner of the Boston Redskins?

15) In 1970, Joe Theismann placed second in the Heisman Trophy balloting. Who won?

16) Who was the very first player drafted by the Washington Redskins?

17) What Redskins quarterback was originally drafted #1 by the St. Louis Cardinals?

18) In Super Bowl VII, who blocked Garo Yepremian's field goal attempt that turned into a Redskins touchdown when Mike Bass intercepted Garo's pass?

19) What Cleveland player was included in the trade that brought Bobby Mitchell to the Redskins?

20) Who holds the Super Bowl record for most passing yards?

21) What was distinctive about quarterback Riley Smith's performance in the Washington Redskins' first-ever game in 1937?

22) How many catches did Charley Taylor make in his career?

23) Who passed for more yardage in his career: Sammy Baugh, Sonny Jurgensen, or Joe Theismann?

24) Who holds the single-season record for most yards passing?

25) Who preceded Bobby Beathard as general manager of the Redskins?

26) What do Curt Knight, Gary Clark, Jeff Bostic, Ted Vactor, Terry Hermeling, Joe Jacoby, Neal Olkewicz, and Jon Jaqua have in common?

27) What do Joe Aguirre, Jim Martin, and Bob Jencks have in common?

28) Which of these NFL stars never became a Redskin? Jim Kiick, Mike Curtis, Jim Youngblood, Pete Retzlaff, Jim Hart, Steve Bartkowski, Tommy Mason.

29) What was the original name of the team?

30) How many different franchises have fielded teams in the NFL? (For example, the Boston Braves, the Boston Redskins, and the Washington Redskins count as one franchise.)
a) 38   b) 51   c) 72   d) 91

31) What did Sammy Baugh do in 1943 that was so unique?

32) Name the three Redskins who won the Heisman Trophy in college.

33) Name the seven Redskins head coaches who compiled winning records while in Washington.

34) Which head coach had the worst winning percentage while in Washington?

35) Name the sites of the Redskins' four Super Bowl appearances.

36) How many catches did Art Monk make in 1984 when he set the NFL record?

37) Who was the first black to sign a Redskins contract?

38) Name the three Redskins quarterbacks who have thrown 99-yard touchdown passes.

39) Between 1970 and 1987, how many times did the Redskins make the playoffs?

40) From 1937 through 1987, how many times have the Washington Redskins won their opening game?
a) 18   b) 24   c) 28   d) 31

41) Who holds the Redskins record for playing in the most consecutive games?

42) Who played the most seasons for the 'Skins?

43) The Redskins have retired seven jerseys in their first 51 years. Who wore them, and what were their numbers?

44) In what year did the Redskins begin their record streak of home-game sellouts?

45) How many times did Sammy Baugh lead the league in passing?

46) What two players share the Redskins' single-game scoring record, and how many points did each score?

47) Name the defensive back that the 'Skins included in the Norm Snead-Sonny Jurgensen trade.

48) Name the only Redskin to play in seven consecutive Pro Bowls.

49) Name the four Redskins running backs with the most career yards rushing.

50) Who holds the Redskins' record for longest run from scrimmage?

Answers on page 335

INDEX

ACKNOWLEDGMENTS

Grateful acknowledgment is made to the following for permission to reprint previously published material:

The Washington Post: Quotes from players and coaches gathered by many *Post* reporters, including: Bob Addie, Bob Alden, David Aldridge, Mark Asher, Paul Attner, Steve Berkowitz, Thomas Boswell, Dave Brady, Christine Brennan, David S. Broder, Bill Burnett, Norman Chad, Al Costello, Ken Denlinger, David DuPree, Tom Friend, William Barry Furlong, William Gildea, Neil H. Greenberger, Blaine Harden, Sally Jenkins, Richard Justice, Dave Kindred, Tony Kornheiser, Angus Phillips, Gary Pomerantz, Shirley Povich, David Remnick, Byron Roberts, Joan Ryan, John Schulian, Dave Sell, Leonard Shapiro, Morris Siegel, George Solomon, Gerald Strine, Kenneth Turan, Jack Walsh, Merrell Whittlesey, and Michael Wilbon.

Leisure Press: Quotes from *Redskin Country: From Baugh to the Super Bowl* by Ken Denlinger and Paul Attner. Copyright © 1983.

Macmillan Publishing Company: Quotes from *The Washington Redskins* (NFL Great Teams, Great Years Series) by Jack Clary. Copyright © 1973 by NFL Properties, Inc.

New American Library: Quote from *Instant Replay* by Jerry Kramer and Dick Schaap. Copyright © 1968.

New American Library: Excerpt from *The Official NFL Encyclopedia of Professional Football*, prepared by National Football League Properties, Inc., Creative Services Division. Copyright © 1982.

Murray Olderman: Quotes from *The Pro Quarterback* by Murray Olderman. Copyright © 1966. Originally published by Prentice-Hall, Inc.

Pocket Books: Quotes from *The Football Hall of Shame* by Bruce Nash and Allan Zullo. Copyright © 1986 by Nash and Zullo Productions, Inc. *The Football Hall of Shame* is a registered trademark of Nash and Zullo Productions, Inc.

Reprinted by permission of Pocket Books, a division of Simon & Schuster, Inc.

Random House, Inc.: Quote from *Always On The Run* by Larry Csonka and Jim Kiick. Copyright © 1973.

Simon & Schuster, Inc.: Quotes from *The New Thinking Man's Guide to Pro Football* by Paul Zimmerman. Copyright © 1984.

Richard Whittingham: Quote from *What a Game They Played* by Richard Whittingham. Copyright © 1984. Originally published by Harper and Row Publishers, Inc.

Dallas Times Herald: Quote of Blackie Sherrod from January 1, 1973, edition. Copyright © 1973.

The Detroit News: Quotes from several editions during the week of November 11, 1956. Reprinted by permission of *The Detroit News*, a Gannett newspaper, copyright © 1956.

The Sporting News: Quote from October 29, 1952, issue. Copyright © 1952. Reprinted by permission of *The Sporting News*.

Sports Illustrated: Quote from August 16, 1976, issue. Copyright © 1976 Time Inc. "Will The Payoff Mean a Playoff" by Robert Jones. All rights reserved.

WMAL Radio: Quote of Frank Herzog from January 17, 1988, radio broacast of NFC Championship game.

ABC Sports: Quotes of Frank Gifford and Joe Namath from November 18, 1985, television broadcast of "Monday Night Football."

CBS Sports: Quotes of Pat Summerall and John Madden from January 17, 1988, television broadcast of NFC Championship game.

NBC Sports: Quote of Merlin Olsen from Super Bowl XVII television broadcast on January 30, 1983.

Washington Redskins: Lyrics to *Hail to the Redskins* by Barnee Breeskin and Corinne Griffith Marshall. Published in 1938 by Leo Feist, Inc., New York.

THANKS

In addition, I would like to thank the following people and organizations for their kind assistance in the creation of this book:

Research:

John Konoza, Director of Information, Washington Redskins

Joe Horrigan, Curator, Pro Football Hall of Fame

Lois Bell, William Christian, Roxanna Deane, Kathryn Ray, and Mary Ternes, Washingtoniana Division, Martin Luther King Library, Washington, D.C.

Dave Kelly, General Reference, Library of Congress

Gail Harris, Recorded Sound Reference Center, Library of Congress

Sam Baugh

Al Demao

Ken Denlinger, *The Washington Post*

Jim Gibbons

Sid Carroll

Jim Heffernan, National Football League

Linda Kirk, National Football League

Steve Hirdt, Elias Sports Bureau

Michael Gibbons, Babe Ruth Museum, Baltimore, Maryland

Barbara Saliba, Detroit Lions

Arthur Havsy, Philadelphia Eagles

Jim Gallagher, Philadelphia Eagles

Greg Aiello, Dallas Cowboys

Steve Legerski, Cleveland Browns

Mrs. Morris A. Bealle

Charley McElwain

Alan Henry

Chuck Snowden

Andy Davis, Redskins Alumni Association

Jack Tulloch

Lewis F. Atchison

Ralph Stowe, Amoco Oil Company

Mrs. Ralph Pittman

Editorial:

John Letterman

Jess Bell

Walter Darring

Photographs:

Gordon W. Beall

Nate Fine

The Washington Redskins

William O'Leary, *The Washington Post*

Katherine Bang, Bettmann Newsphoto, New York

Kevin Terrell and Jeff Oto, NFL Properties, Los Angeles

Tom Freeman, Wide World Photos, Washington, D.C.

Ginny Greene, *St. Paul Pioneer Press Dispatch*

Mike Dickson, *Sports Illustrated*, New York

Ron Sachs, Consolidated News Pictures, Washington, D.C.

Barbara Saliba, Detroit Lions

Design and Production:

Joyce Kachergis, Anne Theilgard, Jess Bell, and Daniel Soileau at Joyce Kachergis Book Design and Production, Pittsboro, North Carolina

Gian Hasbrock, Marathon Typography Service, Inc., Research Triangle Park, North Carolina

Atari Corporation, makers of the 130XE computer and 1050 disk drive

Batteries Included, makers of *PaperClip* word-processing software

Federal Express

Legal:

Gail Ross and Elaine English, Goldfarb & Singer, Washington, D.C.

Encouragement and support:

John Letterman	Dr. Rutillo Romero
Karen Partain	Martin Romero
Gordon and Carol Beall	Dr. Rowen and Patty
Jack Beall, Jr.	Pfeifer
David S. Beall	Clark Williams
Rosemary Beall	Tom and Caroline
Dorothy Beall	Carroll
Rebecca Mock	Bruce Carroll
Keene Ray	John Jiler
David and Joan Bartlett	Liz McGrann
Charley and Susan	Dorothy Barringer
McElwain	Nancy Bagby
Walt and Jean Darring	Bart and David Bolt
Doug and Libby Parks	Liz Reilly
Jim Burke	Pat Piper, Mutual
Denny and Gail Scharf	Broadcasting System
Mead Miller	Belinda Anderson,
Jerry Darring	WRC-TV Sports
Jack Busby	Teri Everett, WJLA-TV
Katherine Newcomb	Del Nayak, Marriott
Bob and Debby Giese	Corporation
Bill and Mary Giese	Patti and Jim Halsey,
Kimberly Bruce	The Stadium Store

OFFICIAL TRIVIA QUIZ ANSWERS

1) b

2) Arkansas A M & N

3) 47

4) Herb Mul-Key

5) Larry Isbell (1951), Jack Scarbath (1952), Ralph Guglielmi (1954), Don Allard (1958), Richie Lucas (1959)

6) Cal Rossi, UCLA

7) Maxie Baughan, Myron Pottios, Jack Pardee

8) Furnace Face, Whiskey, Billy the Kid

9) John Matuszak & Ben Davidson

10) Mike Connell (1980-81)

11) Timmy Smith (204 yards)

12) Marlin McKeever

13) Sam Huff

14) George P. Marshall

15) Jim Plunkett

16) Andy Farkas. (Sammy Baugh was drafted when the team was still in Boston.)

17) George Izo

18) Bill Brundige

19) Leroy Jackson

20) Doug Williams (340 yards)

21) He scored all of Washington's points in a 13-3 victory over the Giants by kicking two field goals, returning an interception for a TD, and kicking the extra point.

22) 649

23) Joe Theismann

24) Jay Schroeder

25) George Allen

26) They were all free agents

27) All three were placekickers who led the Redskins in scoring: Aguirre in '41, '44, and '45; Martin in '64; Jencks in '65.

28) Pete Retzlaff

29) Boston Braves

30) c

31) He led the NFL in passing, punting, and interceptions.

32) Vic Janowicz, Gary Beban, George Rogers

33) Ray Flaherty (54-21-3); Dutch Bergman (6-3-1); Dudley DeGroot (14-5-1); Dick Todd (5-4); Vince Lombardi (7-5-2); George Allen (67-30-1); Joe Gibbs (85-33)

34) Mike Nixon, .167 (4-18-2)

35) Los Angeles, Pasadena, Tampa, San Diego

36) 106

37) Ron Hatcher signed first, but Bobby Mitchell played first

38) Frank Filchock, George Izo, Sonny Jurgensen

39) 10

40) b (overall 24-24-3)

41) Len Hauss, 196

42) Sammy Baugh, 16

43) Jurgensen (9), Houston (27), Baugh (33), Taylor (42), Brown (43), Mitchell (49), Huff (70)

44) 1966

45) 6

46) Dick James and Larry Brown (24 points)

47) Claude Crabb

48) Ken Houston

49) John Riggins (6,795), Larry Brown (5,875), Mike Thomas (3,360), Don Bosseler (3,112)

50) Billy Wells (88 yards)

ORDER BLANKS

You may order copies of *BRAVES ON THE WARPATH* @ $24.95 each, plus $3.00 shipping and handling per copy. D.C. residents, please also include $1.50 sales tax per copy.

Please type or print your name and address on one of the order blanks below. Enclose check or money order made payable to: Kinloch Books. Do not send cash. If you would also like to send a copy to a friend or relative, please fill in his or her name and address on a separate order blank. You may enclose a card or write out a message that will be included with your gift. Please allow 4 weeks for delivery. Thank you.

- -

Mail to: **Kinloch Books**   PO Box 32400   Washington, D.C.   20007

Name _____

Address _____ *Apt.* _____

City _____ *State* _____ *Zip* _____

Telephone _____

Send _____ copies of **BRAVES ON THE WARPATH** *to this address.*
Please enclose a card with this message:

_____

_____

- -

Mail to: **Kinloch Books**   PO Box 32400   Washington, D.C.   20007

Name _____

Address _____ *Apt.* _____

City _____ *State* _____ *Zip* _____

Telephone _____

Send _____ copies of **BRAVES ON THE WARPATH** *to this address.*
Please enclose a card with this message:

_____

_____